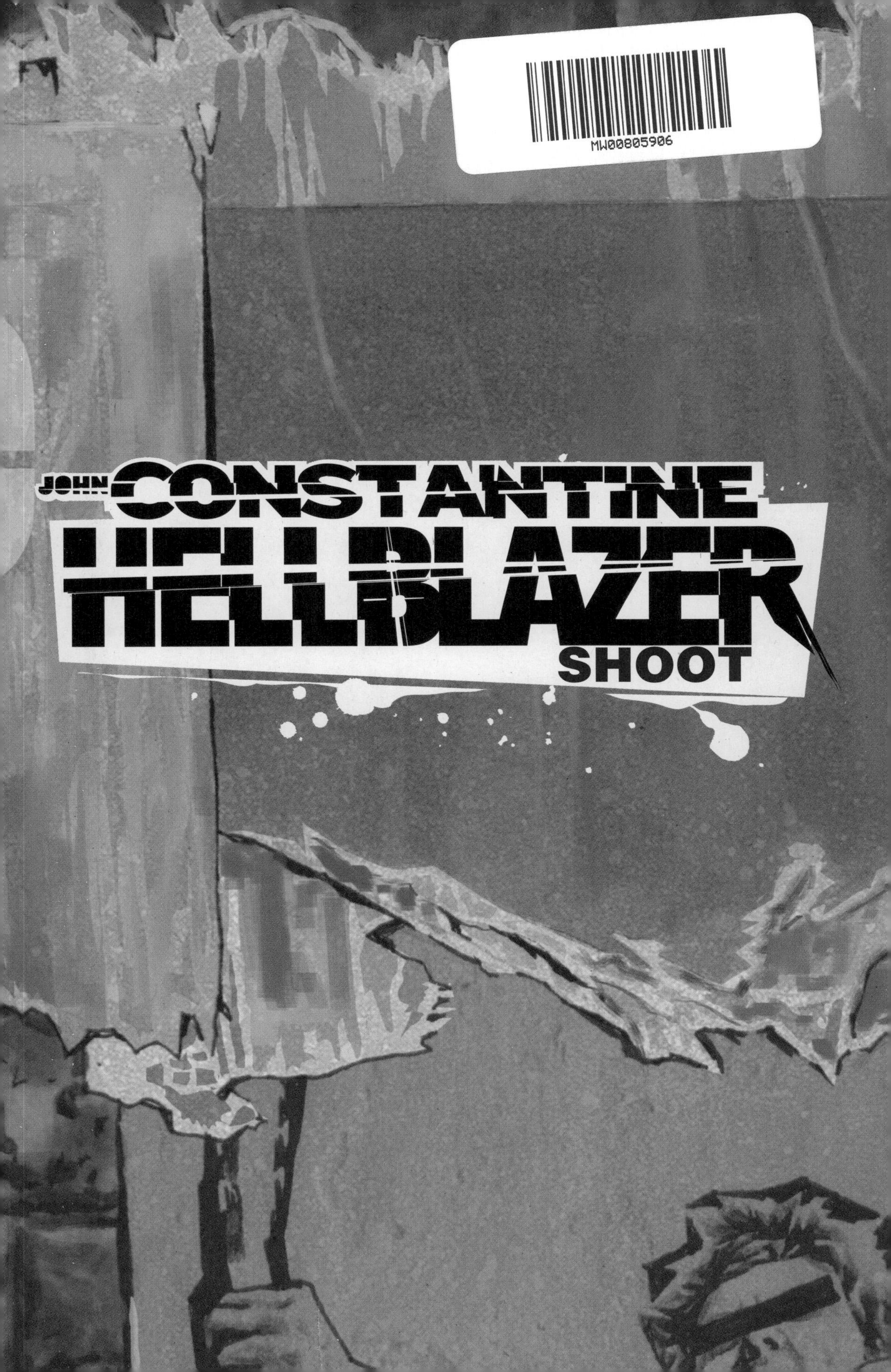
JOHN CONSTANTINE
HELLBLAZER
SHOOT

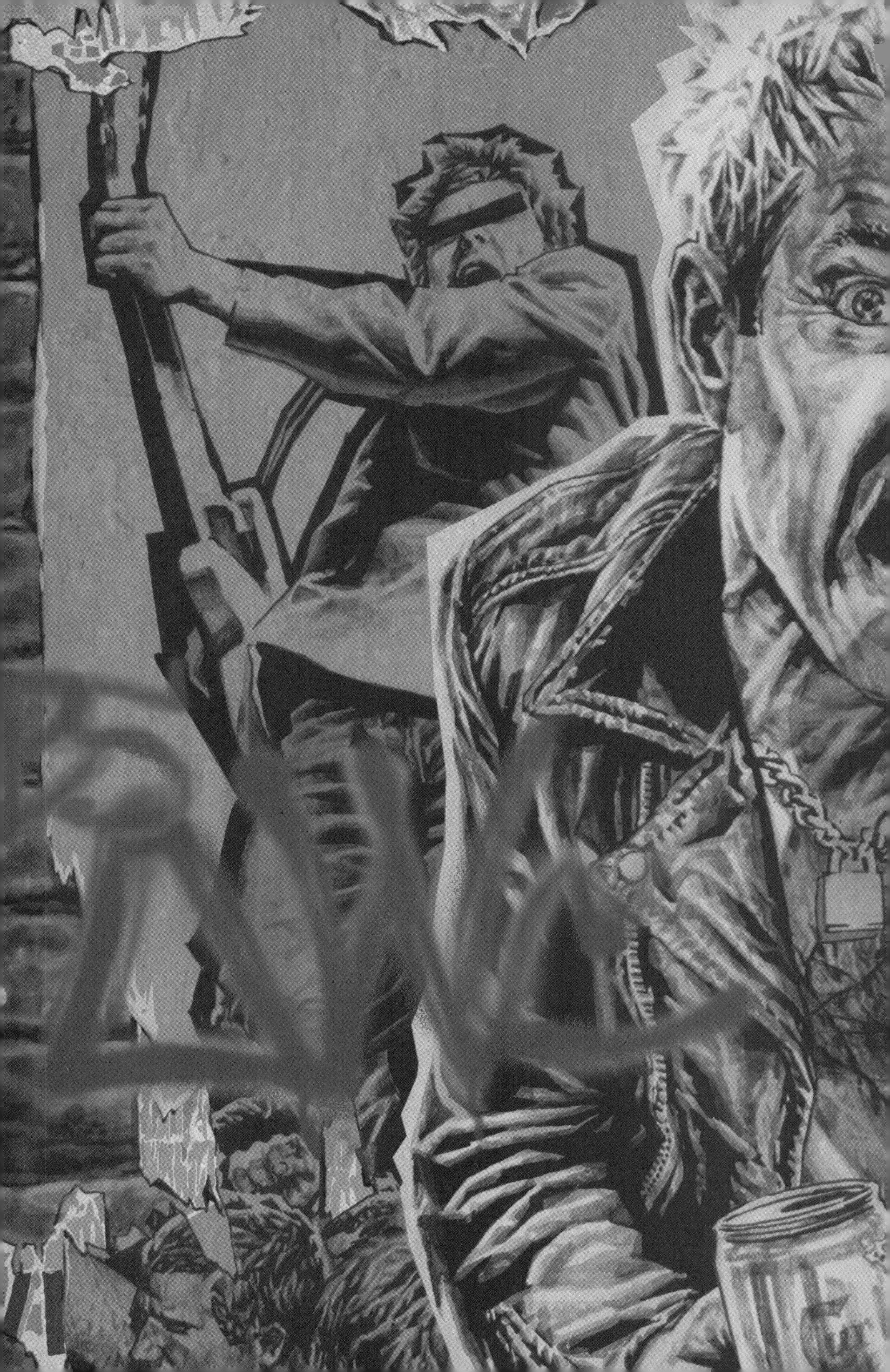

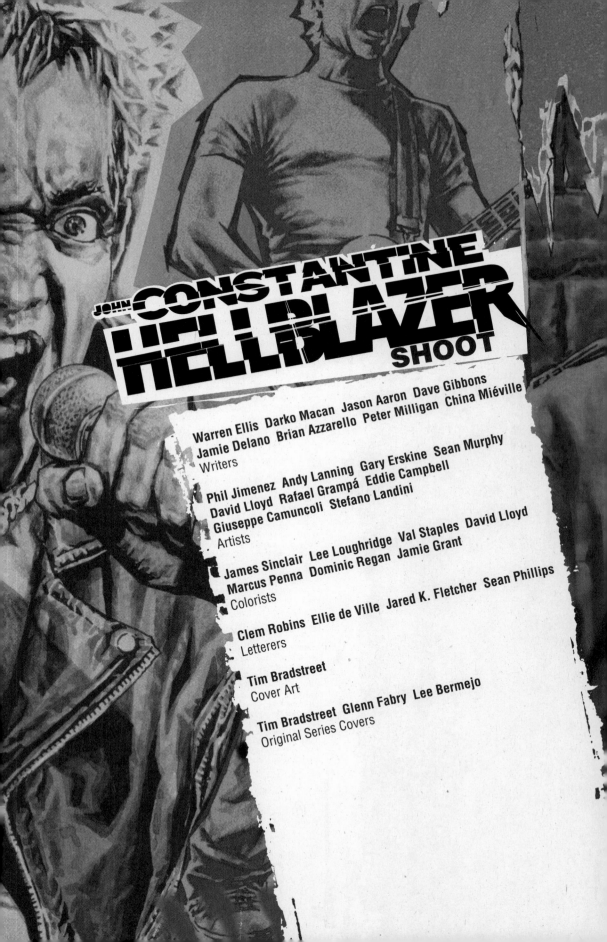

JOHN CONSTANTINE HELLBLAZER
SHOOT

Warren Ellis   Darko Macan   Jason Aaron   Dave Gibbons
Jamie Delano   Brian Azzarello   Peter Milligan   China Miéville
Writers

Phil Jimenez   Andy Lanning   Gary Erskine   Sean Murphy
David Lloyd   Rafael Grampá   Eddie Campbell
Giuseppe Camuncoli   Stefano Landini
Artists

James Sinclair   Lee Loughridge   Val Staples   David Lloyd
Marcus Penna   Dominic Regan   Jamie Grant
Colorists

Clem Robins   Ellie de Ville   Jared K. Fletcher   Sean Phillips
Letterers

Tim Bradstreet
Cover Art

Tim Bradstreet   Glenn Fabry   Lee Bermejo
Original Series Covers

Axel Alonso Casey Seijas Bob Schreck Editors – Original Series
Jennifer Lee Brandon Montclare Assistant Editors – Original Series
Scott Nybakken Editor
Robbin Brosterman Design Director – Books
Louis Prandi Publication Design

Shelly Bond Executive Editor – Vertigo
Hank Kanalz Senior VP – Vertigo & Integrated Publishing

Diane Nelson President
Dan DiDio and Jim Lee Co-Publishers
Geoff Johns Chief Creative Officer
John Rood Executive VP – Sales, Marketing & Business Development
Amy Genkins Senior VP – Business & Legal Affairs
Nairi Gardiner Senior VP – Finance
Jeff Boison VP – Publishing Planning
Mark Chiarello VP – Art Direction & Design
John Cunningham VP – Marketing
Terri Cunningham VP – Editorial Administration
Alison Gill Senior VP – Manufacturing & Operations
Jay Kogan VP – Business & Legal Affairs, Publishing
Jack Mahan VP – Business Affairs, Talent
Nick Napolitano VP – Manufacturing Administration
Sue Pohja VP – Book Sales
Courtney Simmons Senior VP – Publicity
Bob Wayne Senior VP – Sales

JOHN CONSTANTINE, HELLBLAZER: SHOOT

DC Comics, 1700 Broadway, New York, NY 10019
A Warner Bros. Entertainment Company
Printed in the USA. First Printing.
ISBN: 978-1-4012-4748-5

Library of Congress Cataloging-in-Publication Data

Azzarello, Brian.
  Hellblazer : Shoot / Brian Azzarello, Warren Ellis.
     pages cm
  Summary: "An assortment of Hellblazer stories written by Brian Azzarello (100
Bullets), Warren Ellis (Planetary), and others. In these stories by some of comics'
top writers, John Constantine faces school violence, a desperate, occult family,
and more. Plus: A group of documentary filmmakers try to find out what happened
to Mucous Membrane — an up-and-coming punk band led by John Constantine
that met a mysterious end. Collects Hellblazer #144, 145, 245-246, 250, and
Vertigo Resurrected: Hellblazer #1" — Provided by publisher.
  ISBN 978-1-4012-4748-5 (pbk.)
  1. Graphic novels. I. Ellis, Warren. II. Title.
  PN6728.H383A96 2014
  741.5'973—dc23
                              2013045914

Table of Contents

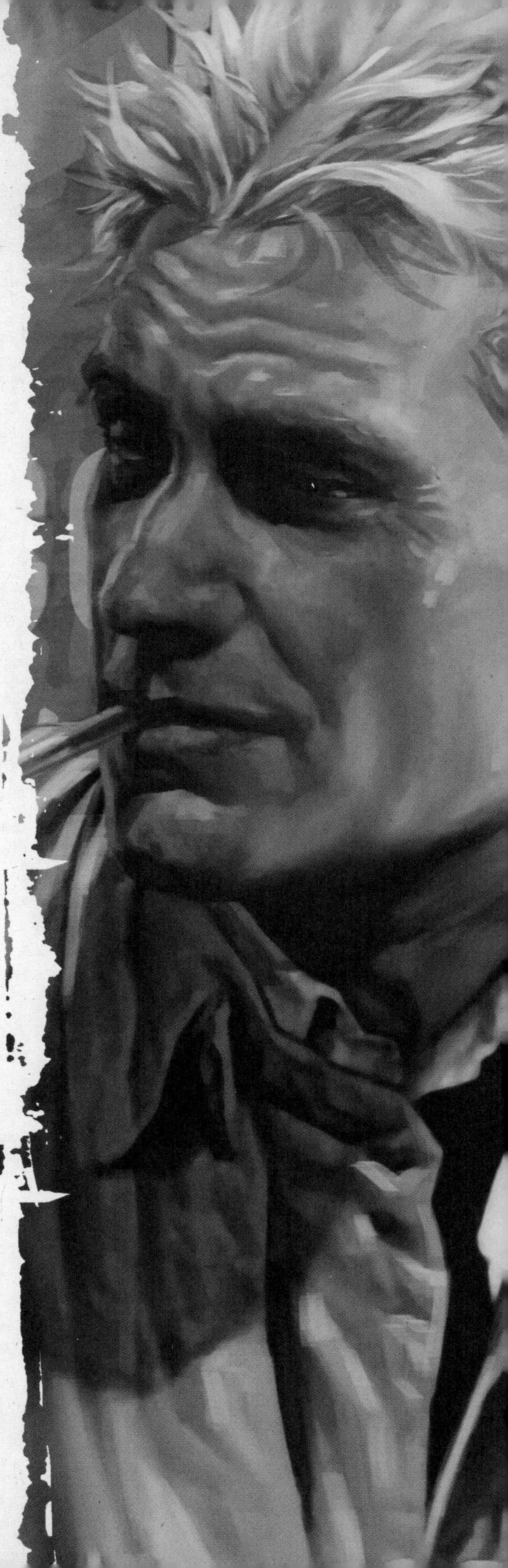

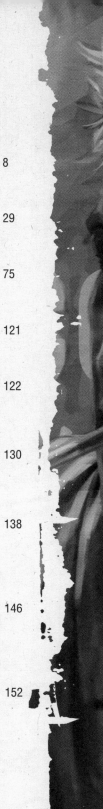

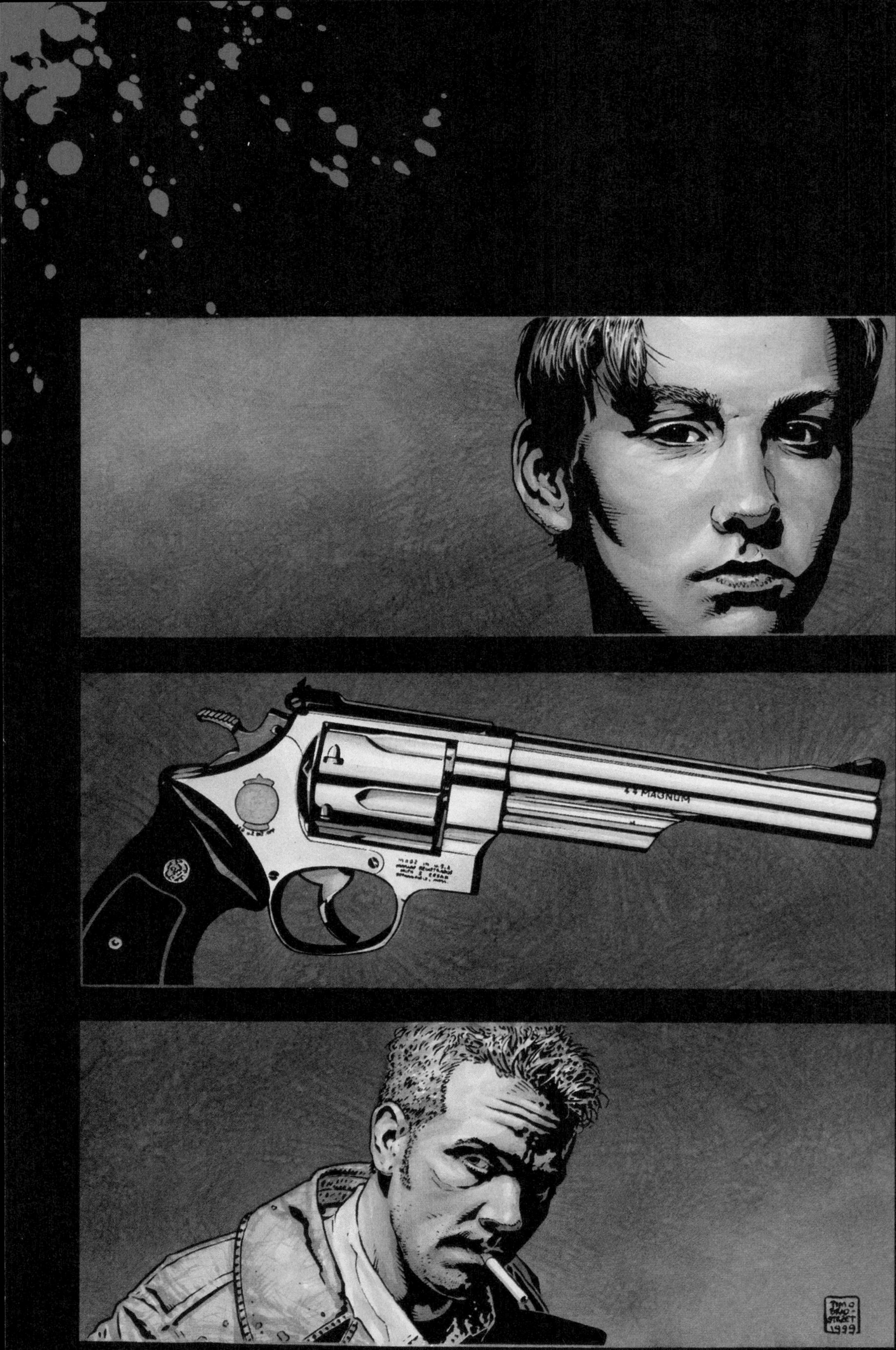
44 MAGNUM
TIM O BRADSTREET 1999

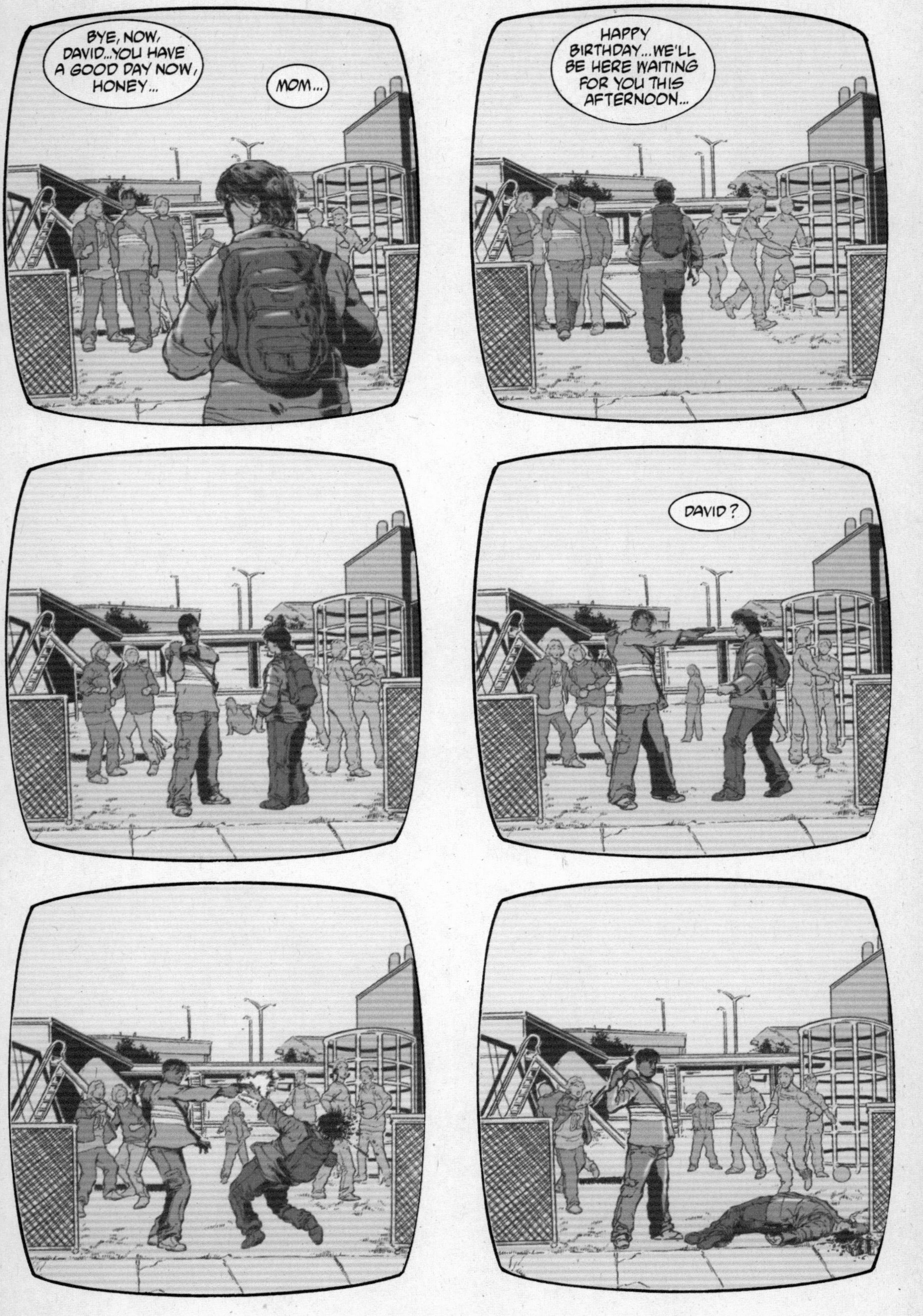
BYE, NOW, DAVID...YOU HAVE A GOOD DAY NOW, HONEY...
MOM...
HAPPY BIRTHDAY...WE'LL BE HERE WAITING FOR YOU THIS AFTERNOON...
DAVID?

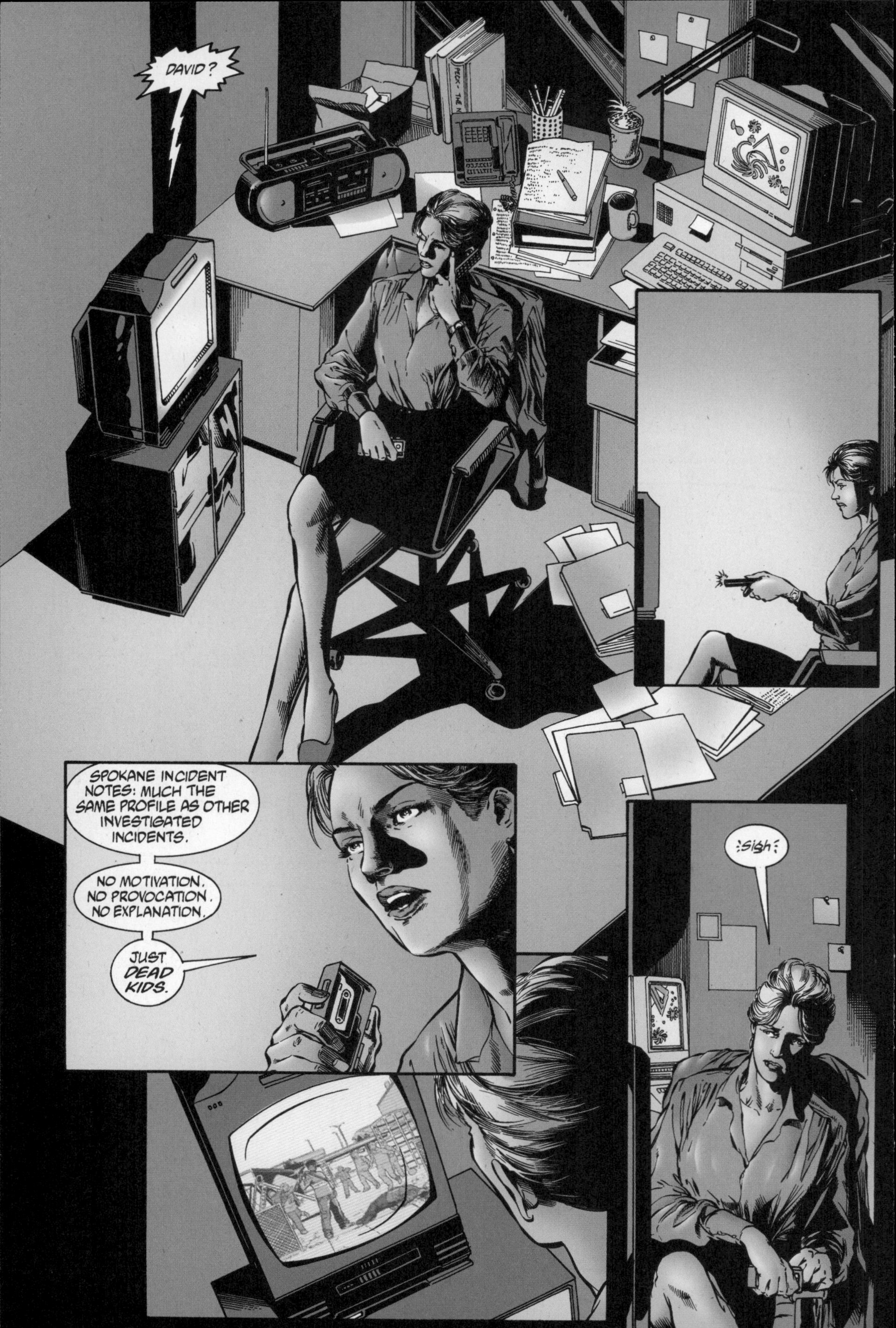
DAVID?
SPOKANE INCIDENT NOTES: MUCH THE SAME PROFILE AS OTHER INVESTIGATED INCIDENTS.
NO MOTIVATION. NO PROVOCATION. NO EXPLANATION.
JUST DEAD KIDS.
SIGH

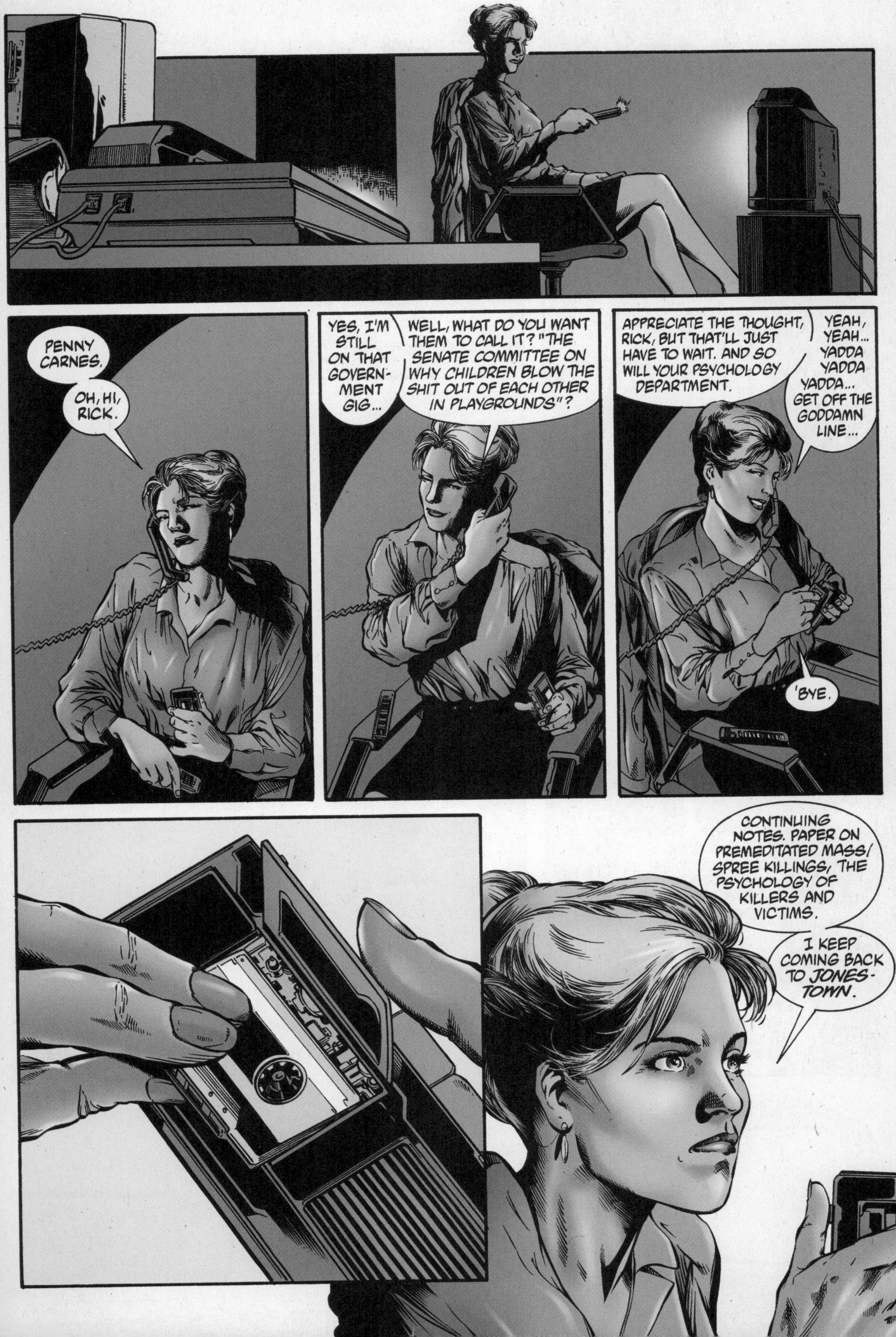
PENNY CARNES.
OH, HI, RICK.
YES, I'M STILL ON THAT GOVERN-MENT GIG...
WELL, WHAT DO YOU WANT THEM TO CALL IT? "THE SENATE COMMITTEE ON WHY CHILDREN BLOW THE SHIT OUT OF EACH OTHER IN PLAYGROUNDS"?
APPRECIATE THE THOUGHT, RICK, BUT THAT'LL JUST HAVE TO WAIT. AND SO WILL YOUR PSYCHOLOGY DEPARTMENT.
YEAH, YEAH... YADDA YADDA YADDA... GET OFF THE GODDAMN LINE...
'BYE.
CONTINUING NOTES. PAPER ON PREMEDITATED MASS/ SPREE KILLINGS, THE PSYCHOLOGY OF KILLERS AND VICTIMS.
I KEEP COMING BACK TO JONES-TOWN.

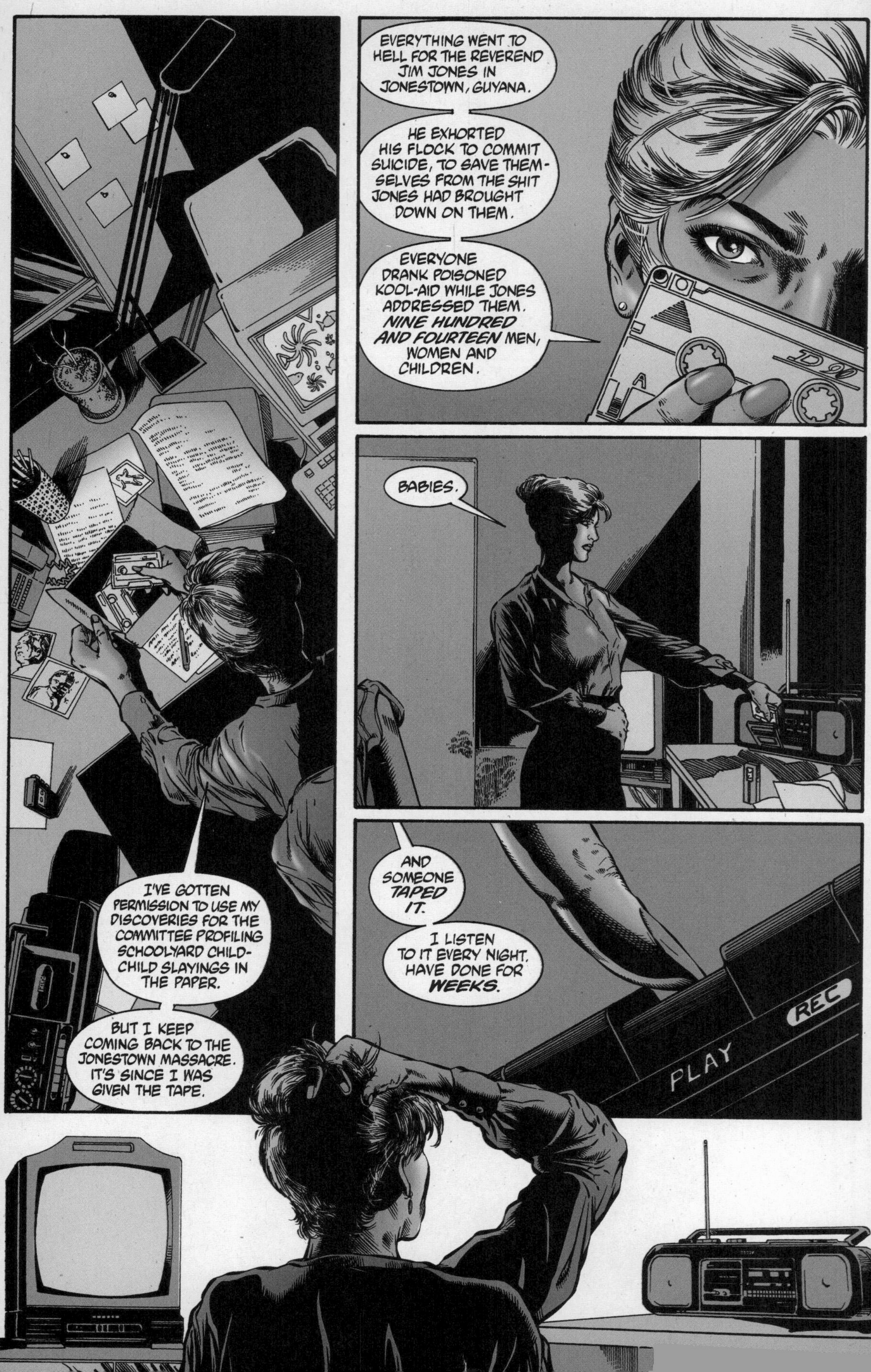
EVERYTHING WENT TO HELL FOR THE REVEREND JIM JONES IN JONESTOWN, GUYANA.
HE EXHORTED HIS FLOCK TO COMMIT SUICIDE, TO SAVE THEM-SELVES FROM THE SHIT JONES HAD BROUGHT DOWN ON THEM.
EVERYONE DRANK POISONED KOOL-AID WHILE JONES ADDRESSED THEM. NINE HUNDRED AND FOURTEEN MEN, WOMEN AND CHILDREN.
I'VE GOTTEN PERMISSION TO USE MY DISCOVERIES FOR THE COMMITTEE PROFILING SCHOOLYARD CHILD-CHILD SLAYINGS IN THE PAPER.
BUT I KEEP COMING BACK TO THE JONESTOWN MASSACRE. IT'S SINCE I WAS GIVEN THE TAPE.
BABIES.
AND SOMEONE TAPED IT.
I LISTEN TO IT EVERY NIGHT. HAVE DONE FOR WEEKS.
REC
PLAY

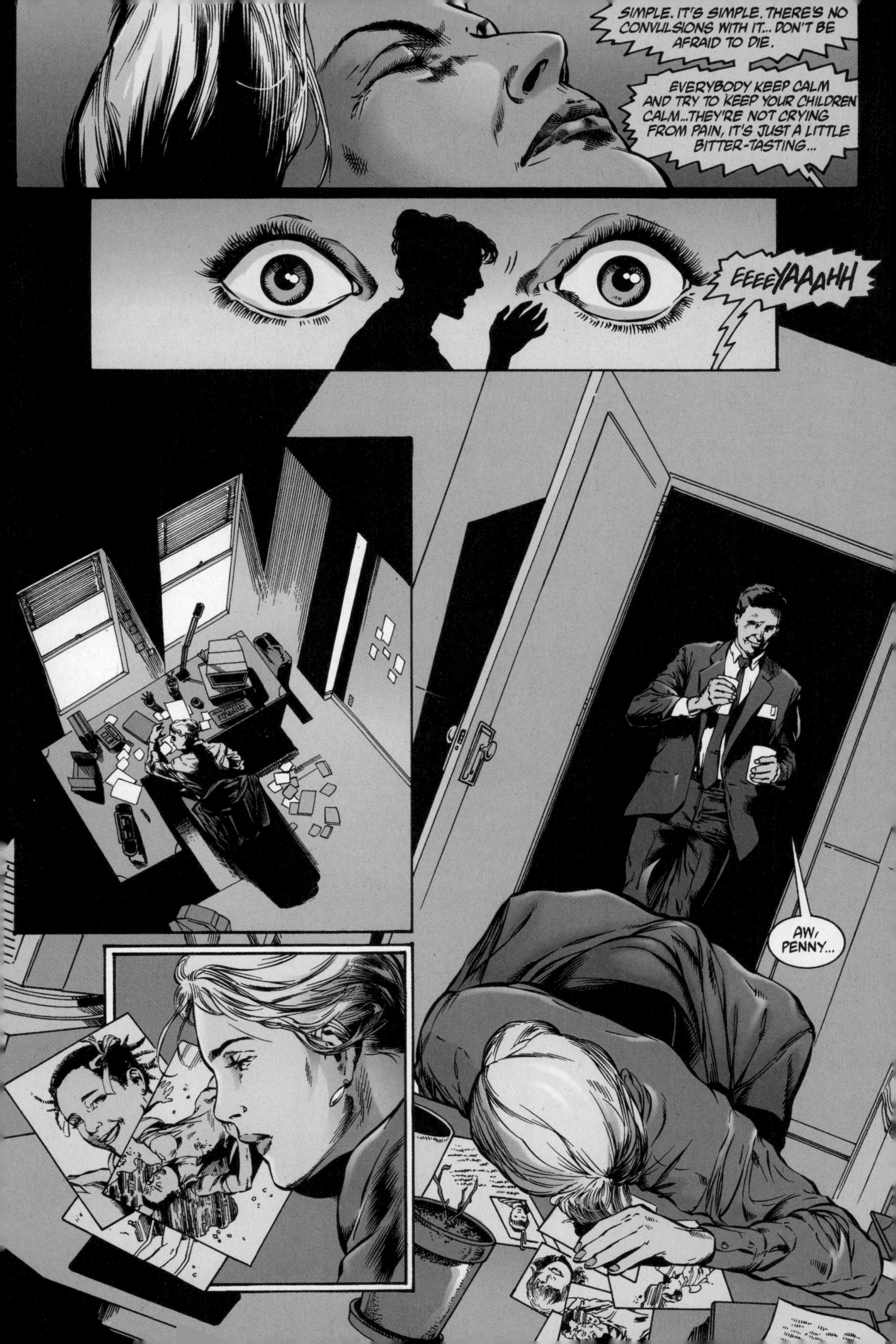
SIMPLE. IT'S SIMPLE. THERE'S NO CONVULSIONS WITH IT... DON'T BE AFRAID TO DIE.
EVERYBODY KEEP CALM AND TRY TO KEEP YOUR CHILDREN CALM...THEY'RE NOT CRYING FROM PAIN, IT'S JUST A LITTLE BITTER-TASTING...
EEEEYAAAHH
AW, PENNY...

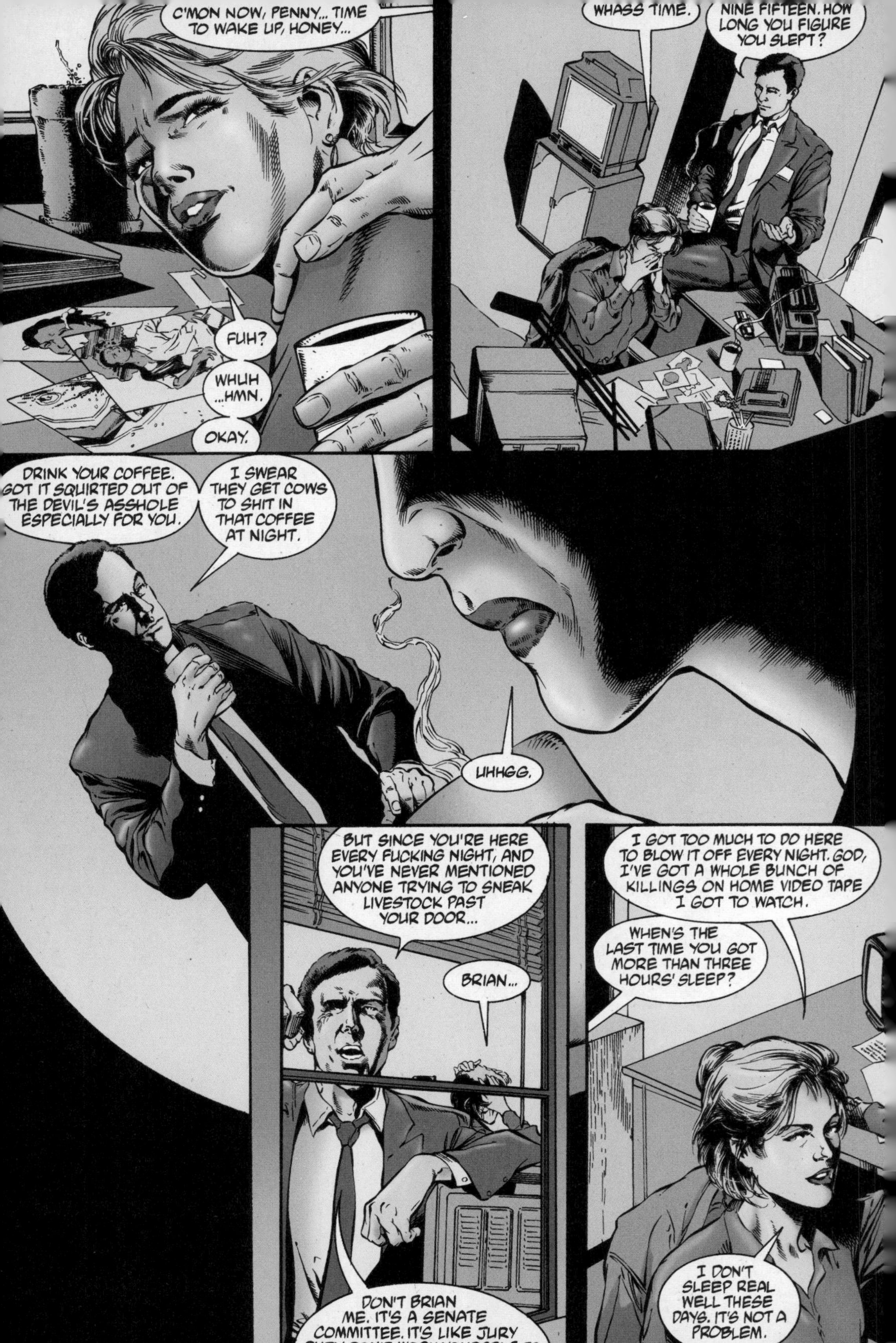
C'MON NOW, PENNY... TIME TO WAKE UP, HONEY...
FUH?
WHUH ...HMN.
OKAY.
WHASS TIME.
NINE FIFTEEN. HOW LONG YOU FIGURE YOU SLEPT?
DRINK YOUR COFFEE. GOT IT SQUIRTED OUT OF THE DEVIL'S ASSHOLE ESPECIALLY FOR YOU.
I SWEAR THEY GET COWS TO SHIT IN THAT COFFEE AT NIGHT.
UHHGG.
BUT SINCE YOU'RE HERE EVERY FUCKING NIGHT, AND YOU'VE NEVER MENTIONED ANYONE TRYING TO SNEAK LIVESTOCK PAST YOUR DOOR...
BRIAN...
DON'T BRIAN ME. IT'S A SENATE COMMITTEE. IT'S LIKE JURY DUTY. DON'T WORK YOURSELF TO DEATH ON IT. NOT WORTH IT.
I GOT TOO MUCH TO DO HERE TO BLOW IT OFF EVERY NIGHT. GOD, I'VE GOT A WHOLE BUNCH OF KILLINGS ON HOME VIDEO TAPE I GOT TO WATCH.
WHEN'S THE LAST TIME YOU GOT MORE THAN THREE HOURS' SLEEP?
I DON'T SLEEP REAL WELL THESE DAYS. IT'S NOT A PROBLEM.

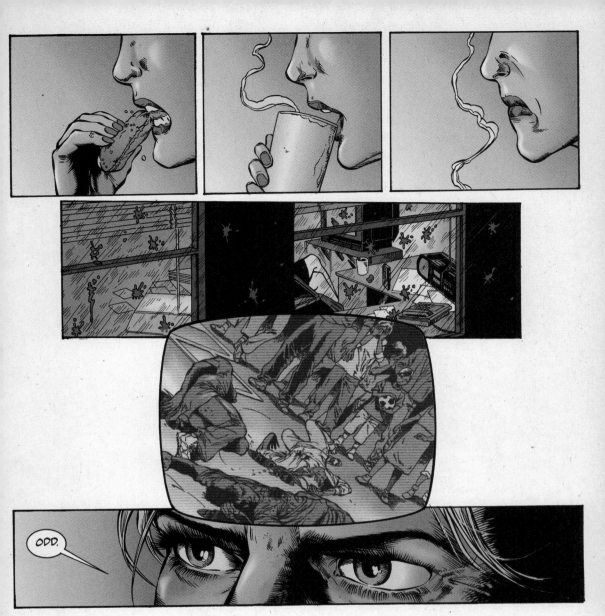

ODD.

I KNOW I'VE SEEN HIM BEFORE.

JACKSONVILLE? HELEN VOLCANO?

HERE.

CAN'T BE.

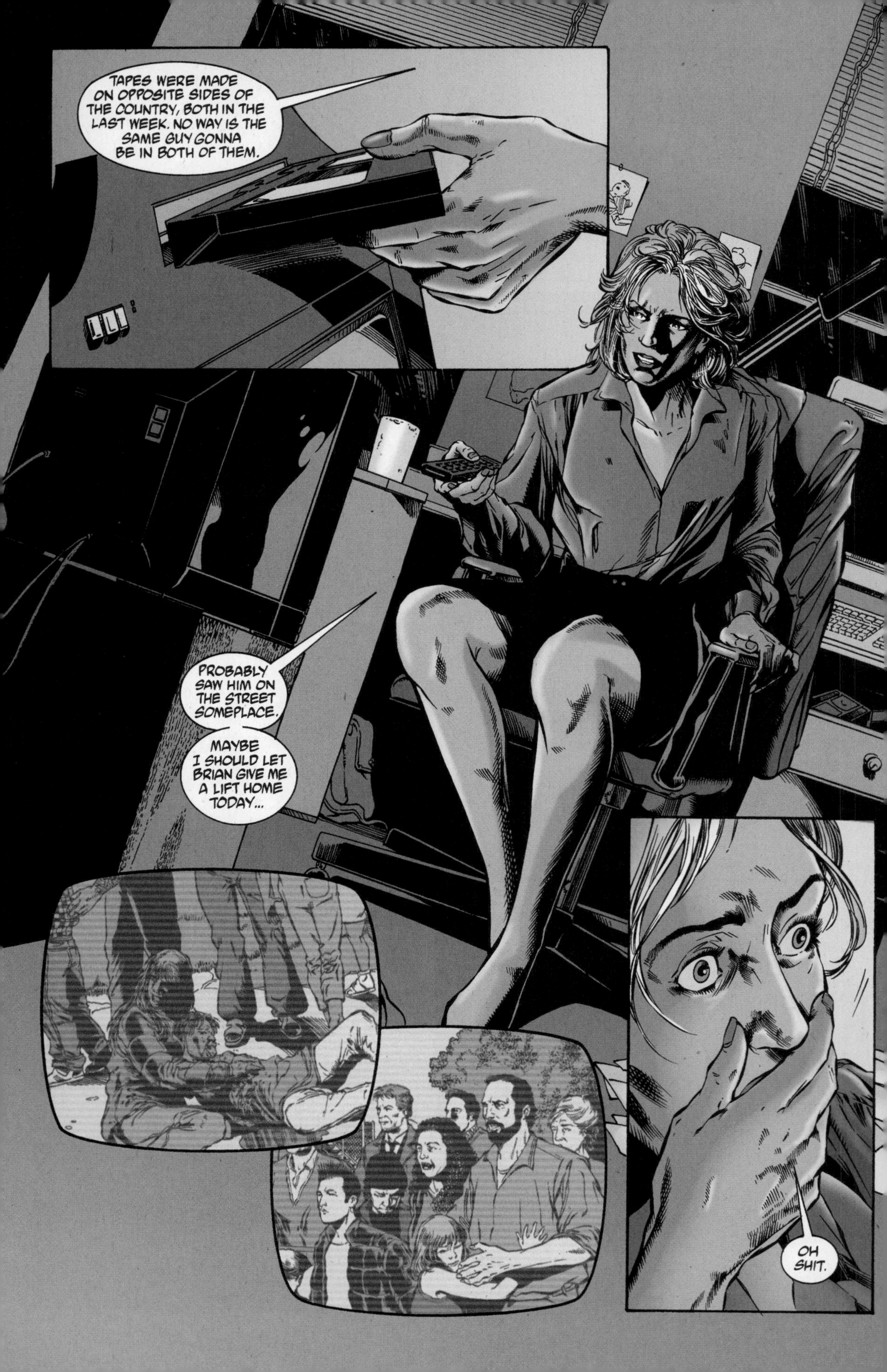
TAPES WERE MADE ON OPPOSITE SIDES OF THE COUNTRY, BOTH IN THE LAST WEEK. NO WAY IS THE SAME GUY GONNA BE IN BOTH OF THEM.
PROBABLY SAW HIM ON THE STREET SOMEPLACE.
MAYBE I SHOULD LET BRIAN GIVE ME A LIFT HOME TODAY...
OH SHIT.

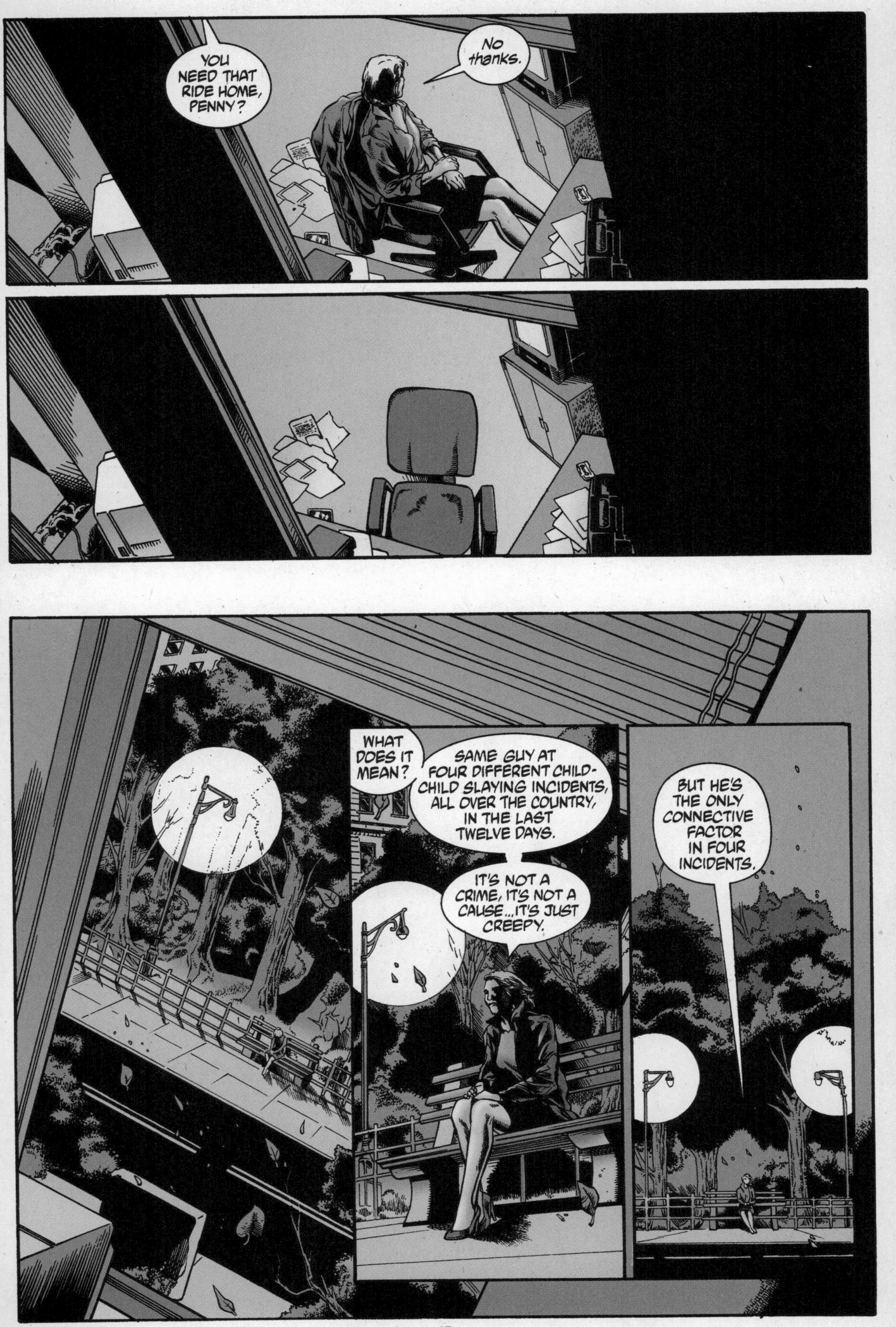
YOU NEED THAT RIDE HOME, PENNY?
No thanks.
WHAT DOES IT MEAN?
SAME GUY AT FOUR DIFFERENT CHILD-CHILD SLAYING INCIDENTS, ALL OVER THE COUNTRY, IN THE LAST TWELVE DAYS.
IT'S NOT A CRIME, IT'S NOT A CAUSE...IT'S JUST CREEPY.
BUT HE'S THE ONLY CONNECTIVE FACTOR IN FOUR INCIDENTS.

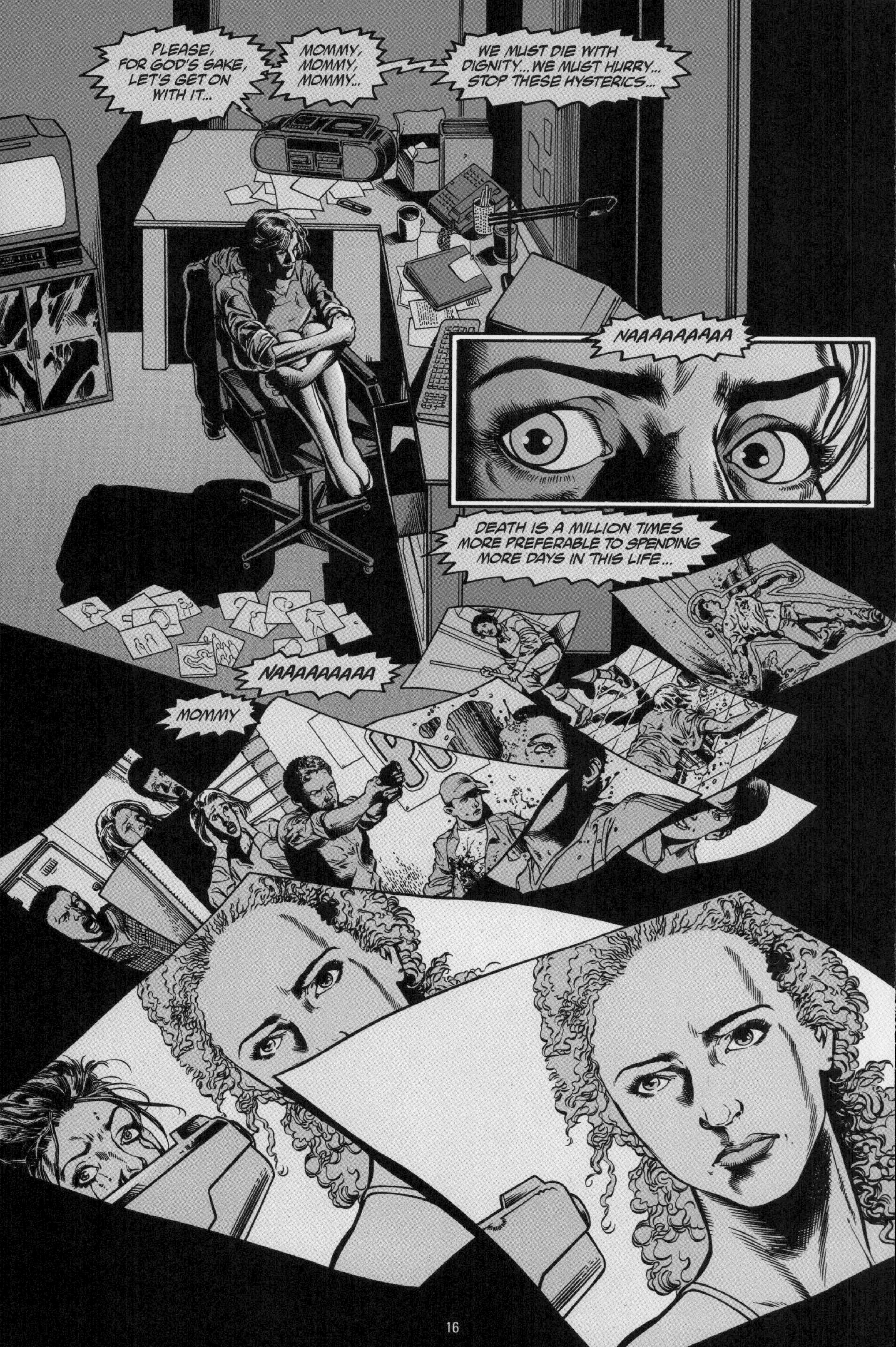
PLEASE, FOR GOD'S SAKE, LET'S GET ON WITH IT...
MOMMY, MOMMY, MOMMY...
WE MUST DIE WITH DIGNITY... WE MUST HURRY... STOP THESE HYSTERICS...
NAAAAAAAAA
DEATH IS A MILLION TIMES MORE PREFERABLE TO SPENDING MORE DAYS IN THIS LIFE...
NAAAAAAAAA
MOMMY

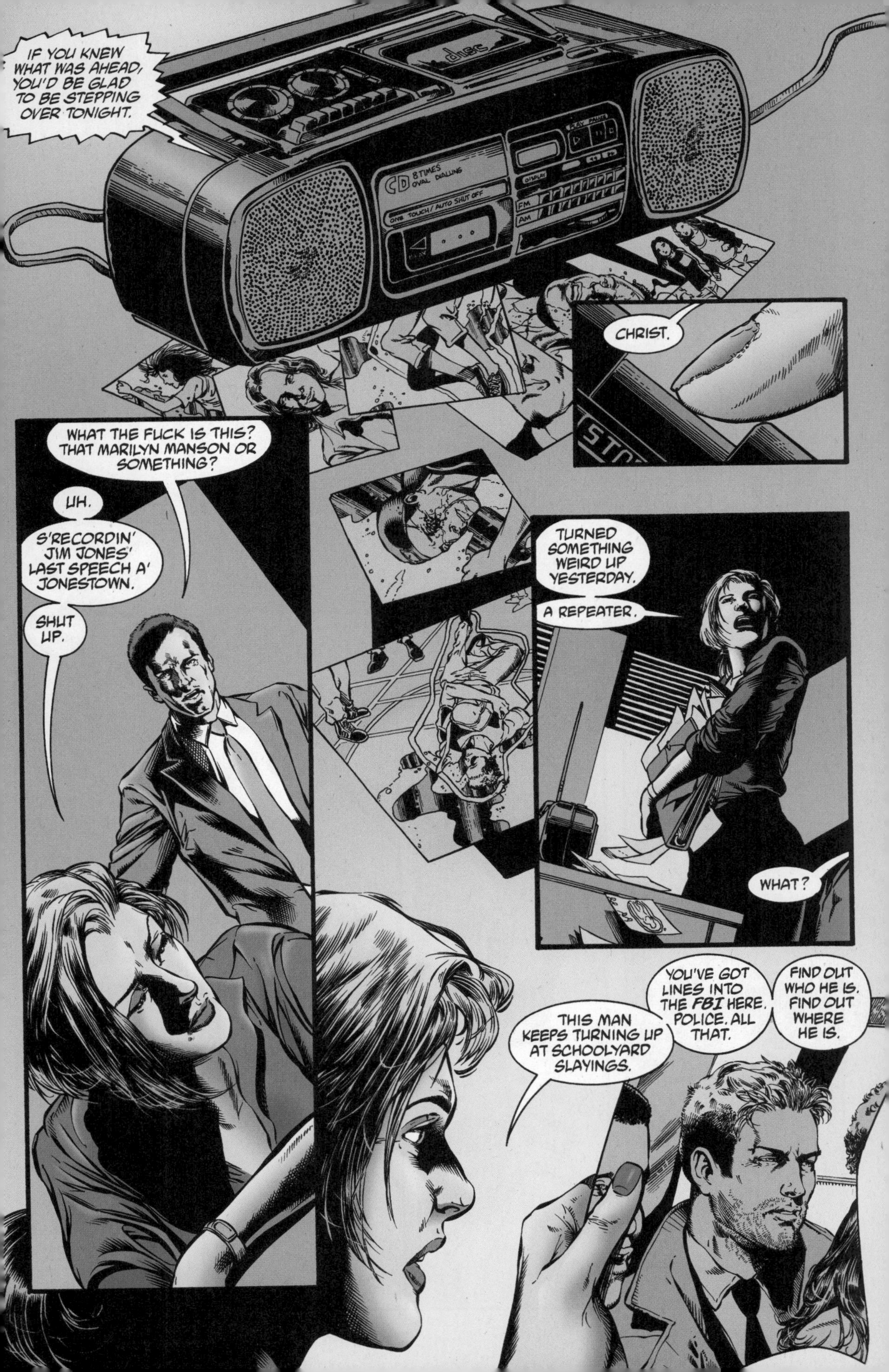

IF YOU KNEW WHAT WAS AHEAD, YOU'D BE GLAD TO BE STEPPING OVER TONIGHT.
CD 8 TIMES OVAL DIALING
ONE TOUCH / AUTO SHUT OFF
FM
AM
PLAY PAUSE
DISPLAY
CHRIST.
WHAT THE FUCK IS THIS? THAT MARILYN MANSON OR SOMETHING?
UH.
S'RECORDIN' JIM JONES' LAST SPEECH A' JONESTOWN.
SHUT UP.
TURNED SOMETHING WEIRD UP YESTERDAY.
A REPEATER.
WHAT?
THIS MAN KEEPS TURNING UP AT SCHOOLYARD SLAYINGS.
YOU'VE GOT LINES INTO THE FBI HERE. POLICE. ALL THAT.
FIND OUT WHO HE IS. FIND OUT WHERE HE IS.

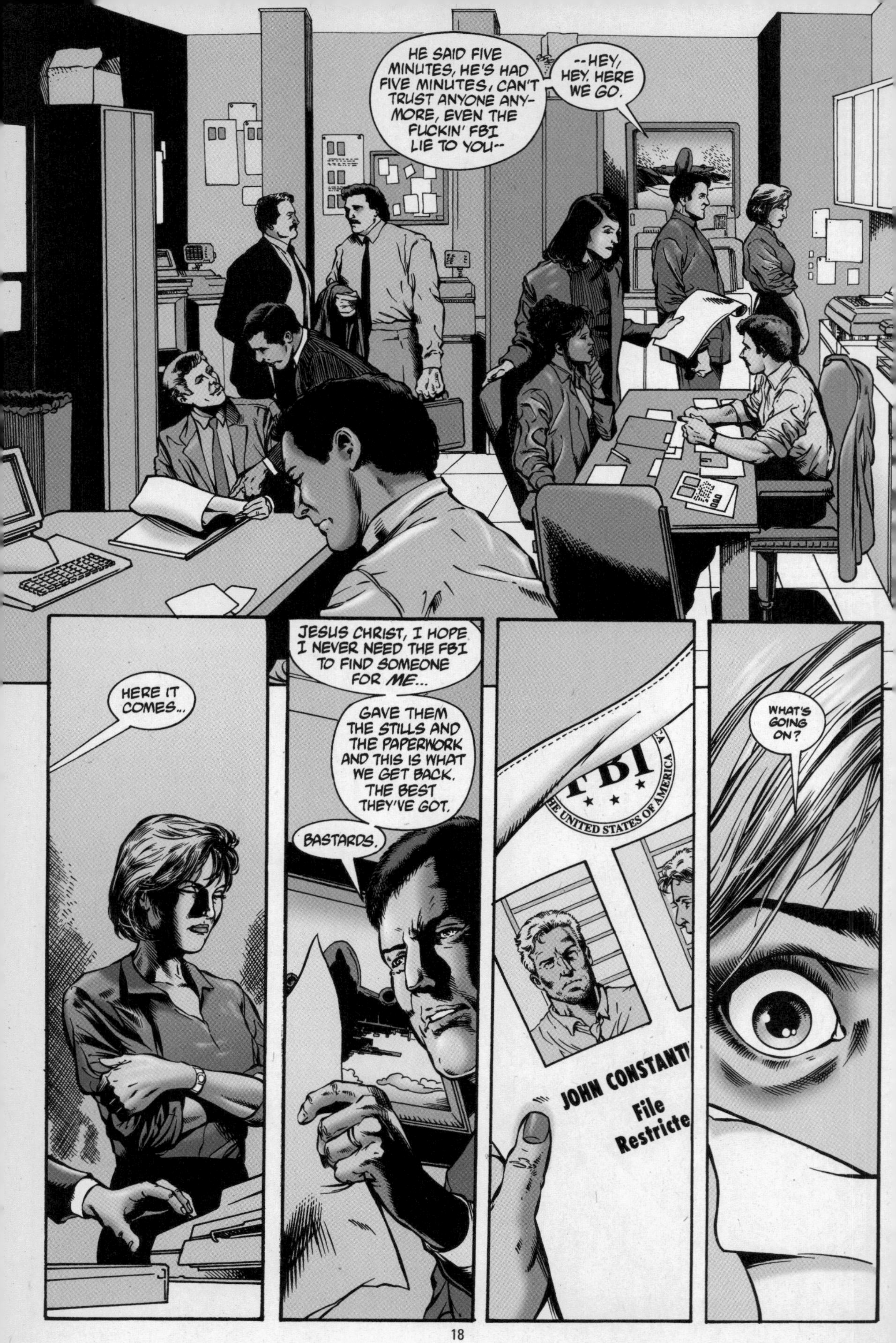
HE SAID FIVE MINUTES, HE'S HAD FIVE MINUTES, CAN'T TRUST ANYONE ANY-MORE, EVEN THE FUCKIN' FBI LIE TO YOU--
--HEY, HEY. HERE WE GO.
HERE IT COMES...
JESUS CHRIST, I HOPE I NEVER NEED THE FBI TO FIND SOMEONE FOR *ME*...
GAVE THEM THE STILLS AND THE PAPERWORK AND THIS IS WHAT WE GET BACK. THE BEST THEY'VE GOT.
BASTARDS.
FBI
THE UNITED STATES OF AMERICA
JOHN CONSTANT
File
Restricte
WHAT'S GOING ON?

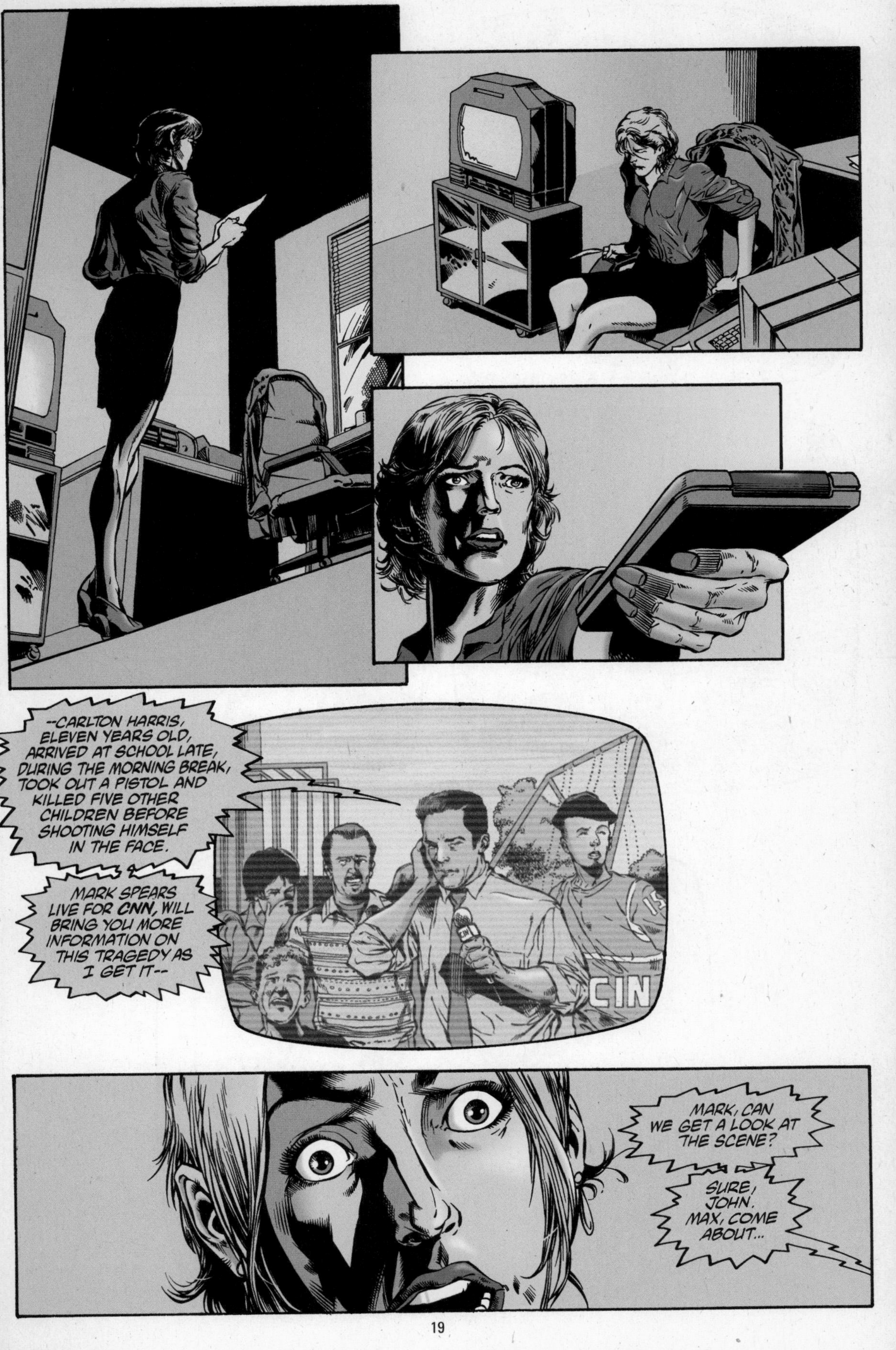
--CARLTON HARRIS, ELEVEN YEARS OLD, ARRIVED AT SCHOOL LATE, DURING THE MORNING BREAK, TOOK OUT A PISTOL AND KILLED FIVE OTHER CHILDREN BEFORE SHOOTING HIMSELF IN THE FACE.
MARK SPEARS LIVE FOR CNN, WILL BRING YOU MORE INFORMATION ON THIS TRAGEDY AS I GET IT--
CIN
MARK, CAN WE GET A LOOK AT THE SCENE?
SURE, JOHN. MAX, COME ABOUT...

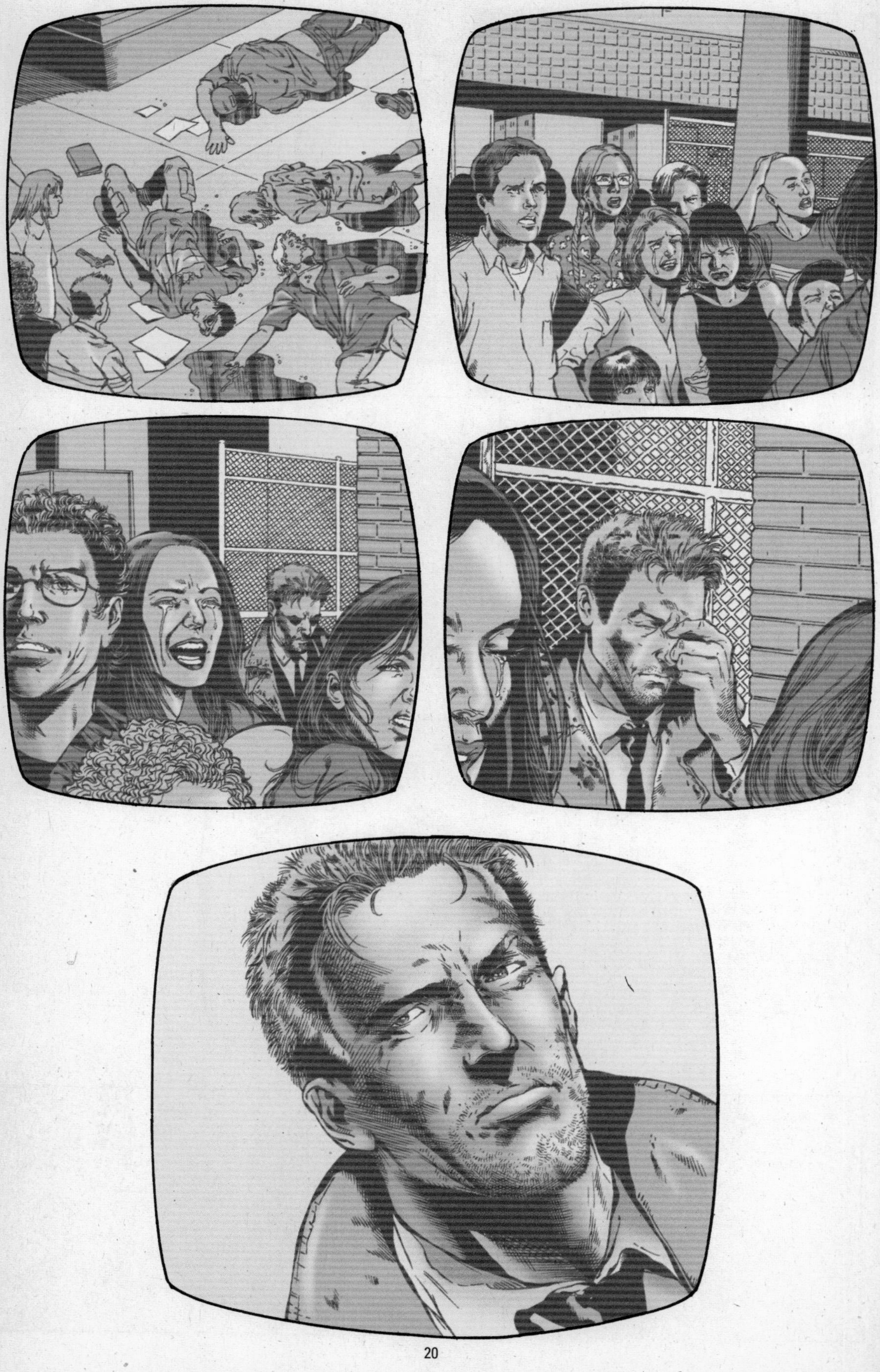

...IT'S DECIDING WHAT TO BLAME, YOU KNOW?

BLAME THE PARENTS FOR KEEPING A GUN IN THE HOUSE? NOT WITHOUT BLAMING THE CONSTITUTION AND PULLING THE NRA'S CHAIN.

THE MOVIES, THE VIDEO GAMES, THE COMIC BOOKS...

MORE KILLERS FIXATE ON AND DRAW INSPIRATION FROM THE BIBLE THAN ANY OTHER PIECE OF CULTURE.

SO IF I DID A NINTENDO THING CALLED "FLYING CHAIN-SAW JESUS" I'D BE RICH?

EW. AND YOU'VE GOT KIDS.

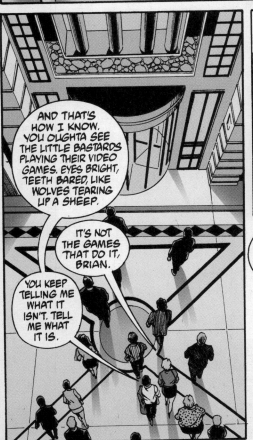

AND THAT'S HOW I KNOW. YOU OUGHTA SEE THE LITTLE BASTARDS PLAYING THEIR VIDEO GAMES. EYES BRIGHT, TEETH BARED, LIKE WOLVES TEARING UP A SHEEP.

IT'S NOT THE GAMES THAT DO IT, BRIAN.

YOU KEEP TELLING ME WHAT IT ISN'T. TELL ME WHAT IT IS.

GOD, IF I KNEW, I'D BOTTLE IT AND SPRAY IT OVER EVERY SCHOOL IN THE COUNTRY ...HOLD ON...

DAMN IT. KNEW THE BAG FELT LIGHT. LEFT MY TAPE RECORDER IN THE OFFICE.

PENNY, I HAVE TO LEAVE LIKE NOW TO PICK UP THE BOYS FROM FOOTBALL PRACTICE...

THEN GO. YOU CAN OWE ME A RIDE, I'LL GET THE BUS HOME.

YOU SURE?

NO BIG DEAL. SEE YOU TOMORROW.

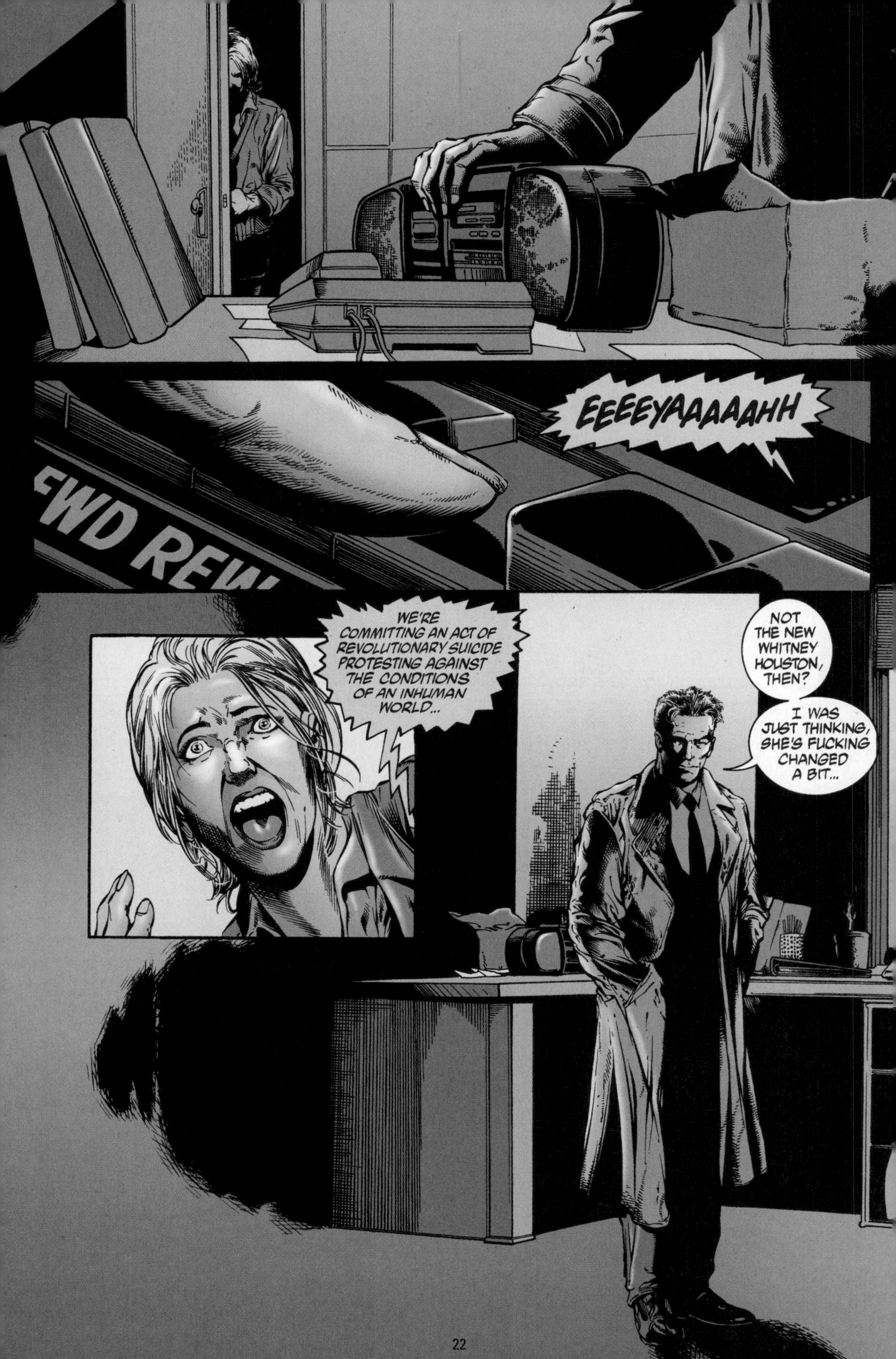

FWD REW
EEEEYAAAAAHH
WE'RE COMMITTING AN ACT OF REVOLUTIONARY SUICIDE PROTESTING AGAINST THE CONDITIONS OF AN INHUMAN WORLD...
NOT THE NEW WHITNEY HOUSTON, THEN?
I WAS JUST THINKING, SHE'S FUCKING CHANGED A BIT...

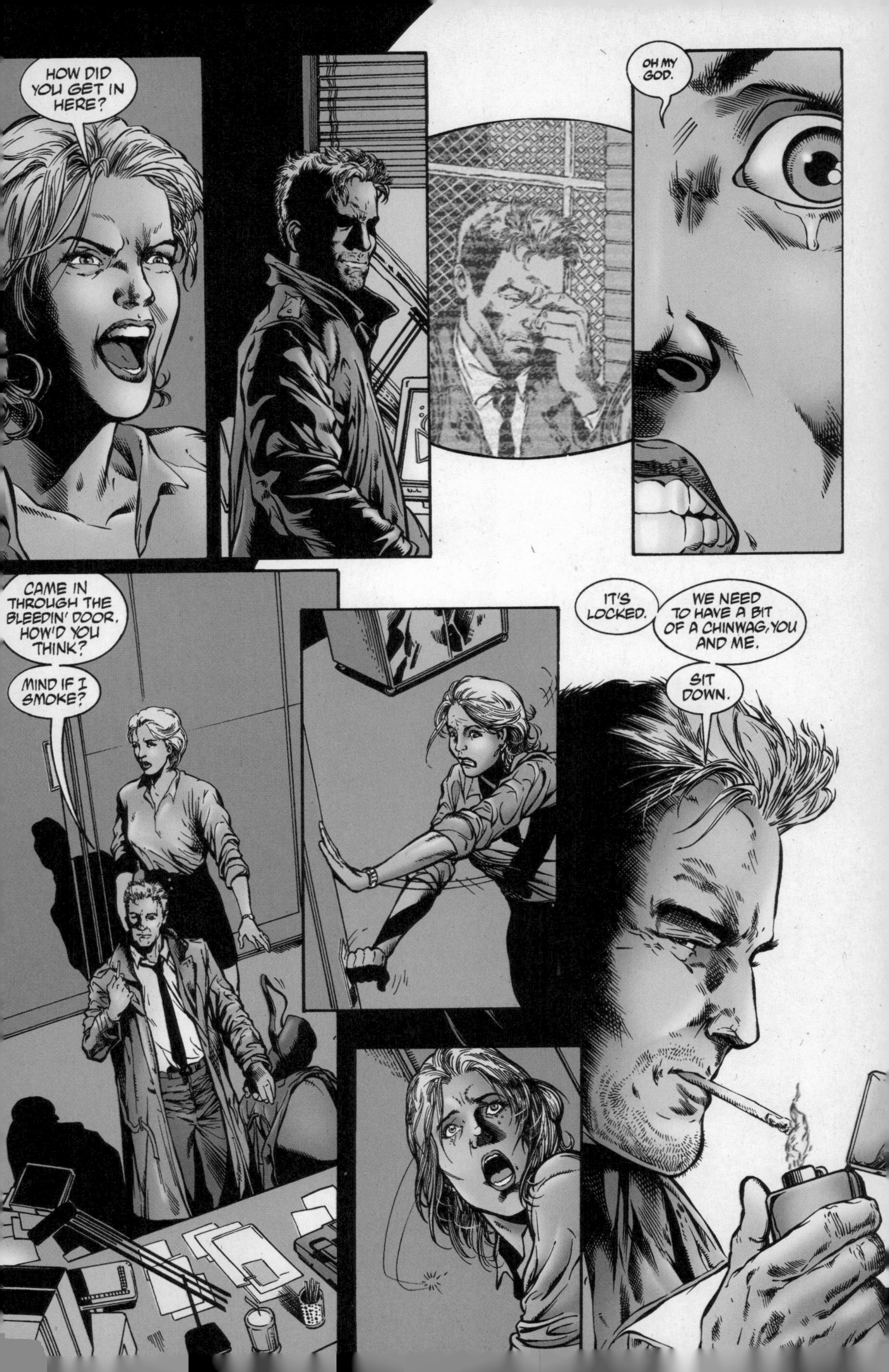
HOW DID YOU GET IN HERE?
OH MY GOD.
CAME IN THROUGH THE BLEEDIN' DOOR, HOW'D YOU THINK?
MIND IF I SMOKE?
IT'S LOCKED.
WE NEED TO HAVE A BIT OF A CHINWAG, YOU AND ME.
SIT DOWN.

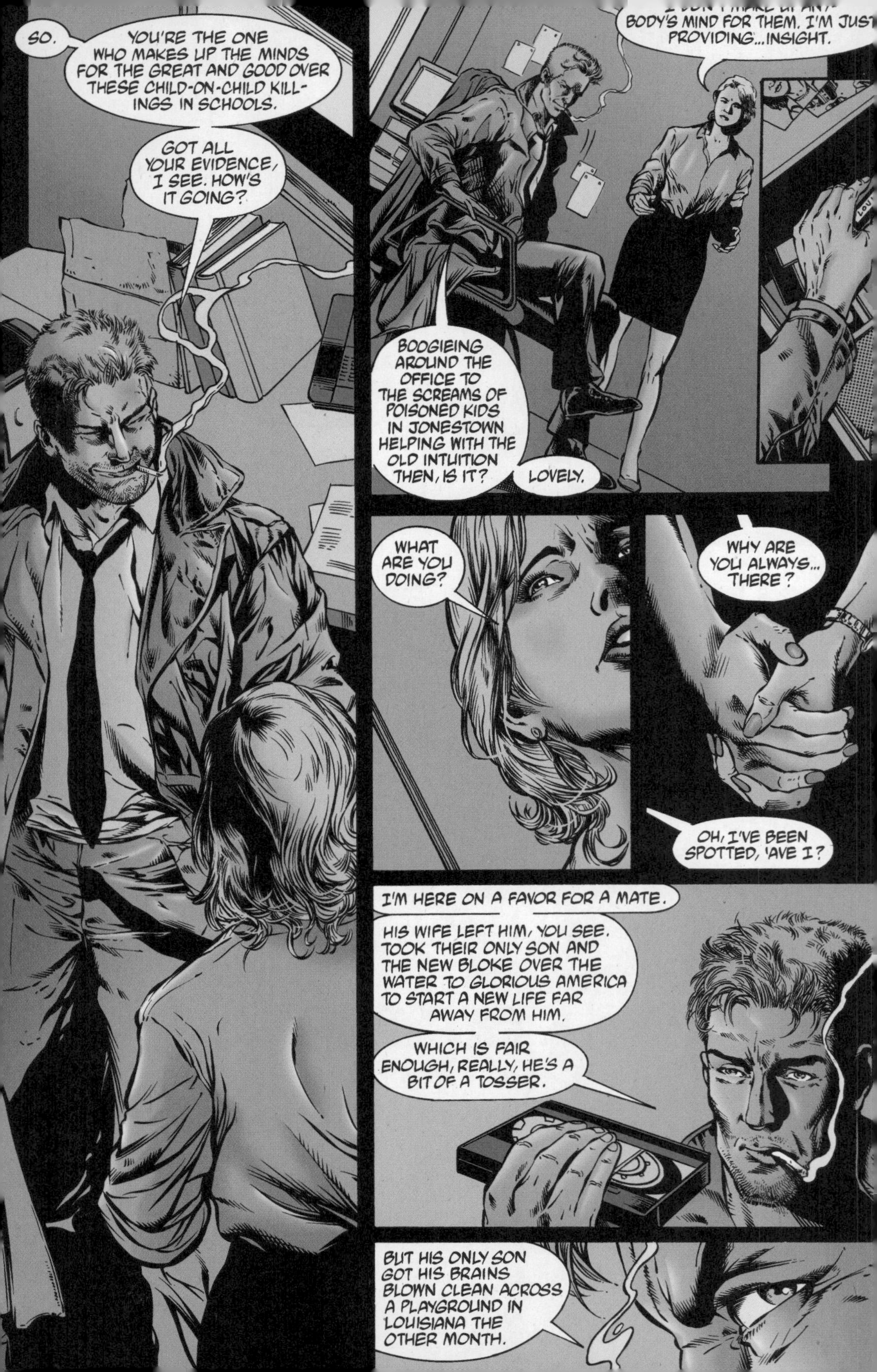
SO.
YOU'RE THE ONE WHO MAKES UP THE MINDS FOR THE GREAT AND GOOD OVER THESE CHILD-ON-CHILD KILL-INGS IN SCHOOLS.
GOT ALL YOUR EVIDENCE, I SEE. HOW'S IT GOING?
BODY'S MIND FOR THEM. I'M JUST PROVIDING...INSIGHT.
BOOGIEING AROUND THE OFFICE TO THE SCREAMS OF POISONED KIDS IN JONESTOWN HELPING WITH THE OLD INTUITION THEN, IS IT?
LOVELY.
WHAT ARE YOU DOING?
WHY ARE YOU ALWAYS... THERE?
OH, I'VE BEEN SPOTTED, 'AVE I?
I'M HERE ON A FAVOR FOR A MATE.
HIS WIFE LEFT HIM, YOU SEE. TOOK THEIR ONLY SON AND THE NEW BLOKE OVER THE WATER TO GLORIOUS AMERICA TO START A NEW LIFE FAR AWAY FROM HIM.
WHICH IS FAIR ENOUGH, REALLY, HE'S A BIT OF A TOSSER.
BUT HIS ONLY SON GOT HIS BRAINS BLOWN CLEAN ACROSS A PLAYGROUND IN LOUISIANA THE OTHER MONTH.

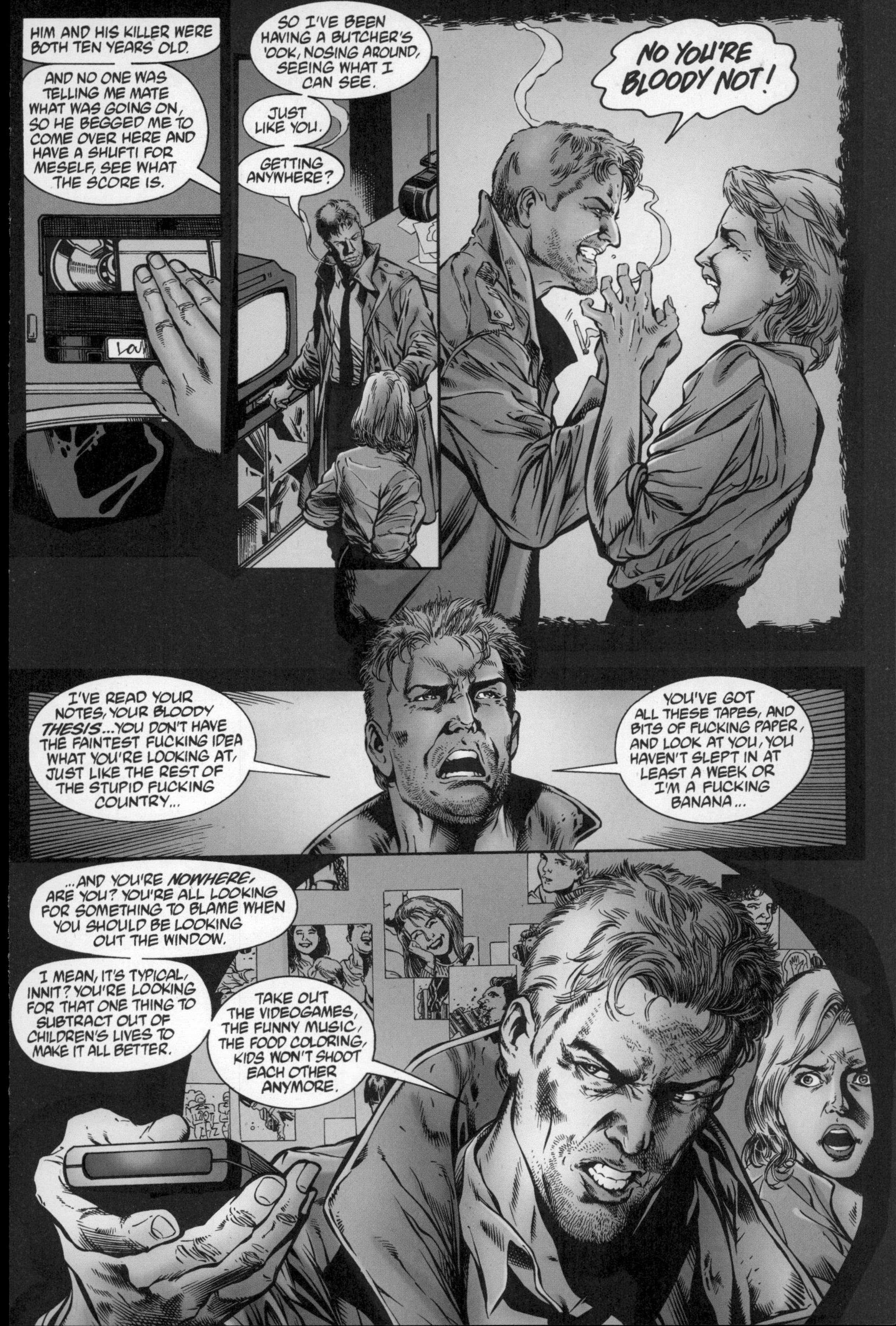
HIM AND HIS KILLER WERE BOTH TEN YEARS OLD.
AND NO ONE WAS TELLING ME MATE WHAT WAS GOING ON, SO HE BEGGED ME TO COME OVER HERE AND HAVE A SHUFTI FOR MESELF, SEE WHAT THE SCORE IS.
SO I'VE BEEN HAVING A BUTCHER'S 'OOK, NOSING AROUND, SEEING WHAT I CAN SEE.
JUST LIKE YOU.
GETTING ANYWHERE?
NO YOU'RE BLOODY NOT!
I'VE READ YOUR NOTES, YOUR BLOODY *THESIS*...YOU DON'T HAVE THE FAINTEST FUCKING IDEA WHAT YOU'RE LOOKING AT, JUST LIKE THE REST OF THE STUPID FUCKING COUNTRY...
YOU'VE GOT ALL THESE TAPES, AND BITS OF FUCKING PAPER, AND LOOK AT YOU, YOU HAVEN'T SLEPT IN AT LEAST A WEEK OR I'M A FUCKING BANANA...
...AND YOU'RE *NOWHERE*, ARE YOU? YOU'RE ALL LOOKING FOR SOMETHING TO BLAME WHEN YOU SHOULD BE LOOKING OUT THE WINDOW.
I MEAN, IT'S TYPICAL, INNIT? YOU'RE LOOKING FOR THAT ONE THING TO SUBTRACT OUT OF CHILDREN'S LIVES TO MAKE IT ALL BETTER.
TAKE OUT THE VIDEOGAMES, THE FUNNY MUSIC, THE FOOD COLORING, KIDS WON'T SHOOT EACH OTHER ANYMORE.

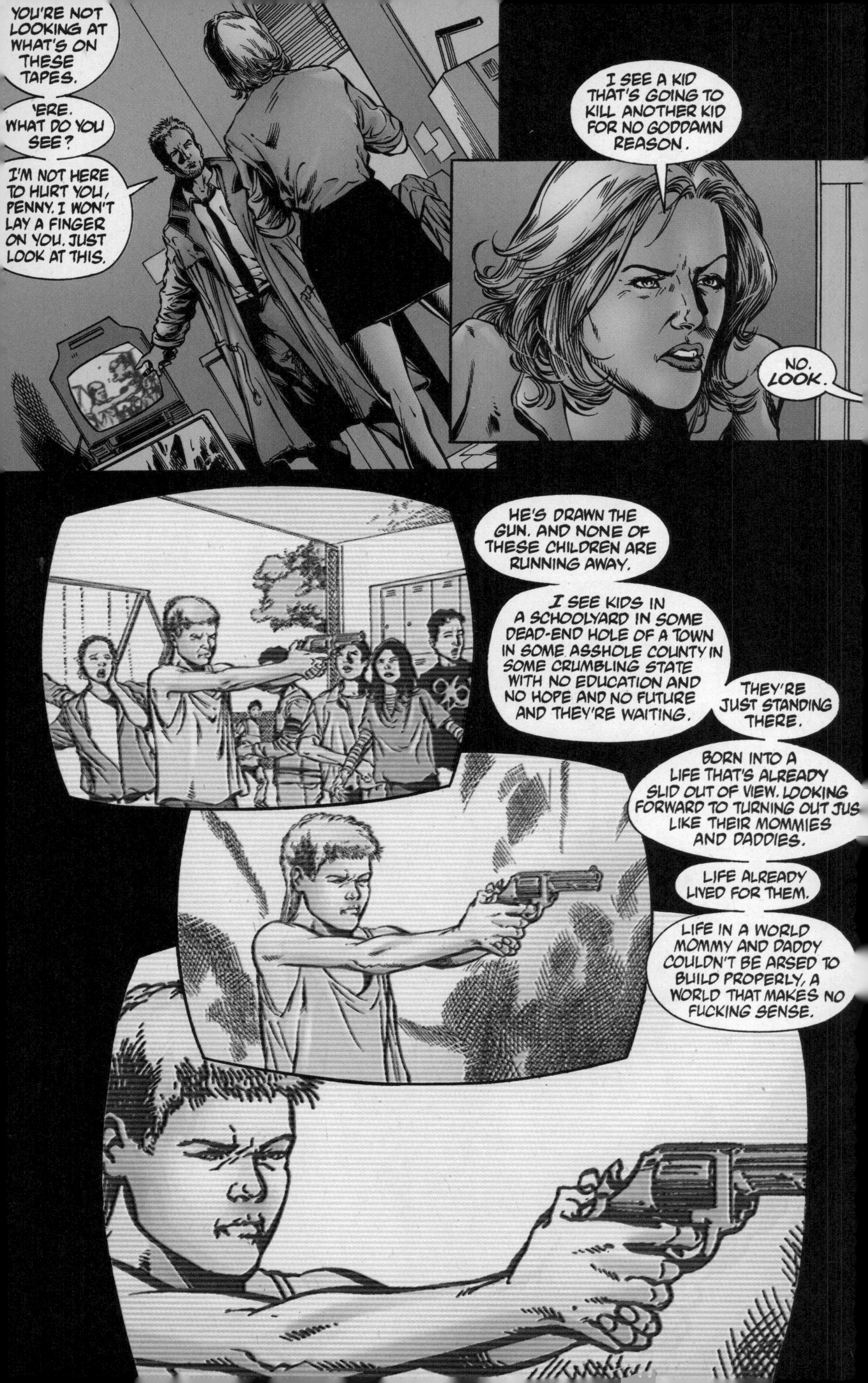

YOU'RE NOT LOOKING AT WHAT'S ON THESE TAPES.
'ERE. WHAT DO YOU SEE?
I'M NOT HERE TO HURT YOU, PENNY. I WON'T LAY A FINGER ON YOU. JUST LOOK AT THIS.
I SEE A KID THAT'S GOING TO KILL ANOTHER KID FOR NO GODDAMN REASON.
NO. LOOK.
HE'S DRAWN THE GUN. AND NONE OF THESE CHILDREN ARE RUNNING AWAY.
I SEE KIDS IN A SCHOOLYARD IN SOME DEAD-END HOLE OF A TOWN IN SOME ASSHOLE COUNTY IN SOME CRUMBLING STATE WITH NO EDUCATION AND NO HOPE AND NO FUTURE AND THEY'RE WAITING.
THEY'RE JUST STANDING THERE.
BORN INTO A LIFE THAT'S ALREADY SLID OUT OF VIEW. LOOKING FORWARD TO TURNING OUT JUS LIKE THEIR MOMMIES AND DADDIES.
LIFE ALREADY LIVED FOR THEM.
LIFE IN A WORLD MOMMY AND DADDY COULDN'T BE ARSED TO BUILD PROPERLY, A WORLD THAT MAKES NO FUCKING SENSE.

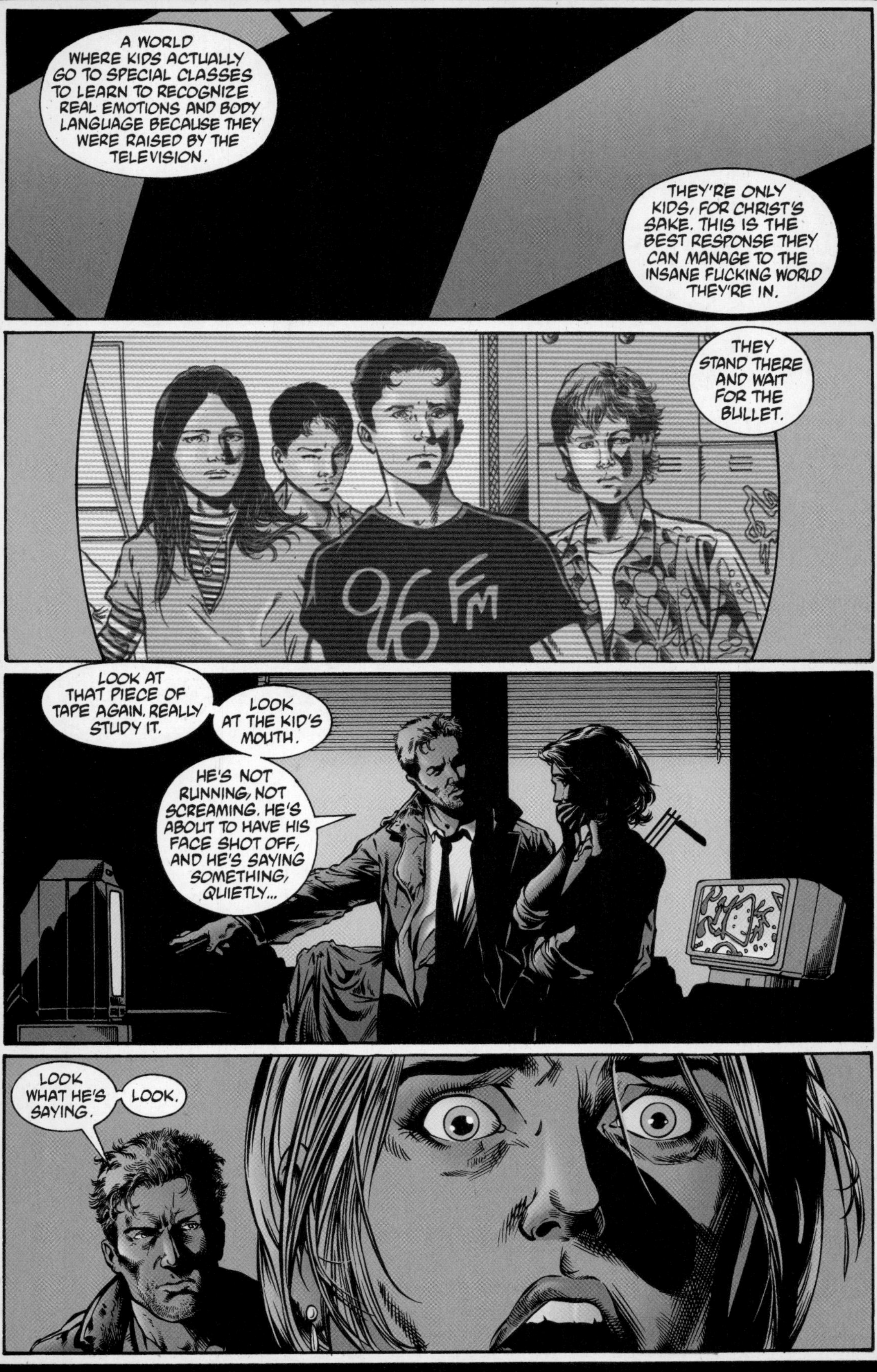
A WORLD WHERE KIDS ACTUALLY GO TO SPECIAL CLASSES TO LEARN TO RECOGNIZE REAL EMOTIONS AND BODY LANGUAGE BECAUSE THEY WERE RAISED BY THE TELEVISION.
THEY'RE ONLY KIDS, FOR CHRIST'S SAKE. THIS IS THE BEST RESPONSE THEY CAN MANAGE TO THE INSANE FUCKING WORLD THEY'RE IN.
THEY STAND THERE AND WAIT FOR THE BULLET.
96 FM
LOOK AT THAT PIECE OF TAPE AGAIN. REALLY STUDY IT.
LOOK AT THE KID'S MOUTH.
HE'S NOT RUNNING, NOT SCREAMING. HE'S ABOUT TO HAVE HIS FACE SHOT OFF, AND HE'S SAYING SOMETHING, QUIETLY...
LOOK WHAT HE'S SAYING.
LOOK.

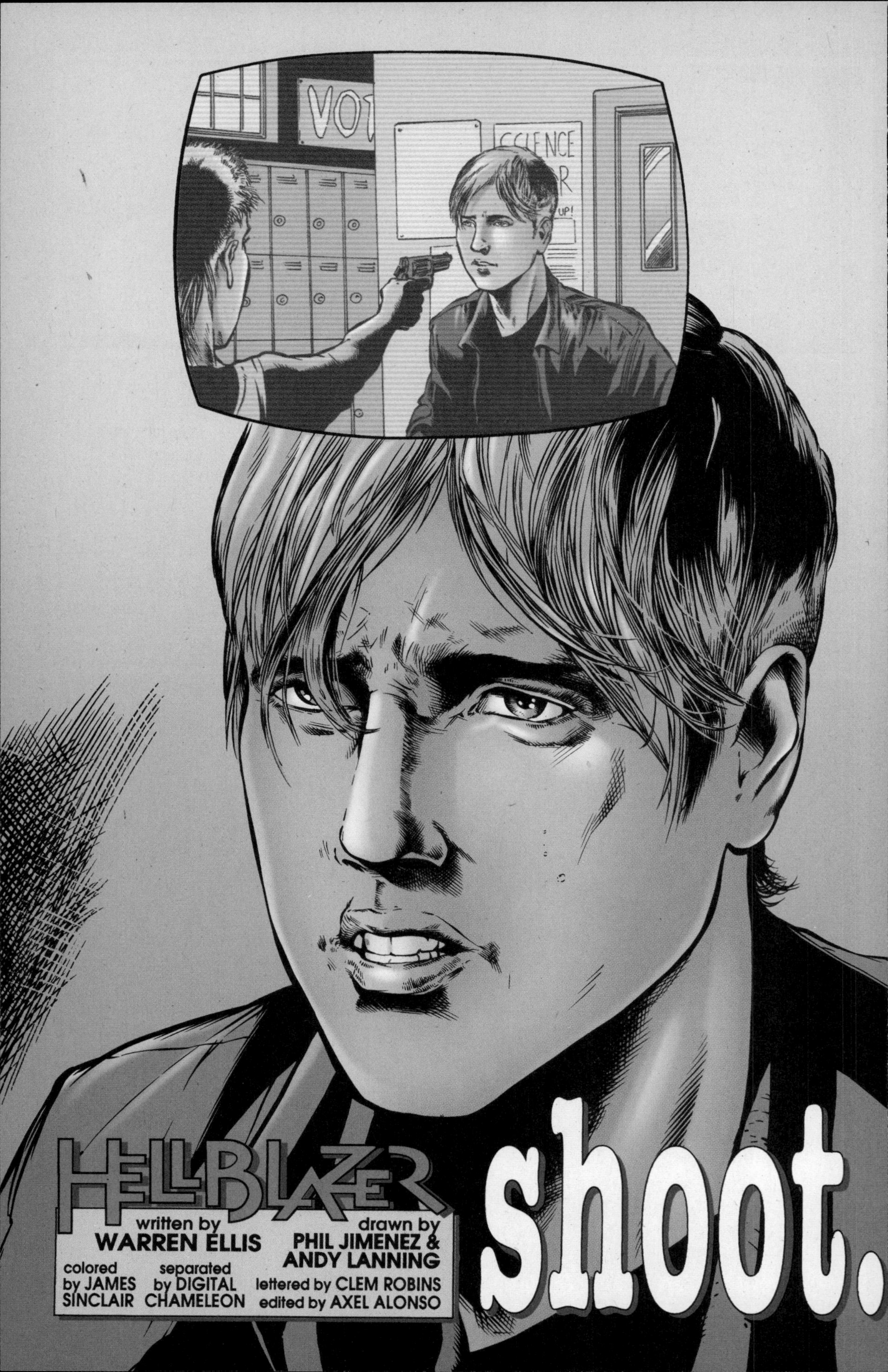
HELLBLAZER
written by
WARREN ELLIS
drawn by
PHIL JIMENEZ &
ANDY LANNING
colored
by JAMES
SINCLAIR
separated
by DIGITAL
CHAMELEON
lettered by CLEM ROBINS
edited by AXEL ALONSO
shoot.

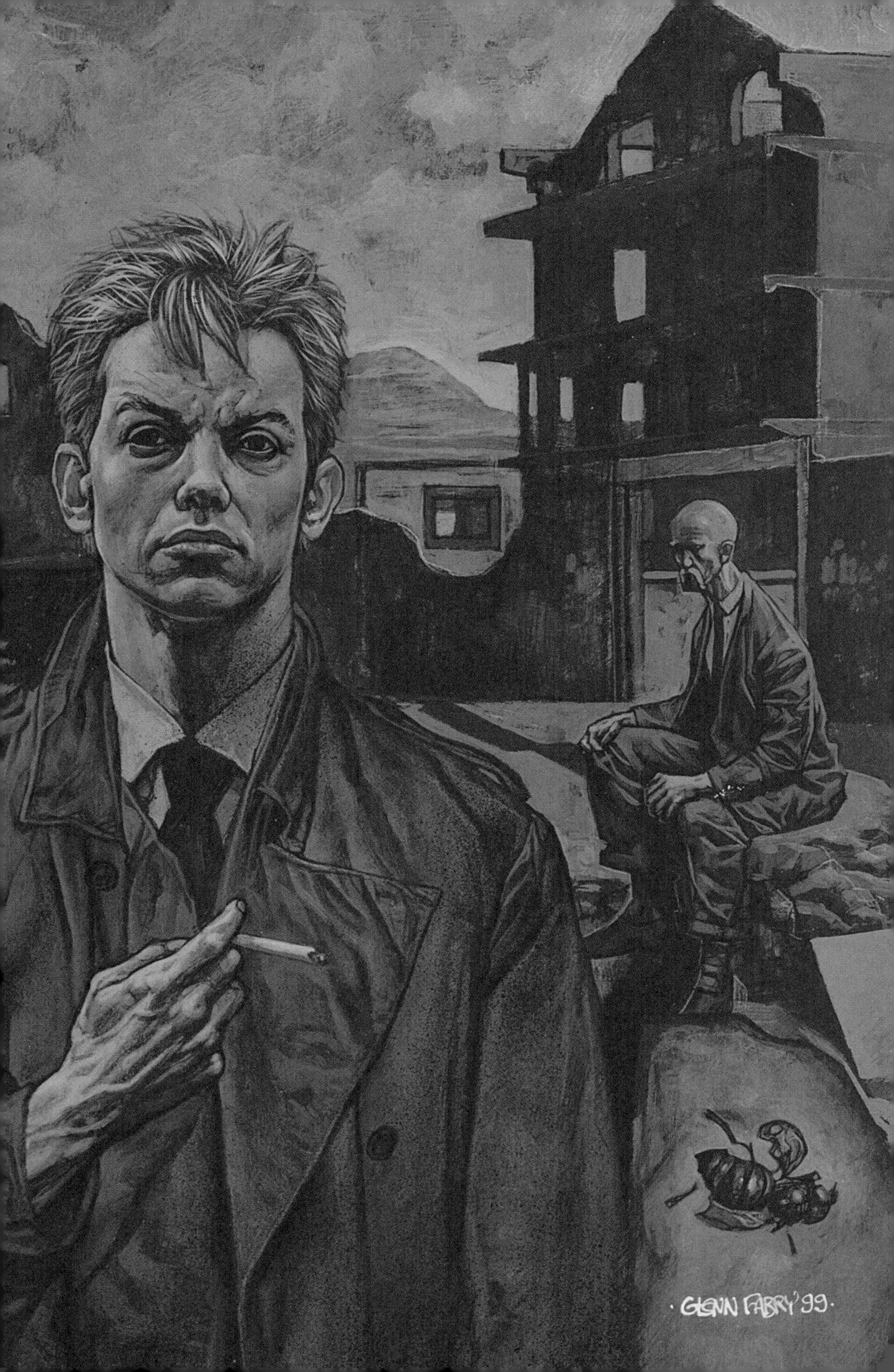
·GLENN FABRY'99·

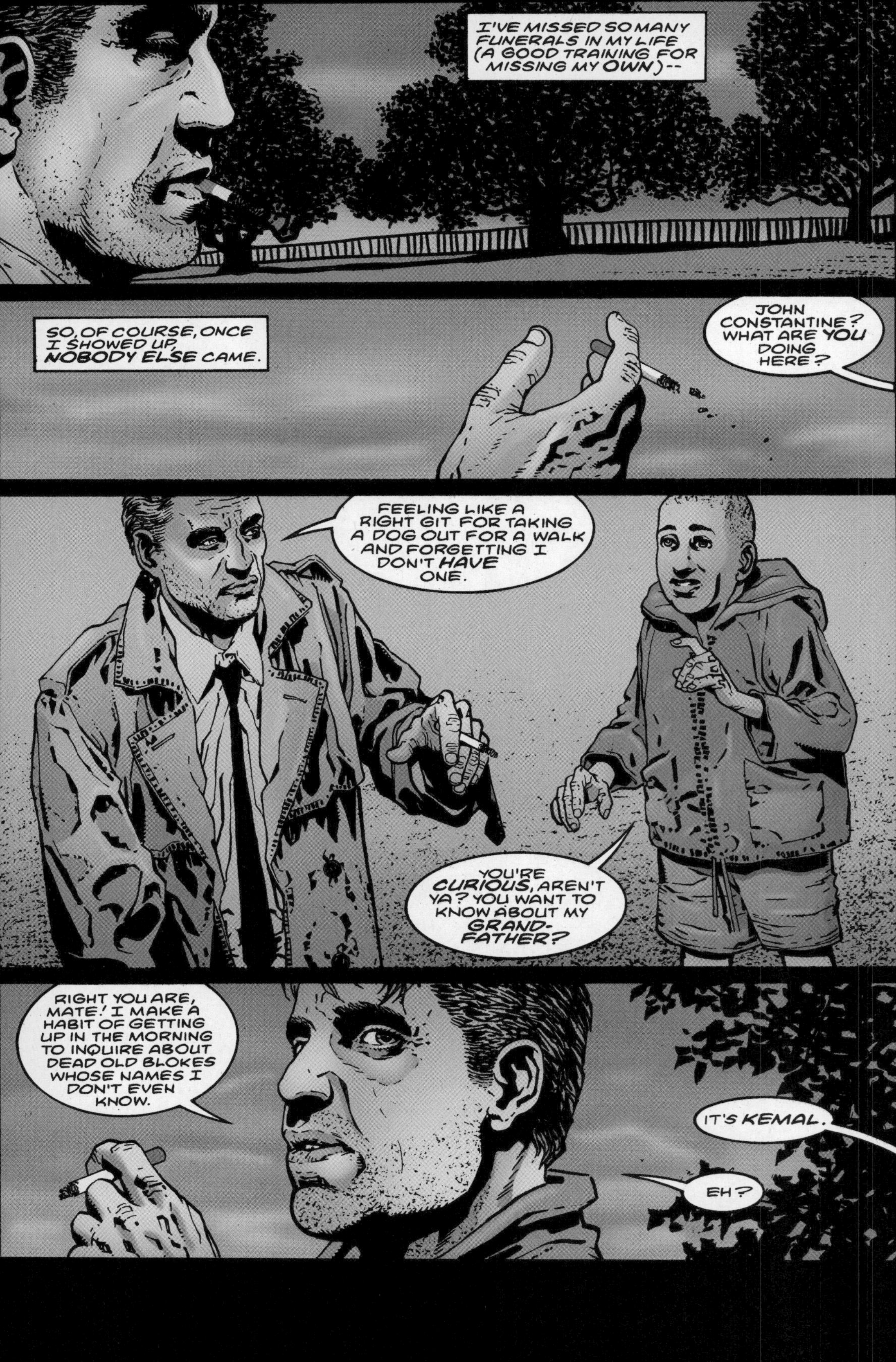
I'VE MISSED SO MANY FUNERALS IN MY LIFE (A GOOD TRAINING FOR MISSING MY OWN) --
SO, OF COURSE, ONCE I SHOWED UP, NOBODY ELSE CAME.
JOHN CONSTANTINE? WHAT ARE YOU DOING HERE?
FEELING LIKE A RIGHT GIT FOR TAKING A DOG OUT FOR A WALK AND FORGETTING I DON'T HAVE ONE.
YOU'RE CURIOUS, AREN'T YA? YOU WANT TO KNOW ABOUT MY GRAND-FATHER?
RIGHT YOU ARE, MATE! I MAKE A HABIT OF GETTING UP IN THE MORNING TO INQUIRE ABOUT DEAD OLD BLOKES WHOSE NAMES I DON'T EVEN KNOW.
IT'S KEMAL.
EH?

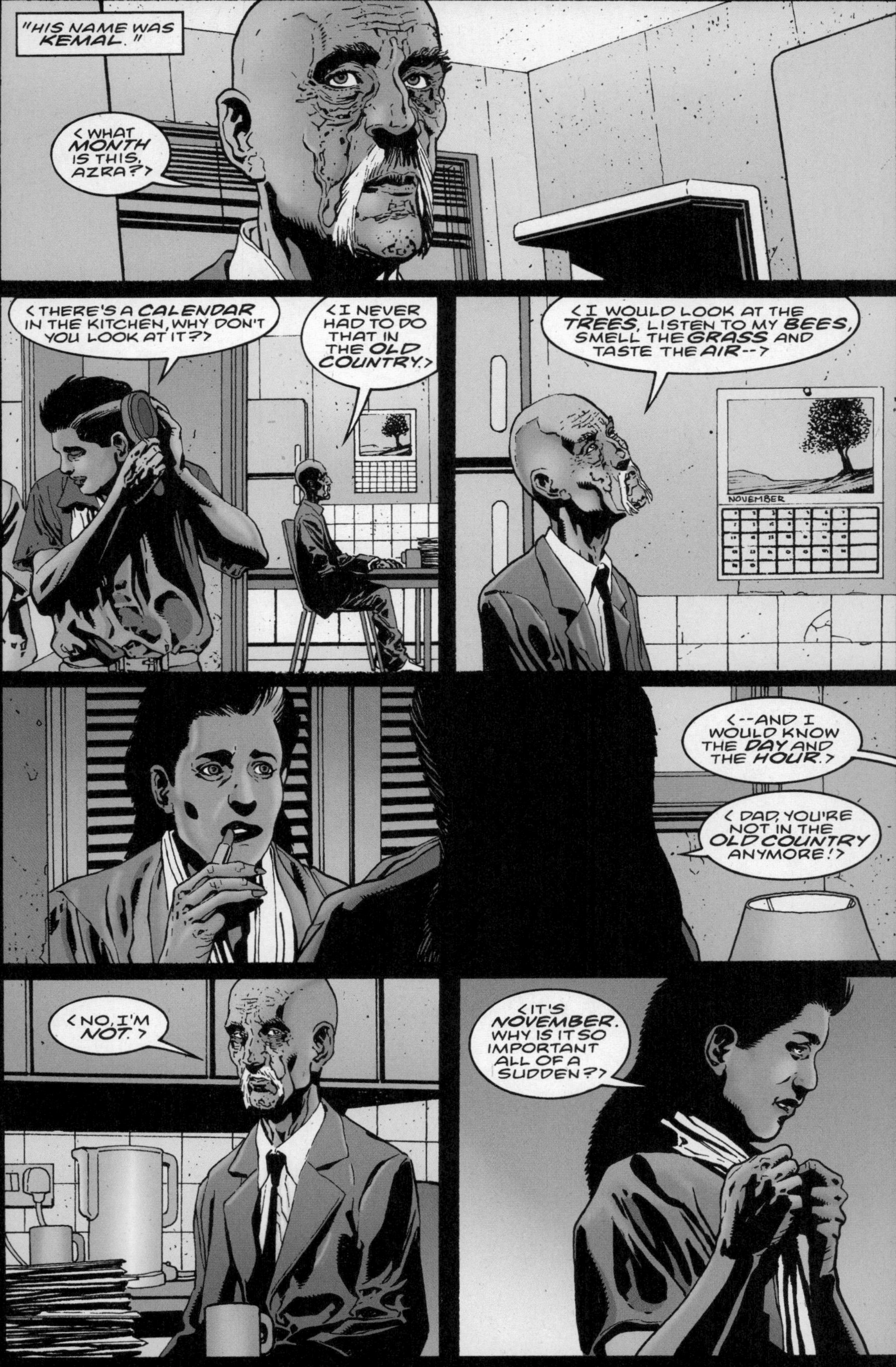
"HIS NAME WAS KEMAL."
<WHAT MONTH IS THIS, AZRA?>
<THERE'S A CALENDAR IN THE KITCHEN, WHY DON'T YOU LOOK AT IT?>
<I NEVER HAD TO DO THAT IN THE OLD COUNTRY.>
<I WOULD LOOK AT THE TREES, LISTEN TO MY BEES, SMELL THE GRASS AND TASTE THE AIR-->
NOVEMBER
<--AND I WOULD KNOW THE DAY AND THE HOUR.>
<DAD, YOU'RE NOT IN THE OLD COUNTRY ANYMORE!>
<NO, I'M NOT.>
<IT'S NOVEMBER. WHY IS IT SO IMPORTANT ALL OF A SUDDEN?>

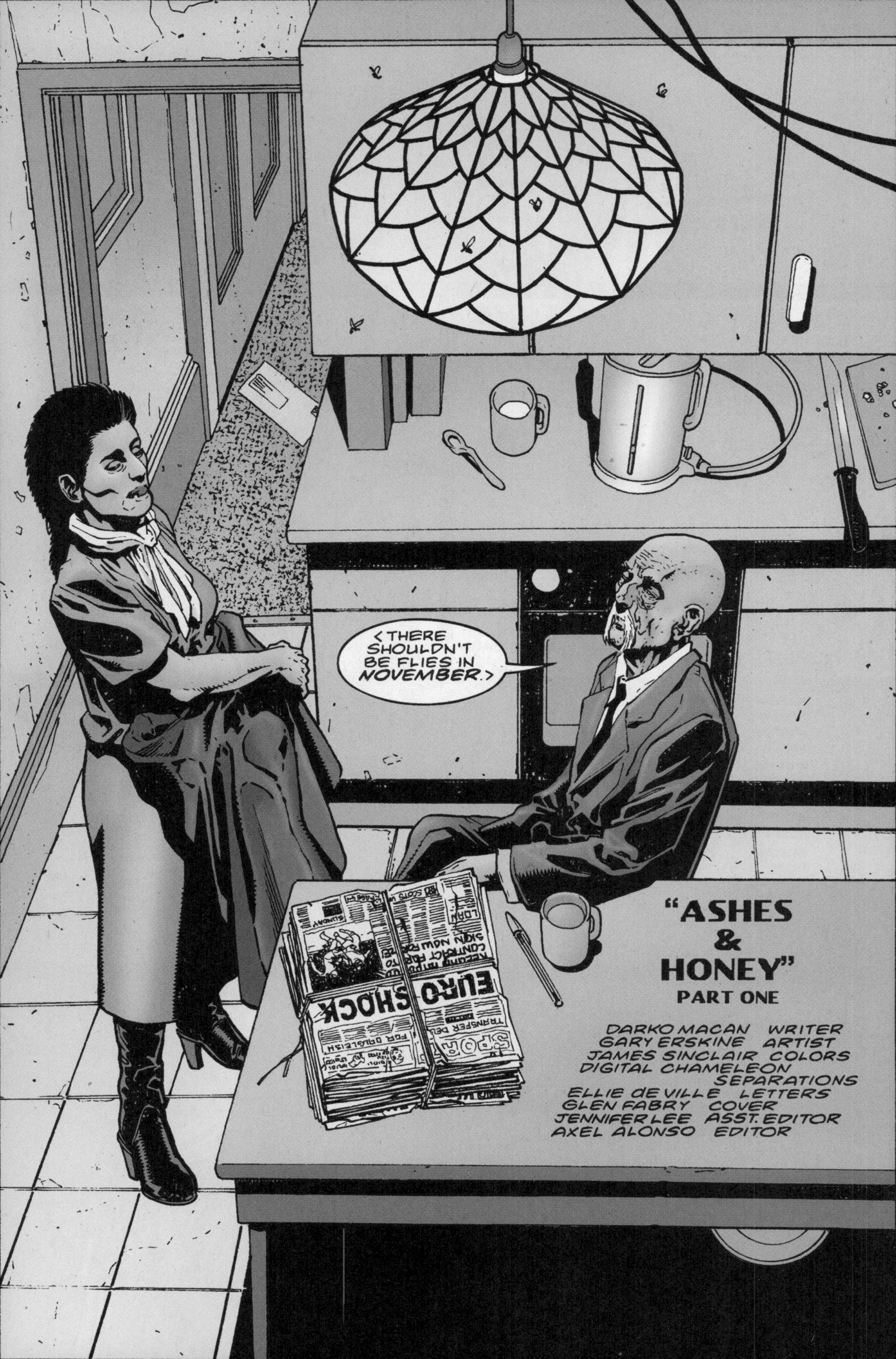

<THERE SHOULDN'T BE FLIES IN NOVEMBER.>
EURO-SHOCK
"ASHES & HONEY"
PART ONE
DARKO MACAN WRITER
GARY ERSKINE ARTIST
JAMES SINCLAIR COLORS
DIGITAL CHAMELEON SEPARATIONS
ELLIE DE VILLE LETTERS
GLEN FABRY COVER
JENNIFER LEE ASST. EDITOR
AXEL ALONSO EDITOR

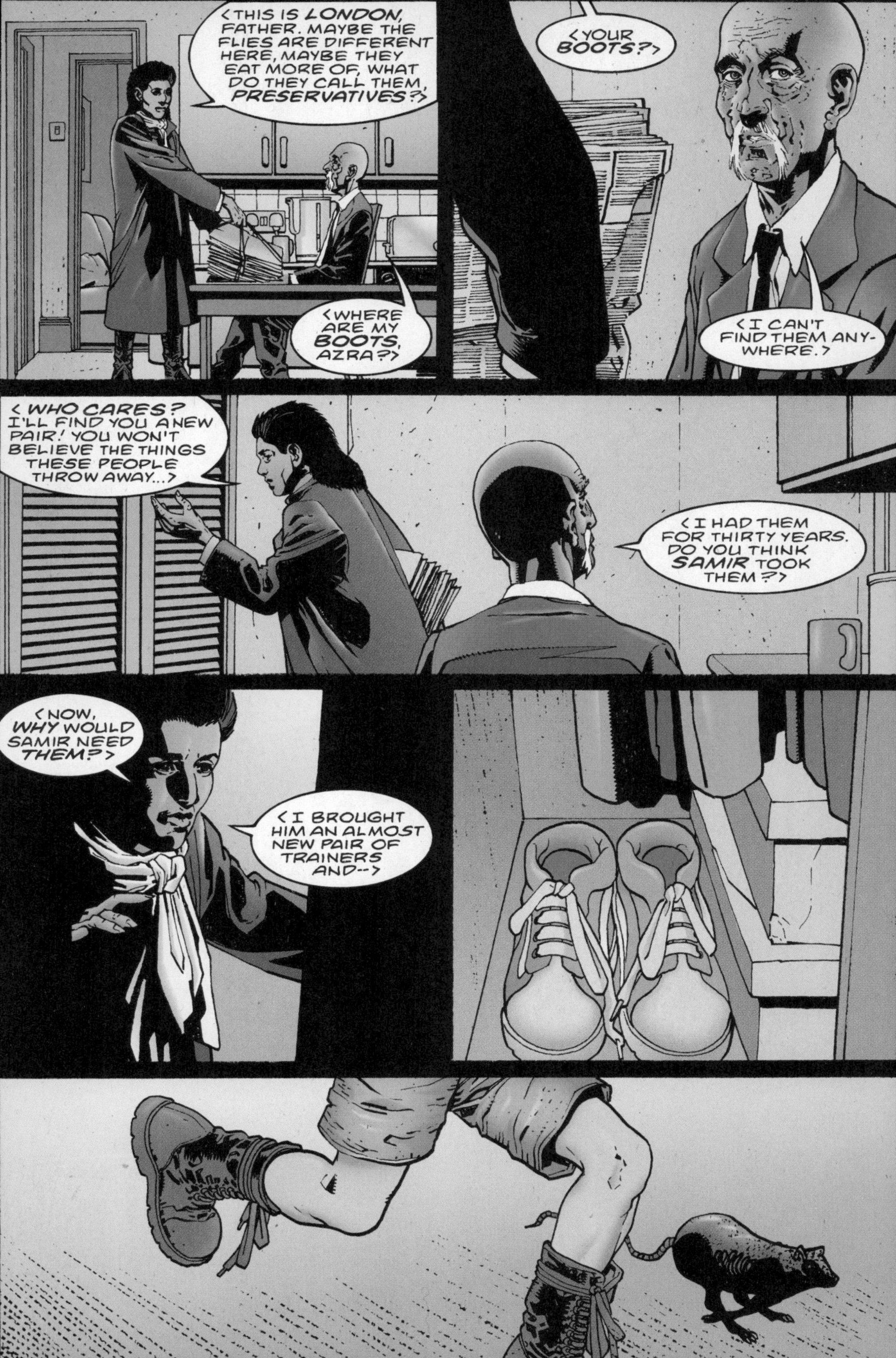
<THIS IS LONDON, FATHER. MAYBE THE FLIES ARE DIFFERENT HERE, MAYBE THEY EAT MORE OF, WHAT DO THEY CALL THEM, PRESERVATIVES?>
<WHERE ARE MY BOOTS, AZRA?>
<YOUR BOOTS?>
<I CAN'T FIND THEM ANY-WHERE.>
<WHO CARES? I'LL FIND YOU A NEW PAIR! YOU WON'T BELIEVE THE THINGS THESE PEOPLE THROW AWAY...>
<I HAD THEM FOR THIRTY YEARS. DO YOU THINK SAMIR TOOK THEM?>
<NOW, WHY WOULD SAMIR NEED THEM?>
<I BROUGHT HIM AN ALMOST NEW PAIR OF TRAINERS AND-->

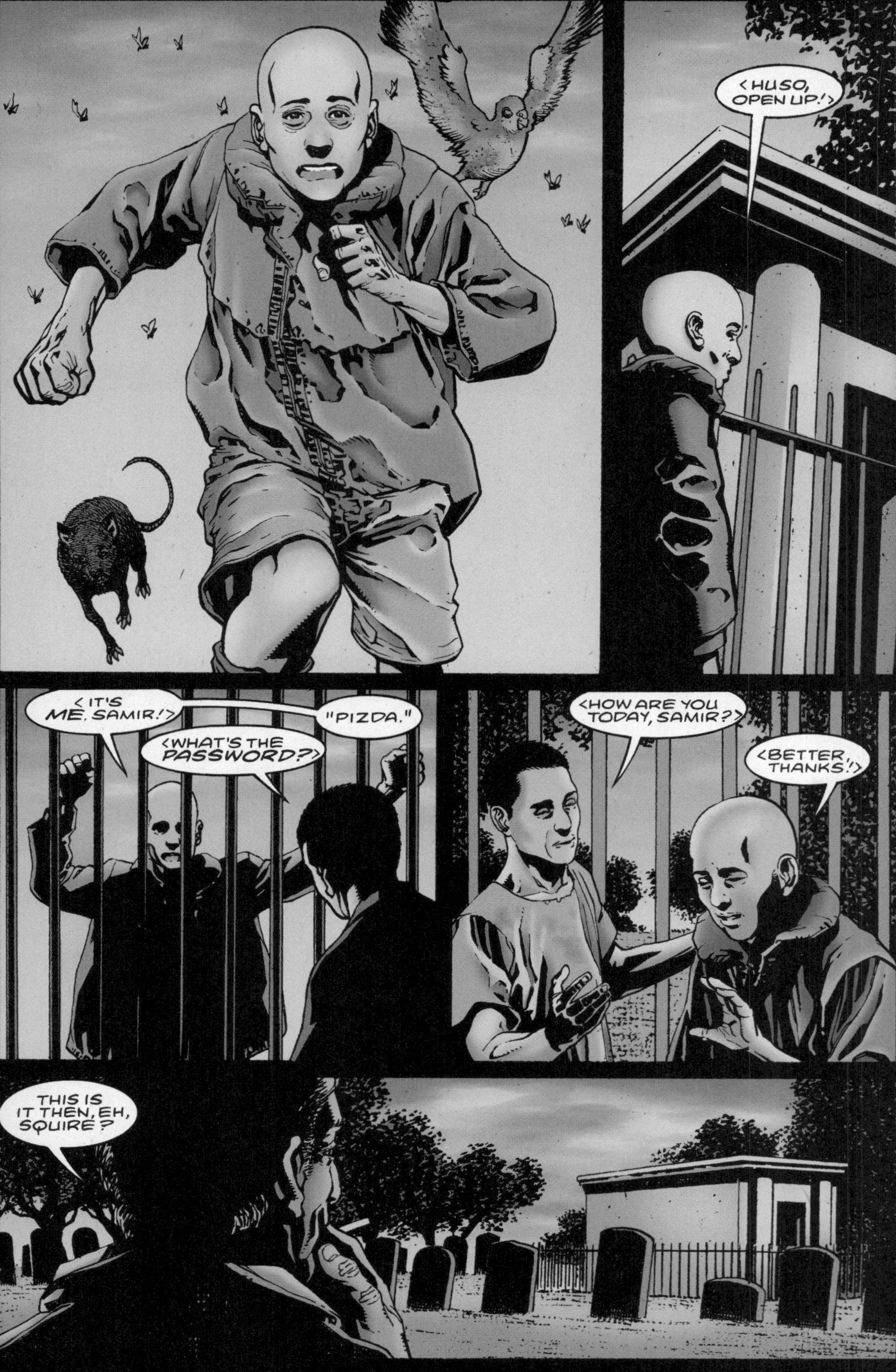
<HUSO, OPEN UP!>
<IT'S ME. SAMIR!>
<WHAT'S THE PASSWORD?>
"PIZDA."
<HOW ARE YOU TODAY, SAMIR?>
<BETTER, THANKS!>
THIS IS IT THEN, EH, SQUIRE?

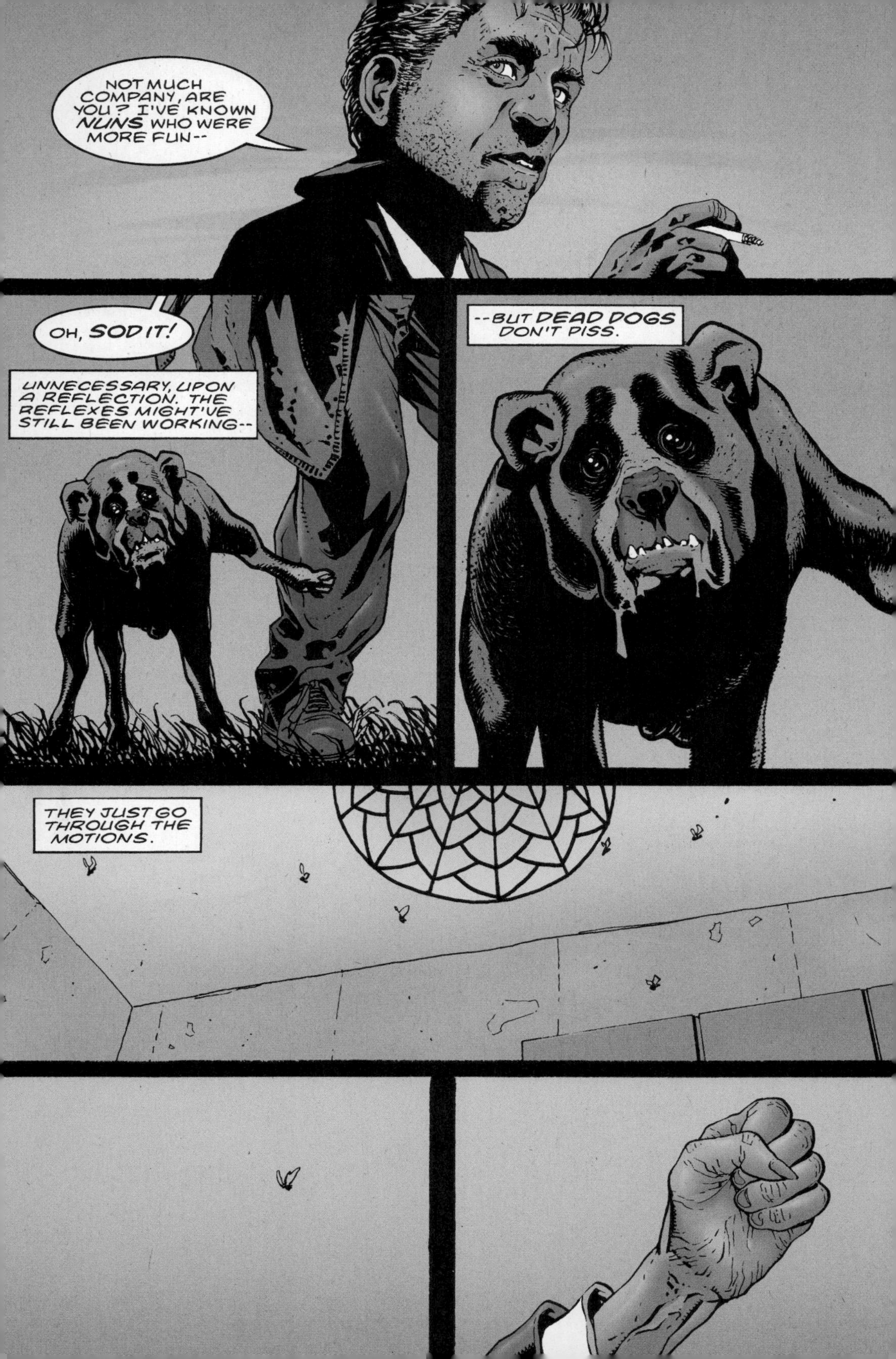
NOT MUCH COMPANY, ARE YOU? I'VE KNOWN NUNS WHO WERE MORE FUN--
OH, SOD IT!
UNNECESSARY, UPON A REFLECTION. THE REFLEXES MIGHT'VE STILL BEEN WORKING--
--BUT DEAD DOGS DON'T PISS.
THEY JUST GO THROUGH THE MOTIONS.

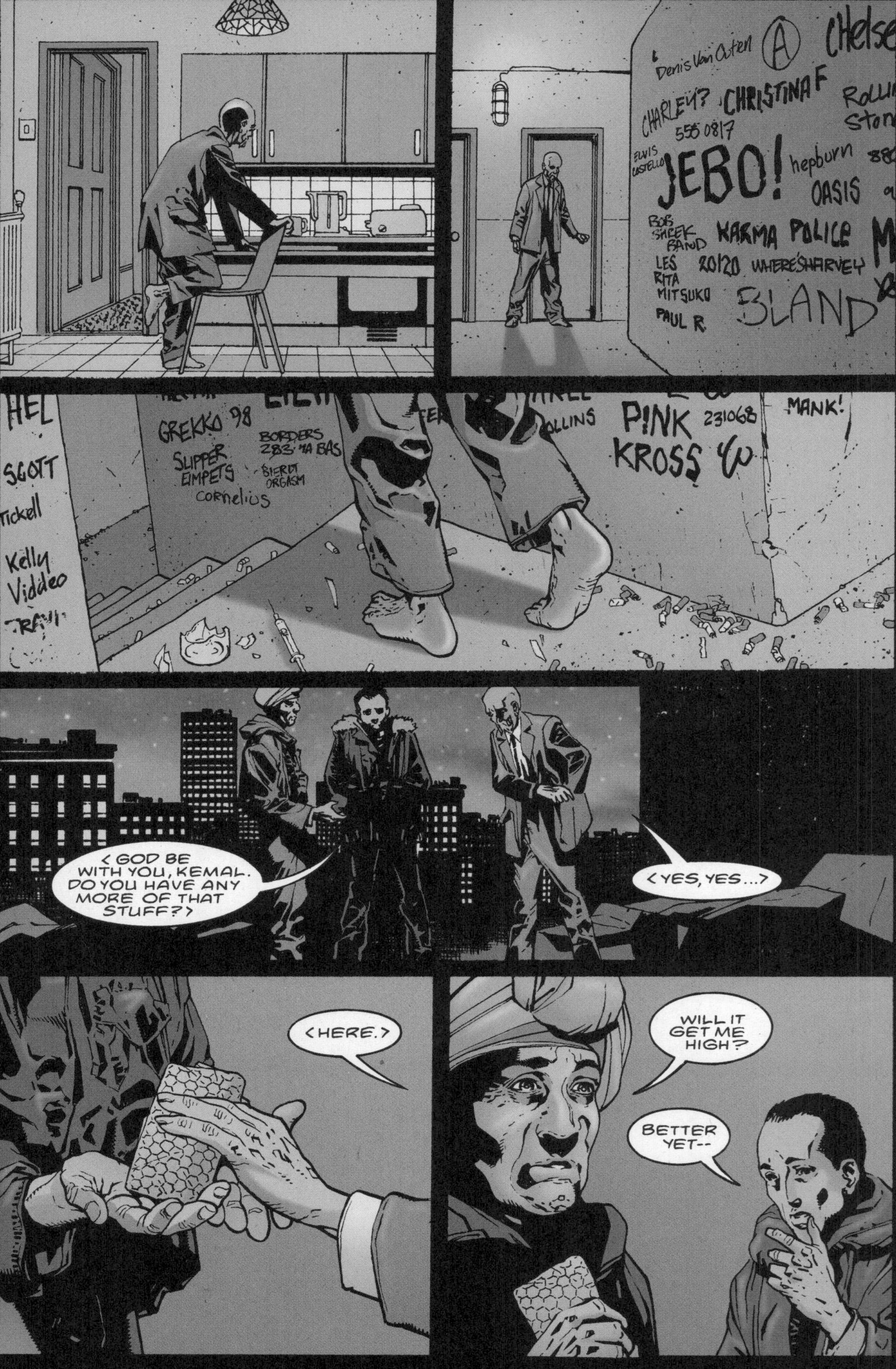
<GOD BE WITH YOU, KEMAL. DO YOU HAVE ANY MORE OF THAT STUFF?>
<YES, YES...>
<HERE.>
WILL IT GET ME HIGH?
BETTER YET--

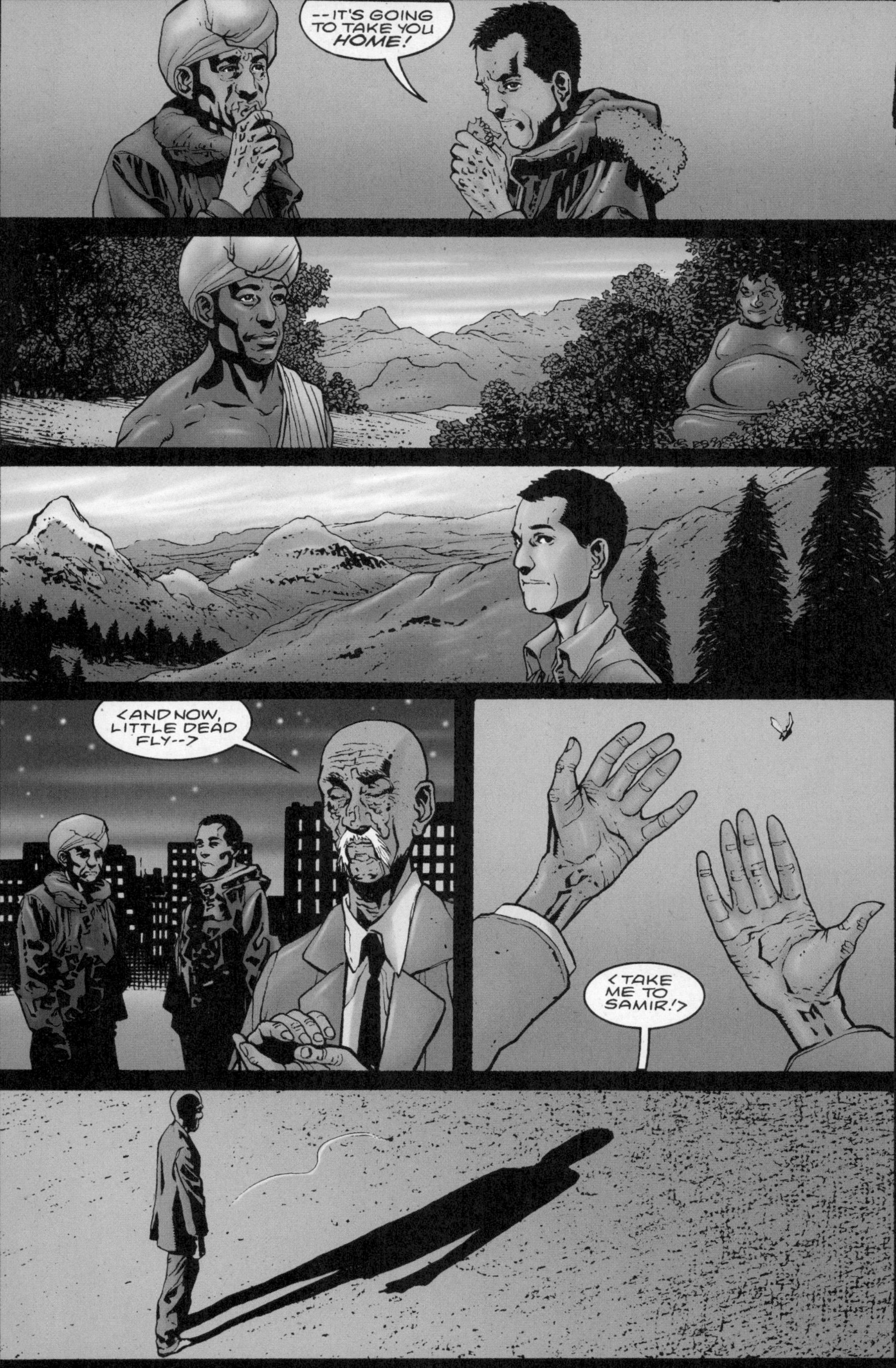
--IT'S GOING TO TAKE YOU HOME!
<AND NOW, LITTLE DEAD FLY-->
<TAKE ME TO SAMIR!>

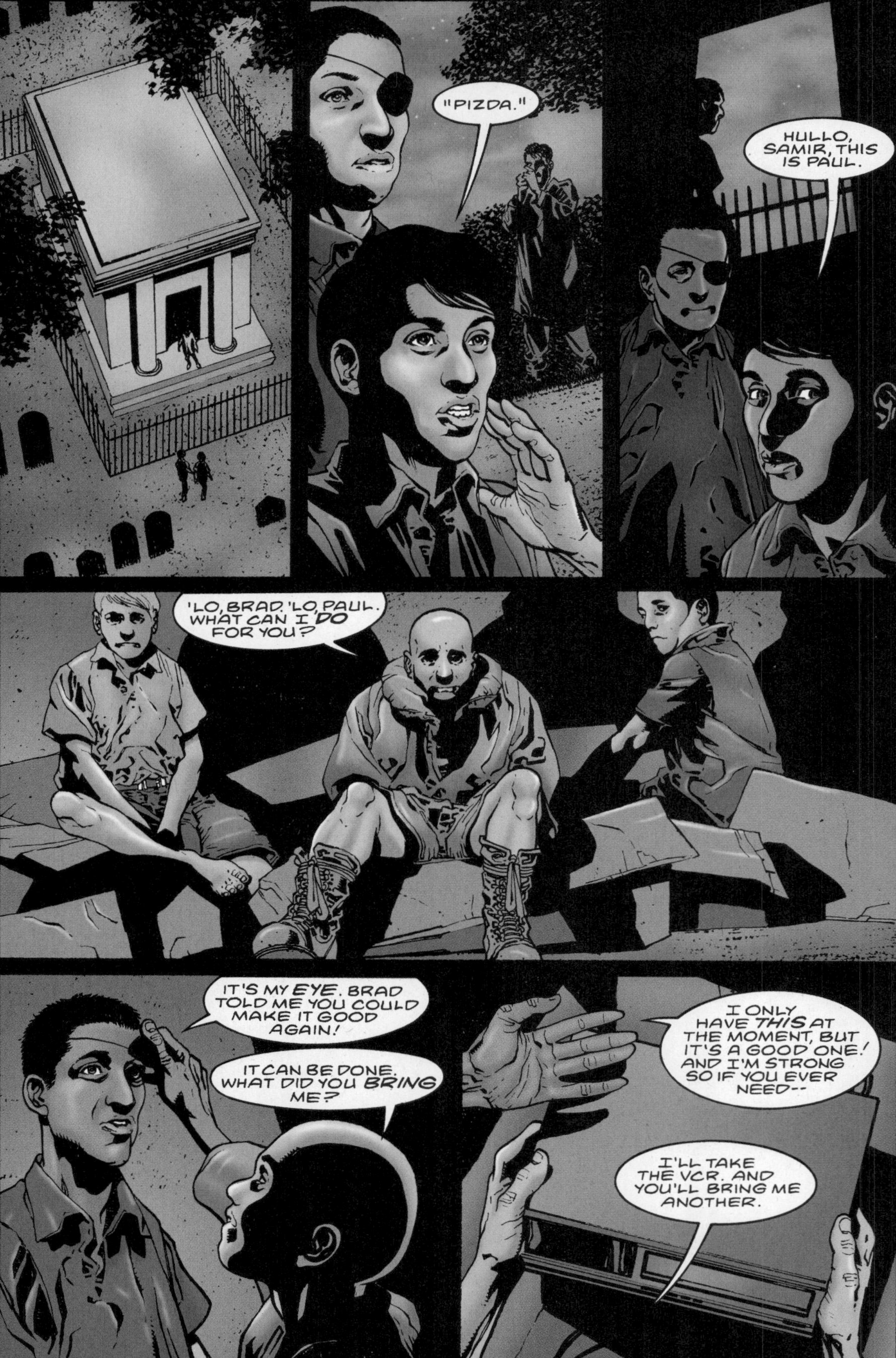
"PIZDA."
HULLO, SAMIR, THIS IS PAUL.
'LO, BRAD. 'LO, PAUL. WHAT CAN I *DO* FOR YOU?
IT'S MY *EYE*. BRAD TOLD ME YOU COULD MAKE IT GOOD AGAIN!
IT CAN BE DONE. WHAT DID YOU *BRING* ME?
I ONLY HAVE *THIS* AT THE MOMENT, BUT IT'S A GOOD ONE! AND I'M STRONG SO IF YOU EVER NEED--
I'LL TAKE THE VCR. AND YOU'LL BRING ME ANOTHER.

STAND STILL NOW.

PRECI MOJI, POMAGAJTE!

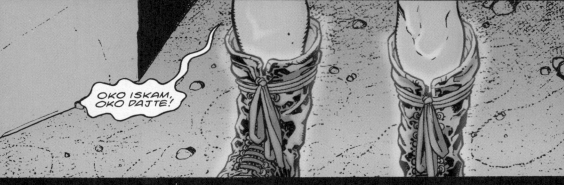

OKO ISKAM, OKO DAJTE!

IT WAS TRUE! I CAN SEE! I CAN SEE!

ARE YOU ALL RIGHT, SAMIR?

FINE, BRAD, FINE...

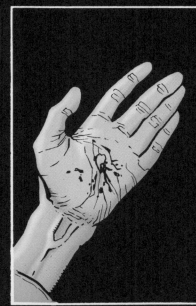

39

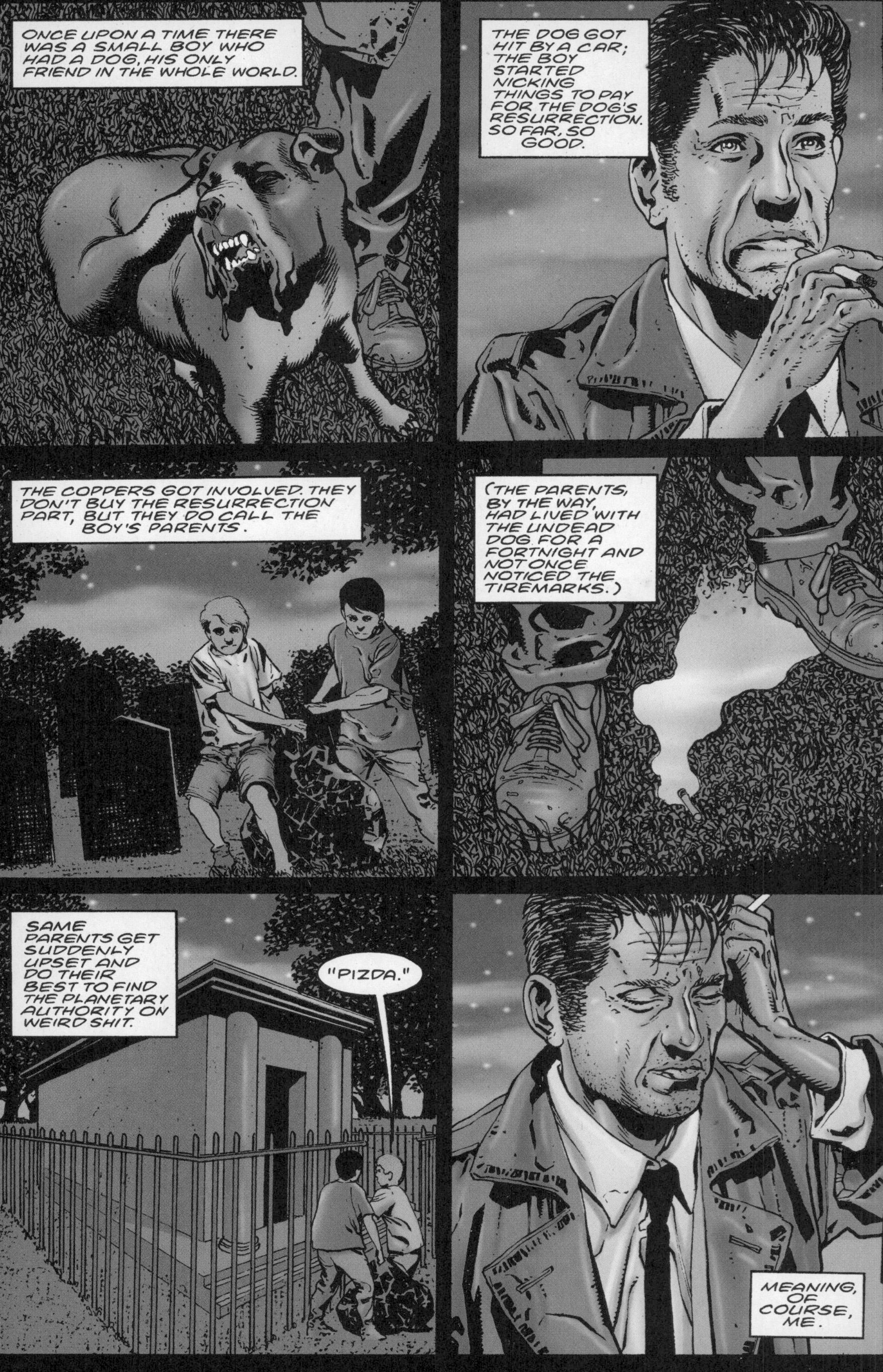
ONCE UPON A TIME THERE WAS A SMALL BOY WHO HAD A DOG, HIS ONLY FRIEND IN THE WHOLE WORLD.
THE DOG GOT HIT BY A CAR; THE BOY STARTED NICKING THINGS TO PAY FOR THE DOG'S RESURRECTION. SO FAR, SO GOOD.
THE COPPERS GOT INVOLVED. THEY DON'T BUY THE RESURRECTION PART, BUT THEY DO CALL THE BOY'S PARENTS.
(THE PARENTS, BY THE WAY, HAD LIVED WITH THE UNDEAD DOG FOR A FORTNIGHT AND NOT ONCE NOTICED THE TIREMARKS.)
SAME PARENTS GET SUDDENLY UPSET AND DO THEIR BEST TO FIND THE PLANETARY AUTHORITY ON WEIRD SHIT.
"PIZDA."
MEANING, OF COURSE, ME.

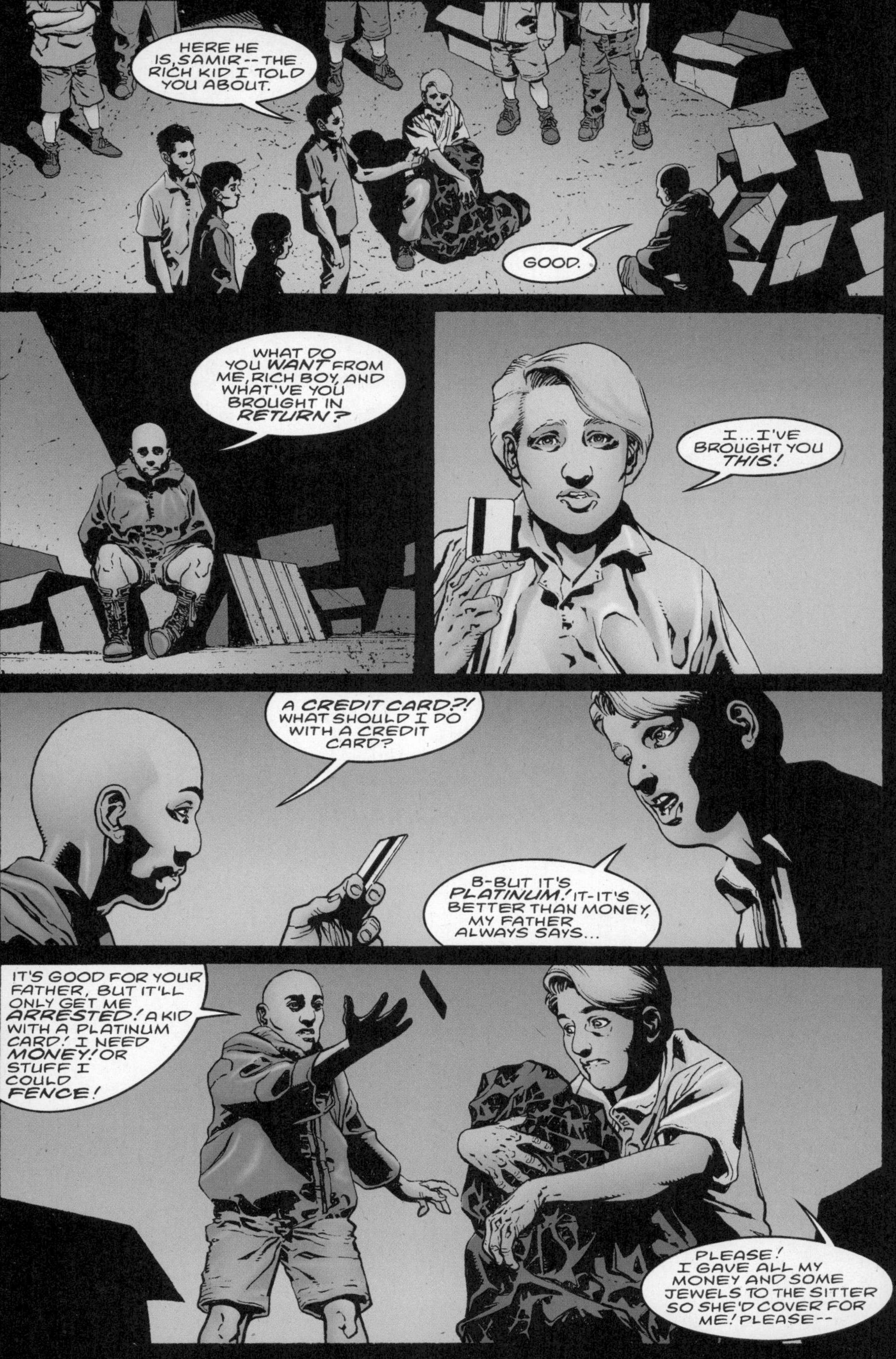
HERE HE IS, SAMIR -- THE RICH KID I TOLD YOU ABOUT.
GOOD.
WHAT DO YOU WANT FROM ME, RICH BOY, AND WHAT'VE YOU BROUGHT IN RETURN?
I... I'VE BROUGHT YOU THIS!
A CREDIT CARD?! WHAT SHOULD I DO WITH A CREDIT CARD?
B-BUT IT'S PLATINUM! IT-IT'S BETTER THAN MONEY, MY FATHER ALWAYS SAYS...
IT'S GOOD FOR YOUR FATHER, BUT IT'LL ONLY GET ME ARRESTED! A KID WITH A PLATINUM CARD! I NEED MONEY! OR STUFF I COULD FENCE!
PLEASE! I GAVE ALL MY MONEY AND SOME JEWELS TO THE SITTER SO SHE'D COVER FOR ME! PLEASE--

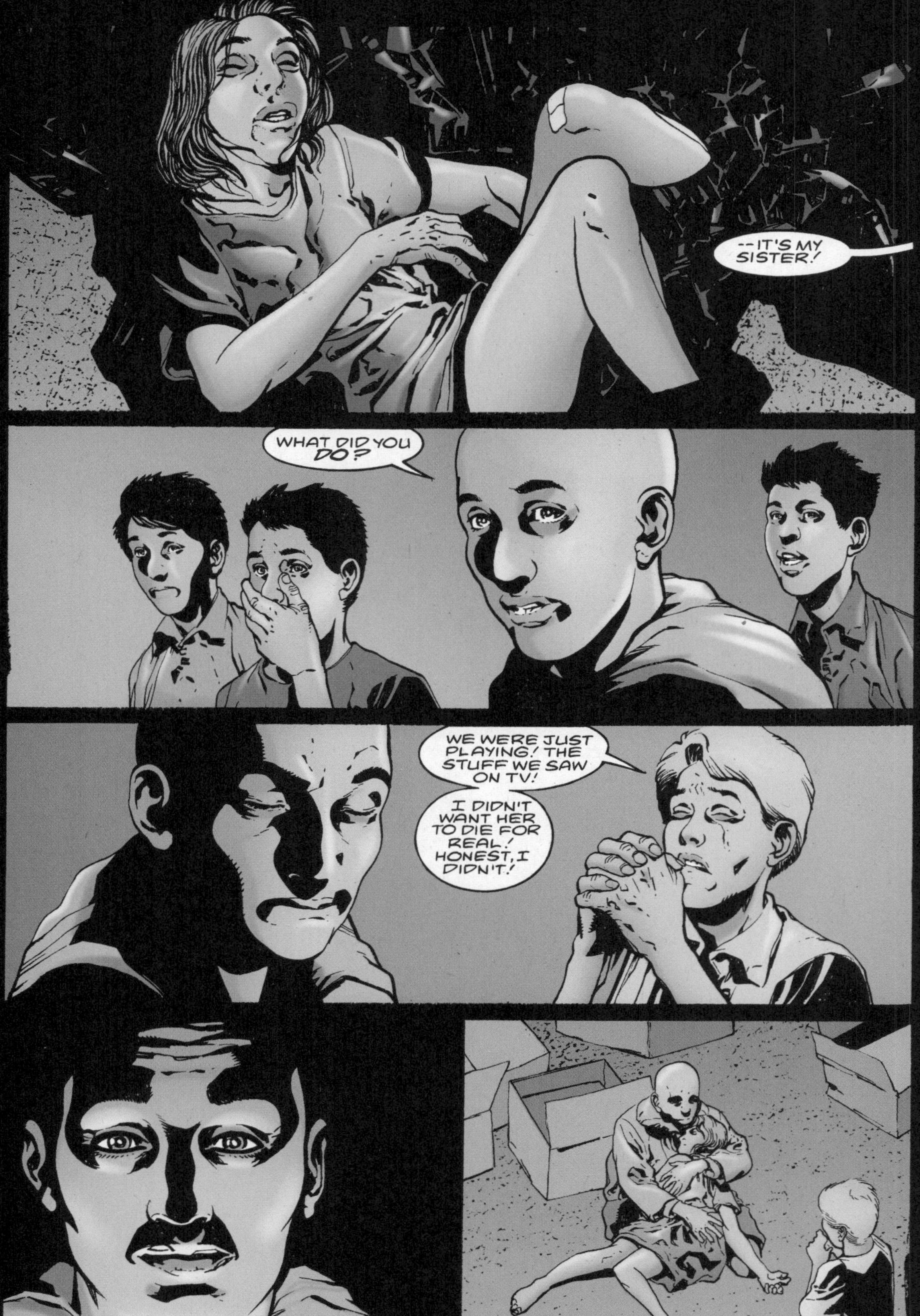
--IT'S MY SISTER!
WHAT DID YOU DO?
WE WERE JUST PLAYING! THE STUFF WE SAW ON TV!
I DIDN'T WANT HER TO DIE FOR REAL! HONEST, I DIDN'T!
SHUT UP, I'LL DO IT!

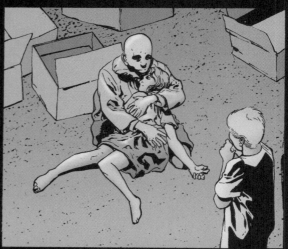

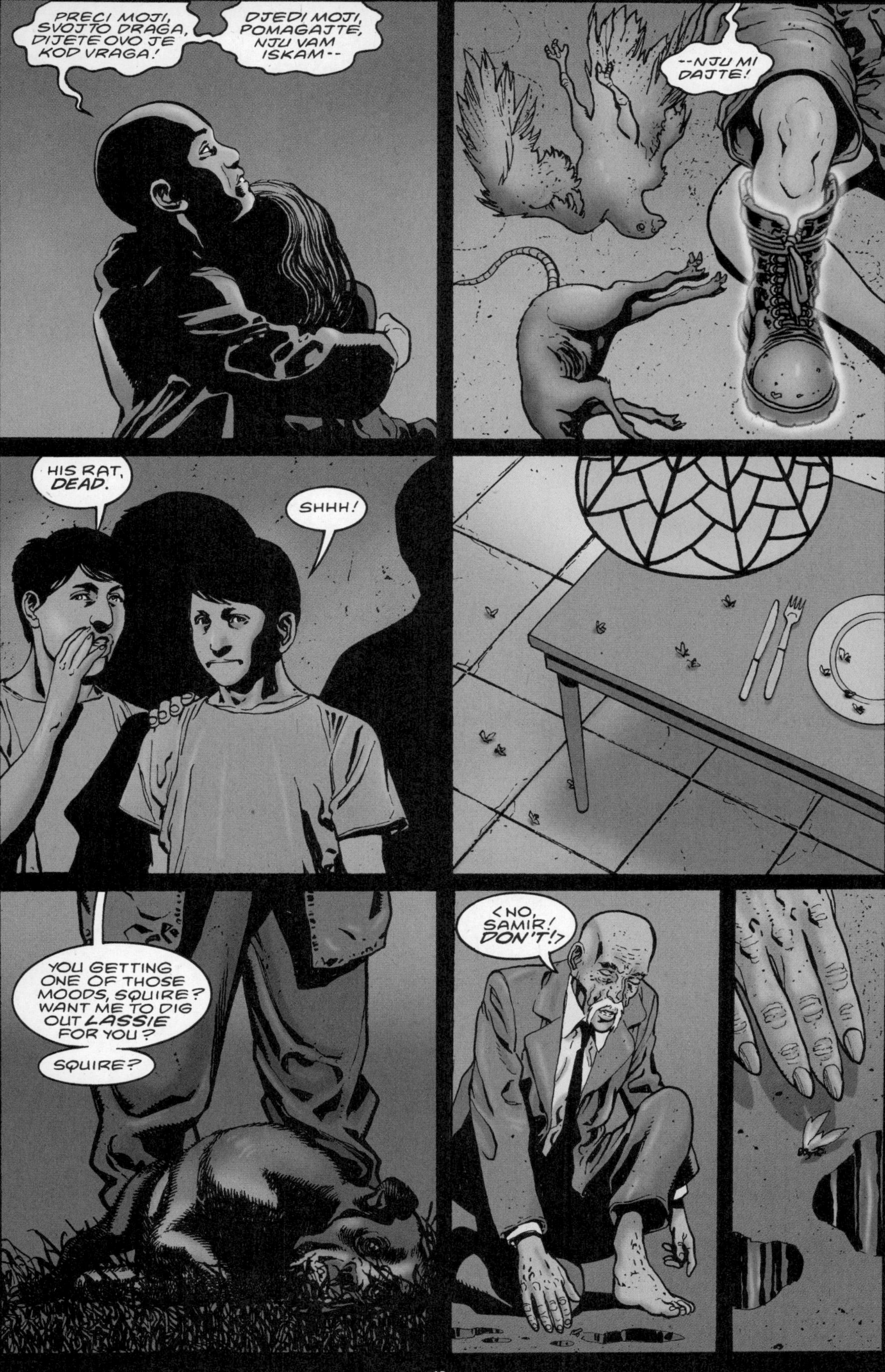
PRECI MOJI, SVOJTO DRAGA, DIJETE OVO JE KOD VRAGA!
DJEDI MOJI, POMAGAJTE, NJU VAM ISKAM --
--NJU MI DAJTE!
HIS RAT, DEAD.
SHHH!
YOU GETTING ONE OF THOSE MOODS, SQUIRE? WANT ME TO DIG OUT LASSIE FOR YOU?
SQUIRE?
<NO, SAMIR! DON'T!>

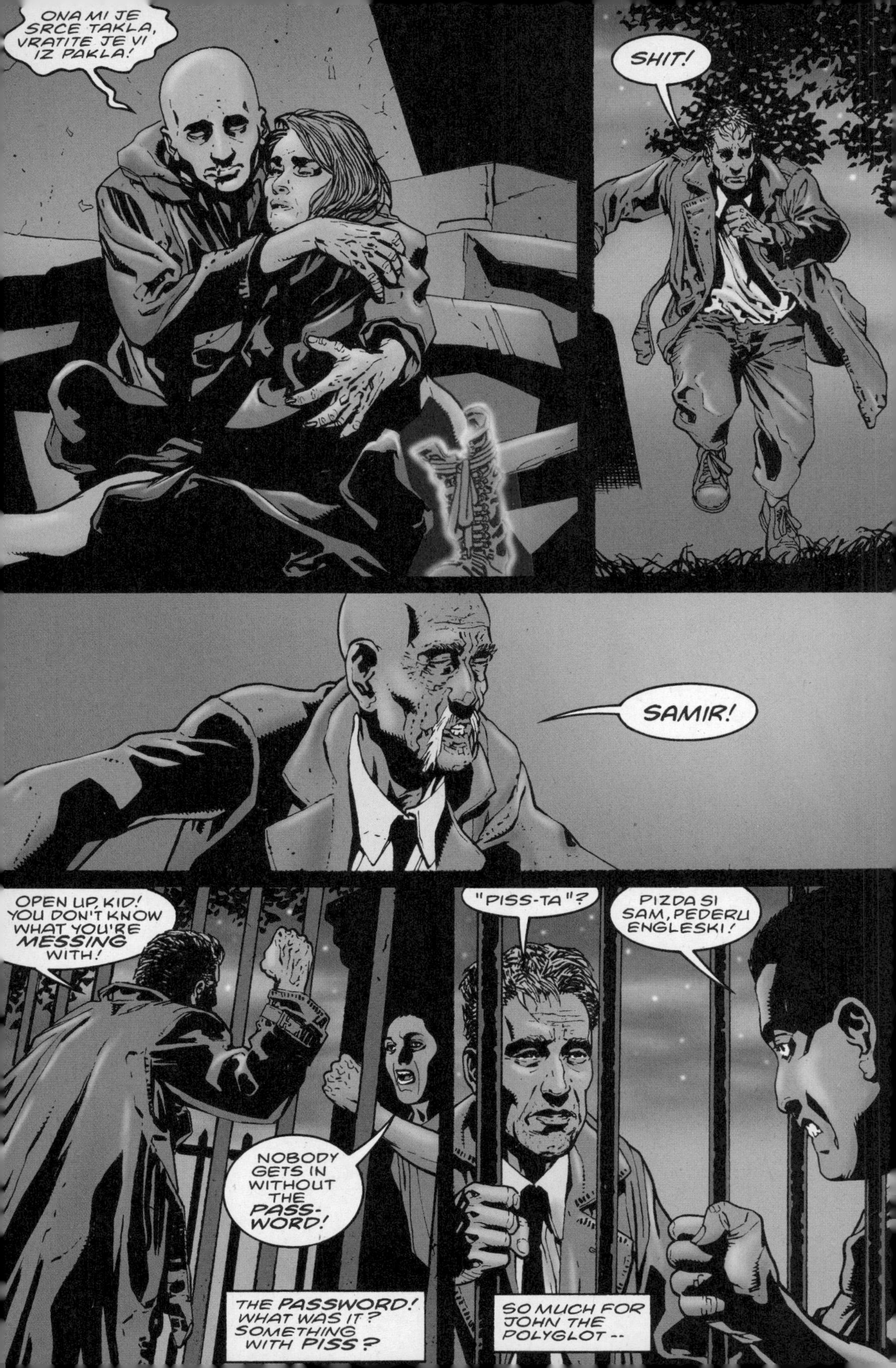
ONA MI JE SRCE TAKLA, VRATITE JE VI IZ PAKLA!
SHIT!
SAMIR!
OPEN UP, KID! YOU DON'T KNOW WHAT YOU'RE MESSING WITH!
NOBODY GETS IN WITHOUT THE PASS-WORD!
THE PASSWORD! WHAT WAS IT? SOMETHING WITH PISS?
"PISS-TA"?
PIZDA SI SAM, PEDERU ENGLESKI!
SO MUCH FOR JOHN THE POLYGLOT --

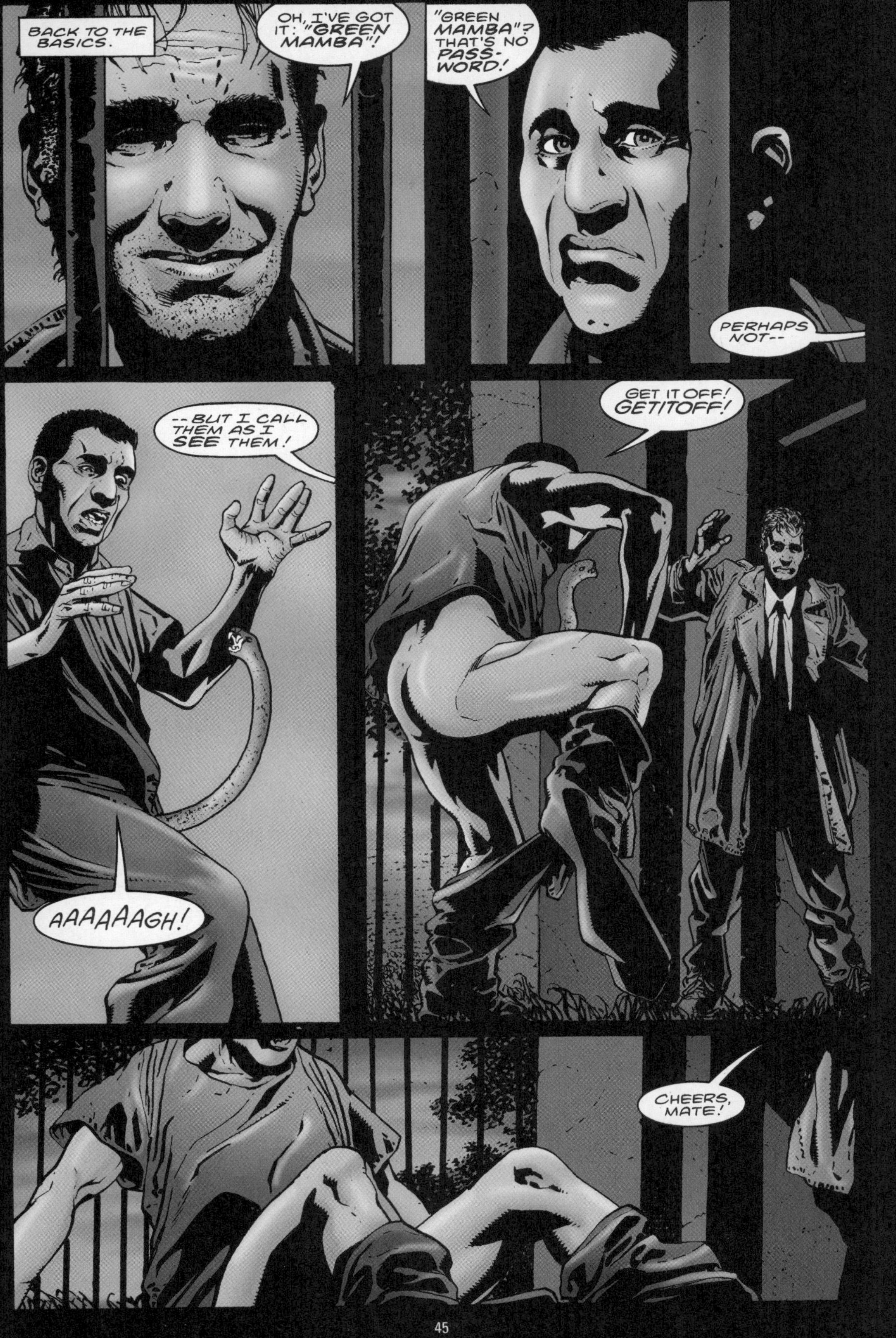
BACK TO THE BASICS.
OH, I'VE GOT IT: "GREEN MAMBA"!
"GREEN MAMBA"? THAT'S NO PASSWORD!
PERHAPS NOT--
--BUT I CALL THEM AS I SEE THEM!
AAAAAAGH!
GET IT OFF! GETITOFF!
CHEERS, MATE!

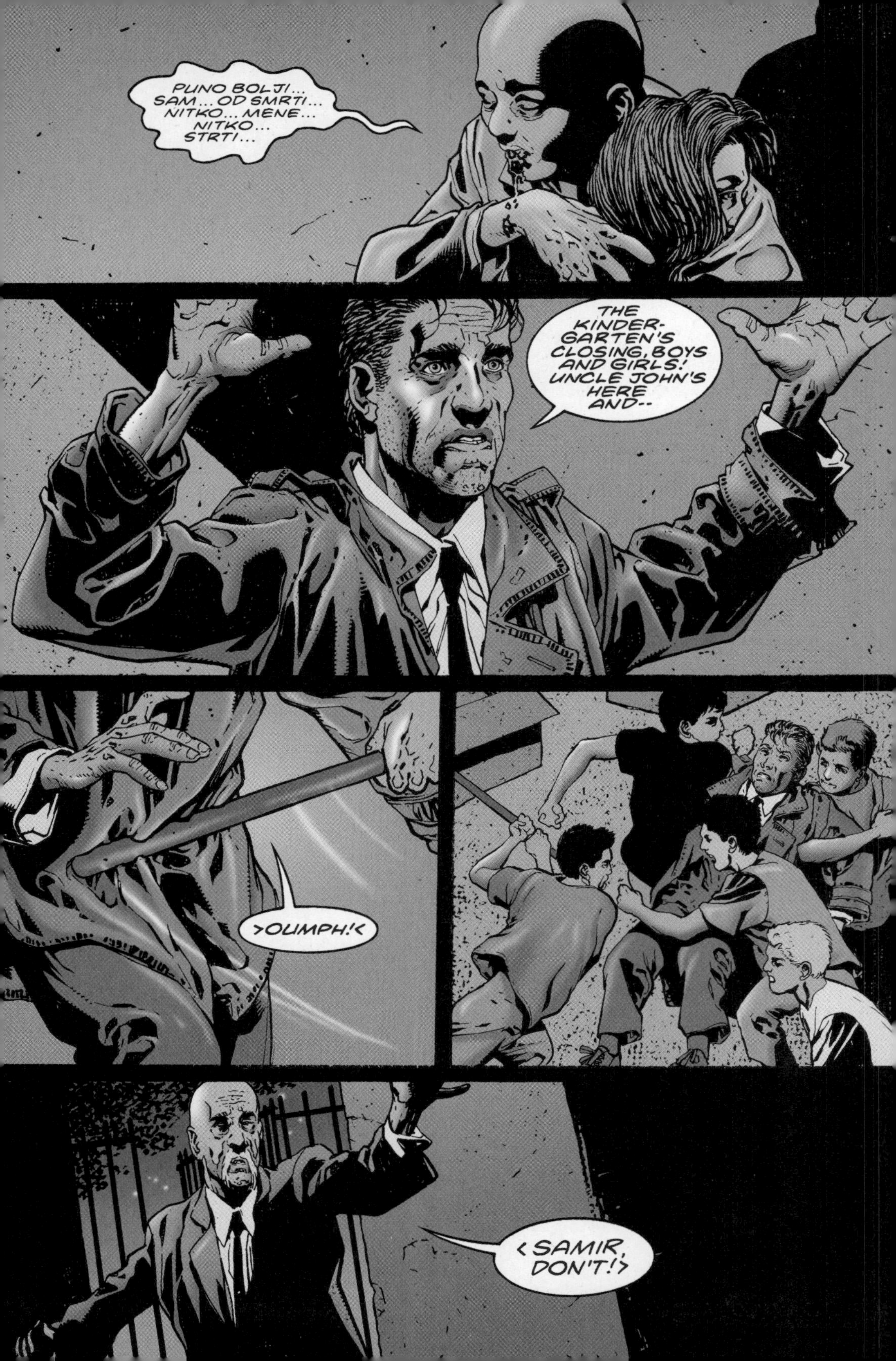
PUNO BOLJI... SAM... OD SMRTI... NITKO... MENE... NITKO... STRTI...
THE KINDER-GARTEN'S CLOSING, BOYS AND GIRLS! UNCLE JOHN'S HERE AND--
>OUMPH!<
<SAMIR, DON'T!>

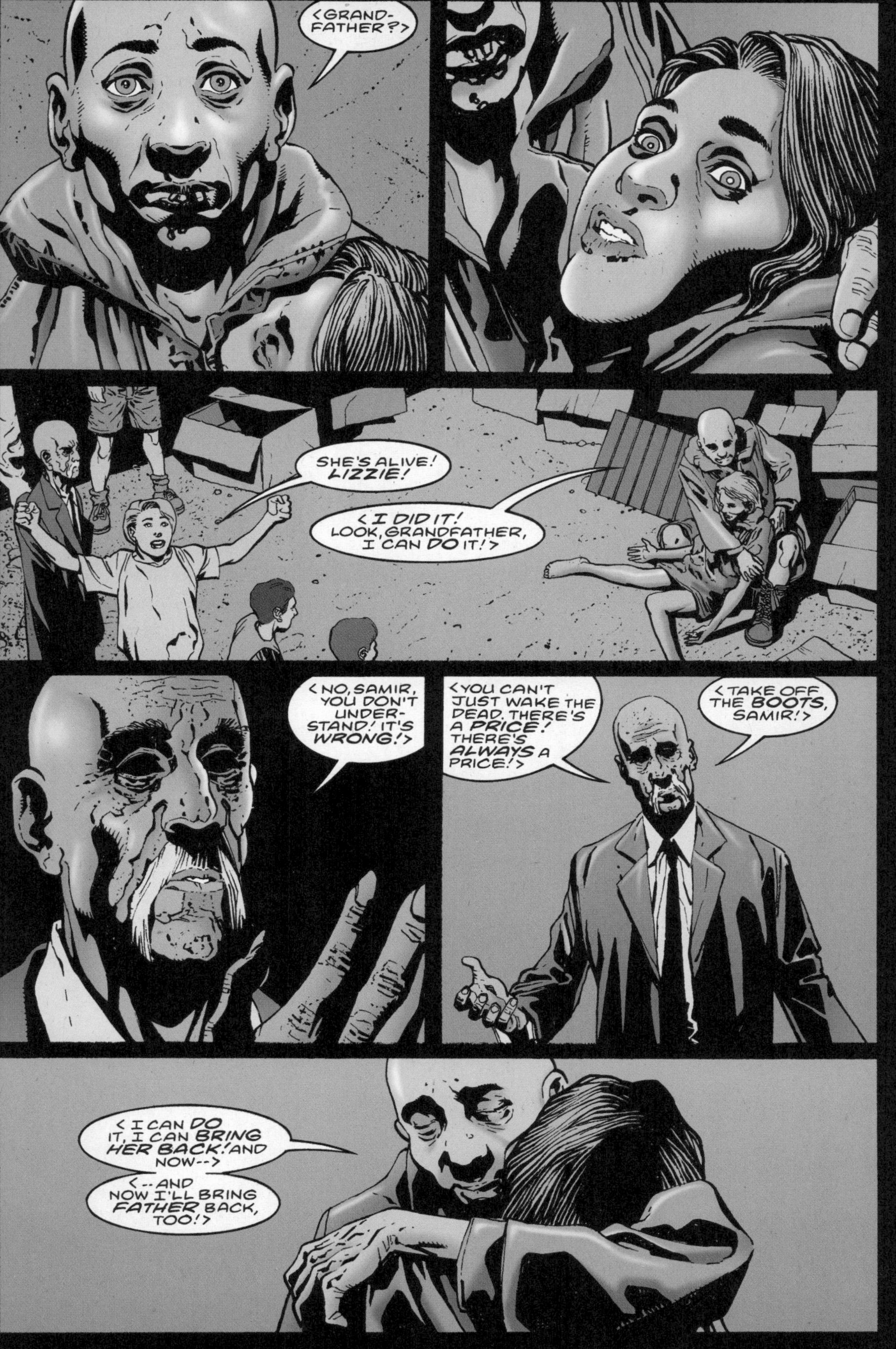

<GRAND-FATHER?>
SHE'S ALIVE! LIZZIE!
<I DID IT! LOOK, GRANDFATHER, I CAN DO IT!>
<NO, SAMIR, YOU DON'T UNDER-STAND! IT'S WRONG!>
<YOU CAN'T JUST WAKE THE DEAD. THERE'S A PRICE! THERE'S ALWAYS A PRICE!>
<TAKE OFF THE BOOTS, SAMIR!>
<I CAN DO IT, I CAN BRING HER BACK! AND NOW-->
<--AND NOW I'LL BRING FATHER BACK, TOO!>

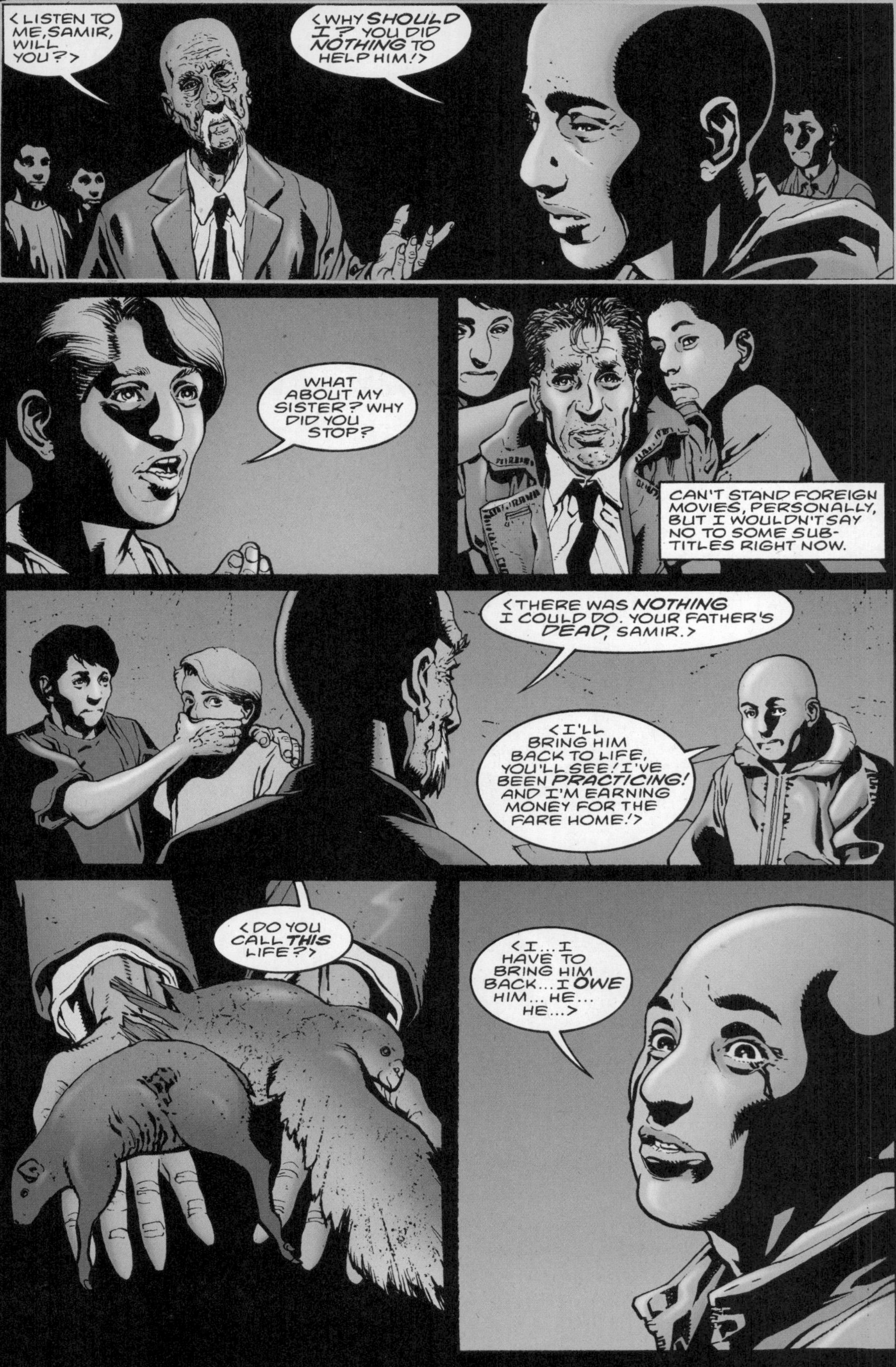

<LISTEN TO ME, SAMIR, WILL YOU?>
<WHY SHOULD I? YOU DID NOTHING TO HELP HIM!>
WHAT ABOUT MY SISTER? WHY DID YOU STOP?
CAN'T STAND FOREIGN MOVIES, PERSONALLY, BUT I WOULDN'T SAY NO TO SOME SUB-TITLES RIGHT NOW.
<THERE WAS NOTHING I COULD DO. YOUR FATHER'S DEAD, SAMIR.>
<I'LL BRING HIM BACK TO LIFE, YOU'LL SEE! I'VE BEEN PRACTICING! AND I'M EARNING MONEY FOR THE FARE HOME!>
<DO YOU CALL THIS LIFE?>
<I... I HAVE TO BRING HIM BACK... I OWE HIM... HE... HE...>

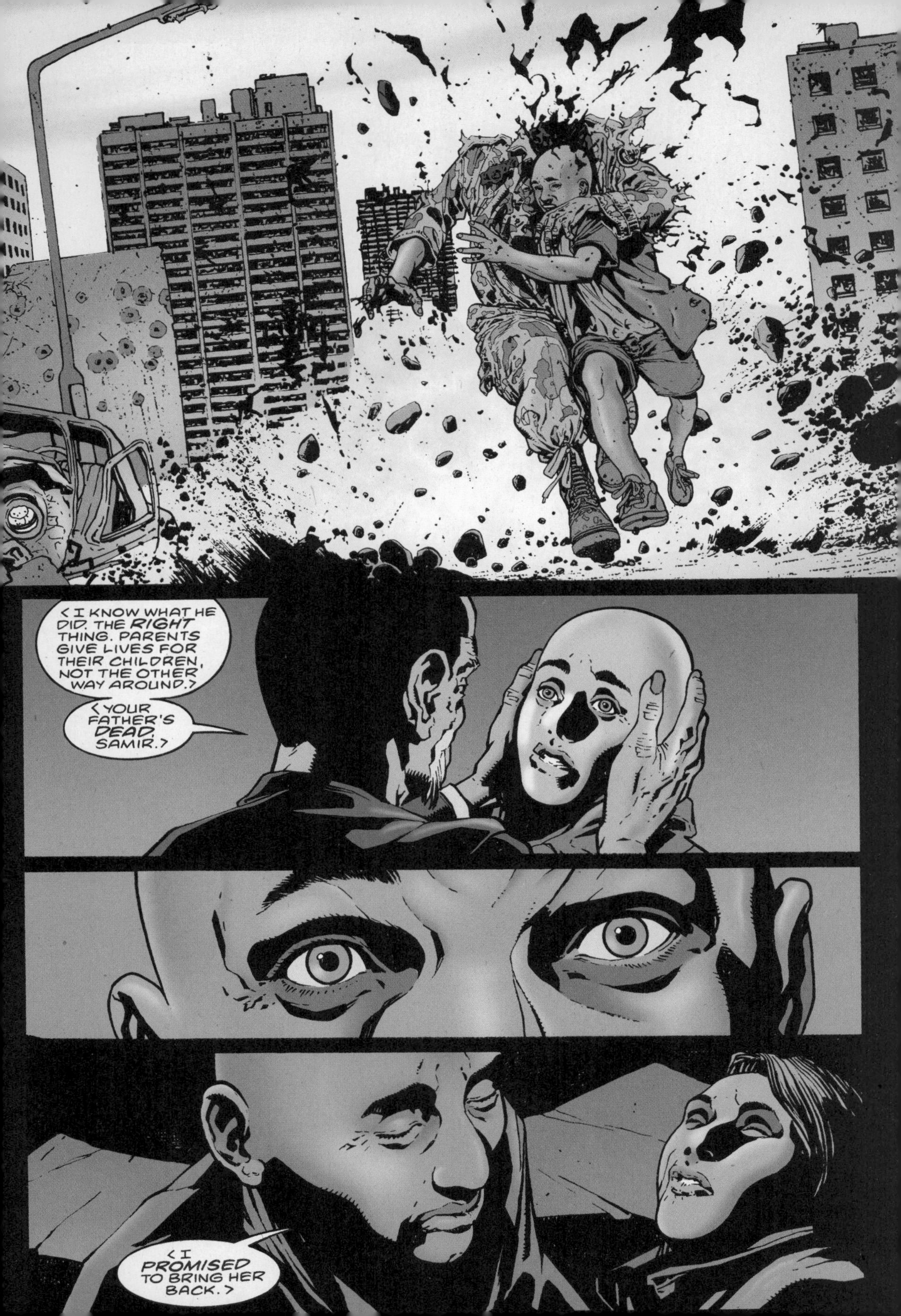
< I KNOW WHAT HE DID. THE RIGHT THING. PARENTS GIVE LIVES FOR THEIR CHILDREN, NOT THE OTHER WAY AROUND. >
< YOUR FATHER'S DEAD, SAMIR. >
< I PROMISED TO BRING HER BACK. >

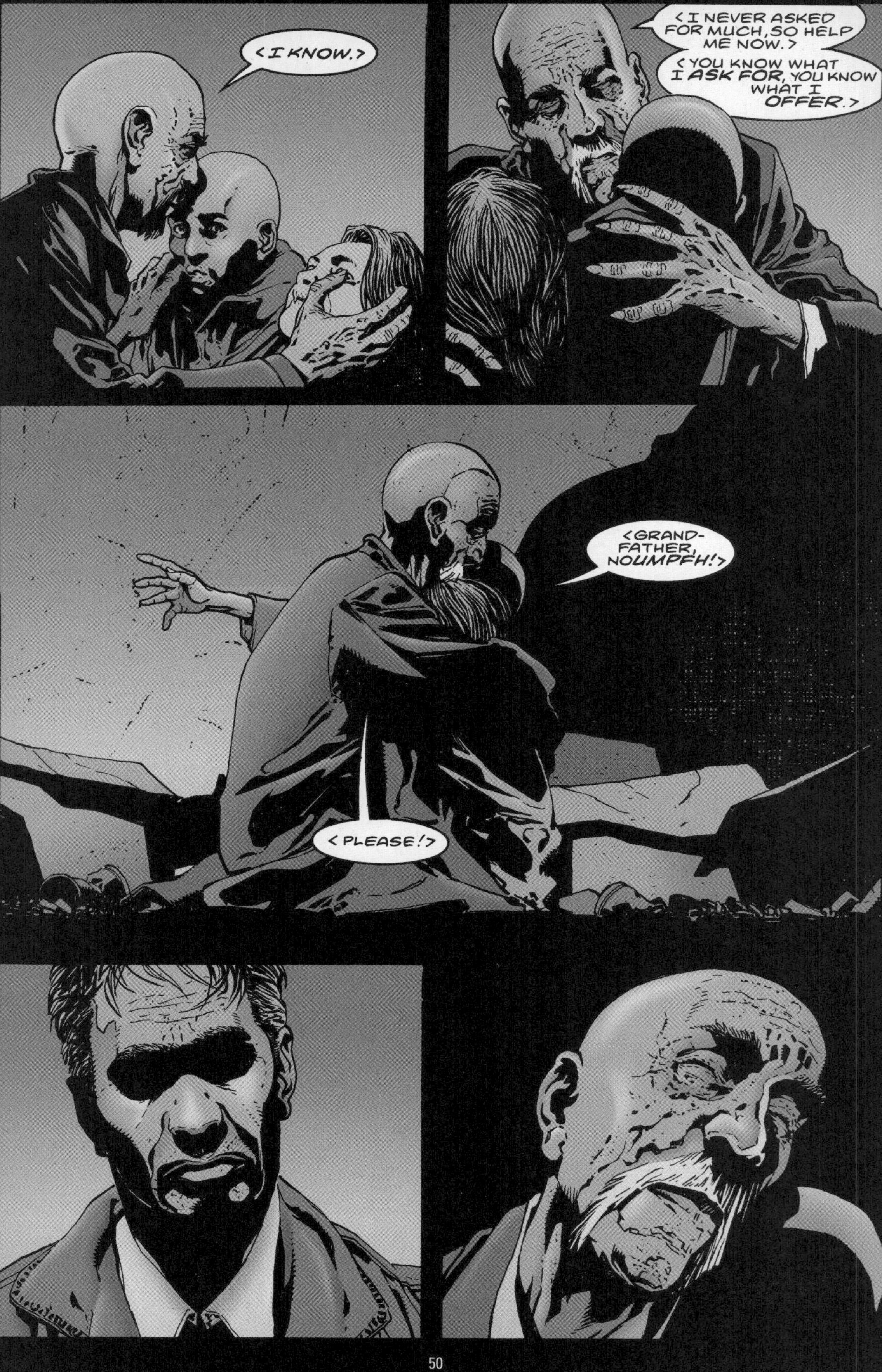
<I KNOW.>
<I NEVER ASKED FOR MUCH, SO HELP ME NOW.>
<YOU KNOW WHAT I ASK FOR, YOU KNOW WHAT I OFFER.>
<GRAND-FATHER, NOUMPFH!>
<PLEASE!>

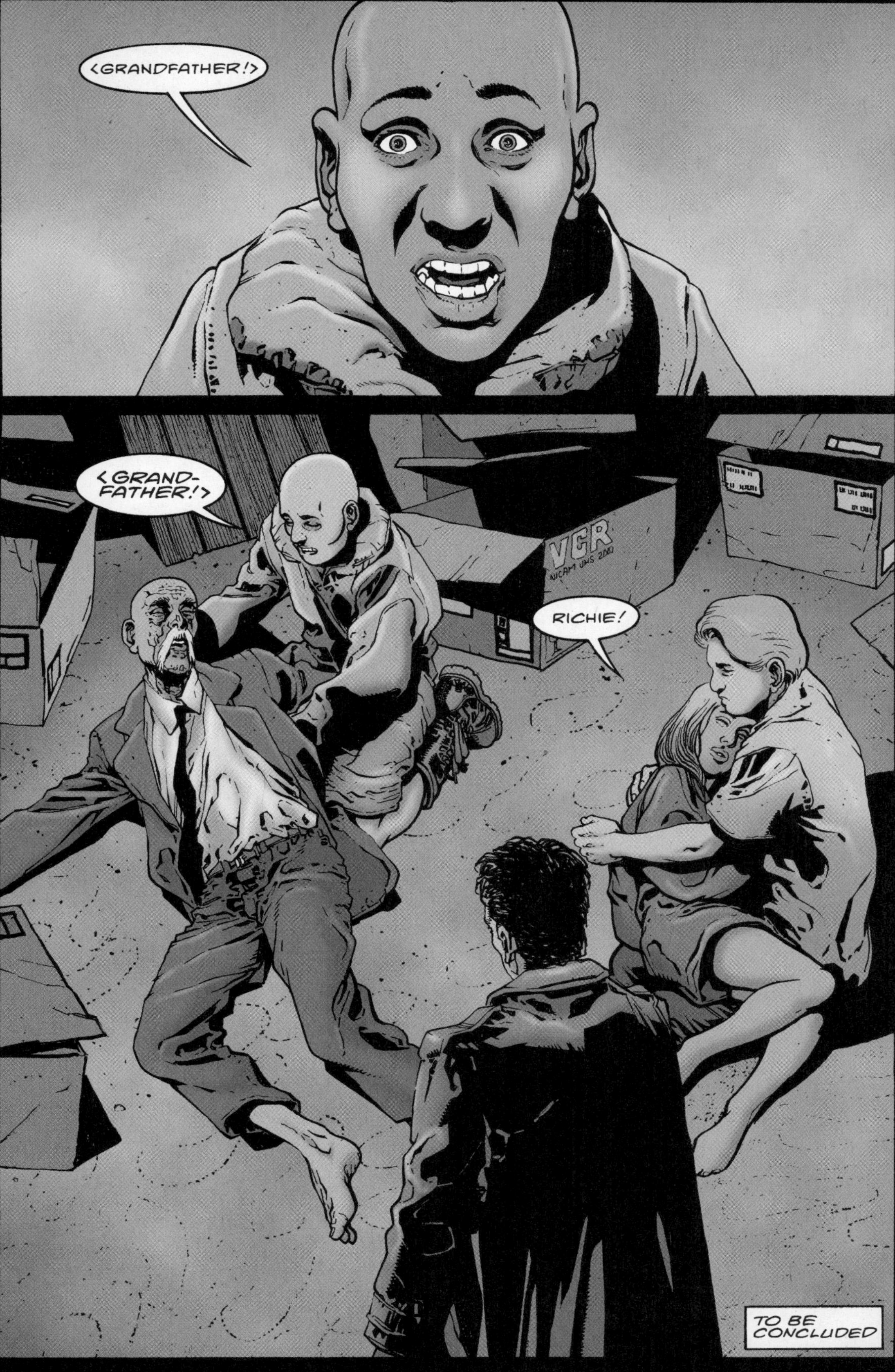
<GRANDFATHER!>
<GRAND-FATHER!>
VCR
RICHIE!
TO BE CONCLUDED

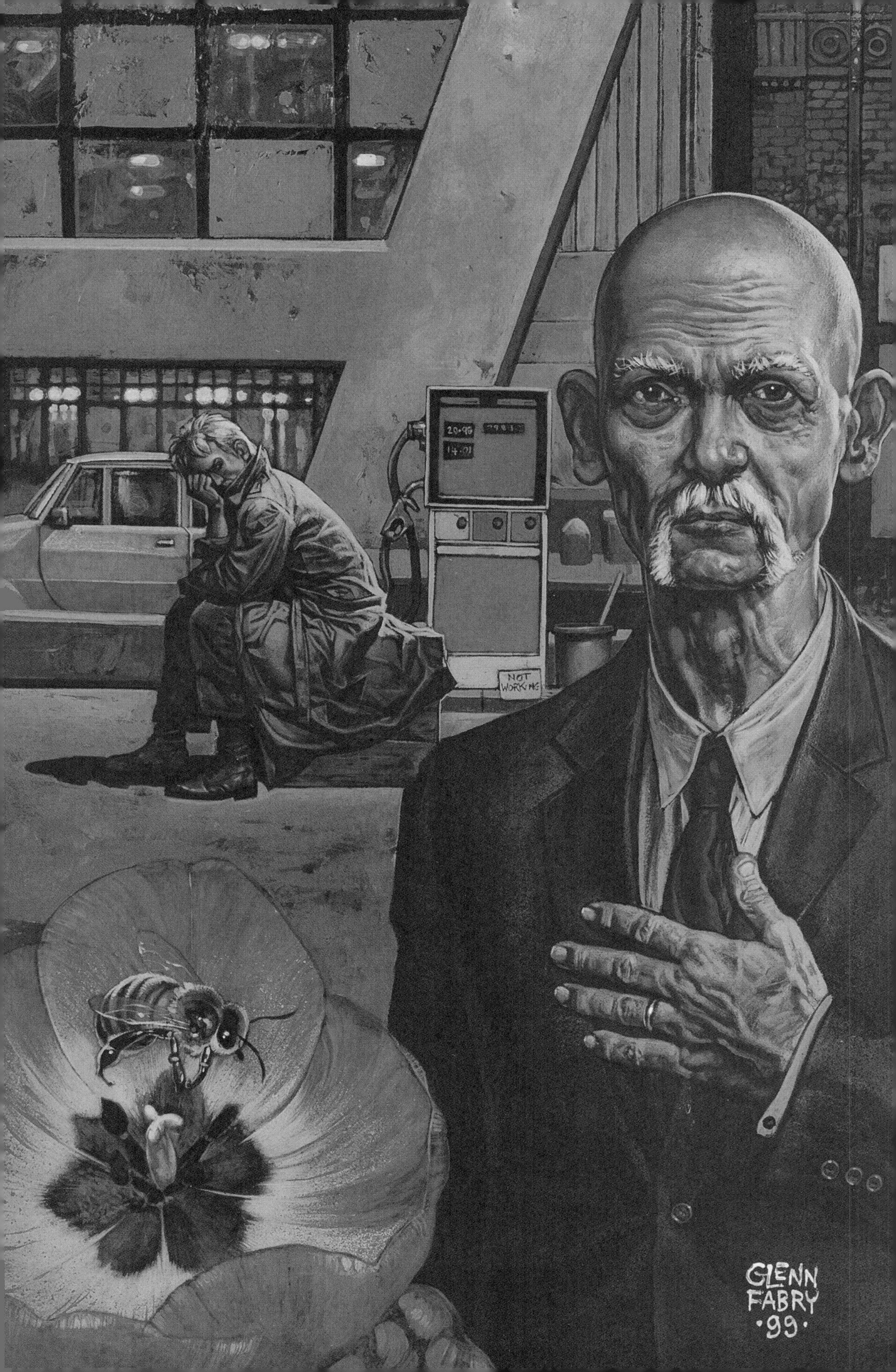
NOT WORKING
GLENN FABRY ·99·

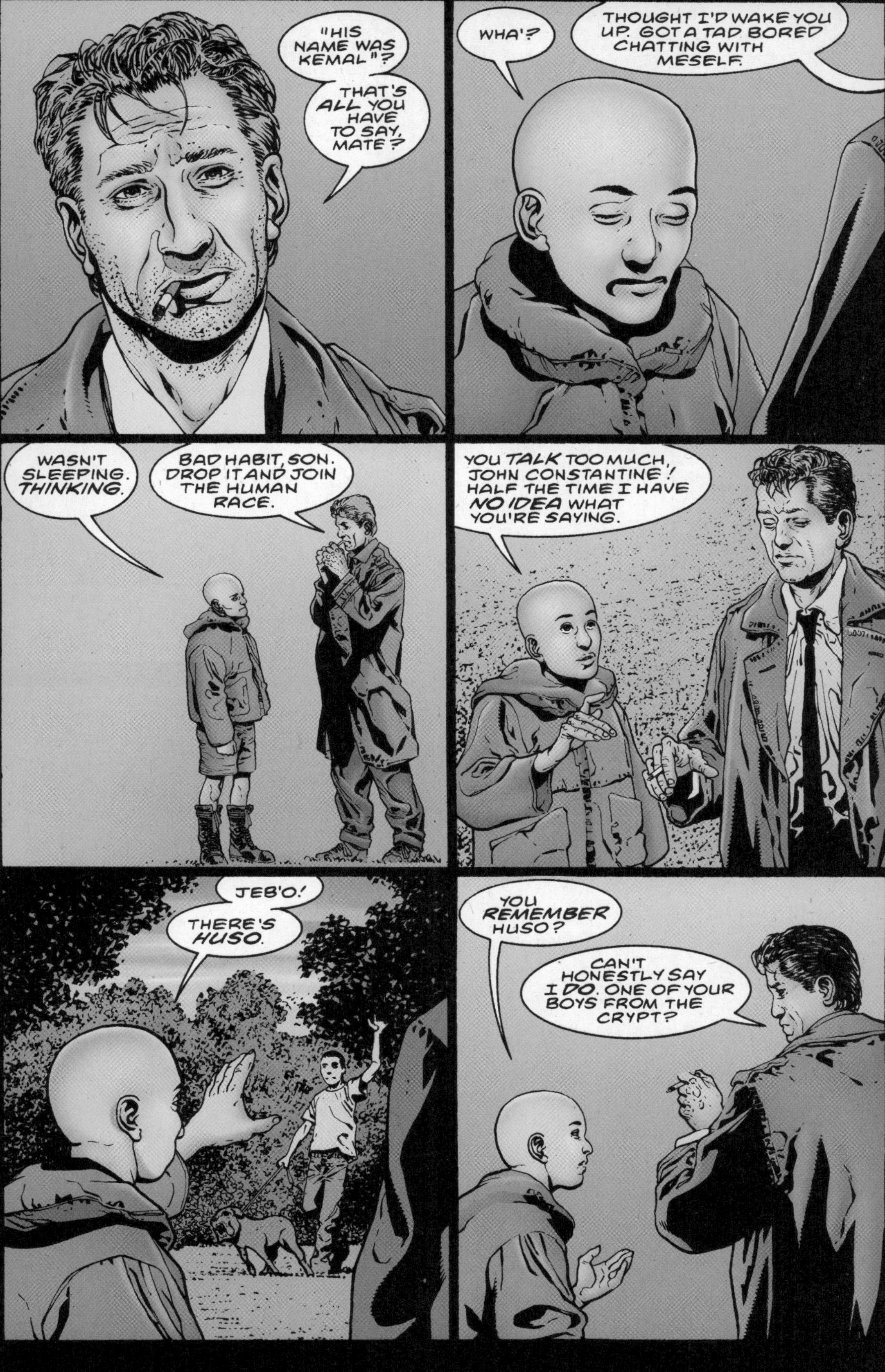
"HIS NAME WAS KEMAL"?
THAT'S ALL YOU HAVE TO SAY, MATE?
WHA'?
THOUGHT I'D WAKE YOU UP. GOT A TAD BORED CHATTING WITH MESELF.
WASN'T SLEEPING. THINKING.
BAD HABIT, SON. DROP IT AND JOIN THE HUMAN RACE.
YOU TALK TOO MUCH, JOHN CONSTANTINE! HALF THE TIME I HAVE NO IDEA WHAT YOU'RE SAYING.
JEB'O!
THERE'S HUSO.
YOU REMEMBER HUSO?
CAN'T HONESTLY SAY I DO. ONE OF YOUR BOYS FROM THE CRYPT?

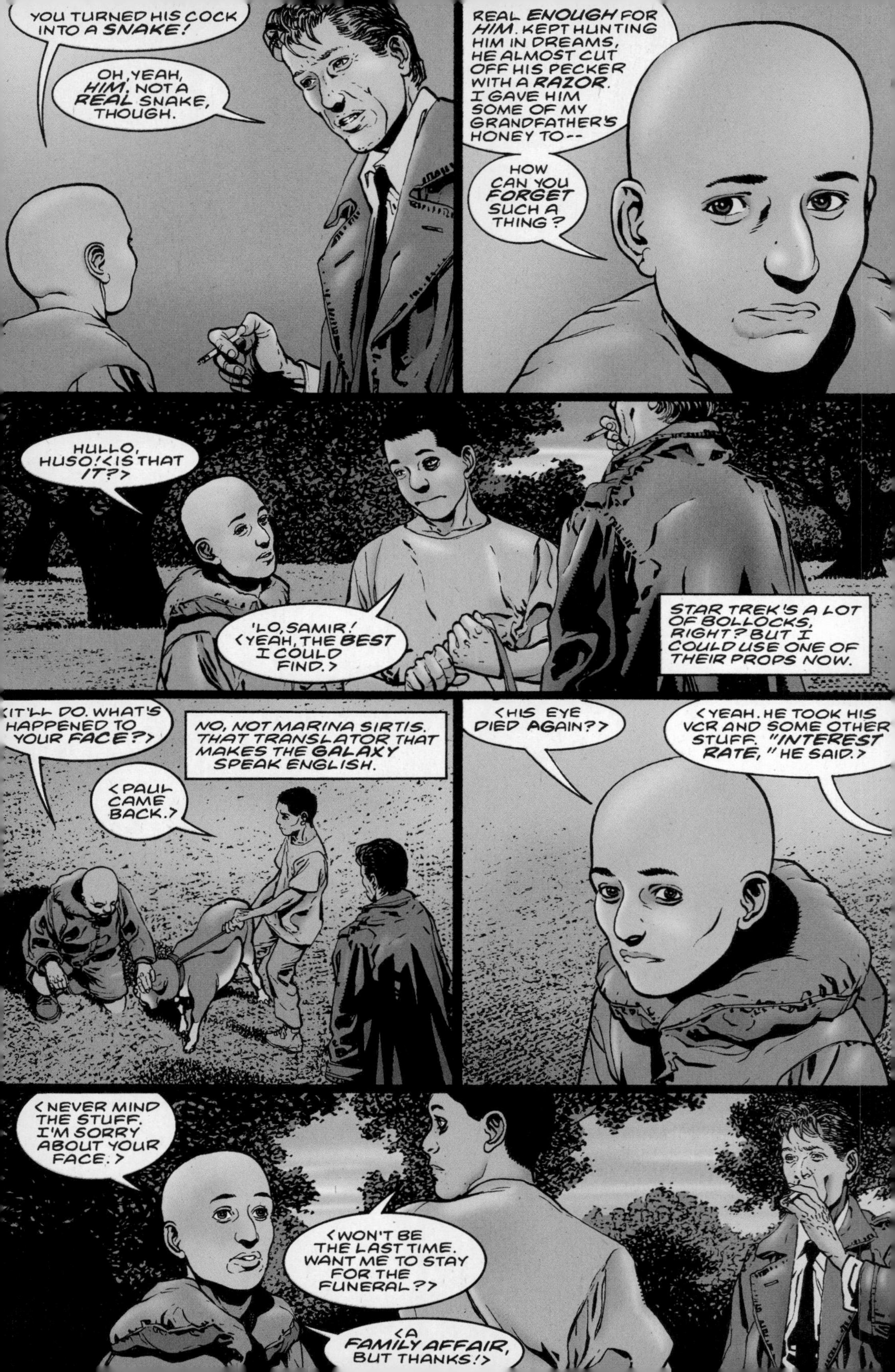
YOU TURNED HIS COCK INTO A SNAKE!
OH, YEAH, HIM. NOT A REAL SNAKE, THOUGH.
REAL ENOUGH FOR HIM. KEPT HUNTING HIM IN DREAMS, HE ALMOST CUT OFF HIS PECKER WITH A RAZOR. I GAVE HIM SOME OF MY GRANDFATHER'S HONEY TO--
HOW CAN YOU FORGET SUCH A THING?
HULLO, HUSO! <IS THAT IT?>
'LO, SAMIR! <YEAH, THE BEST I COULD FIND.>
STAR TREK'S A LOT OF BOLLOCKS, RIGHT? BUT I COULD USE ONE OF THEIR PROPS NOW.
<IT'LL DO. WHAT'S HAPPENED TO YOUR FACE?>
NO, NOT MARINA SIRTIS. THAT TRANSLATOR THAT MAKES THE GALAXY SPEAK ENGLISH.
<PAUL CAME BACK.>
<HIS EYE DIED AGAIN?>
<YEAH. HE TOOK HIS VCR AND SOME OTHER STUFF. "INTEREST RATE," HE SAID.>
<NEVER MIND THE STUFF. I'M SORRY ABOUT YOUR FACE.>
<WON'T BE THE LAST TIME. WANT ME TO STAY FOR THE FUNERAL?>
<A FAMILY AFFAIR, BUT THANKS!>

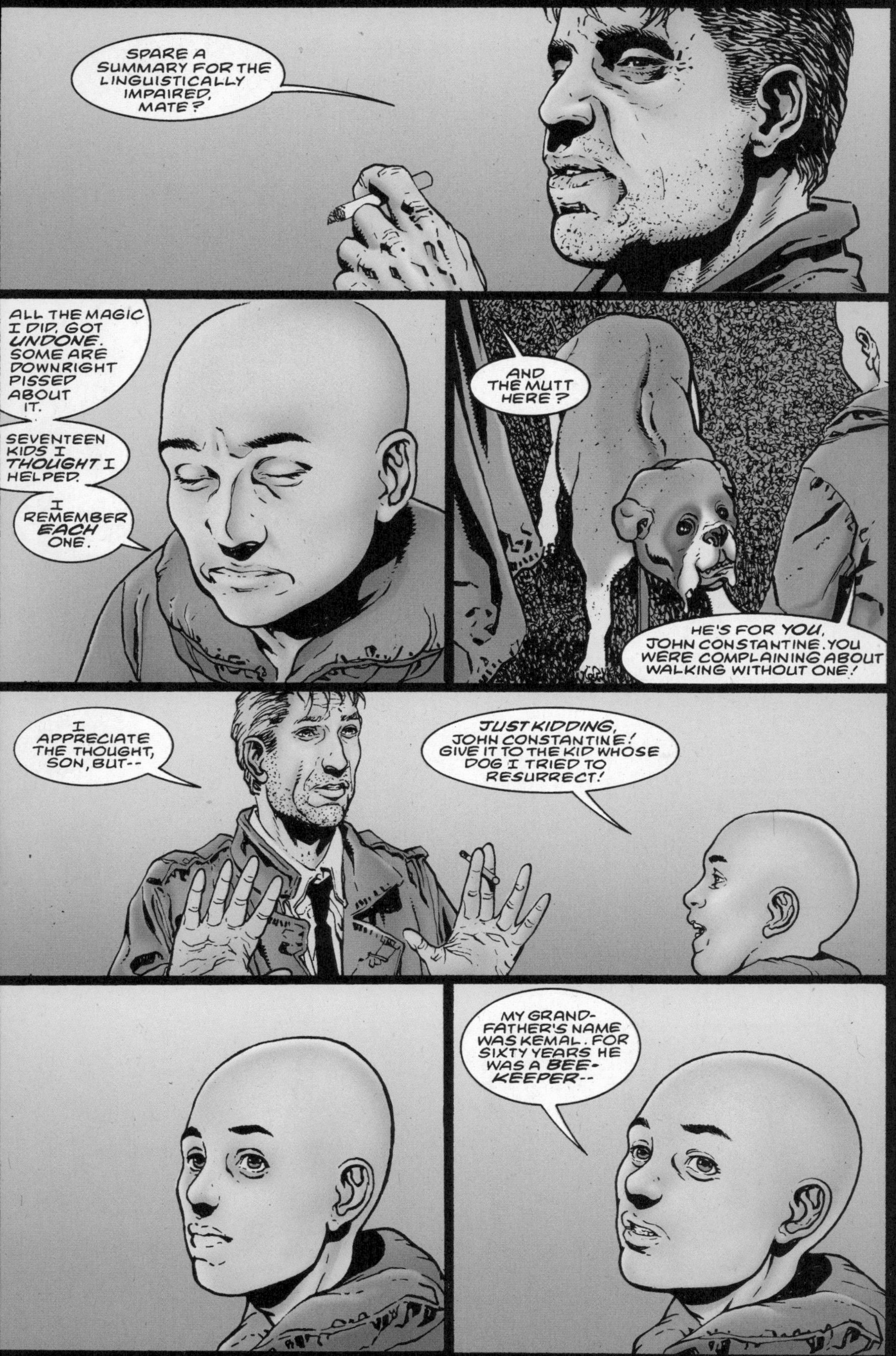
SPARE A SUMMARY FOR THE LINGUISTICALLY IMPAIRED, MATE?
ALL THE MAGIC I DID, GOT UNDONE. SOME ARE DOWNRIGHT PISSED ABOUT IT.
SEVENTEEN KIDS I THOUGHT I HELPED.
I REMEMBER EACH ONE.
AND THE MUTT HERE?
HE'S FOR YOU, JOHN CONSTANTINE. YOU WERE COMPLAINING ABOUT WALKING WITHOUT ONE!
I APPRECIATE THE THOUGHT, SON, BUT--
JUST KIDDING, JOHN CONSTANTINE! GIVE IT TO THE KID WHOSE DOG I TRIED TO RESURRECT!
MY GRANDFATHER'S NAME WAS KEMAL. FOR SIXTY YEARS HE WAS A BEEKEEPER--

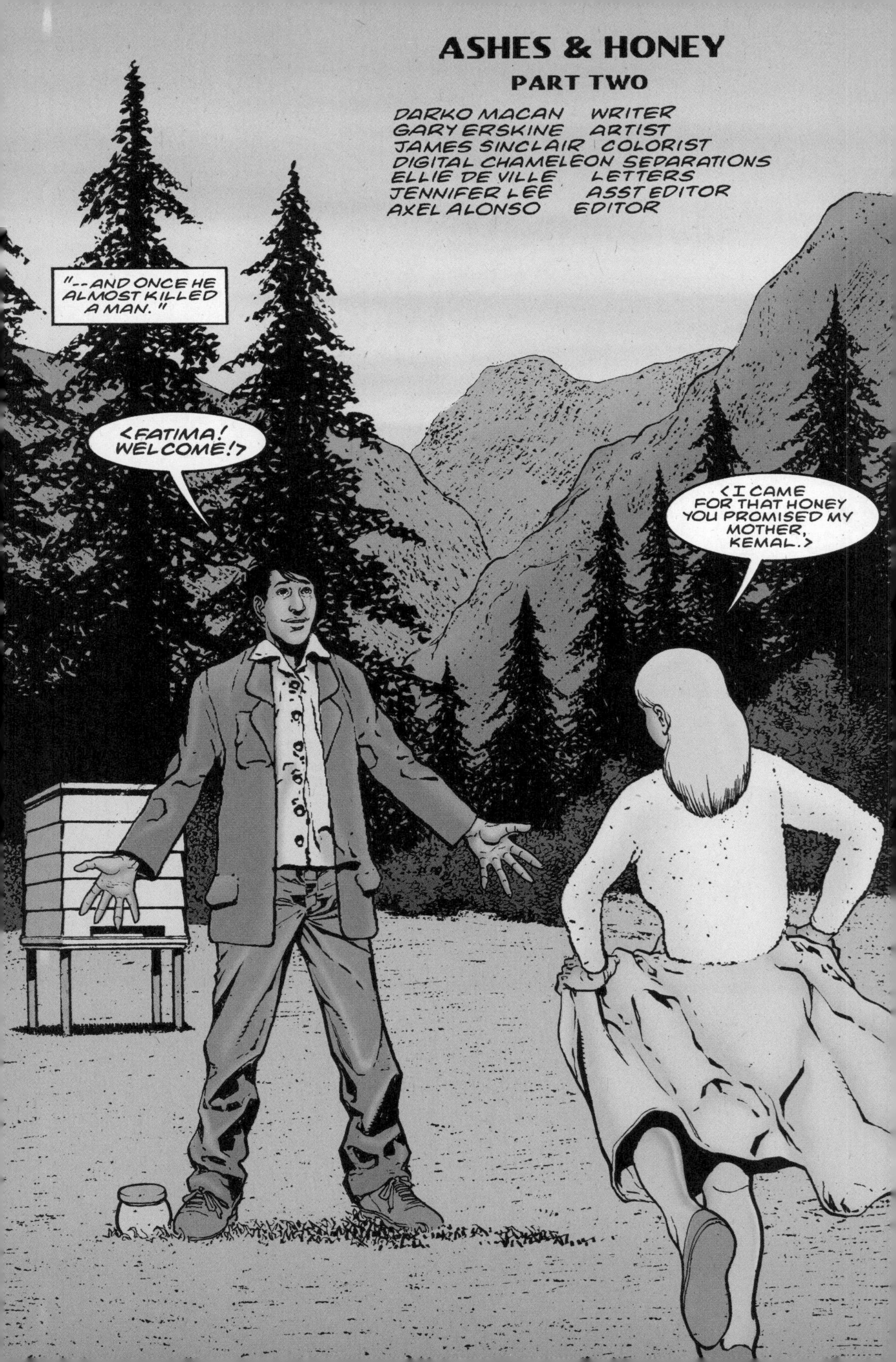
ASHES & HONEY
PART TWO
DARKO MACAN WRITER
GARY ERSKINE ARTIST
JAMES SINCLAIR COLORIST
DIGITAL CHAMELEON SEPARATIONS
ELLIE DE VILLE LETTERS
JENNIFER LEE ASST EDITOR
AXEL ALONSO EDITOR
"--AND ONCE HE ALMOST KILLED A MAN."
<FATIMA! WELCOME!>
<I CAME FOR THAT HONEY YOU PROMISED MY MOTHER, KEMAL.>

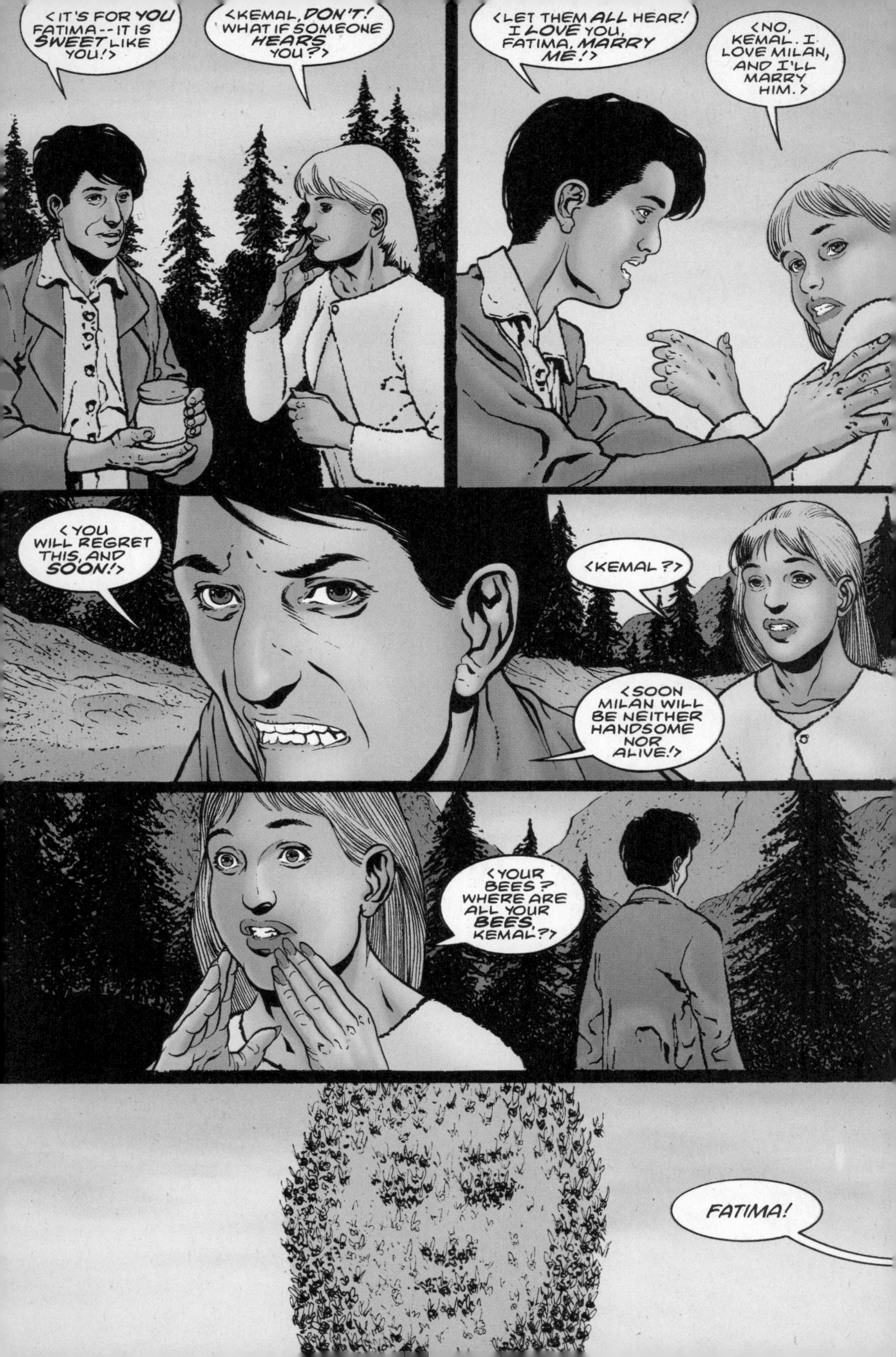
<IT'S FOR YOU FATIMA--IT IS SWEET LIKE YOU!>
<KEMAL, DON'T! WHAT IF SOMEONE HEARS YOU?>
<LET THEM ALL HEAR! I LOVE YOU, FATIMA, MARRY ME!>
<NO, KEMAL. I LOVE MILAN, AND I'LL MARRY HIM.>
<YOU WILL REGRET THIS, AND SOON!>
<KEMAL?>
<SOON MILAN WILL BE NEITHER HANDSOME NOR ALIVE!>
<YOUR BEES? WHERE ARE ALL YOUR BEES, KEMAL?>
FATIMA!

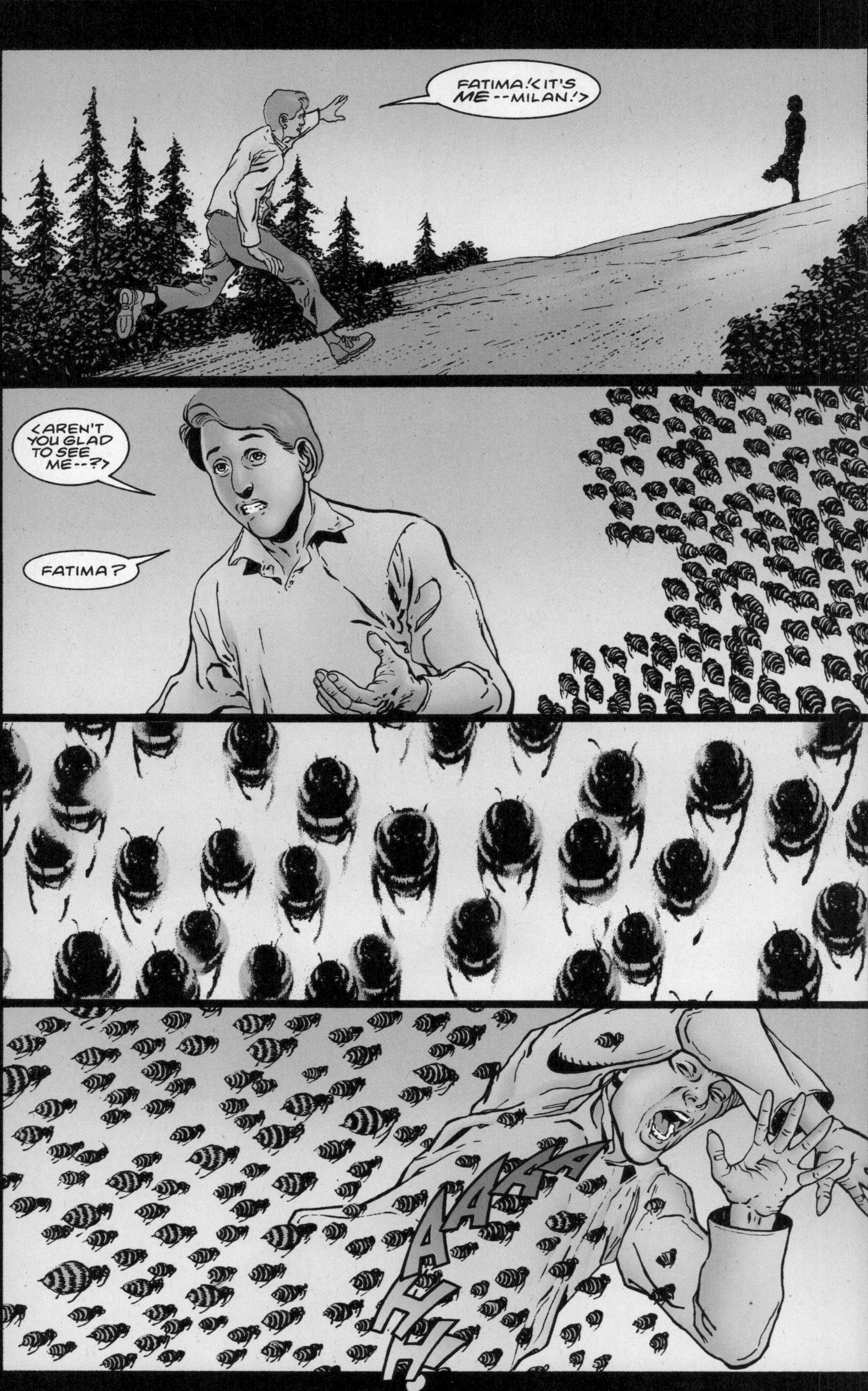
FATIMA! <IT'S ME--MILAN!>
<AREN'T YOU GLAD TO SEE ME--?>
FATIMA?
AAAAAHH!

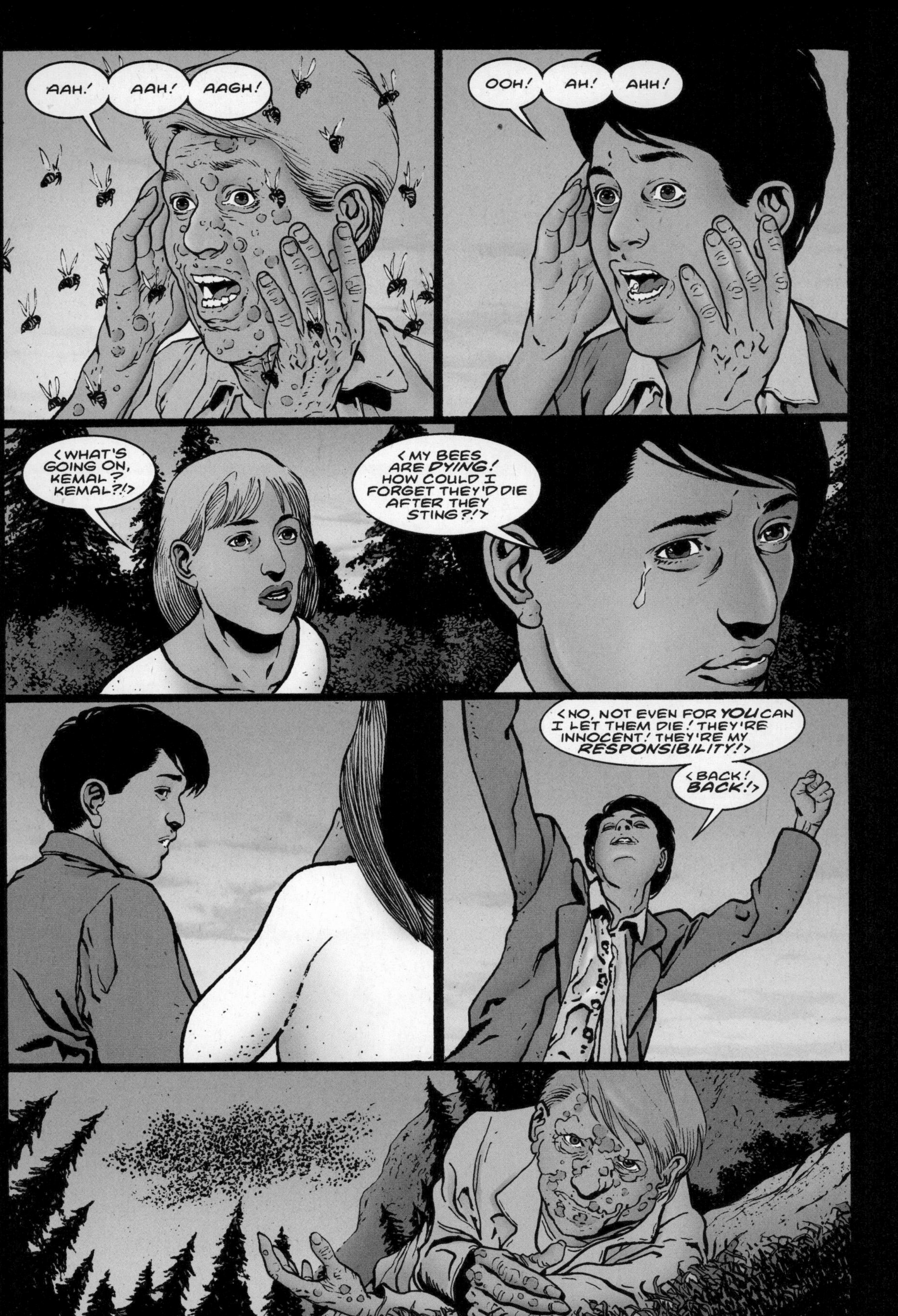
AAH!
AAH!
AAGH!
OOH!
AH!
AHH!
< WHAT'S GOING ON, KEMAL? KEMAL?!>
< MY BEES ARE DYING! HOW COULD I FORGET THEY'D DIE AFTER THEY STING?!>
< NO, NOT EVEN FOR YOU CAN I LET THEM DIE! THEY'RE INNOCENT! THEY'RE MY RESPONSIBILITY!>
< BACK! BACK!>

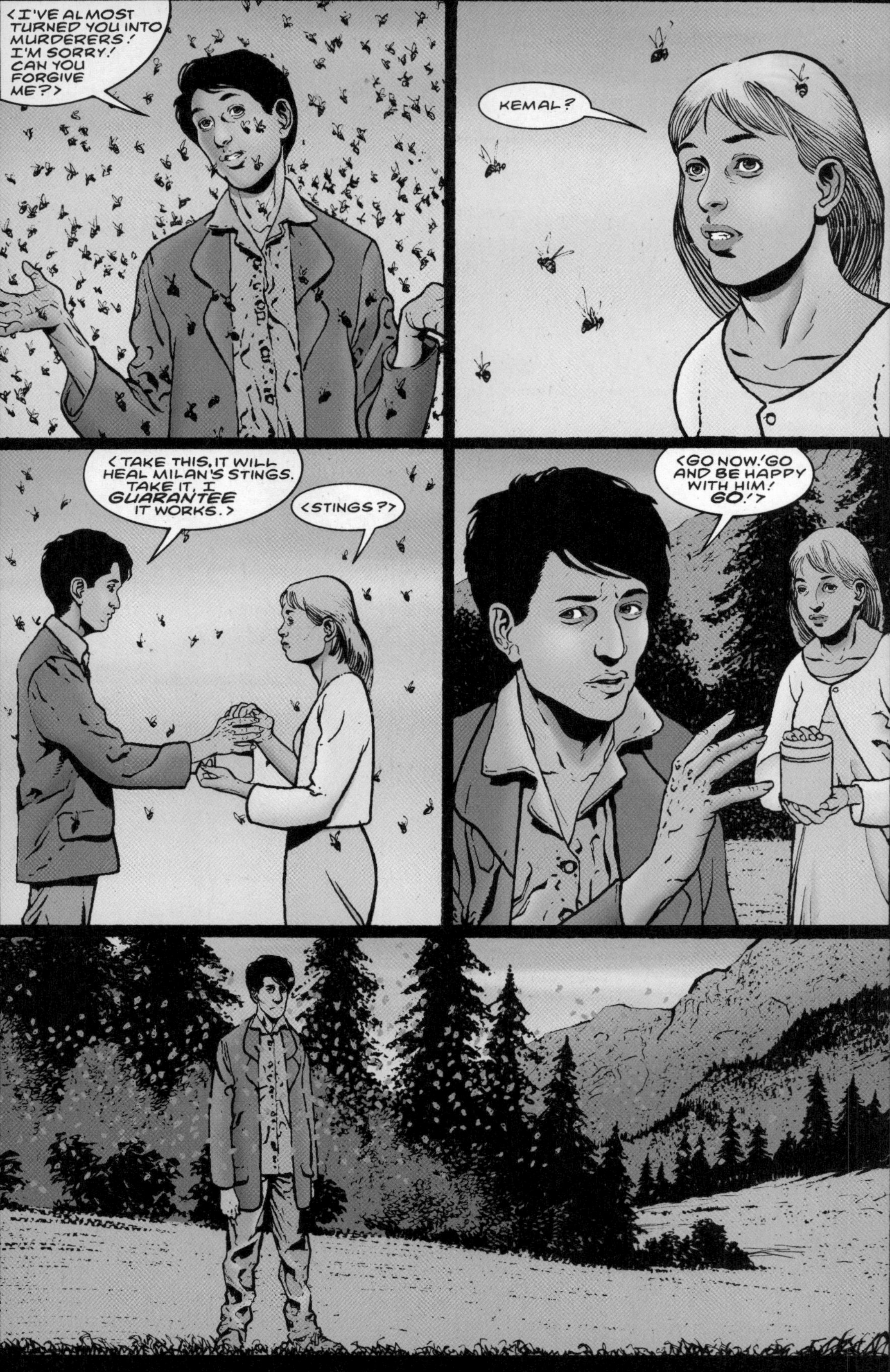
<I'VE ALMOST TURNED YOU INTO MURDERERS! I'M SORRY! CAN YOU FORGIVE ME?>
KEMAL?
<TAKE THIS, IT WILL HEAL MILAN'S STINGS. TAKE IT, I GUARANTEE IT WORKS.>
<STINGS?>
<GO NOW! GO AND BE HAPPY WITH HIM! GO!>

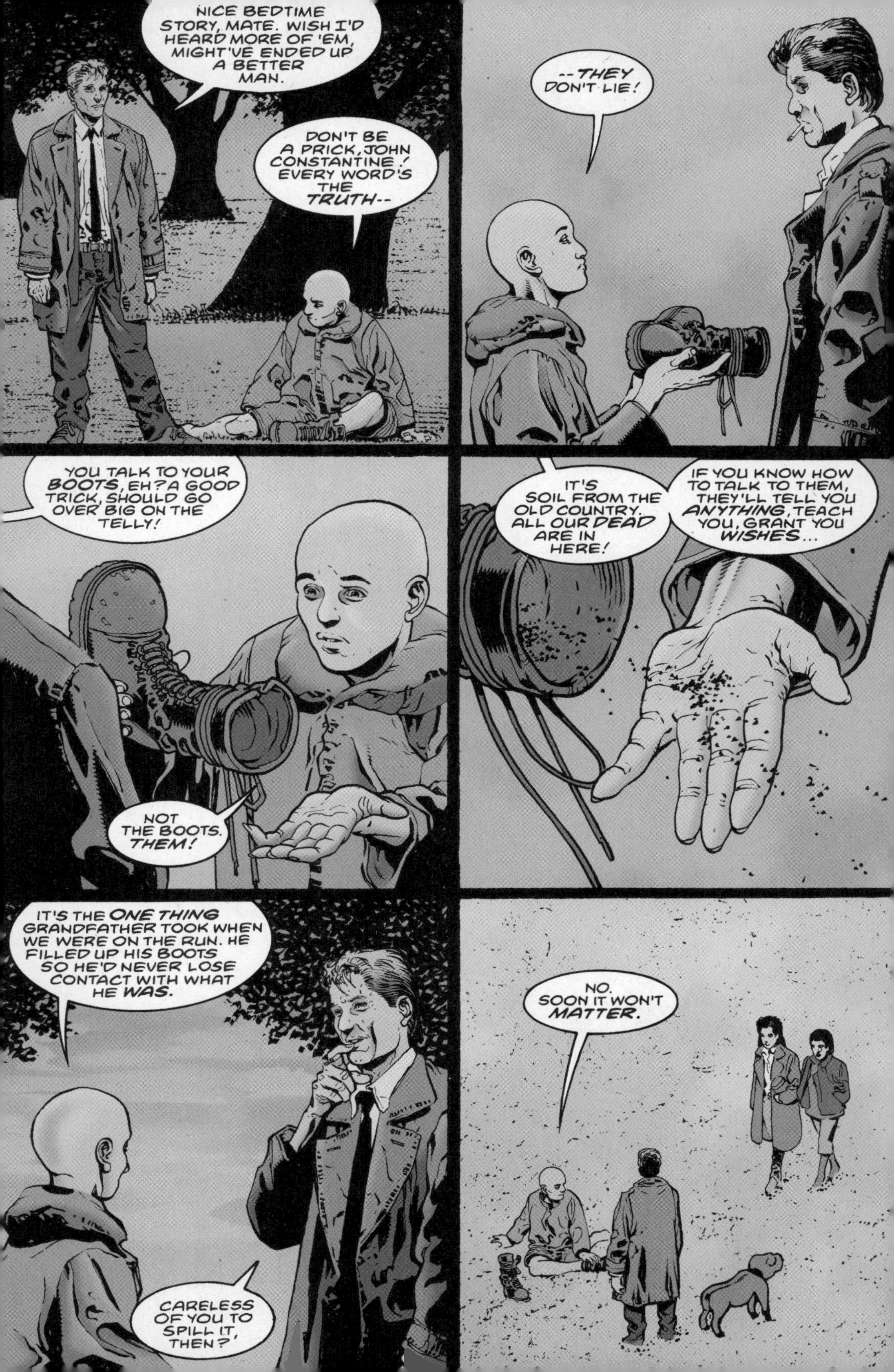

NICE BEDTIME STORY, MATE. WISH I'D HEARD MORE OF 'EM, MIGHT'VE ENDED UP A BETTER MAN.
DON'T BE A PRICK, JOHN CONSTANTINE! EVERY WORD'S THE *TRUTH*--
--*THEY* DON'T LIE!
YOU TALK TO YOUR *BOOTS*, EH? A GOOD TRICK, SHOULD GO OVER BIG ON THE TELLY!
NOT THE BOOTS. *THEM!*
IT'S SOIL FROM THE OLD COUNTRY. ALL OUR *DEAD* ARE IN HERE!
IF YOU KNOW HOW TO TALK TO THEM, THEY'LL TELL YOU *ANYTHING*, TEACH YOU, GRANT YOU *WISHES*...
IT'S THE *ONE THING* GRANDFATHER TOOK WHEN WE WERE ON THE RUN. HE FILLED UP HIS BOOTS SO HE'D NEVER LOSE CONTACT WITH WHAT HE **WAS**.
CARELESS OF YOU TO SPILL IT, THEN?
NO. SOON IT WON'T *MATTER*.

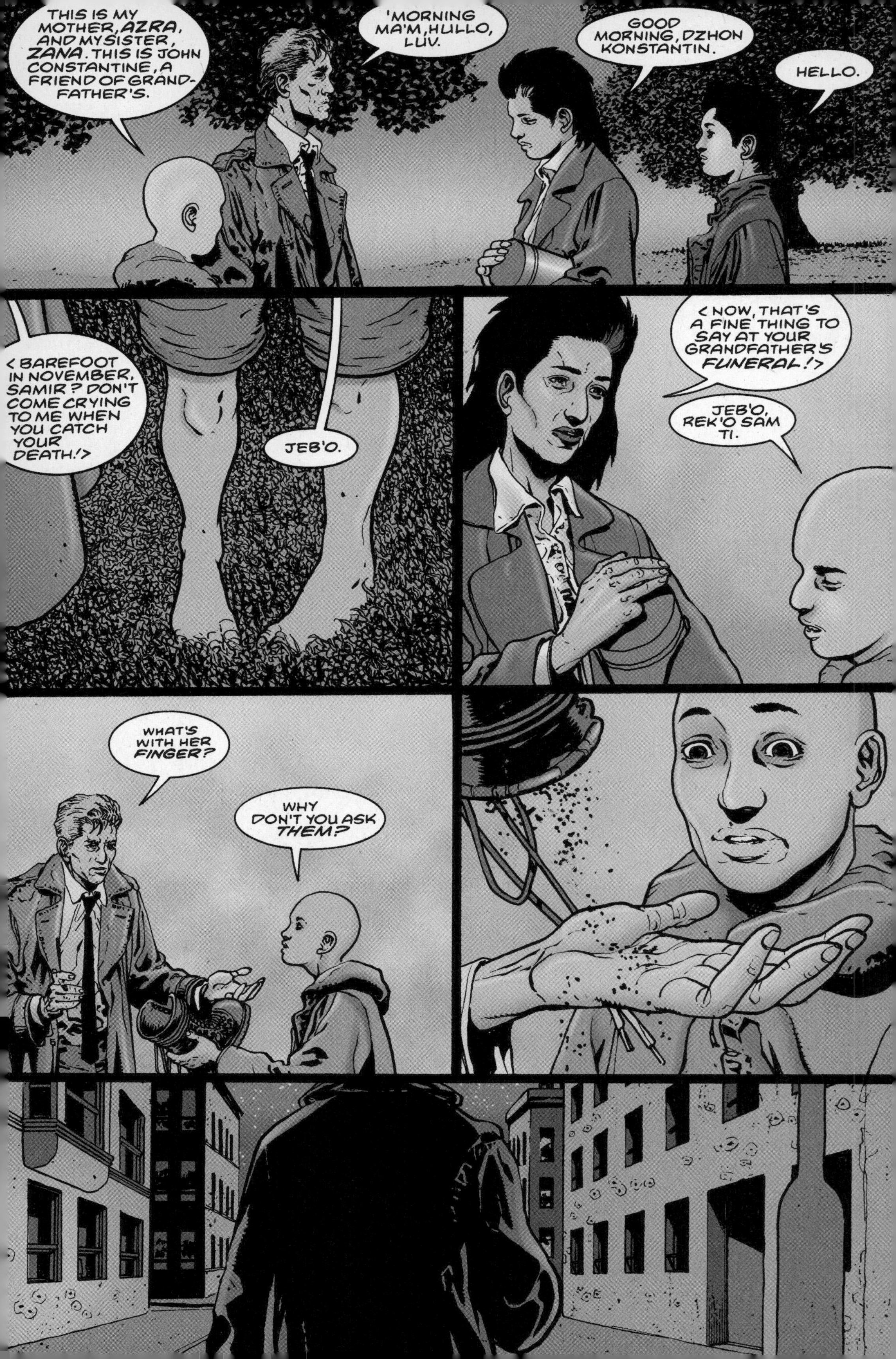

THIS IS MY MOTHER, AZRA, AND MY SISTER, ZANA. THIS IS JOHN CONSTANTINE, A FRIEND OF GRAND-FATHER'S.
'MORNING MA'M, HULLO, LUV.
GOOD MORNING, DZHON KONSTANTIN.
HELLO.
< BAREFOOT IN NOVEMBER, SAMIR? DON'T COME CRYING TO ME WHEN YOU CATCH YOUR DEATH!>
JEB'O.
< NOW, THAT'S A FINE THING TO SAY AT YOUR GRANDFATHER'S FUNERAL!>
JEB'O, REK'O SAM TI.
WHAT'S WITH HER FINGER?
WHY DON'T YOU ASK THEM?

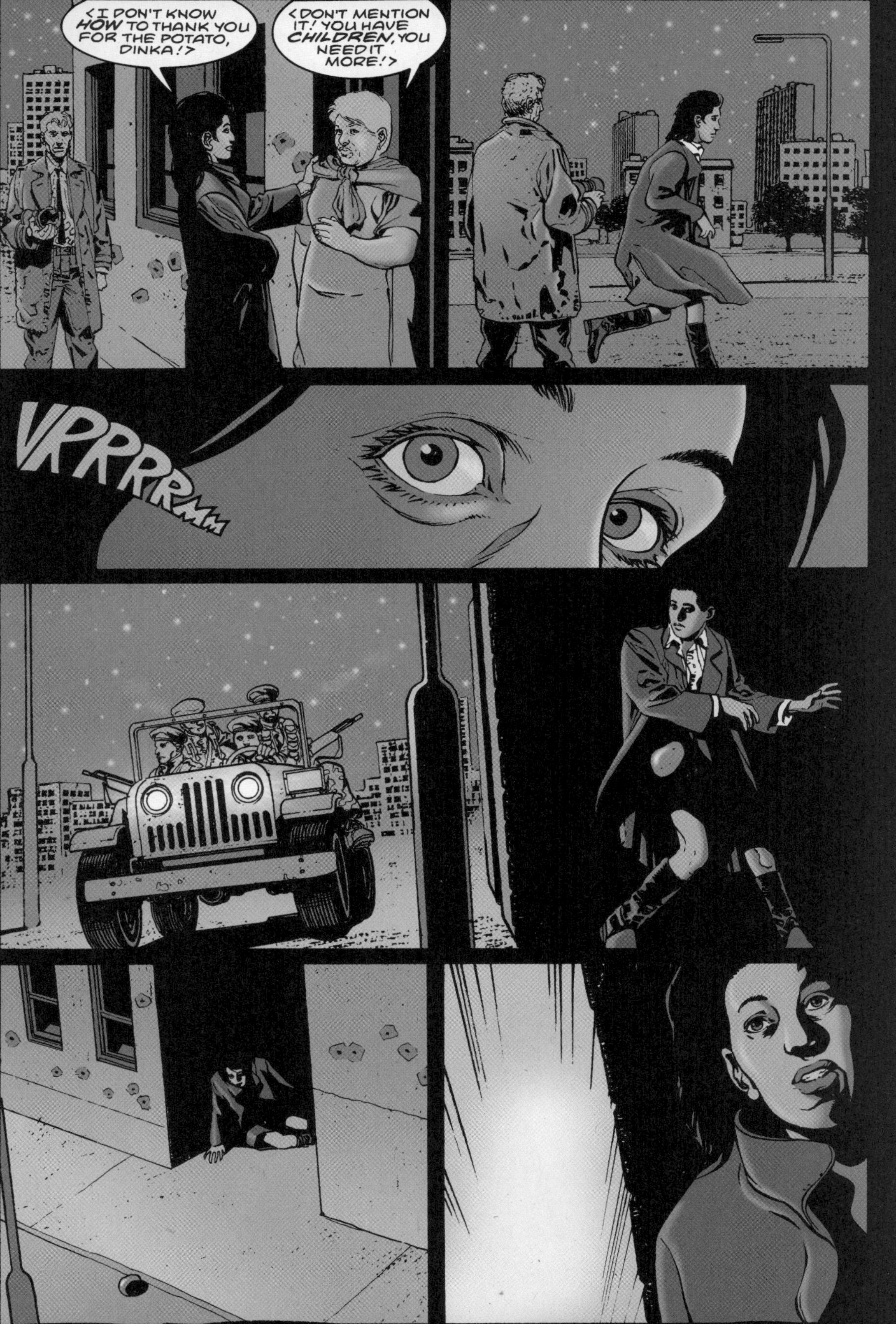

<I DON'T KNOW HOW TO THANK YOU FOR THE POTATO, DINKA!>
<DON'T MENTION IT! YOU HAVE CHILDREN, YOU NEED IT MORE!>
VRRRRRMM

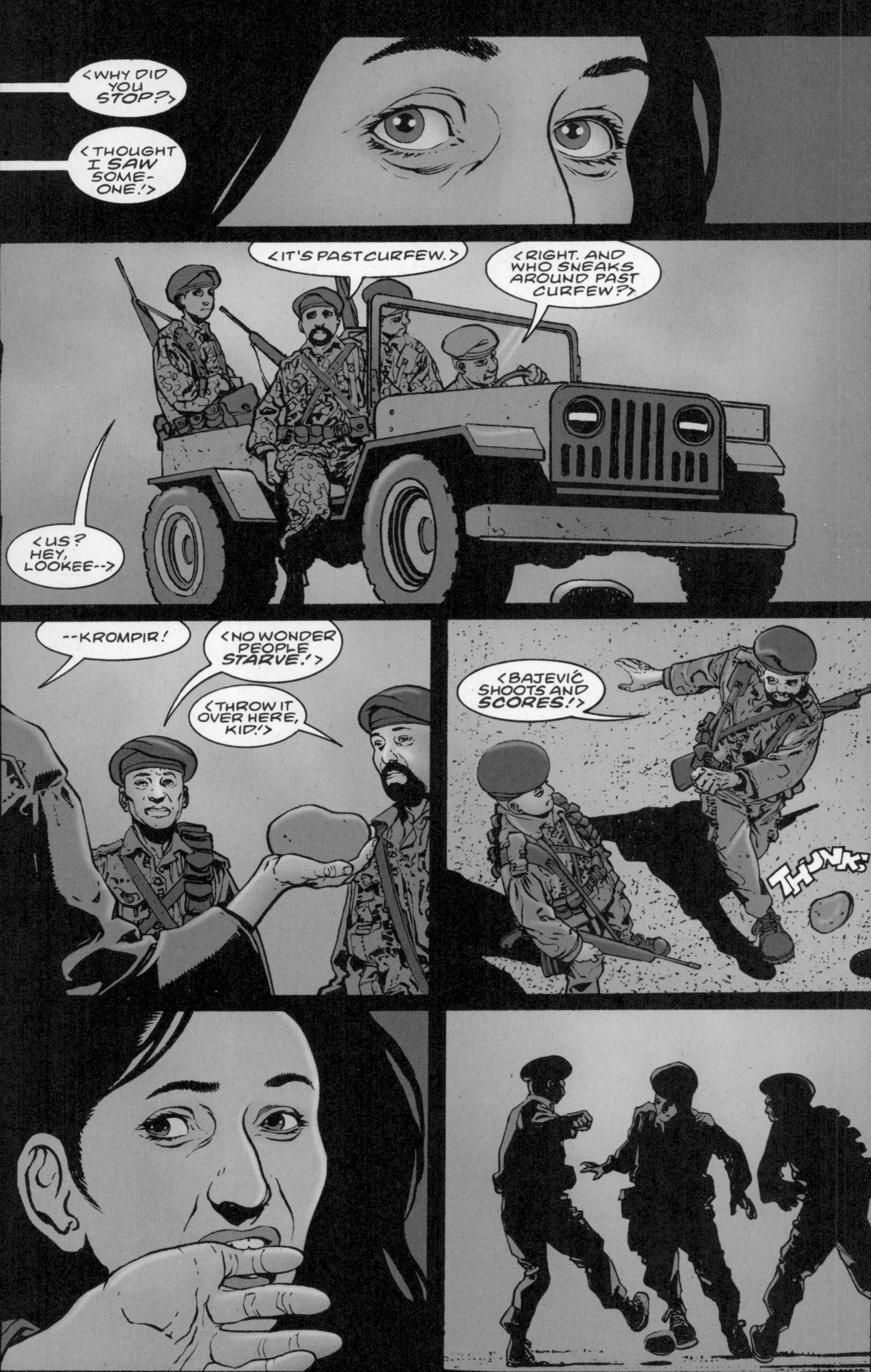

<WHY DID YOU STOP?>
<THOUGHT I SAW SOME-ONE.!>
<IT'S PAST CURFEW.>
<RIGHT. AND WHO SNEAKS AROUND PAST CURFEW?>
<US? HEY, LOOKEE-->
--KROMPIR!
<NO WONDER PEOPLE STARVE.!>
<THROW IT OVER HERE, KID!>
<BAJEVIĆ SHOOTS AND SCORES.!>
THUNK!

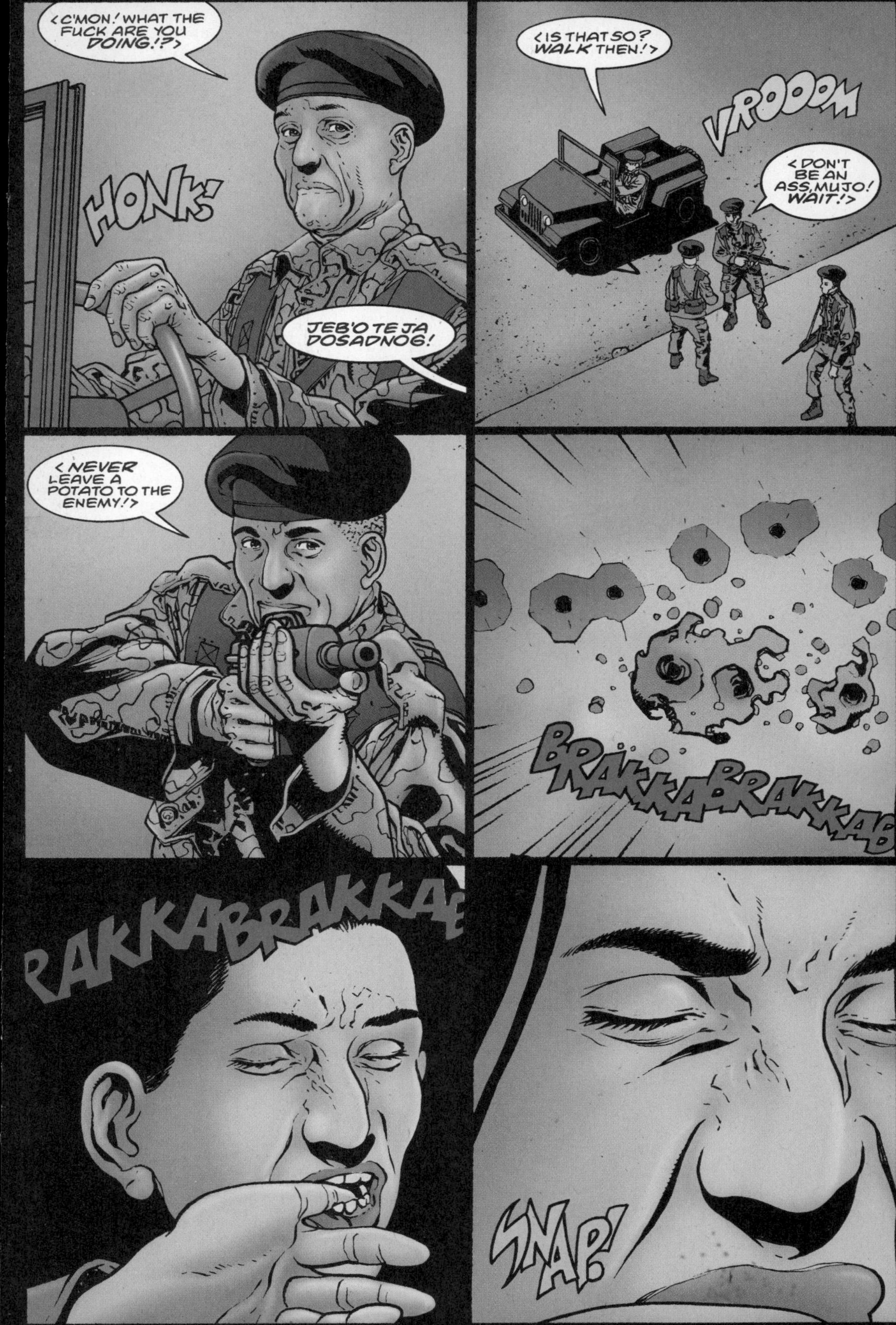

<C'MON! WHAT THE FUCK ARE YOU DOING!?>
HONK!
JEB'O TE JA DOSADNOG!
<IS THAT SO? WALK THEN!>
VROOOM
<DON'T BE AN ASS, MUJO! WAIT!>
<NEVER LEAVE A POTATO TO THE ENEMY!>
BRAKKABRAKKAB
RAKKABRAKKAB
SNAP!

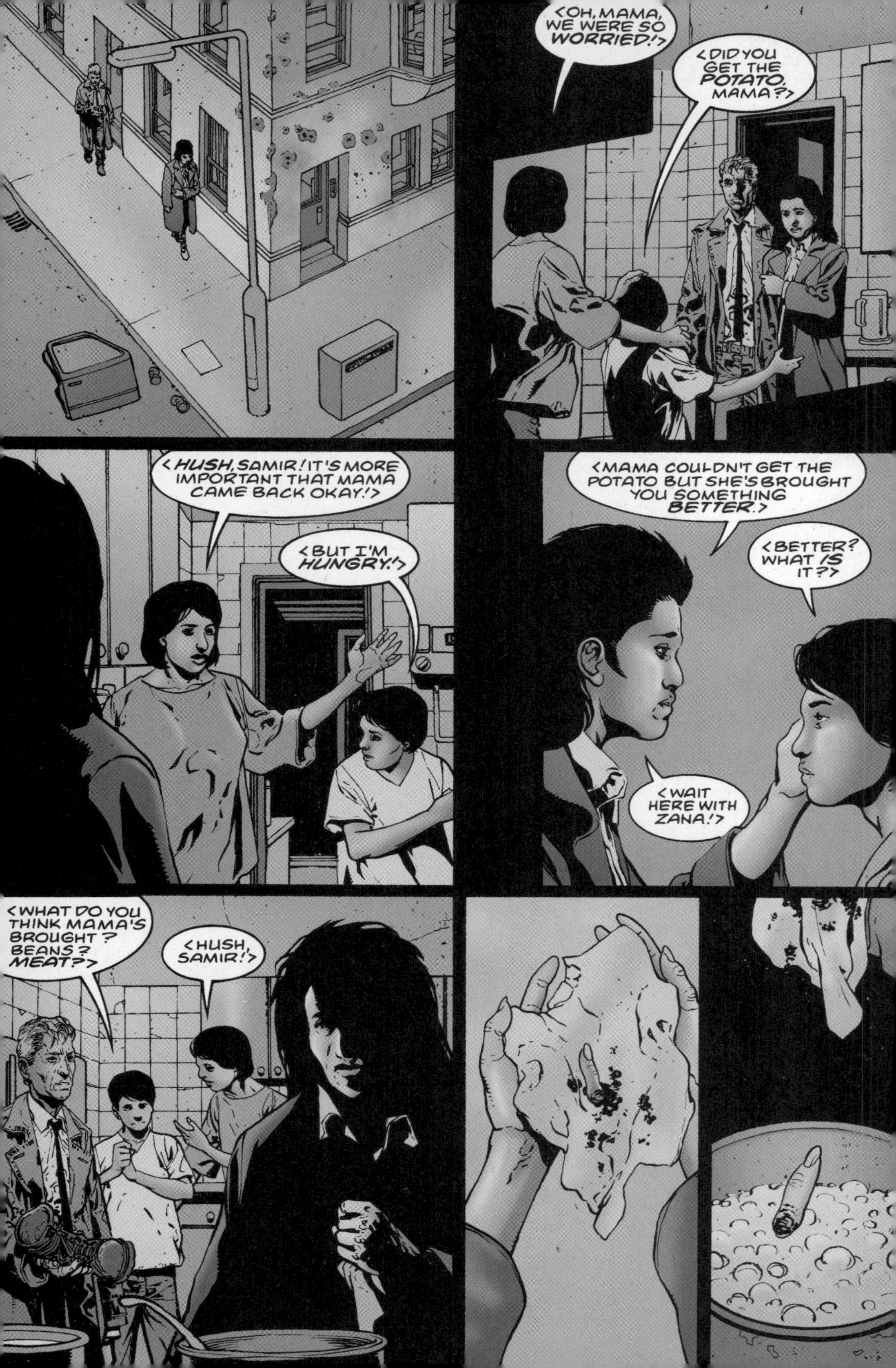

<OH, MAMA, WE WERE SO WORRIED!>
<DID YOU GET THE POTATO, MAMA?>
<HUSH, SAMIR! IT'S MORE IMPORTANT THAT MAMA CAME BACK OKAY!>
<BUT I'M HUNGRY!>
<MAMA COULDN'T GET THE POTATO BUT SHE'S BROUGHT YOU SOMETHING BETTER.>
<BETTER? WHAT IS IT?>
<WAIT HERE WITH ZANA!>
<WHAT DO YOU THINK MAMA'S BROUGHT? BEANS? MEAT?>
<HUSH, SAMIR!>

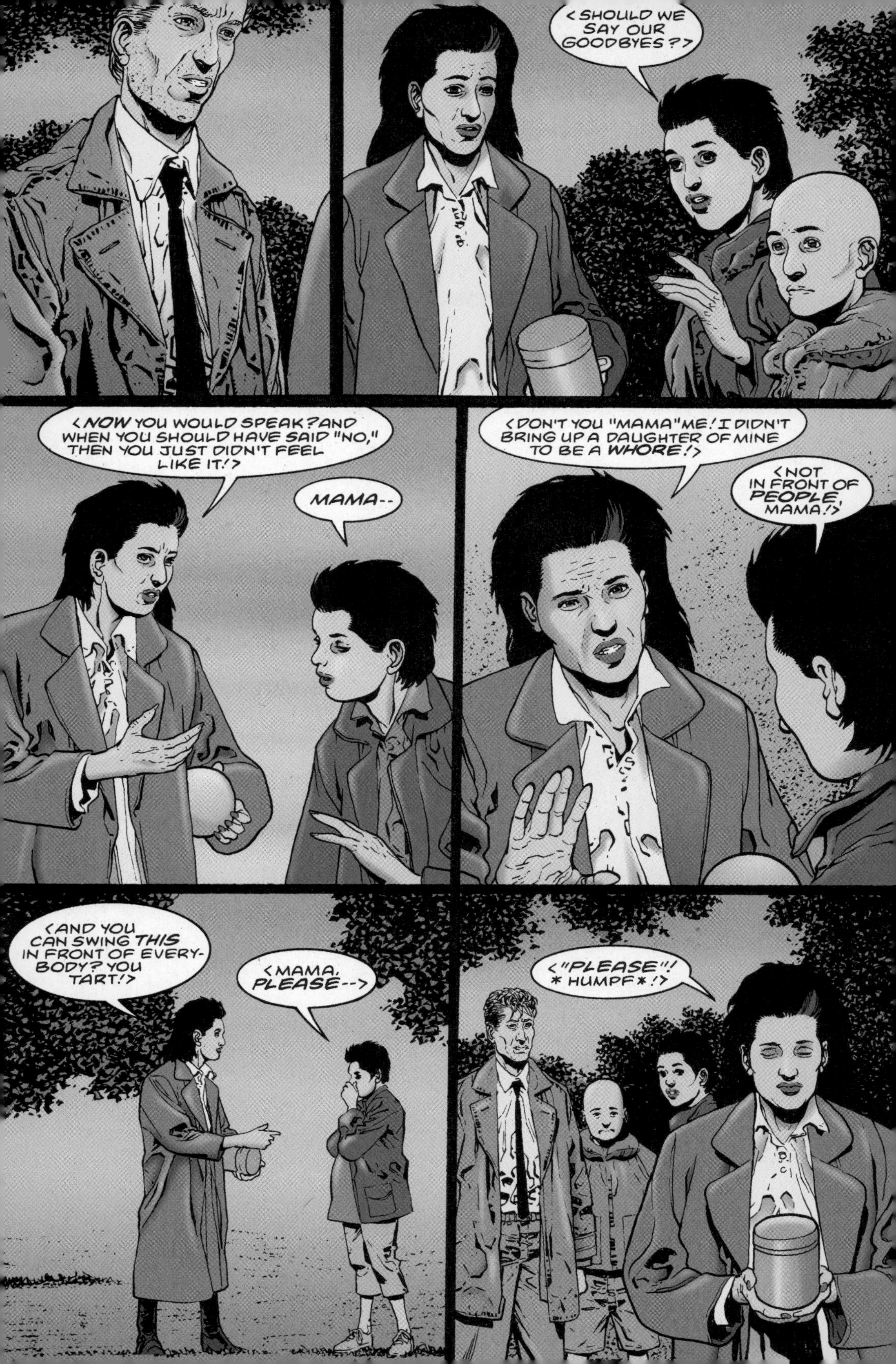
<SHOULD WE SAY OUR GOODBYES?>
<NOW YOU WOULD SPEAK? AND WHEN YOU SHOULD HAVE SAID "NO," THEN YOU JUST DIDN'T FEEL LIKE IT!>
MAMA--
<DON'T YOU "MAMA" ME! I DIDN'T BRING UP A DAUGHTER OF MINE TO BE A WHORE!>
<NOT IN FRONT OF PEOPLE, MAMA!>
<AND YOU CAN SWING THIS IN FRONT OF EVERY-BODY? YOU TART!>
<MAMA, PLEASE-->
<"PLEASE"! *HUMPF*!>

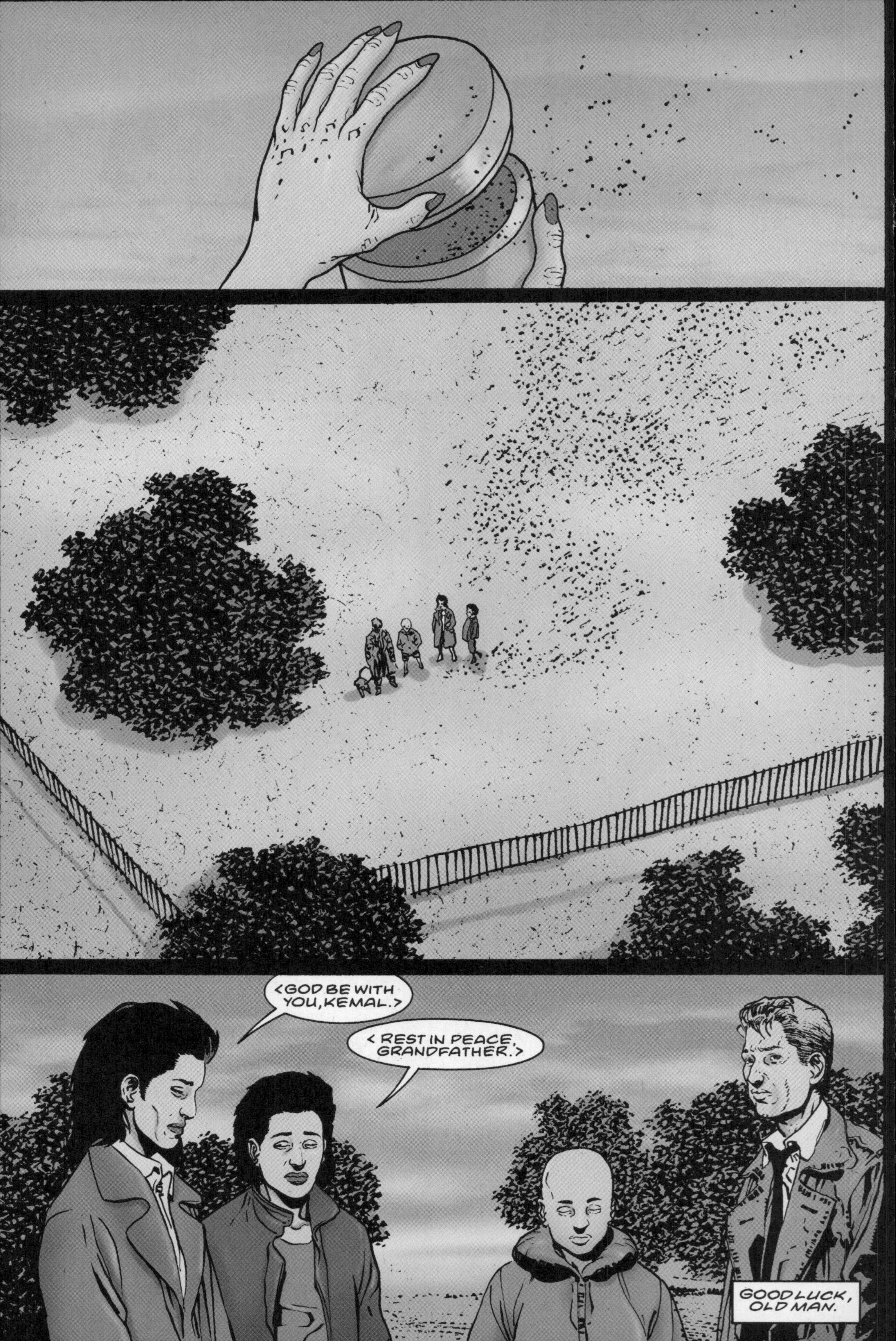

<GOD BE WITH YOU, KEMAL.>
< REST IN PEACE, GRANDFATHER.>
GOOD LUCK, OLD MAN.

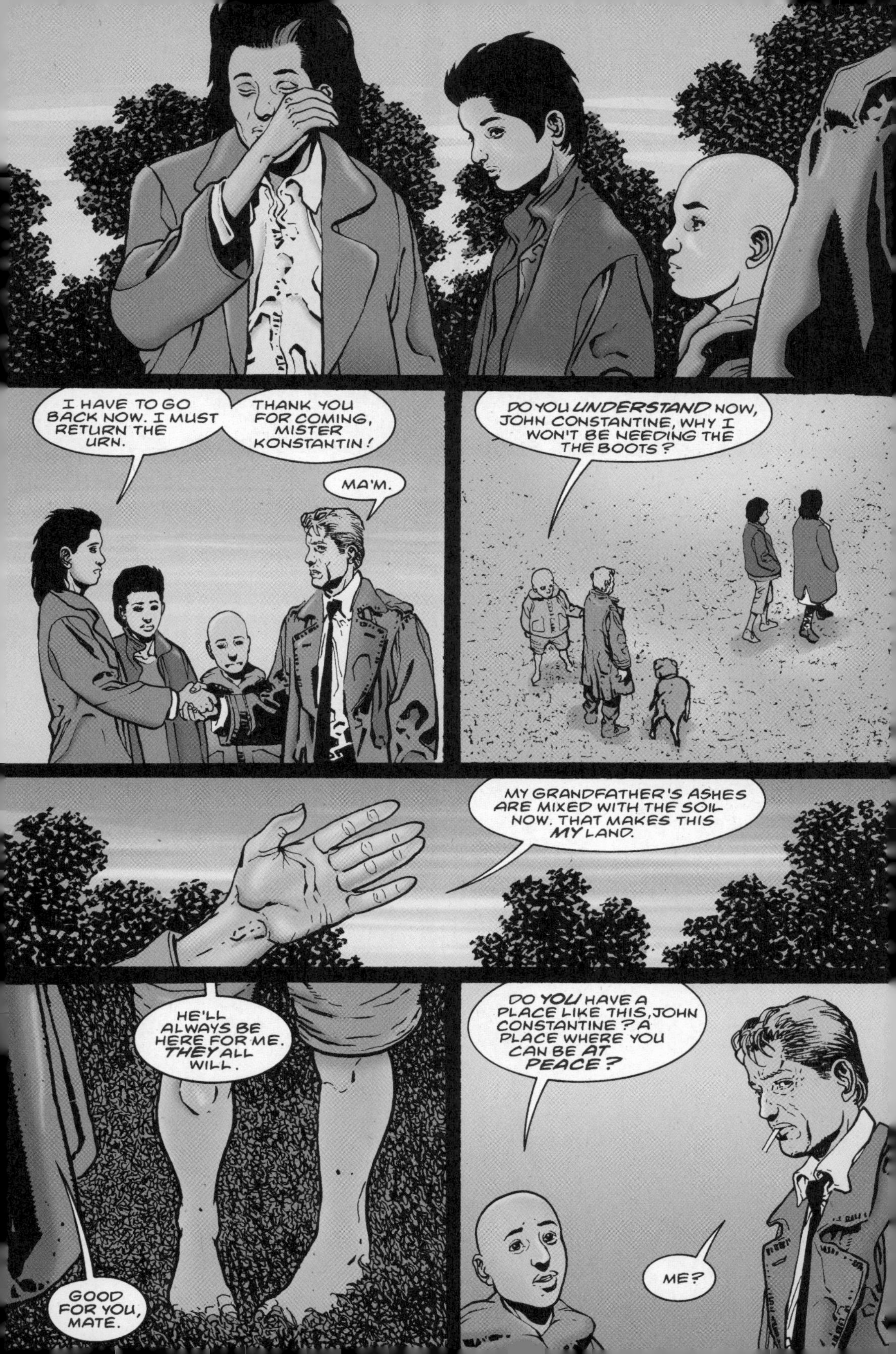

I HAVE TO GO BACK NOW. I MUST RETURN THE URN.
THANK YOU FOR COMING, MISTER KONSTANTIN!
MA'M.
DO YOU *UNDERSTAND* NOW, JOHN CONSTANTINE, WHY I WON'T BE NEEDING THE THE BOOTS?
MY GRANDFATHER'S ASHES ARE MIXED WITH THE SOIL NOW. THAT MAKES THIS *MY* LAND.
HE'LL ALWAYS BE HERE FOR ME. *THEY* ALL WILL.
GOOD FOR YOU, MATE.
DO *YOU* HAVE A PLACE LIKE THIS, JOHN CONSTANTINE? A PLACE WHERE YOU CAN BE *AT PEACE*?
ME?

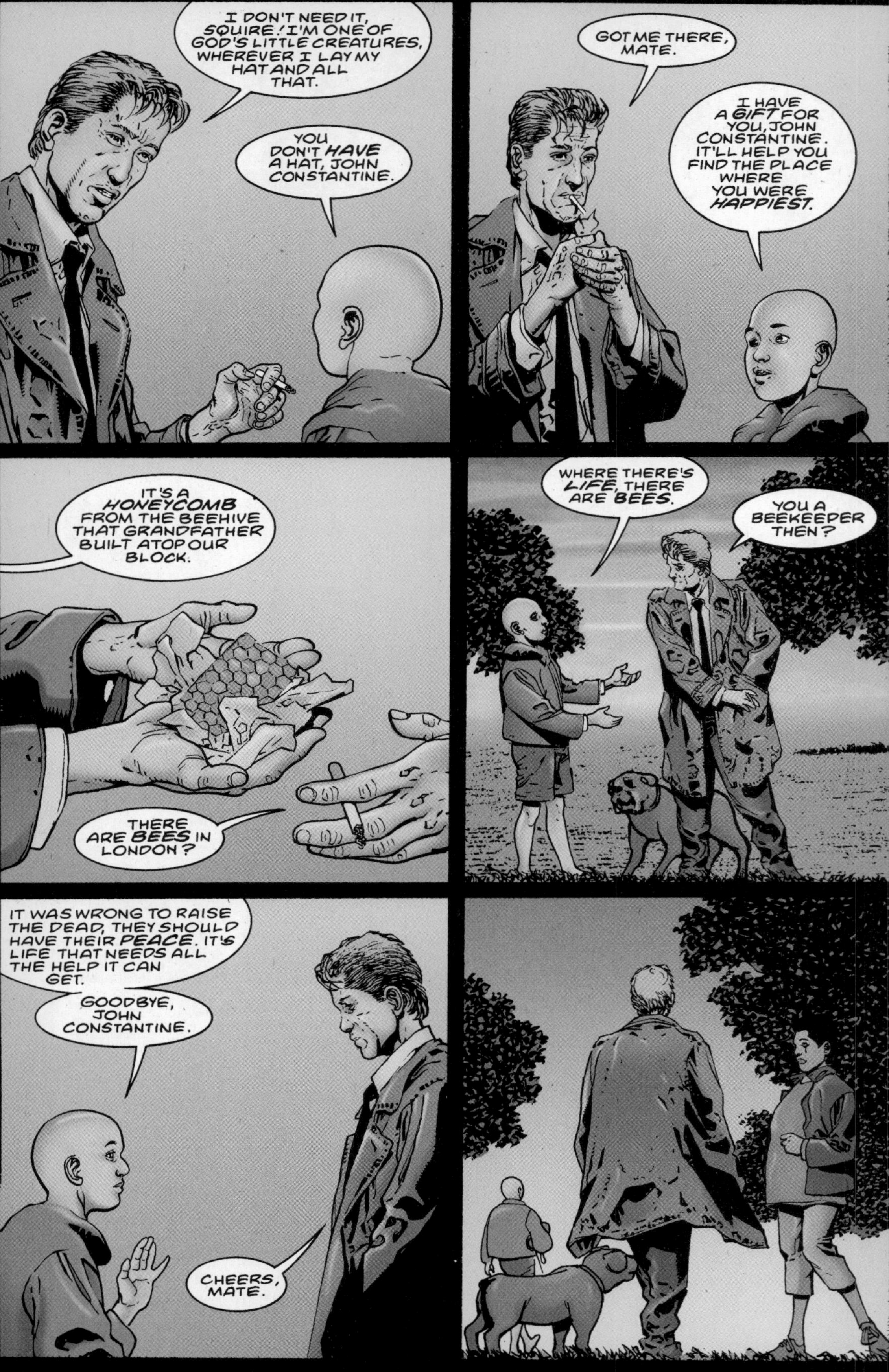
I DON'T NEED IT, SQUIRE! I'M ONE OF GOD'S LITTLE CREATURES, WHEREVER I LAY MY HAT AND ALL THAT.
YOU DON'T HAVE A HAT, JOHN CONSTANTINE.
GOT ME THERE, MATE.
I HAVE A GIFT FOR YOU, JOHN CONSTANTINE. IT'LL HELP YOU FIND THE PLACE WHERE YOU WERE HAPPIEST.
IT'S A HONEYCOMB FROM THE BEEHIVE THAT GRANDFATHER BUILT ATOP OUR BLOCK.
THERE ARE BEES IN LONDON?
WHERE THERE'S LIFE, THERE ARE BEES.
YOU A BEEKEEPER THEN?
IT WAS WRONG TO RAISE THE DEAD, THEY SHOULD HAVE THEIR PEACE. IT'S LIFE THAT NEEDS ALL THE HELP IT CAN GET.
GOODBYE, JOHN CONSTANTINE.
CHEERS, MATE.

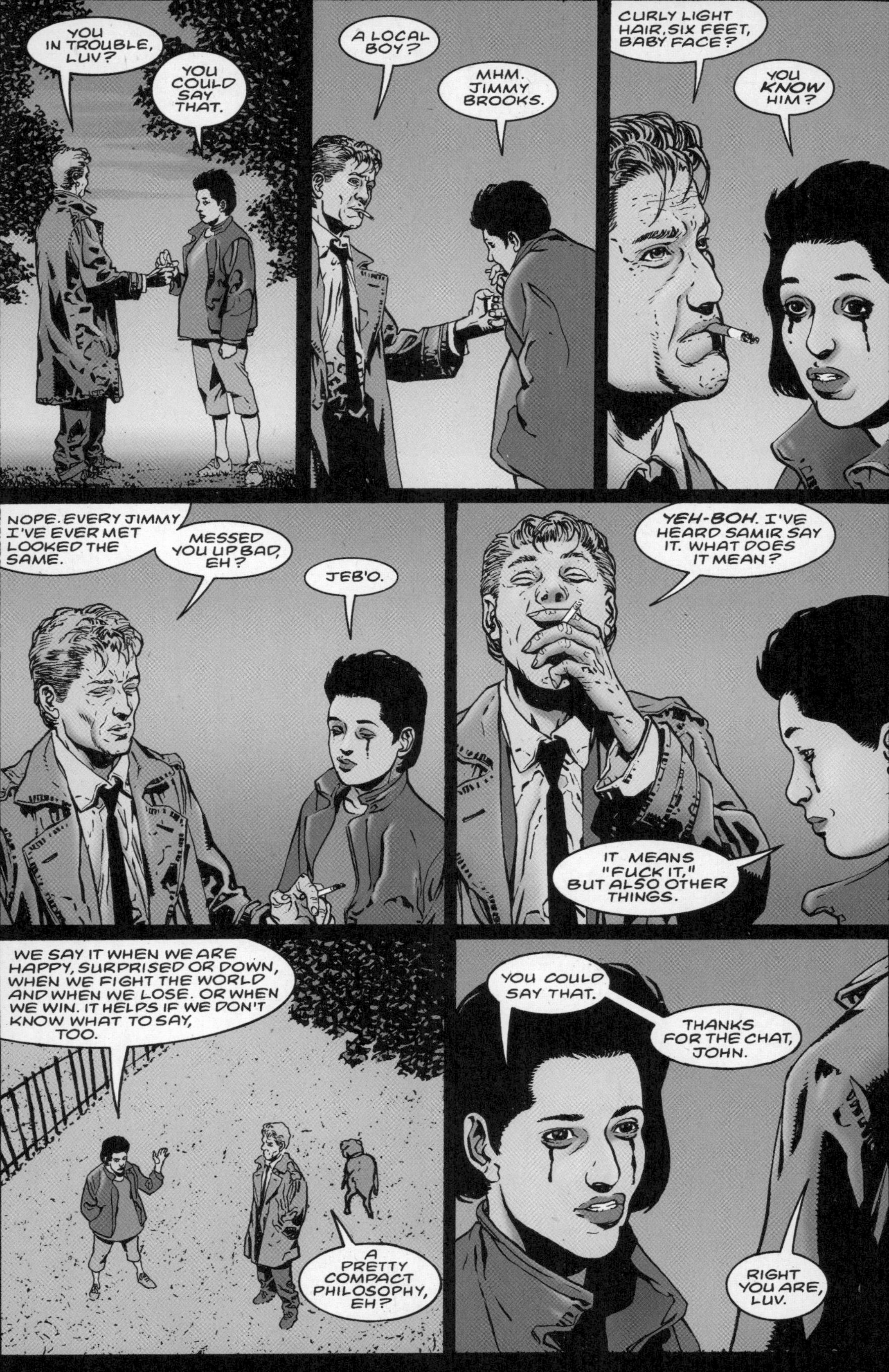
YOU IN TROUBLE, LUV?
YOU COULD SAY THAT.
A LOCAL BOY?
MHM. JIMMY BROOKS.
CURLY LIGHT HAIR, SIX FEET, BABY FACE?
YOU KNOW HIM?
NOPE. EVERY JIMMY I'VE EVER MET LOOKED THE SAME.
MESSED YOU UP BAD, EH?
JEB'O.
YEH-BOH. I'VE HEARD SAMIR SAY IT. WHAT DOES IT MEAN?
IT MEANS "FUCK IT," BUT ALSO OTHER THINGS.
WE SAY IT WHEN WE ARE HAPPY, SURPRISED OR DOWN, WHEN WE FIGHT THE WORLD AND WHEN WE LOSE. OR WHEN WE WIN. IT HELPS IF WE DON'T KNOW WHAT TO SAY, TOO.
A PRETTY COMPACT PHILOSOPHY, EH?
YOU COULD SAY THAT.
THANKS FOR THE CHAT, JOHN.
RIGHT YOU ARE, LUV.

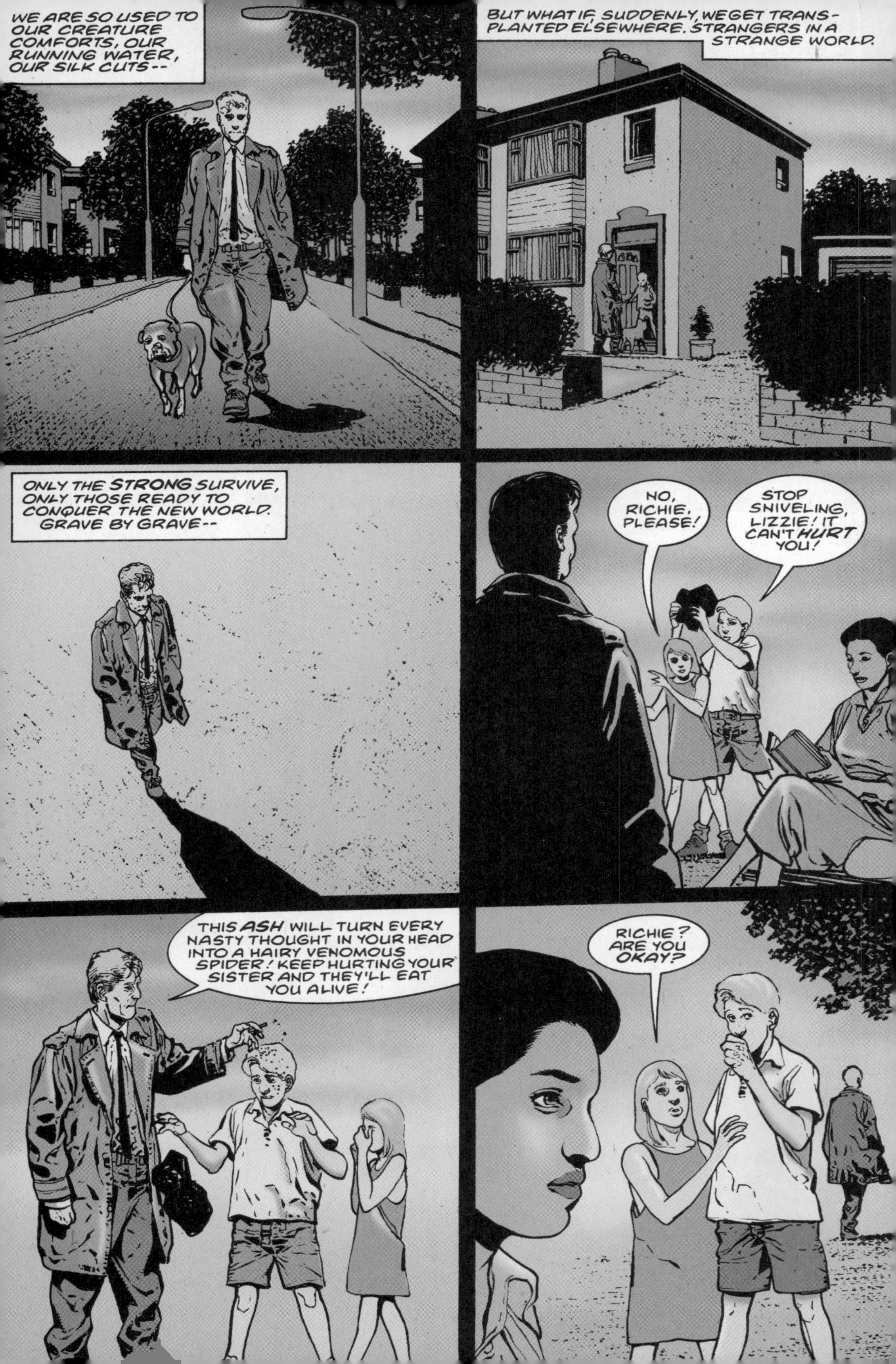
WE ARE SO USED TO OUR CREATURE COMFORTS, OUR RUNNING WATER, OUR SILK CUTS--
BUT WHAT IF, SUDDENLY, WE GET TRANS-PLANTED ELSEWHERE. STRANGERS IN A STRANGE WORLD.
ONLY THE STRONG SURVIVE, ONLY THOSE READY TO CONQUER THE NEW WORLD. GRAVE BY GRAVE--
NO, RICHIE, PLEASE!
STOP SNIVELING, LIZZIE! IT CAN'T HURT YOU!
THIS ASH WILL TURN EVERY NASTY THOUGHT IN YOUR HEAD INTO A HAIRY VENOMOUS SPIDER! KEEP HURTING YOUR SISTER AND THEY'LL EAT YOU ALIVE!
RICHIE? ARE YOU OKAY?

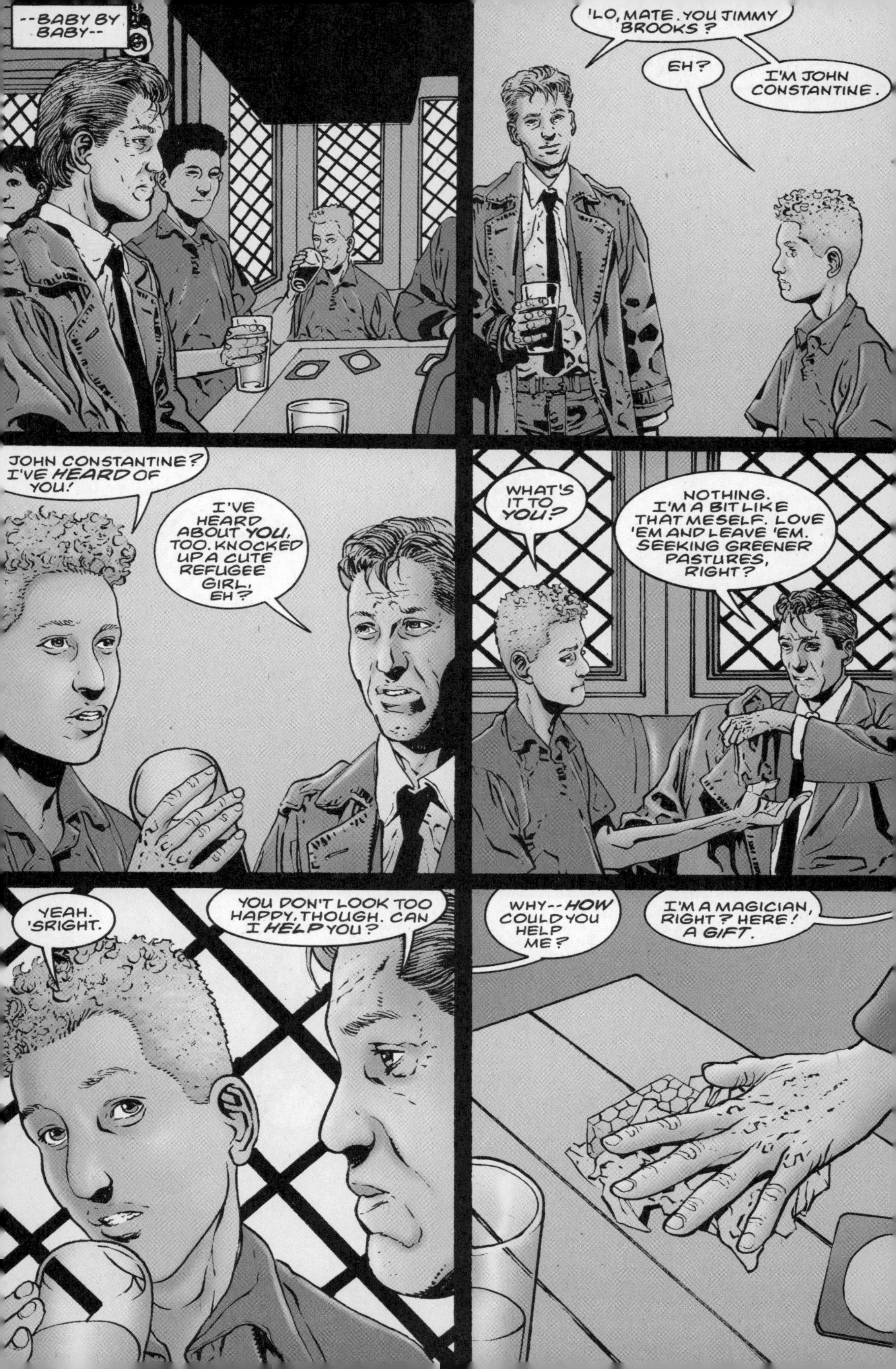
--BABY BY BABY--
'LO, MATE. YOU JIMMY BROOKS?
EH?
I'M JOHN CONSTANTINE.
JOHN CONSTANTINE? I'VE *HEARD* OF YOU!
I'VE HEARD ABOUT *YOU*, TOO. KNOCKED UP A CUTE REFUGEE GIRL, EH?
WHAT'S IT TO *YOU*?
NOTHING. I'M A BIT LIKE THAT MESELF. LOVE 'EM AND LEAVE 'EM. SEEKING GREENER PASTURES, RIGHT?
YEAH. 'SRIGHT.
YOU DON'T LOOK TOO HAPPY, THOUGH. CAN I *HELP* YOU?
WHY-- *HOW* COULD YOU HELP ME?
I'M A MAGICIAN, RIGHT? HERE! A *GIFT*.

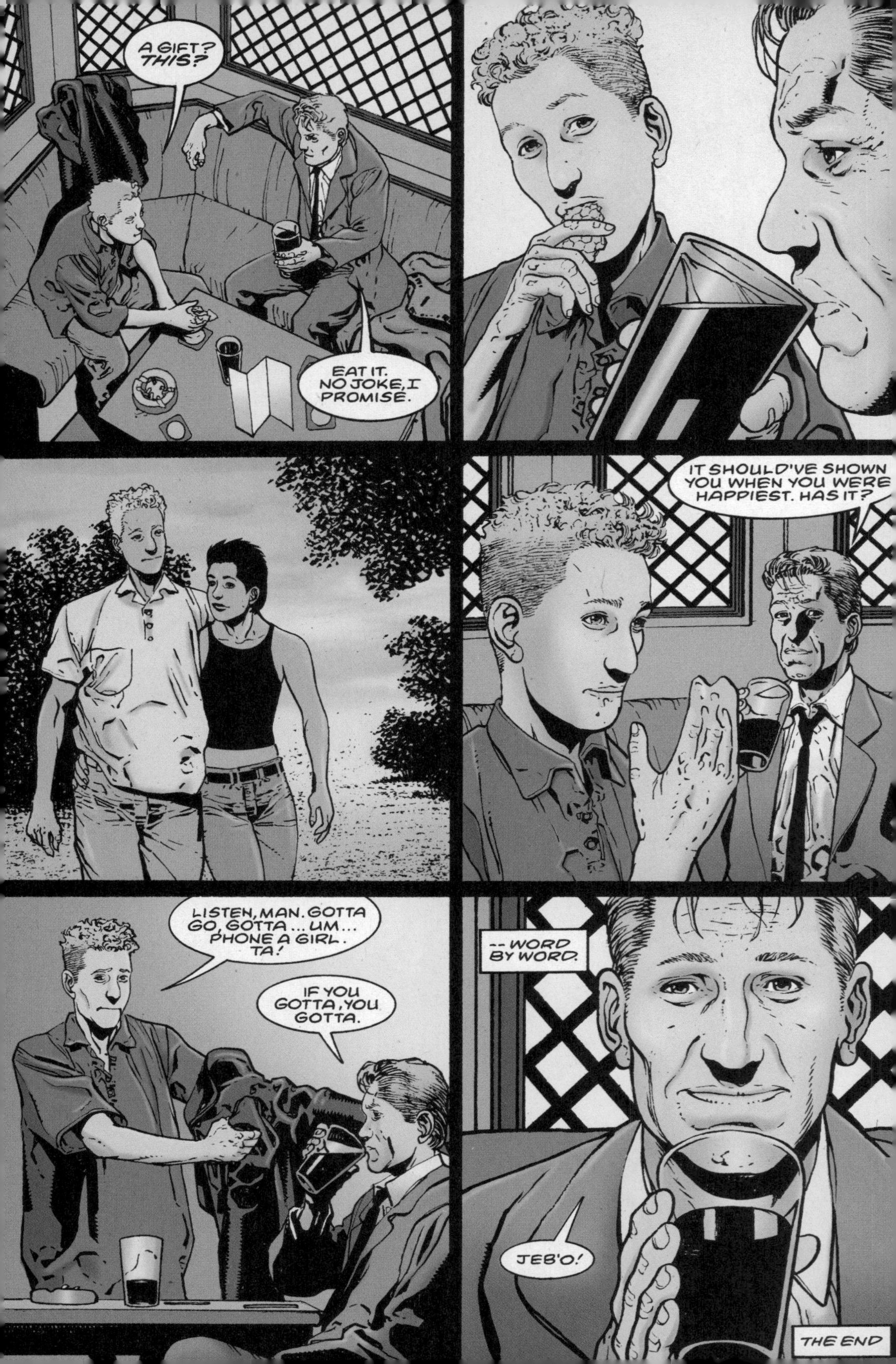
A GIFT? THIS?
EAT IT. NO JOKE, I PROMISE.
IT SHOULD'VE SHOWN YOU WHEN YOU WERE HAPPIEST. HAS IT?
LISTEN, MAN. GOTTA GO, GOTTA ... UM ... PHONE A GIRL. TA!
IF YOU GOTTA, YOU GOTTA.
-- WORD BY WORD.
JEB'O!
THE END

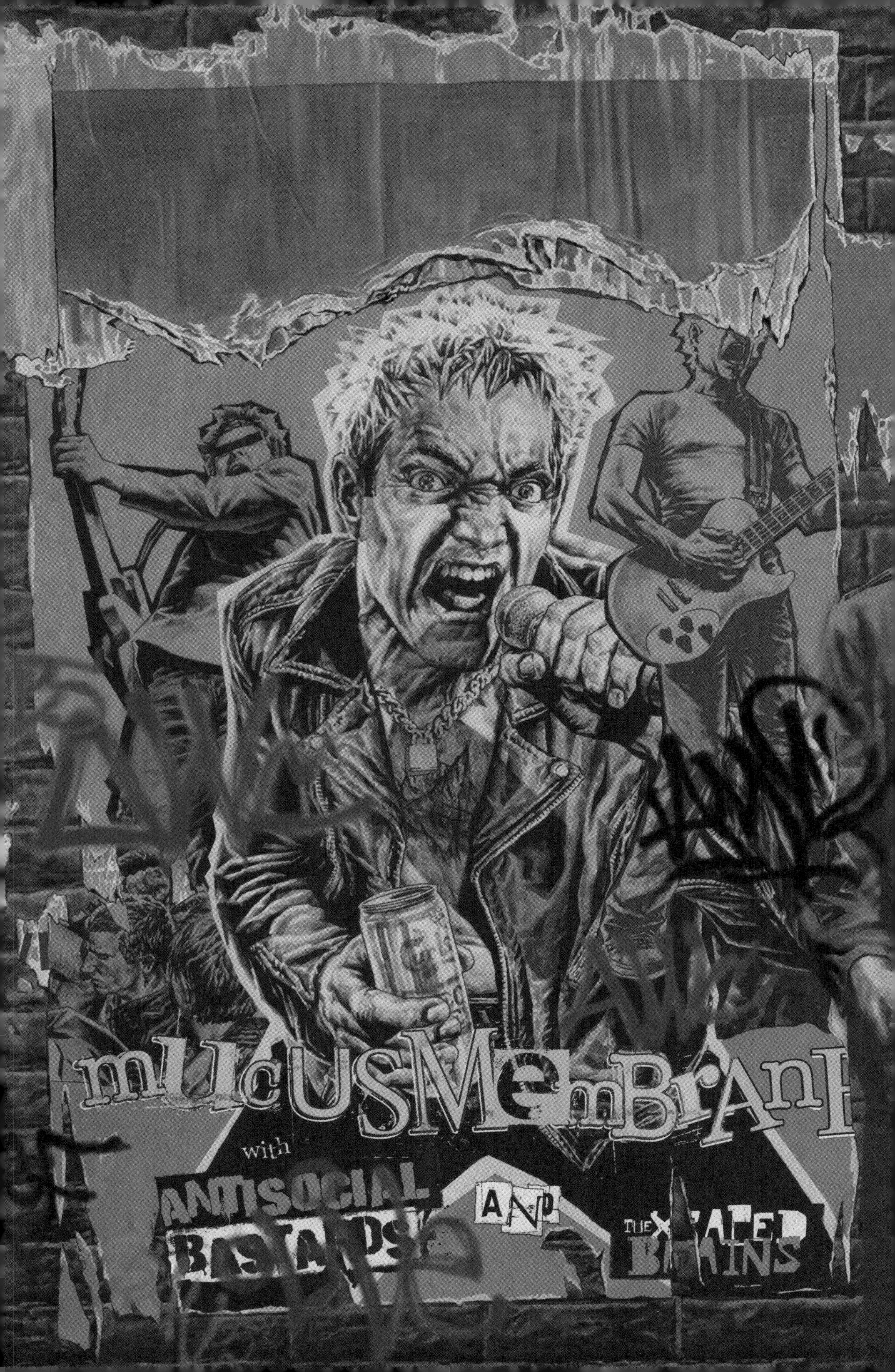
mUcUSMeMBrAnE
with
ANTISOCIAL BASTARDS
AND
THE X-RATED BRAINS

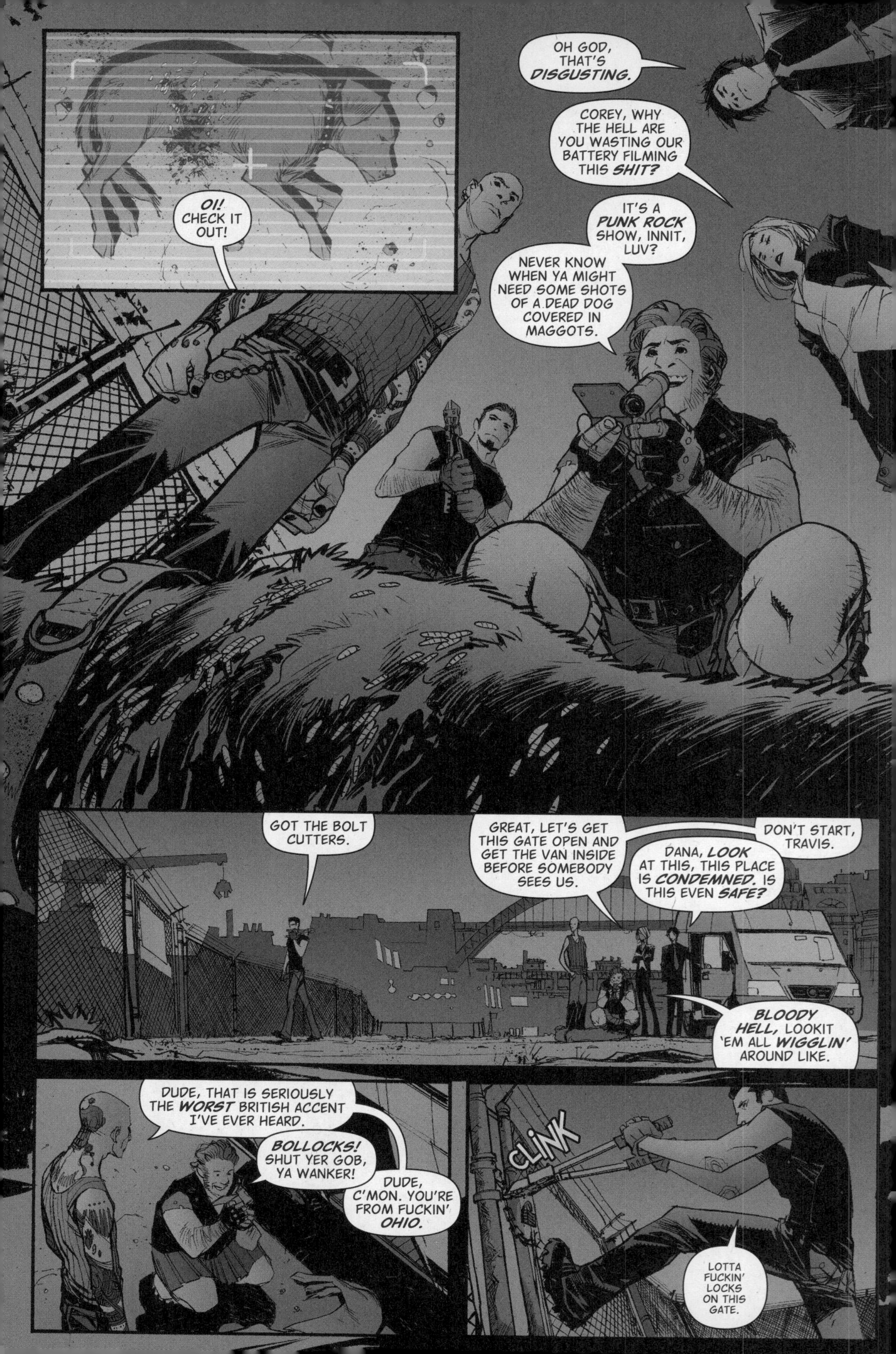

OI! CHECK IT OUT!
OH GOD, THAT'S DISGUSTING.
COREY, WHY THE HELL ARE YOU WASTING OUR BATTERY FILMING THIS SHIT?
IT'S A PUNK ROCK SHOW, INNIT, LUV?
NEVER KNOW WHEN YA MIGHT NEED SOME SHOTS OF A DEAD DOG COVERED IN MAGGOTS.
GOT THE BOLT CUTTERS.
GREAT, LET'S GET THIS GATE OPEN AND GET THE VAN INSIDE BEFORE SOMEBODY SEES US.
DON'T START, TRAVIS.
DANA, LOOK AT THIS, THIS PLACE IS CONDEMNED. IS THIS EVEN SAFE?
BLOODY HELL, LOOKIT 'EM ALL WIGGLIN' AROUND LIKE.
DUDE, THAT IS SERIOUSLY THE WORST BRITISH ACCENT I'VE EVER HEARD.
BOLLOCKS! SHUT YER GOB, YA WANKER!
DUDE, C'MON. YOU'RE FROM FUCKIN' OHIO.
CLINK
LOTTA FUCKIN' LOCKS ON THIS GATE.

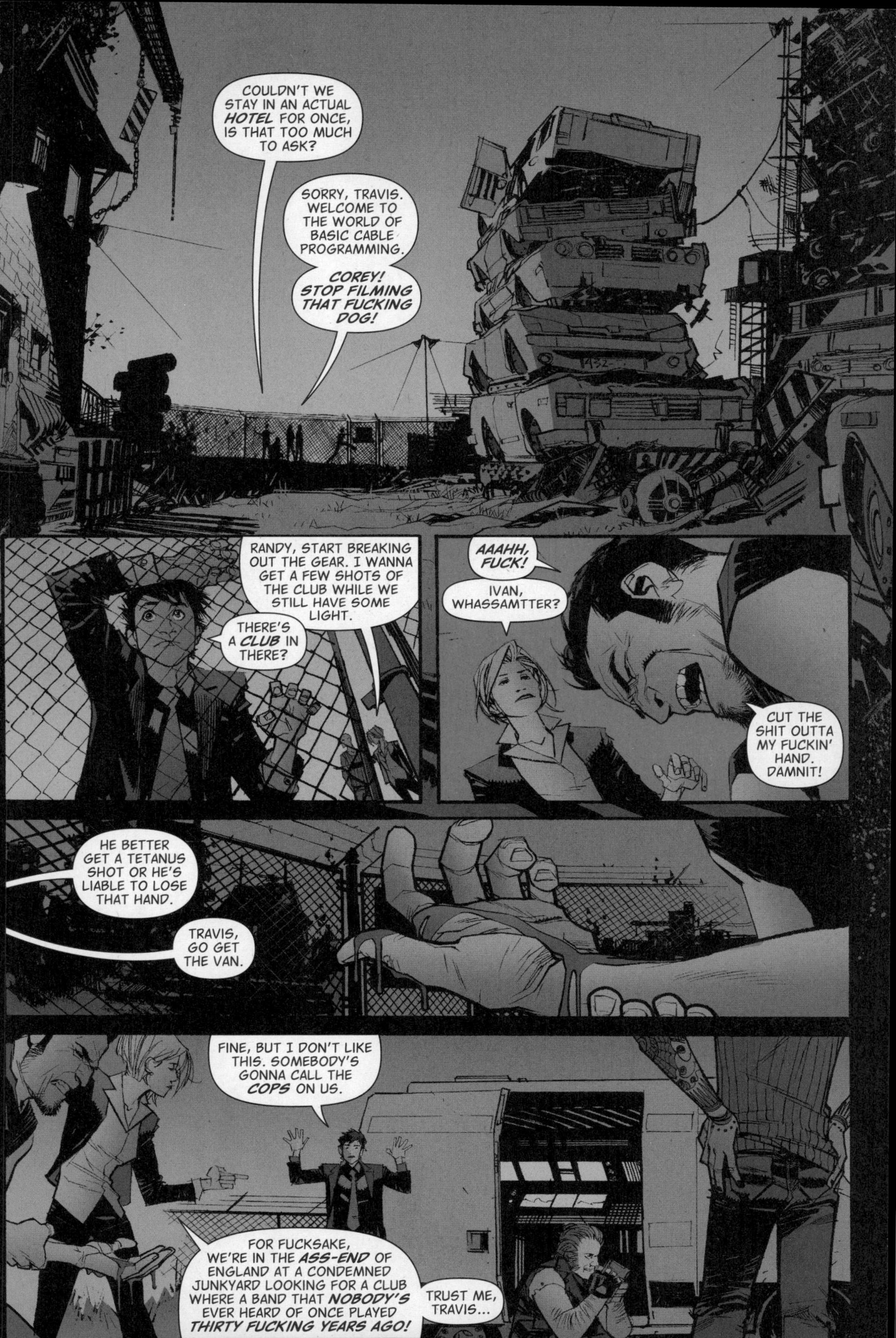
COULDN'T WE STAY IN AN ACTUAL HOTEL FOR ONCE, IS THAT TOO MUCH TO ASK?
SORRY, TRAVIS. WELCOME TO THE WORLD OF BASIC CABLE PROGRAMMING.
COREY! STOP FILMING THAT FUCKING DOG!
RANDY, START BREAKING OUT THE GEAR. I WANNA GET A FEW SHOTS OF THE CLUB WHILE WE STILL HAVE SOME LIGHT.
THERE'S A CLUB IN THERE?
AAAHH, FUCK!
IVAN, WHASSAMTTER?
CUT THE SHIT OUTTA MY FUCKIN' HAND. DAMNIT!
HE BETTER GET A TETANUS SHOT OR HE'S LIABLE TO LOSE THAT HAND.
TRAVIS, GO GET THE VAN.
FINE, BUT I DON'T LIKE THIS. SOMEBODY'S GONNA CALL THE COPS ON US.
FOR FUCKSAKE, WE'RE IN THE ASS-END OF ENGLAND AT A CONDEMNED JUNKYARD LOOKING FOR A CLUB WHERE A BAND THAT NOBODY'S EVER HEARD OF ONCE PLAYED THIRTY FUCKING YEARS AGO!
TRUST ME, TRAVIS...

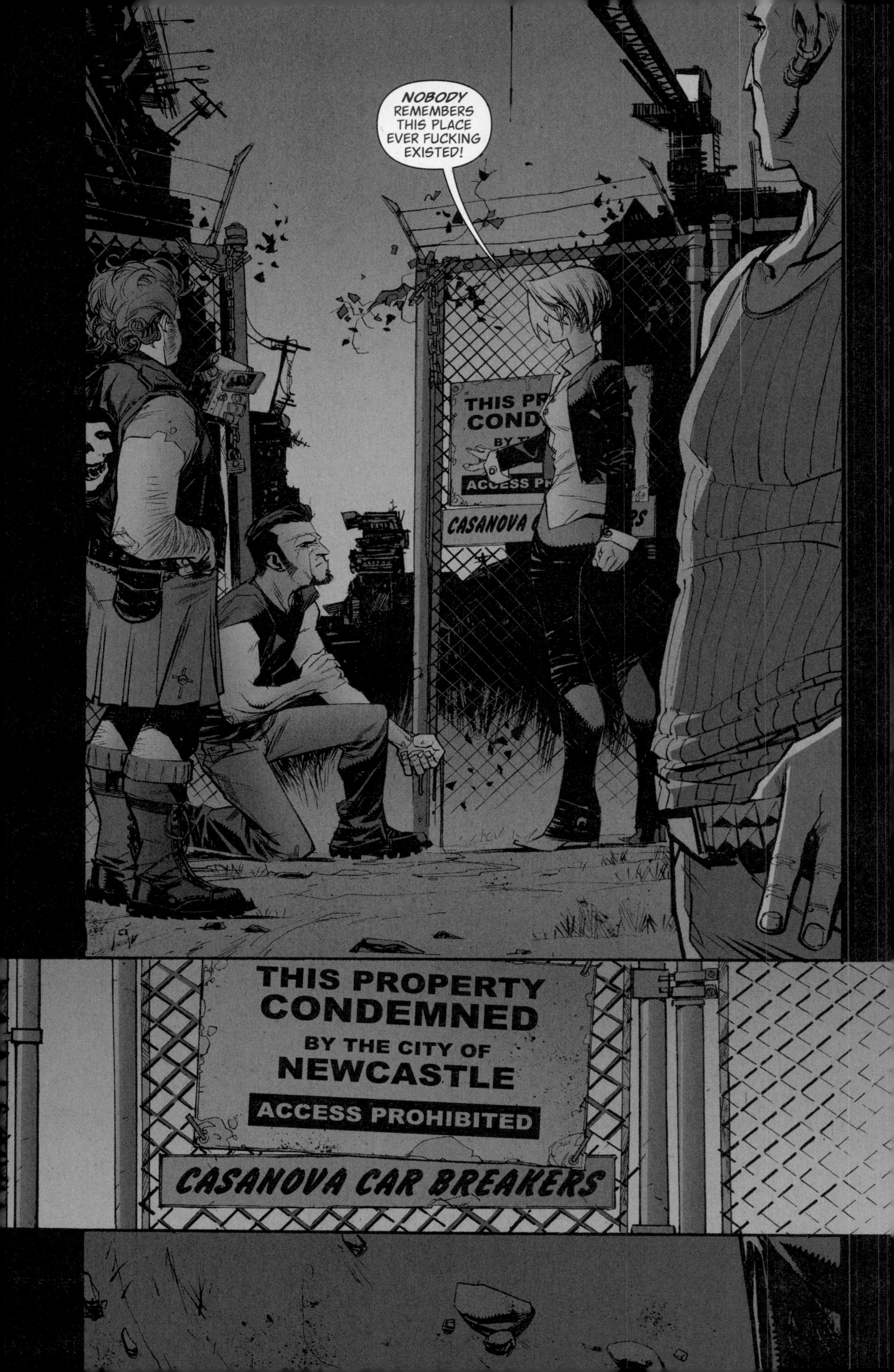
NOBODY REMEMBERS THIS PLACE EVER FUCKING EXISTED!
THIS PROPERTY CONDEMNED BY THE CITY OF NEWCASTLE
ACCESS PROHIBITED
CASANOVA CAR BREAKERS

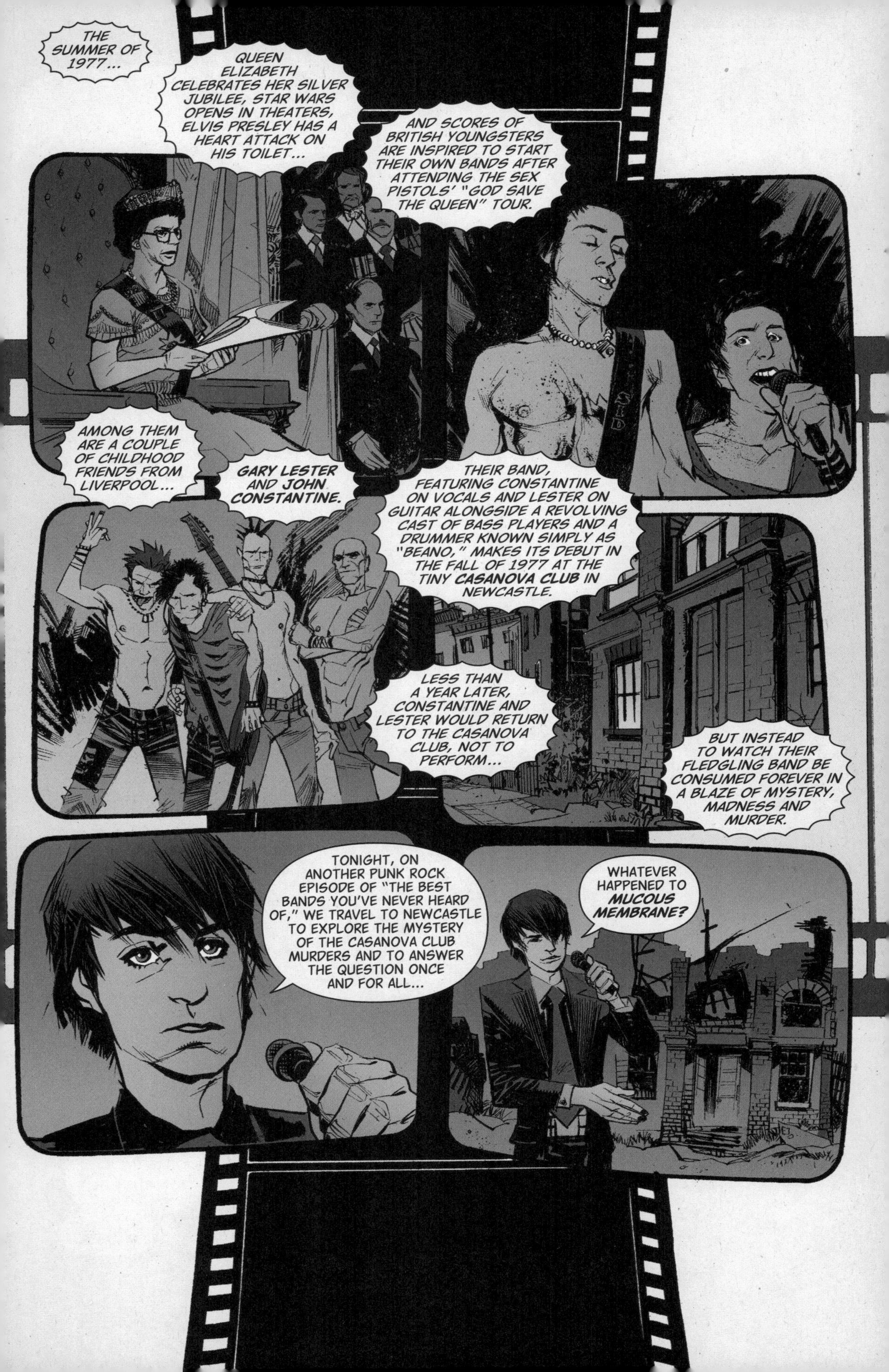
THE SUMMER OF 1977...
QUEEN ELIZABETH CELEBRATES HER SILVER JUBILEE, STAR WARS OPENS IN THEATERS, ELVIS PRESLEY HAS A HEART ATTACK ON HIS TOILET...
AND SCORES OF BRITISH YOUNGSTERS ARE INSPIRED TO START THEIR OWN BANDS AFTER ATTENDING THE SEX PISTOLS' "GOD SAVE THE QUEEN" TOUR.
SID
AMONG THEM ARE A COUPLE OF CHILDHOOD FRIENDS FROM LIVERPOOL...
GARY LESTER AND JOHN CONSTANTINE.
THEIR BAND, FEATURING CONSTANTINE ON VOCALS AND LESTER ON GUITAR ALONGSIDE A REVOLVING CAST OF BASS PLAYERS AND A DRUMMER KNOWN SIMPLY AS "BEANO," MAKES ITS DEBUT IN THE FALL OF 1977 AT THE TINY CASANOVA CLUB IN NEWCASTLE.
LESS THAN A YEAR LATER, CONSTANTINE AND LESTER WOULD RETURN TO THE CASANOVA CLUB, NOT TO PERFORM...
BUT INSTEAD TO WATCH THEIR FLEDGLING BAND BE CONSUMED FOREVER IN A BLAZE OF MYSTERY, MADNESS AND MURDER.
TONIGHT, ON ANOTHER PUNK ROCK EPISODE OF "THE BEST BANDS YOU'VE NEVER HEARD OF," WE TRAVEL TO NEWCASTLE TO EXPLORE THE MYSTERY OF THE CASANOVA CLUB MURDERS AND TO ANSWER THE QUESTION ONCE AND FOR ALL...
WHATEVER HAPPENED TO MUCOUS MEMBRANE?

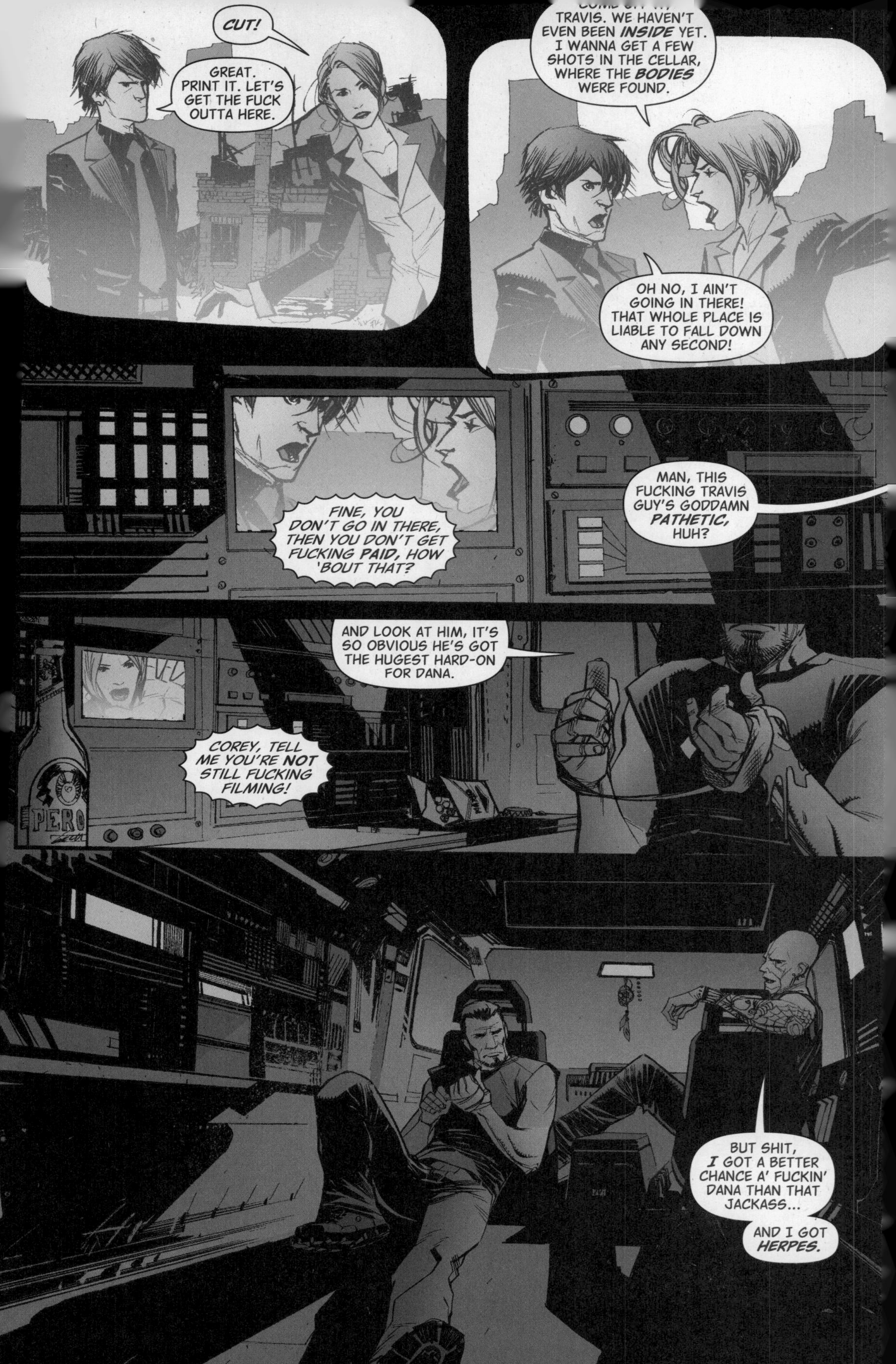
CUT!
GREAT. PRINT IT. LET'S GET THE FUCK OUTTA HERE.
TRAVIS. WE HAVEN'T EVEN BEEN *INSIDE* YET. I WANNA GET A FEW SHOTS IN THE CELLAR, WHERE THE *BODIES* WERE FOUND.
OH NO, I AIN'T GOING IN THERE! THAT WHOLE PLACE IS LIABLE TO FALL DOWN ANY SECOND!
FINE, YOU DON'T GO IN THERE, THEN YOU DON'T GET FUCKING *PAID*, HOW 'BOUT THAT?
MAN, THIS FUCKING TRAVIS GUY'S GODDAMN *PATHETIC*, HUH?
AND LOOK AT HIM, IT'S SO OBVIOUS HE'S GOT THE HUGEST HARD-ON FOR DANA.
COREY, TELL ME YOU'RE *NOT* STILL FUCKING FILMING!
PERO
BUT SHIT, *I* GOT A BETTER CHANCE A' FUCKIN' DANA THAN THAT JACKASS...
AND I GOT *HERPES.*

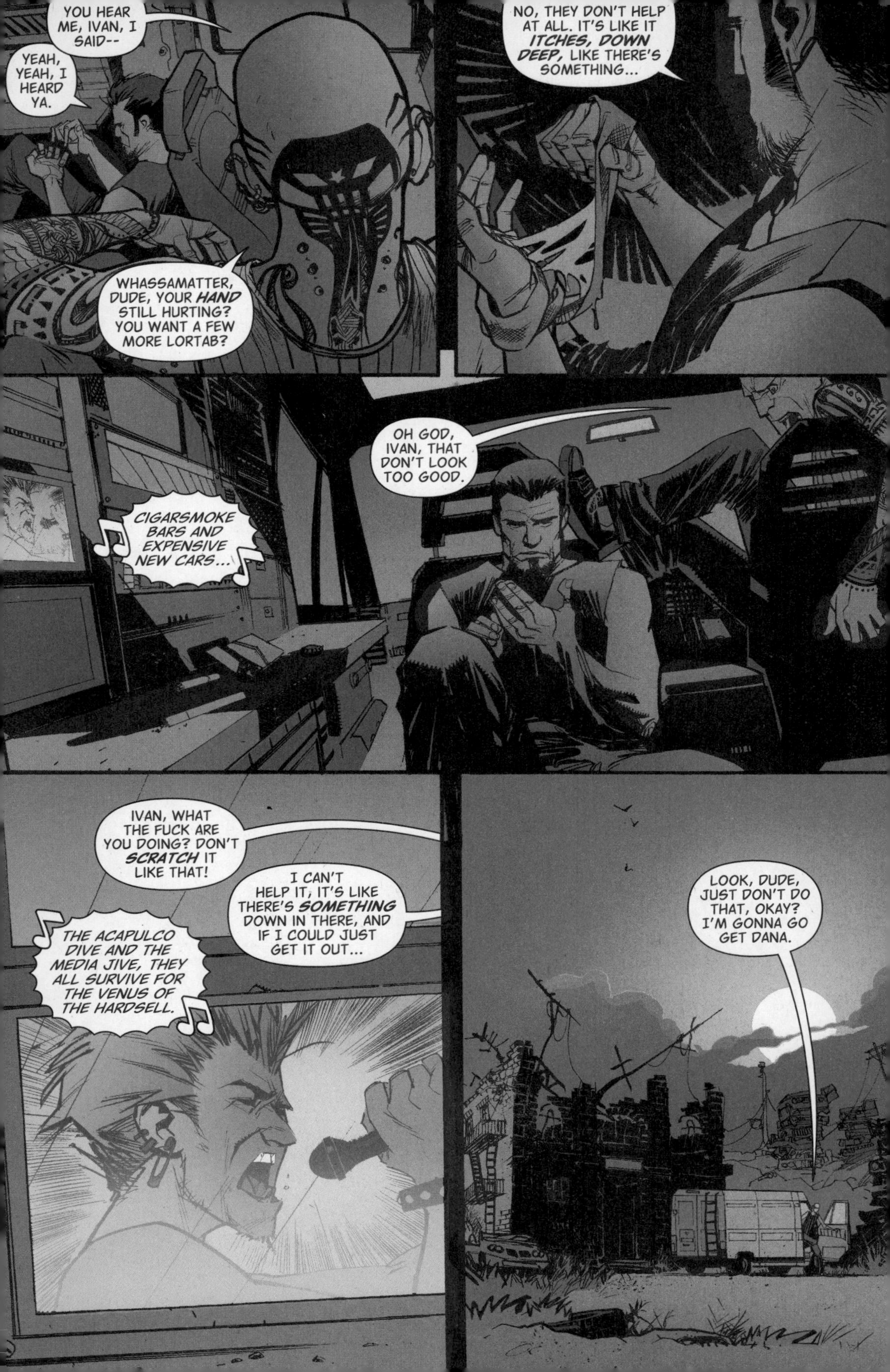
YOU HEAR ME, IVAN, I SAID--
YEAH, YEAH, I HEARD YA.
WHASSAMATTER, DUDE, YOUR HAND STILL HURTING? YOU WANT A FEW MORE LORTAB?
NO, THEY DON'T HELP AT ALL. IT'S LIKE IT ITCHES, DOWN DEEP, LIKE THERE'S SOMETHING...
OH GOD, IVAN, THAT DON'T LOOK TOO GOOD.
CIGARSMOKE BARS AND EXPENSIVE NEW CARS...
IVAN, WHAT THE FUCK ARE YOU DOING? DON'T SCRATCH IT LIKE THAT!
I CAN'T HELP IT, IT'S LIKE THERE'S SOMETHING DOWN IN THERE, AND IF I COULD JUST GET IT OUT...
THE ACAPULCO DIVE AND THE MEDIA JIVE, THEY ALL SURVIVE FOR THE VENUS OF THE HARDSELL.
LOOK, DUDE, JUST DON'T DO THAT, OKAY? I'M GONNA GO GET DANA.

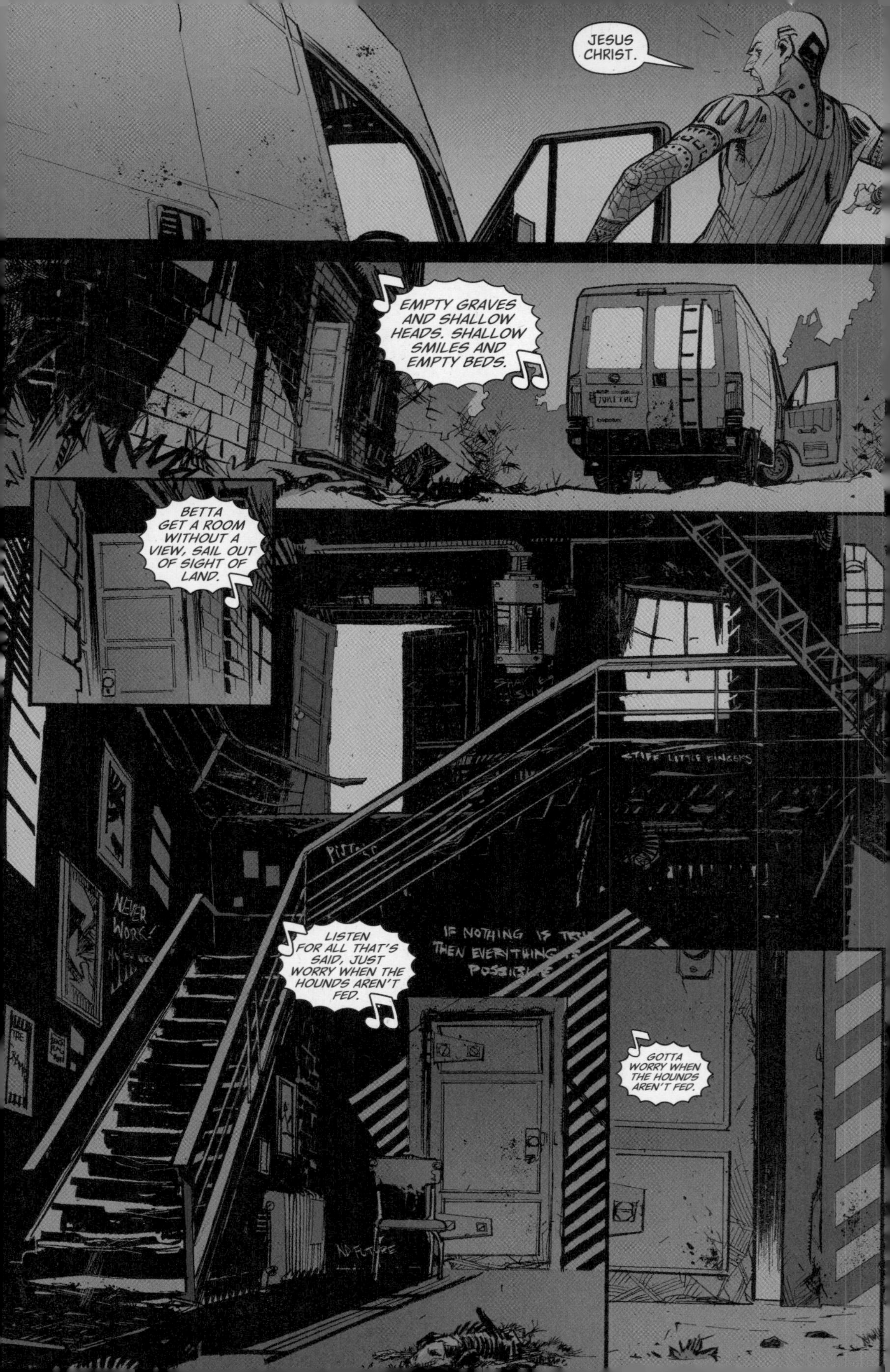
JESUS CHRIST.
EMPTY GRAVES AND SHALLOW HEADS. SHALLOW SMILES AND EMPTY BEDS.
BETTA GET A ROOM WITHOUT A VIEW, SAIL OUT OF SIGHT OF LAND.
STIFF LITTLE FINGERS
NEVER WORK!
LISTEN FOR ALL THAT'S SAID, JUST WORRY WHEN THE HOUNDS AREN'T FED.
GOTTA WORRY WHEN THE HOUNDS AREN'T FED.
NO FUTURE

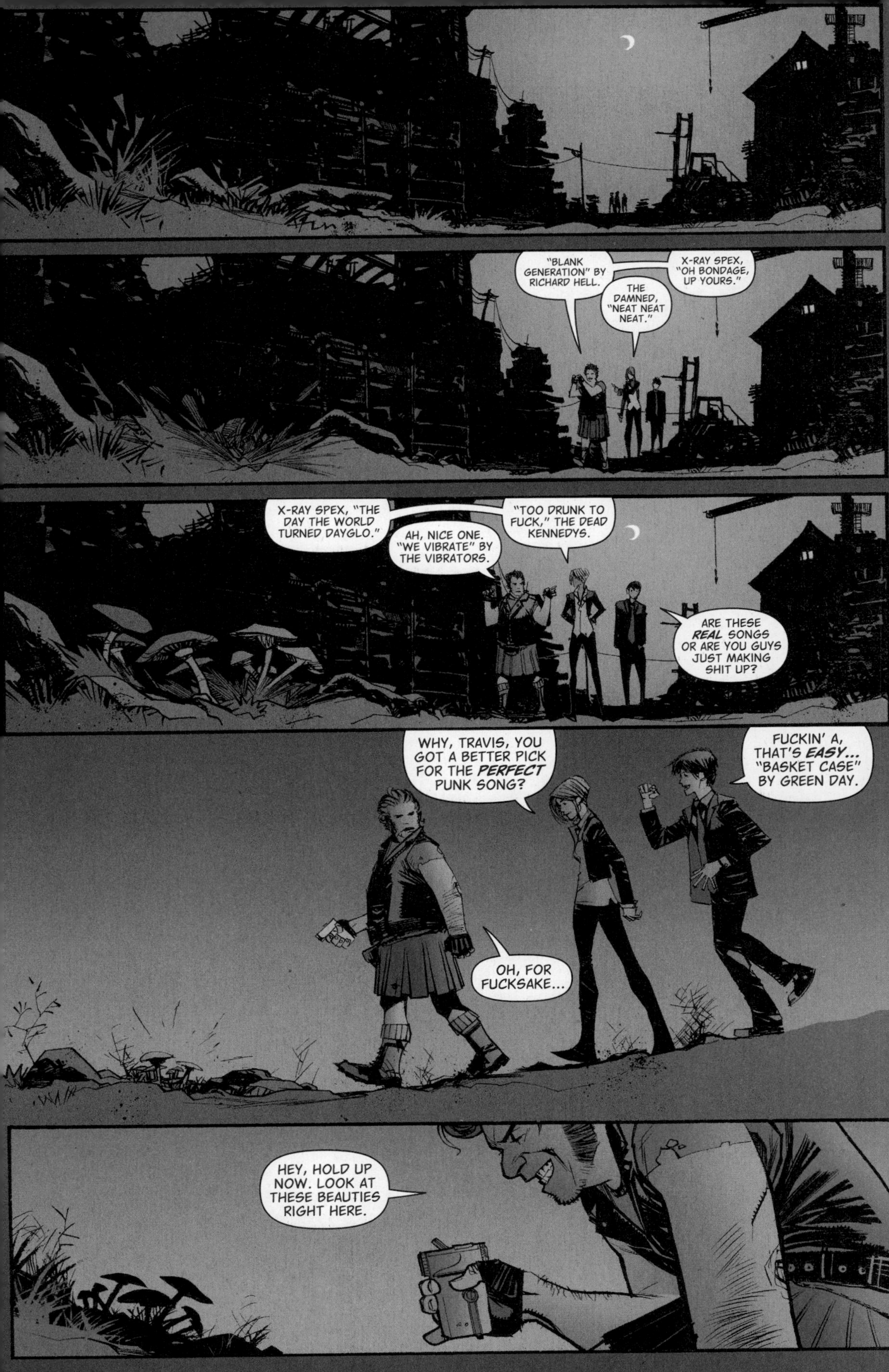
"BLANK GENERATION" BY RICHARD HELL.
X-RAY SPEX, "OH BONDAGE, UP YOURS."
THE DAMNED, "NEAT NEAT NEAT."
X-RAY SPEX, "THE DAY THE WORLD TURNED DAYGLO."
"TOO DRUNK TO FUCK," THE DEAD KENNEDYS.
AH, NICE ONE. "WE VIBRATE" BY THE VIBRATORS.
ARE THESE REAL SONGS OR ARE YOU GUYS JUST MAKING SHIT UP?
WHY, TRAVIS, YOU GOT A BETTER PICK FOR THE PERFECT PUNK SONG?
FUCKIN' A, THAT'S EASY... "BASKET CASE" BY GREEN DAY.
OH, FOR FUCKSAKE...
HEY, HOLD UP NOW. LOOK AT THESE BEAUTIES RIGHT HERE.

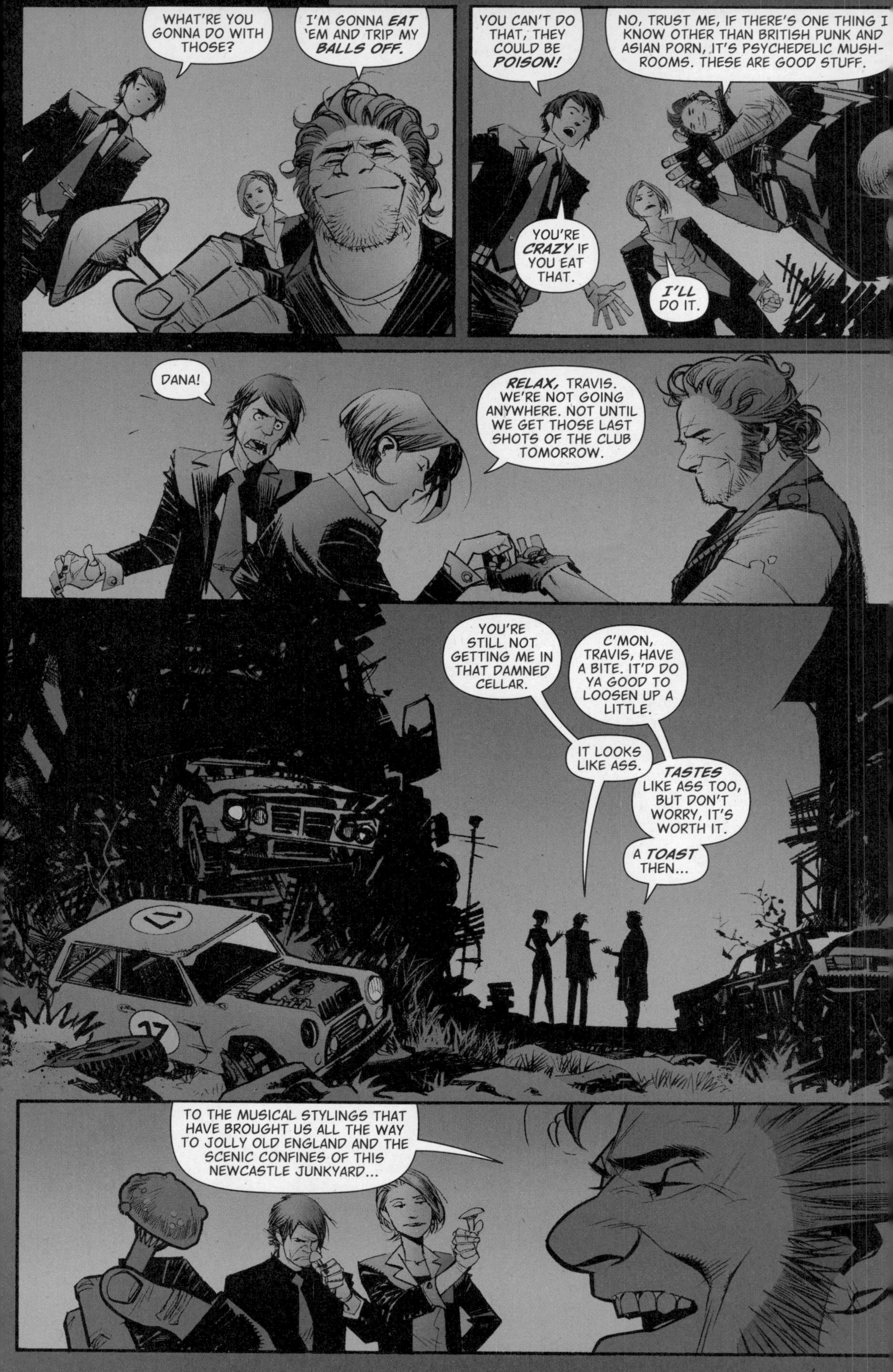
WHAT'RE YOU GONNA DO WITH THOSE?
I'M GONNA EAT 'EM AND TRIP MY BALLS OFF.
YOU CAN'T DO THAT, THEY COULD BE POISON!
NO, TRUST ME, IF THERE'S ONE THING I KNOW OTHER THAN BRITISH PUNK AND ASIAN PORN, IT'S PSYCHEDELIC MUSH-ROOMS. THESE ARE GOOD STUFF.
YOU'RE CRAZY IF YOU EAT THAT.
I'LL DO IT.
DANA!
RELAX, TRAVIS. WE'RE NOT GOING ANYWHERE. NOT UNTIL WE GET THOSE LAST SHOTS OF THE CLUB TOMORROW.
YOU'RE STILL NOT GETTING ME IN THAT DAMNED CELLAR.
C'MON, TRAVIS, HAVE A BITE. IT'D DO YA GOOD TO LOOSEN UP A LITTLE.
IT LOOKS LIKE ASS.
TASTES LIKE ASS TOO, BUT DON'T WORRY, IT'S WORTH IT.
A TOAST THEN...
TO THE MUSICAL STYLINGS THAT HAVE BROUGHT US ALL THE WAY TO JOLLY OLD ENGLAND AND THE SCENIC CONFINES OF THIS NEWCASTLE JUNKYARD...

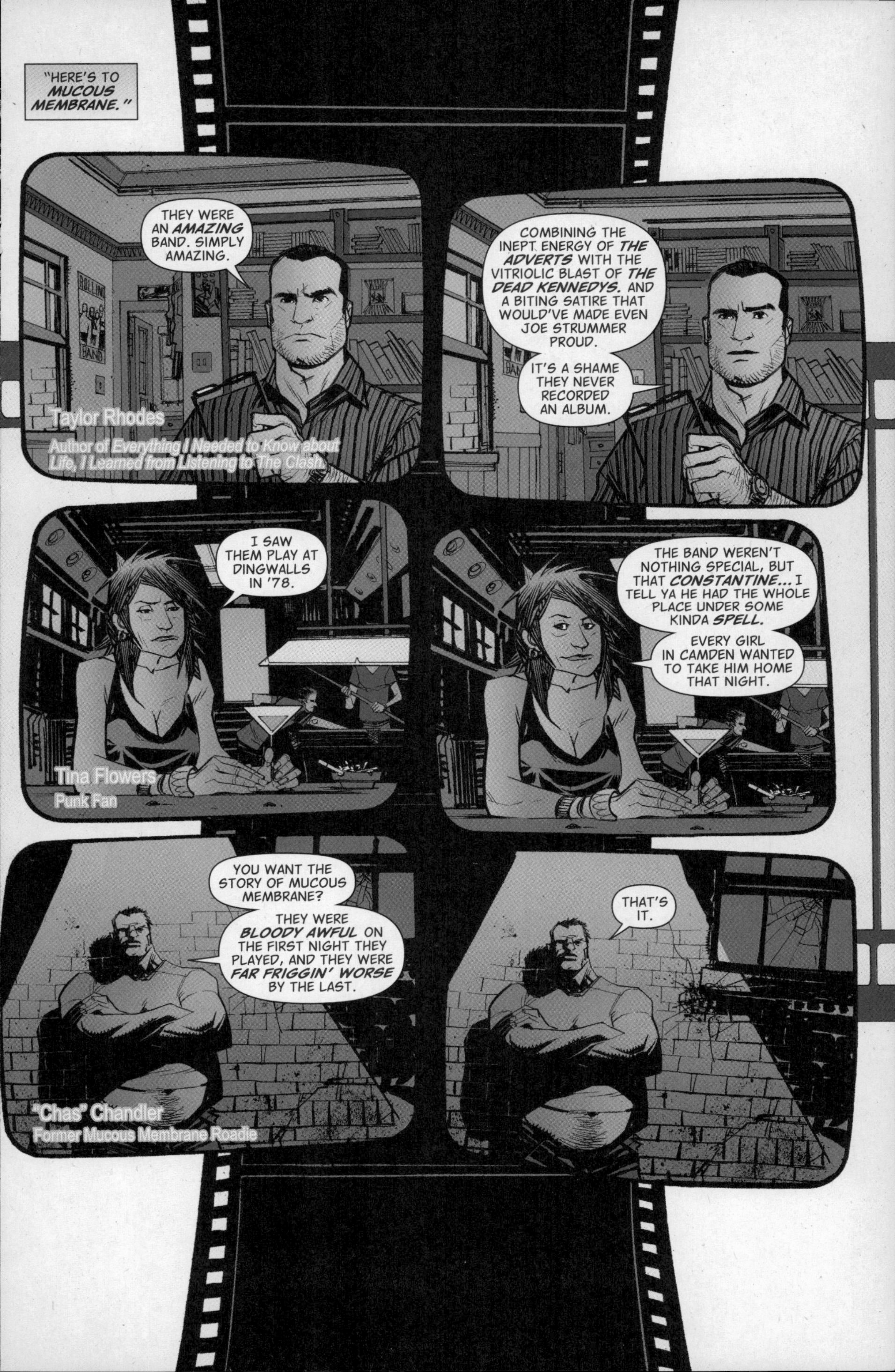
"HERE'S TO MUCOUS MEMBRANE."
THEY WERE AN AMAZING BAND. SIMPLY AMAZING.
Taylor Rhodes
Author of Everything I Needed to Know about Life, I Learned from Listening to The Clash.
COMBINING THE INEPT ENERGY OF THE ADVERTS WITH THE VITRIOLIC BLAST OF THE DEAD KENNEDYS. AND A BITING SATIRE THAT WOULD'VE MADE EVEN JOE STRUMMER PROUD.
IT'S A SHAME THEY NEVER RECORDED AN ALBUM.
I SAW THEM PLAY AT DINGWALLS IN '78.
Tina Flowers
Punk Fan
THE BAND WEREN'T NOTHING SPECIAL, BUT THAT CONSTANTINE... I TELL YA HE HAD THE WHOLE PLACE UNDER SOME KINDA SPELL.
EVERY GIRL IN CAMDEN WANTED TO TAKE HIM HOME THAT NIGHT.
YOU WANT THE STORY OF MUCOUS MEMBRANE?
THEY WERE BLOODY AWFUL ON THE FIRST NIGHT THEY PLAYED, AND THEY WERE FAR FRIGGIN' WORSE BY THE LAST.
"Chas" Chandler
Former Mucous Membrane Roadie
THAT'S IT.

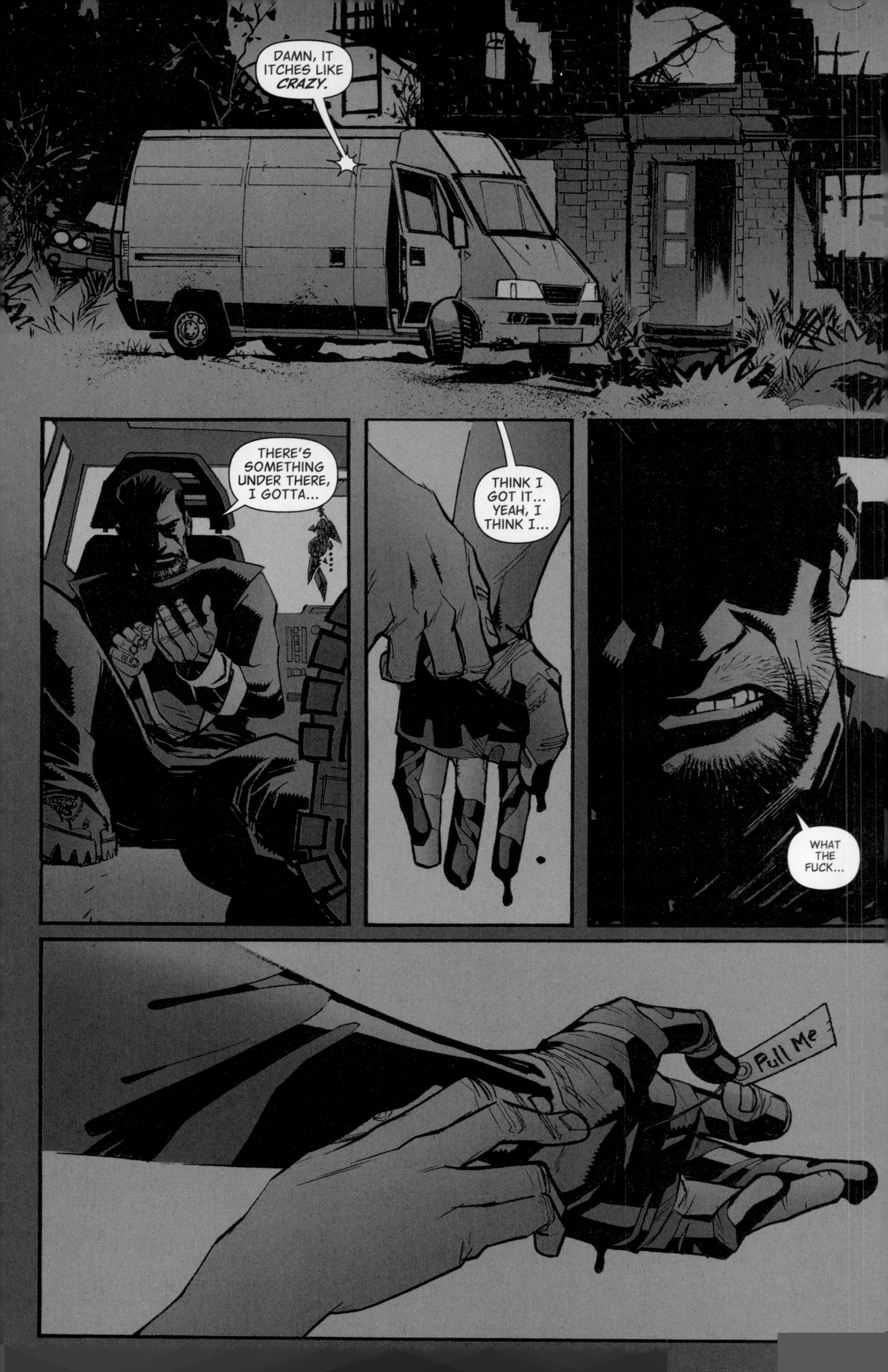
DAMN, IT ITCHES LIKE CRAZY.
THERE'S SOMETHING UNDER THERE, I GOTTA...
THINK I GOT IT... YEAH, I THINK I...
WHAT THE FUCK...
Pull Me

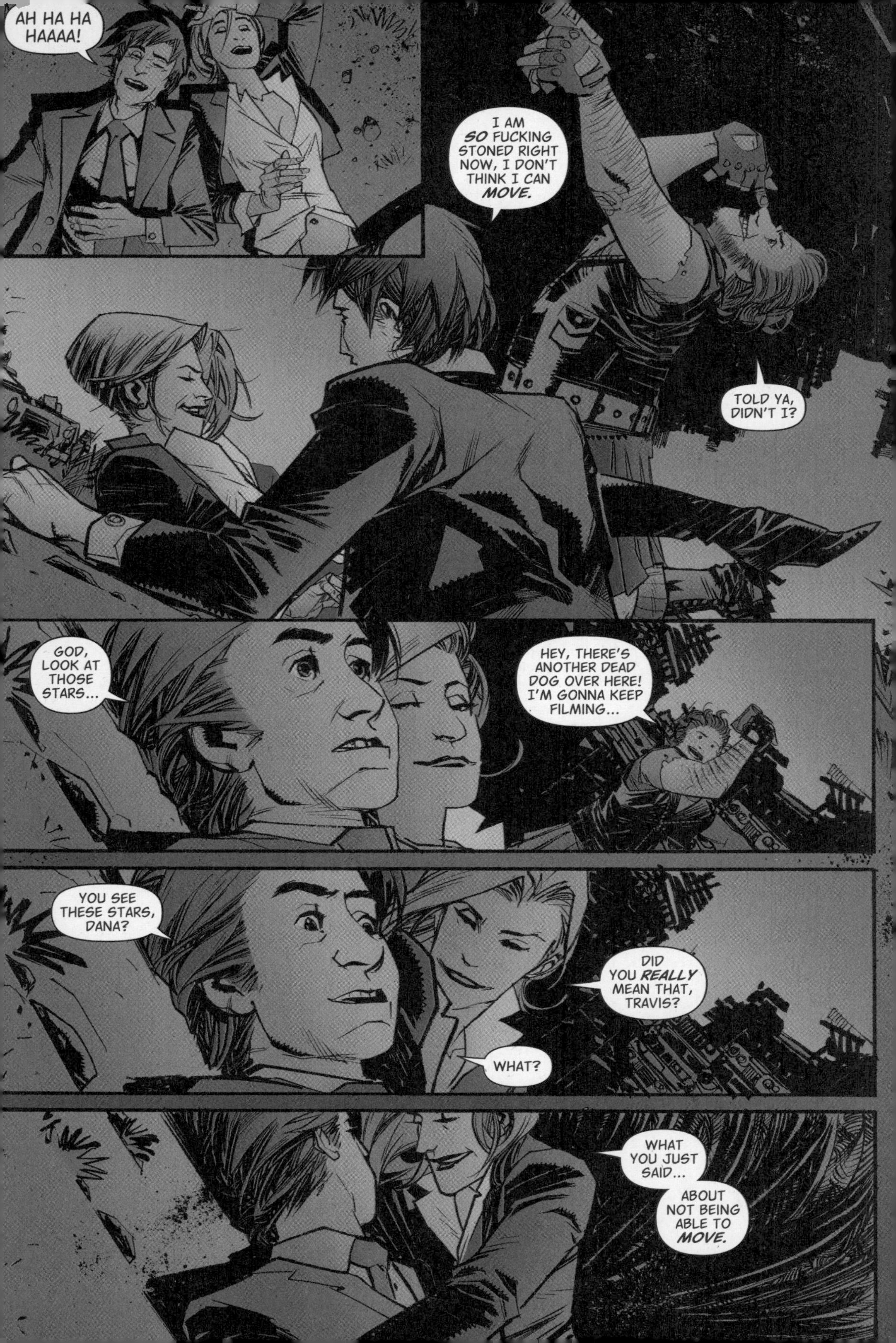
AH HA HA HAAAA!
I AM SO FUCKING STONED RIGHT NOW, I DON'T THINK I CAN MOVE.
TOLD YA, DIDN'T I?
GOD, LOOK AT THOSE STARS...
HEY, THERE'S ANOTHER DEAD DOG OVER HERE! I'M GONNA KEEP FILMING...
YOU SEE THESE STARS, DANA?
DID YOU REALLY MEAN THAT, TRAVIS?
WHAT?
WHAT YOU JUST SAID...
ABOUT NOT BEING ABLE TO MOVE.

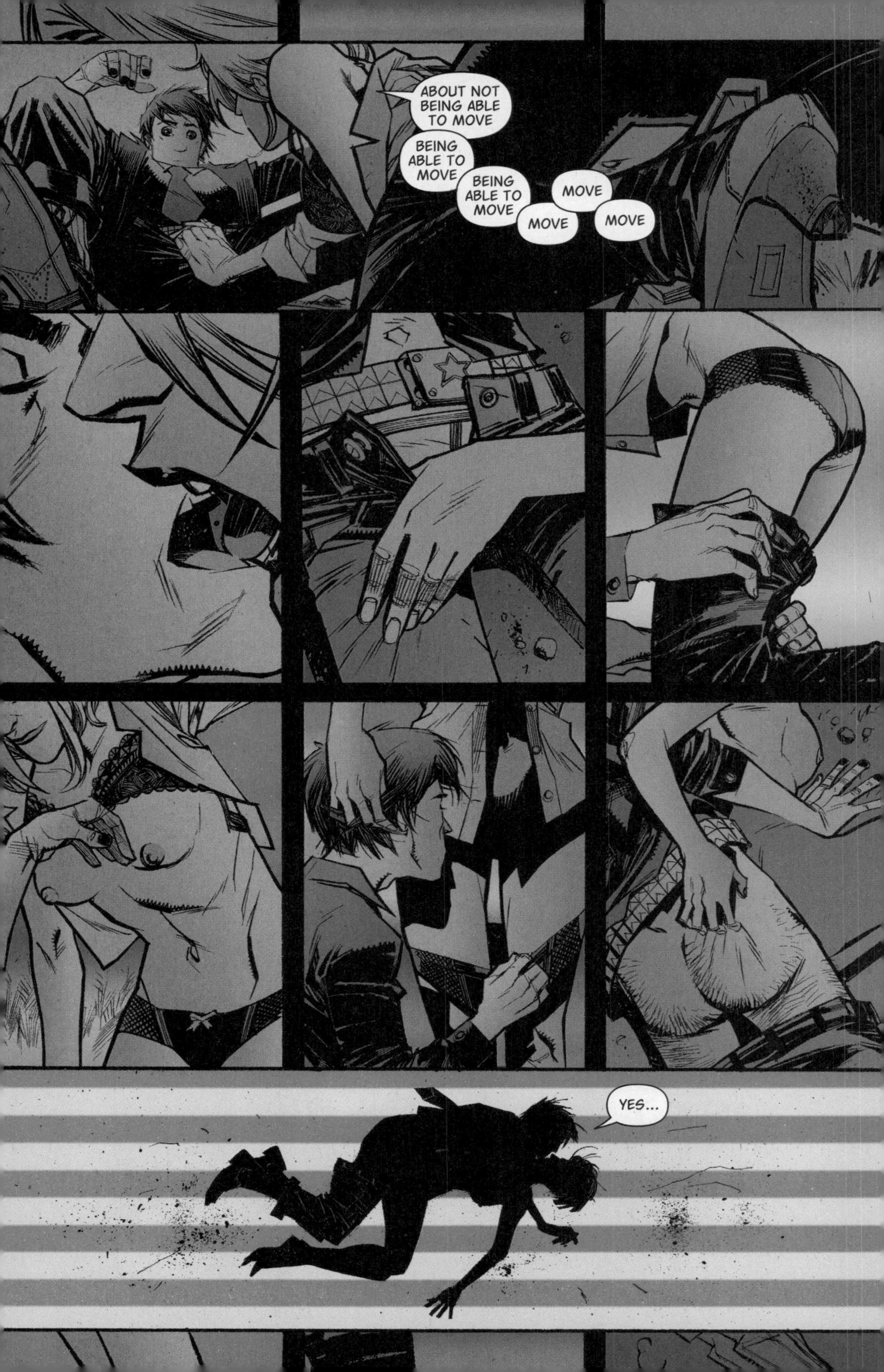
ABOUT NOT BEING ABLE TO MOVE
BEING ABLE TO MOVE
BEING ABLE TO MOVE
MOVE
MOVE
MOVE
YES...

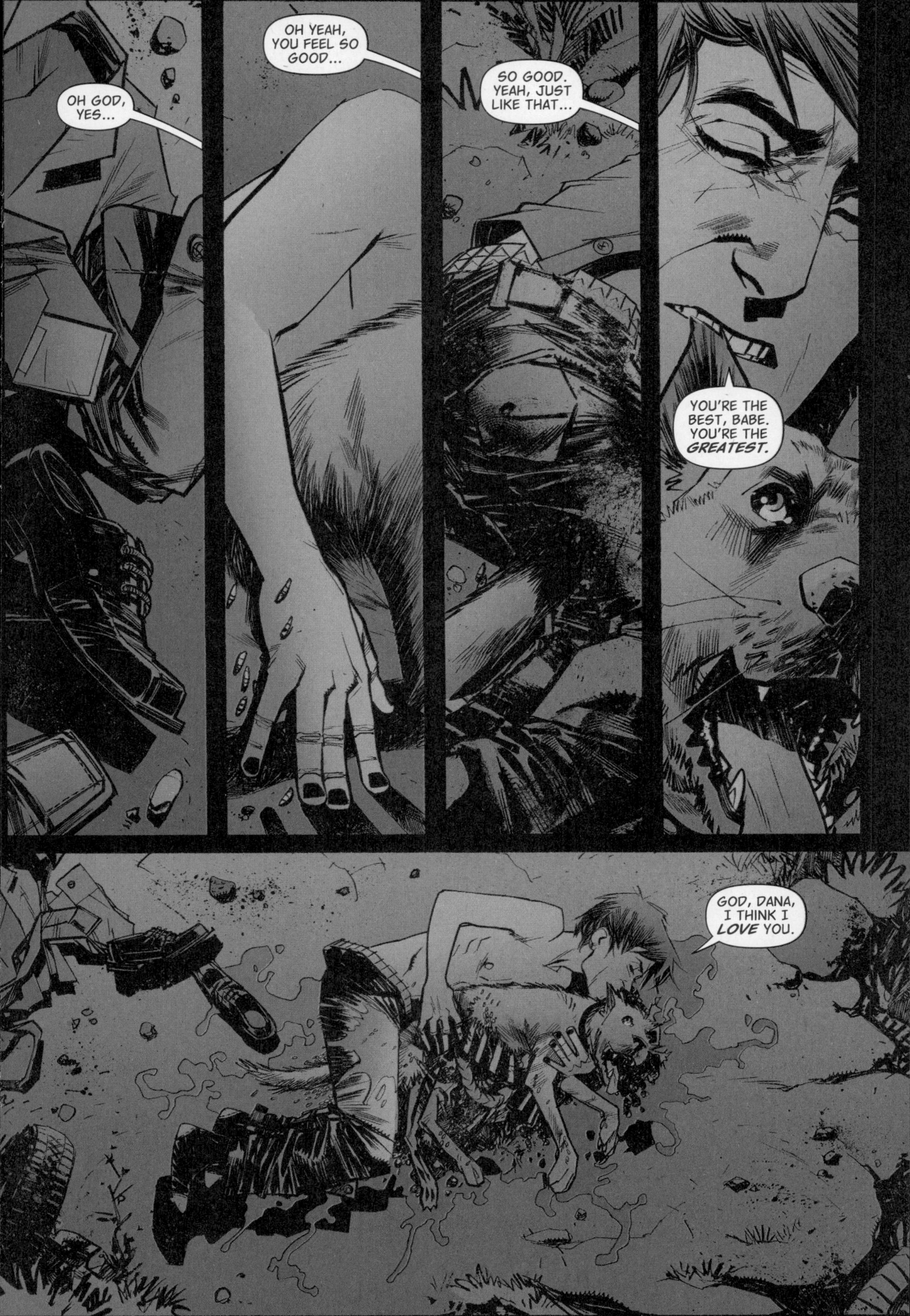
OH GOD, YES...
OH YEAH, YOU FEEL SO GOOD...
SO GOOD. YEAH, JUST LIKE THAT...
YOU'RE THE BEST, BABE. YOU'RE THE *GREATEST.*
GOD, DANA, I THINK I *LOVE* YOU.

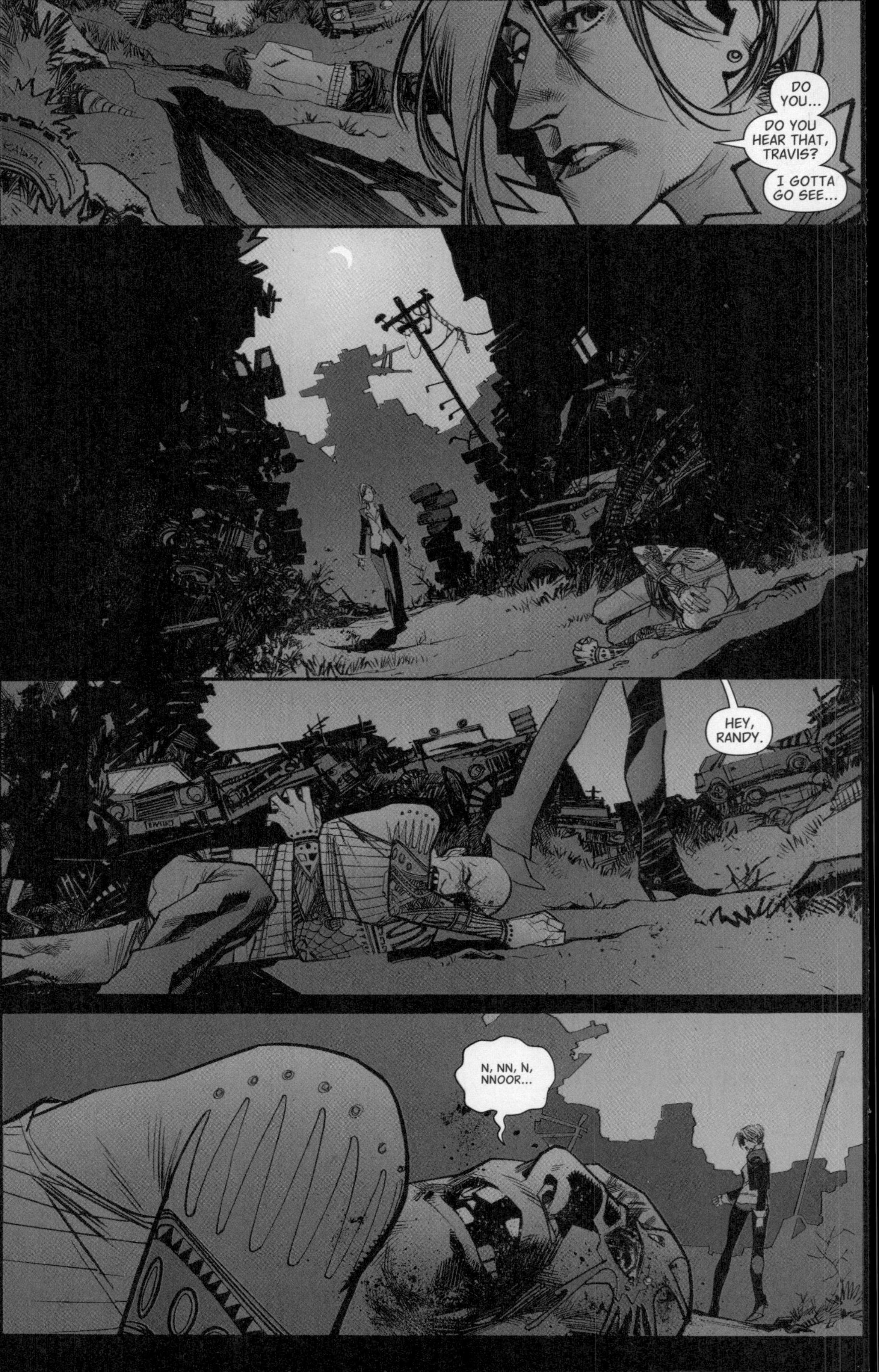
DO YOU...
DO YOU HEAR THAT, TRAVIS?
I GOTTA GO SEE...
HEY, RANDY.
N, NN, N, NNOOR...

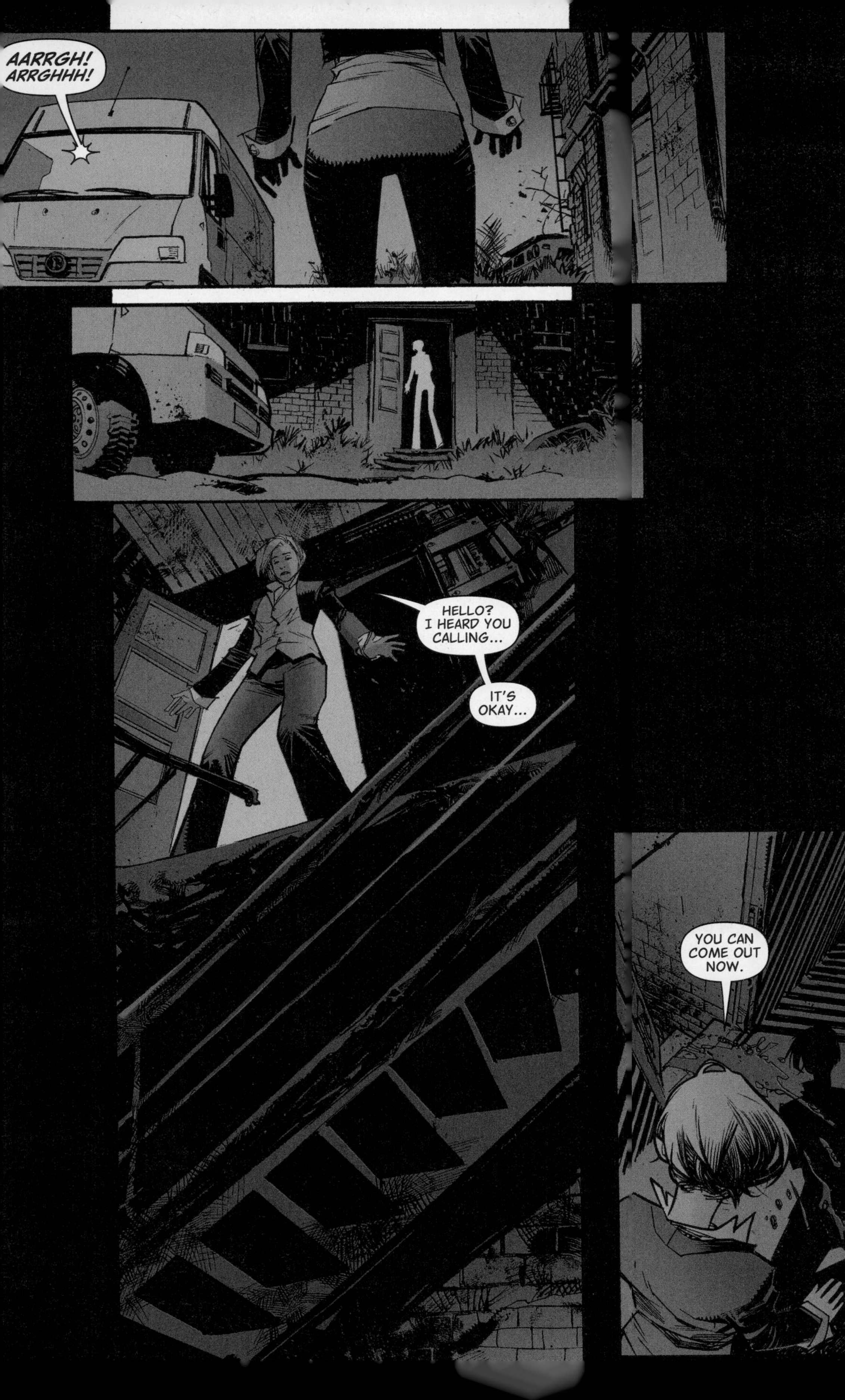
AARRGH! ARRGHHH!
HELLO? I HEARD YOU CALLING...
IT'S OKAY...
YOU CAN COME OUT NOW.

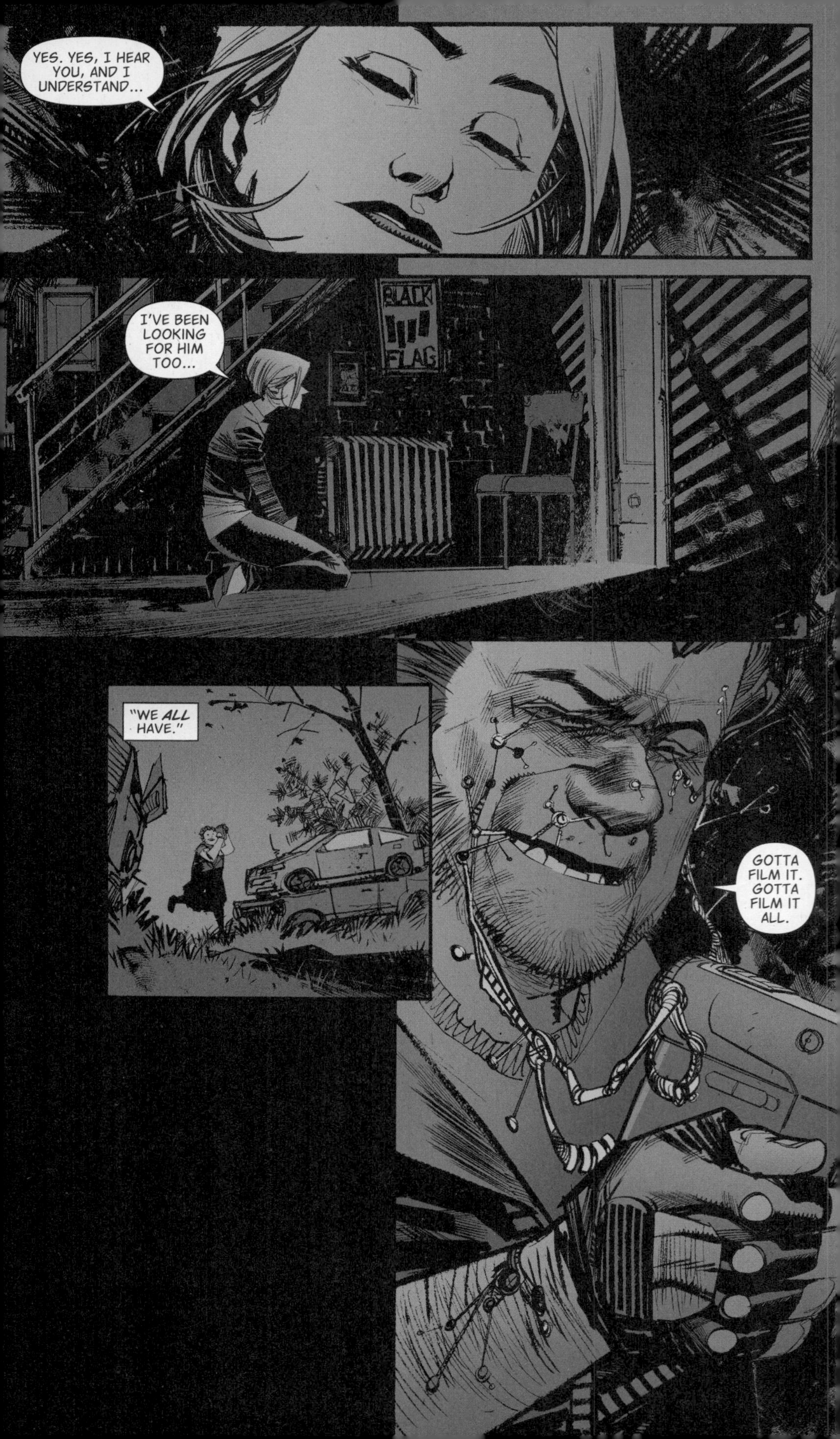
YES. YES, I HEAR YOU, AND I UNDERSTAND...
I'VE BEEN LOOKING FOR HIM TOO...
BLACK FLAG
"WE ALL HAVE."
GOTTA FILM IT. GOTTA FILM IT ALL.

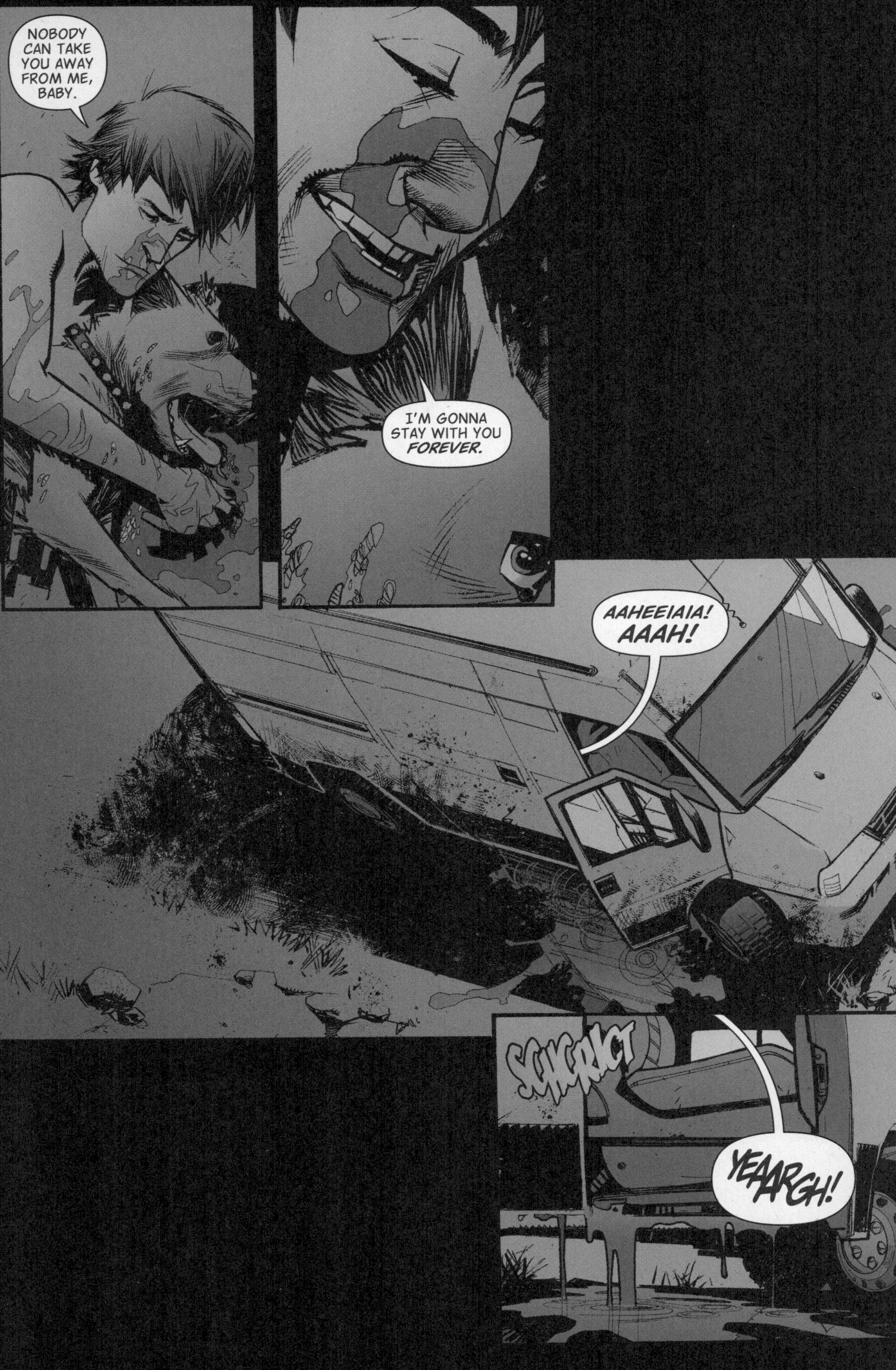
NOBODY CAN TAKE YOU AWAY FROM ME, BABY.
I'M GONNA STAY WITH YOU *FOREVER.*
AAHEEIAIA! AAAH!
SCHGRICT
YEAARGH!

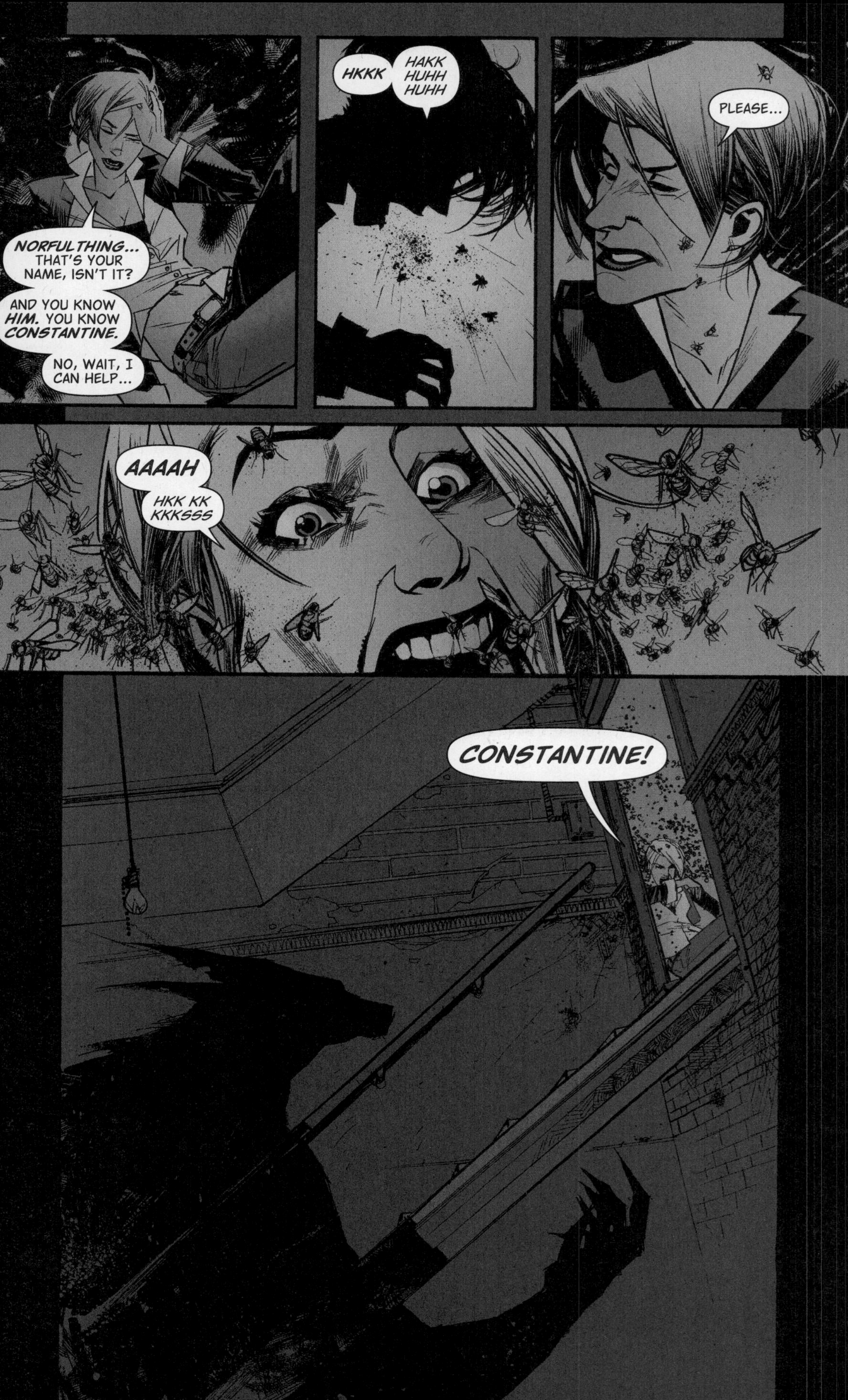
NORFULTHING... THAT'S YOUR NAME, ISN'T IT?
AND YOU KNOW HIM. YOU KNOW CONSTANTINE.
NO, WAIT, I CAN HELP...
HKKK
HAKK HUHH HUHH
PLEASE...
AAAAH
HKK KK KKKSSS
CONSTANTINE!

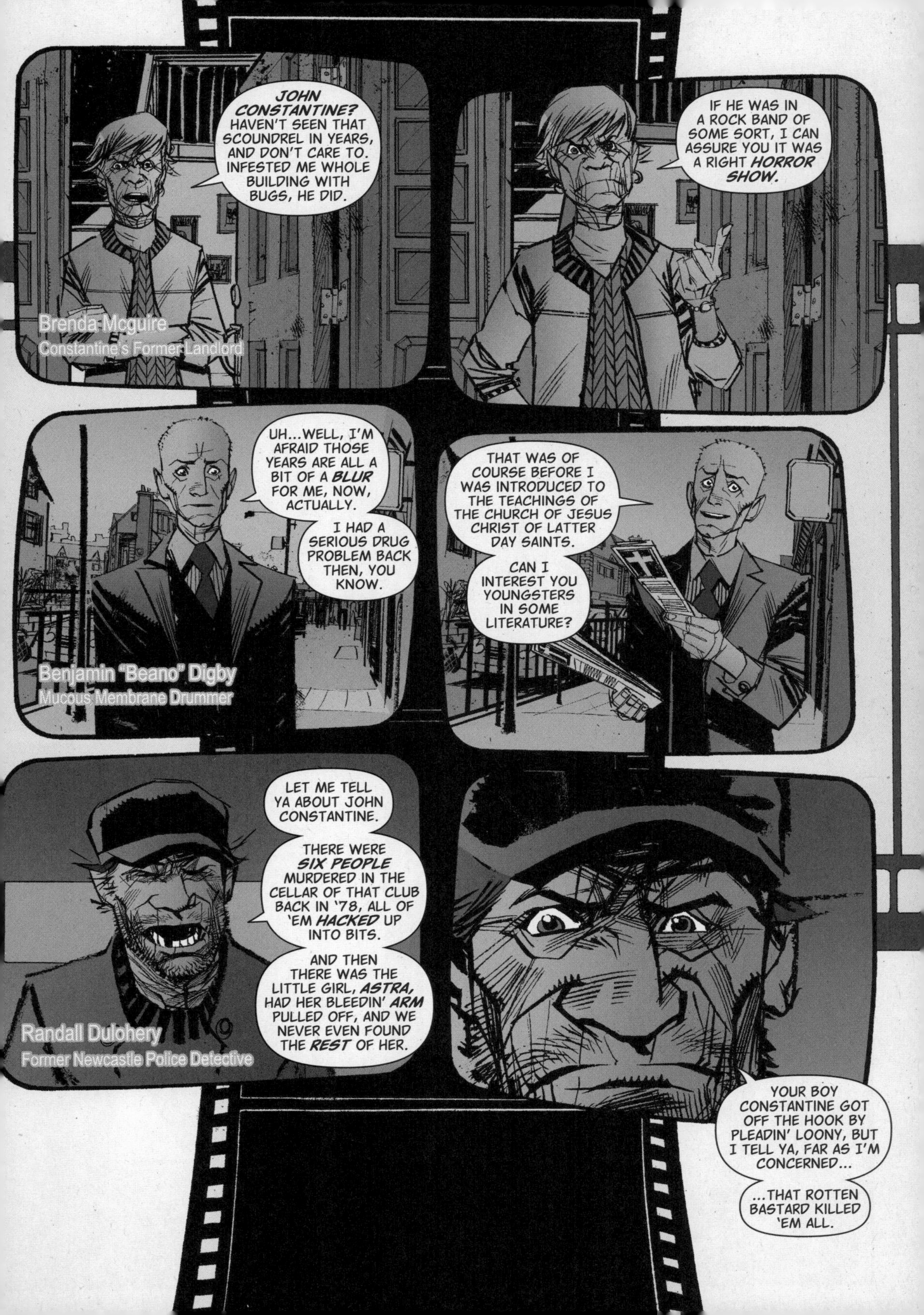
JOHN CONSTANTINE? HAVEN'T SEEN THAT SCOUNDREL IN YEARS, AND DON'T CARE TO. INFESTED ME WHOLE BUILDING WITH BUGS, HE DID.
Brenda Mcguire
Constantine's Former Landlord
IF HE WAS IN A ROCK BAND OF SOME SORT, I CAN ASSURE YOU IT WAS A RIGHT HORROR SHOW.
UH...WELL, I'M AFRAID THOSE YEARS ARE ALL A BIT OF A BLUR FOR ME, NOW, ACTUALLY.
I HAD A SERIOUS DRUG PROBLEM BACK THEN, YOU KNOW.
Benjamin "Beano" Digby
Mucous Membrane Drummer
THAT WAS OF COURSE BEFORE I WAS INTRODUCED TO THE TEACHINGS OF THE CHURCH OF JESUS CHRIST OF LATTER DAY SAINTS.
CAN I INTEREST YOU YOUNGSTERS IN SOME LITERATURE?
LET ME TELL YA ABOUT JOHN CONSTANTINE.
THERE WERE SIX PEOPLE MURDERED IN THE CELLAR OF THAT CLUB BACK IN '78, ALL OF 'EM HACKED UP INTO BITS.
AND THEN THERE WAS THE LITTLE GIRL, ASTRA, HAD HER BLEEDIN' ARM PULLED OFF, AND WE NEVER EVEN FOUND THE REST OF HER.
Randall Dulohery
Former Newcastle Police Detective
YOUR BOY CONSTANTINE GOT OFF THE HOOK BY PLEADIN' LOONY, BUT I TELL YA, FAR AS I'M CONCERNED...
...THAT ROTTEN BASTARD KILLED 'EM ALL.

ONE TICKET ON THE NEXT TRAIN TO *NEWCASTLE*, PLEASE, LUV.

NEWCASTLE, EH? HAD ME HEN PARTY THERE IN THE BIGG MARKET. RIGHT FINE *KNEES UP* THAT WAS. SEEMS LIKE A THOUSAND YEARS AGO NOW, THOUGH.

IF YOU'RE LOOKIN' FOR A GOOD *PUB*, YA COULD DO WORSE THAN THE BLACKIE BOY OR THE PIG AND WHISTLE.

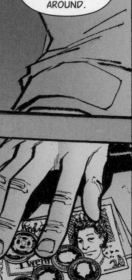

'PRECIATE THE TIP, BUT I DOUBT WE'LL MAKE IT DOWN THE PUB THIS TIME AROUND.

BUSINESS TRIP?

ALWAYS BUSINESS, I'M AFRAID, 'LEAST WHEN IT COMES TO NEWCASTLE.

SHAME.

WILL YOU BE CARRYING ANY *BAGGAGE* WITH YOU THEN?

OH *AYE*, LUV...

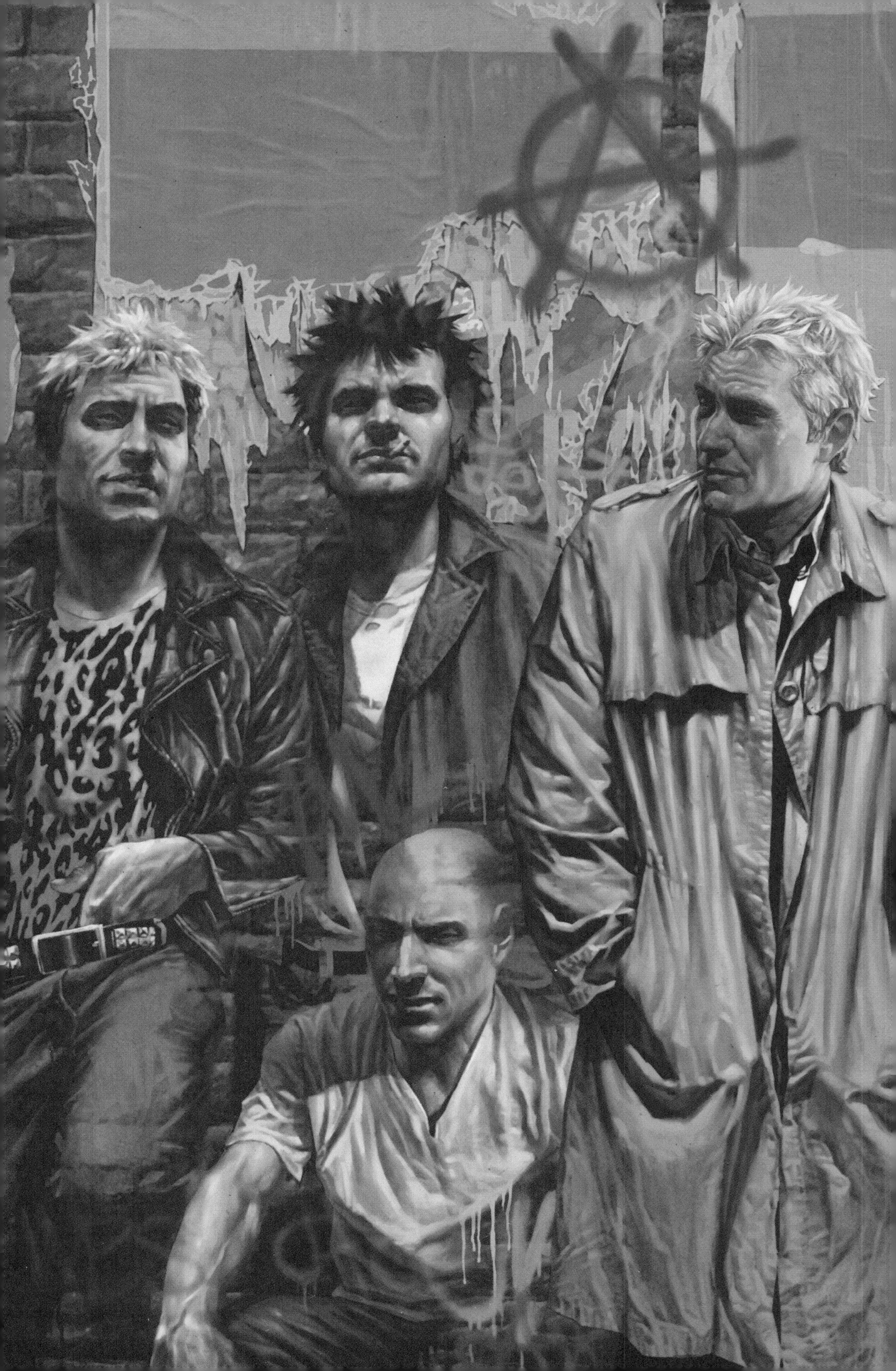

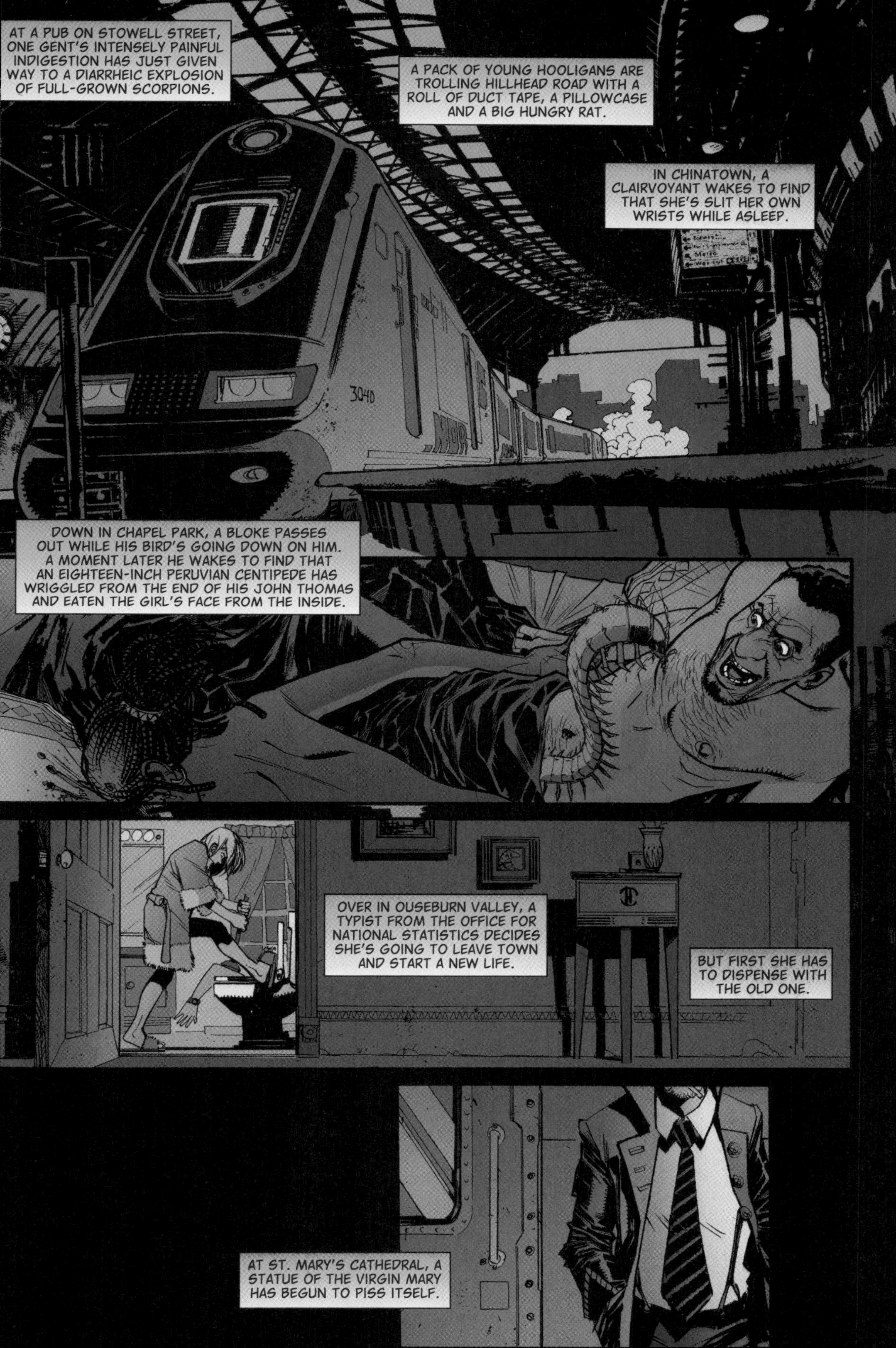
AT A PUB ON STOWELL STREET, ONE GENT'S INTENSELY PAINFUL INDIGESTION HAS JUST GIVEN WAY TO A DIARRHEIC EXPLOSION OF FULL-GROWN SCORPIONS.
A PACK OF YOUNG HOOLIGANS ARE TROLLING HILLHEAD ROAD WITH A ROLL OF DUCT TAPE, A PILLOWCASE AND A BIG HUNGRY RAT.
IN CHINATOWN, A CLAIRVOYANT WAKES TO FIND THAT SHE'S SLIT HER OWN WRISTS WHILE ASLEEP.
3040
DOWN IN CHAPEL PARK, A BLOKE PASSES OUT WHILE HIS BIRD'S GOING DOWN ON HIM. A MOMENT LATER HE WAKES TO FIND THAT AN EIGHTEEN-INCH PERUVIAN CENTIPEDE HAS WRIGGLED FROM THE END OF HIS JOHN THOMAS AND EATEN THE GIRL'S FACE FROM THE INSIDE.
OVER IN OUSEBURN VALLEY, A TYPIST FROM THE OFFICE FOR NATIONAL STATISTICS DECIDES SHE'S GOING TO LEAVE TOWN AND START A NEW LIFE.
BUT FIRST SHE HAS TO DISPENSE WITH THE OLD ONE.
AT ST. MARY'S CATHEDRAL, A STATUE OF THE VIRGIN MARY HAS BEGUN TO PISS ITSELF.

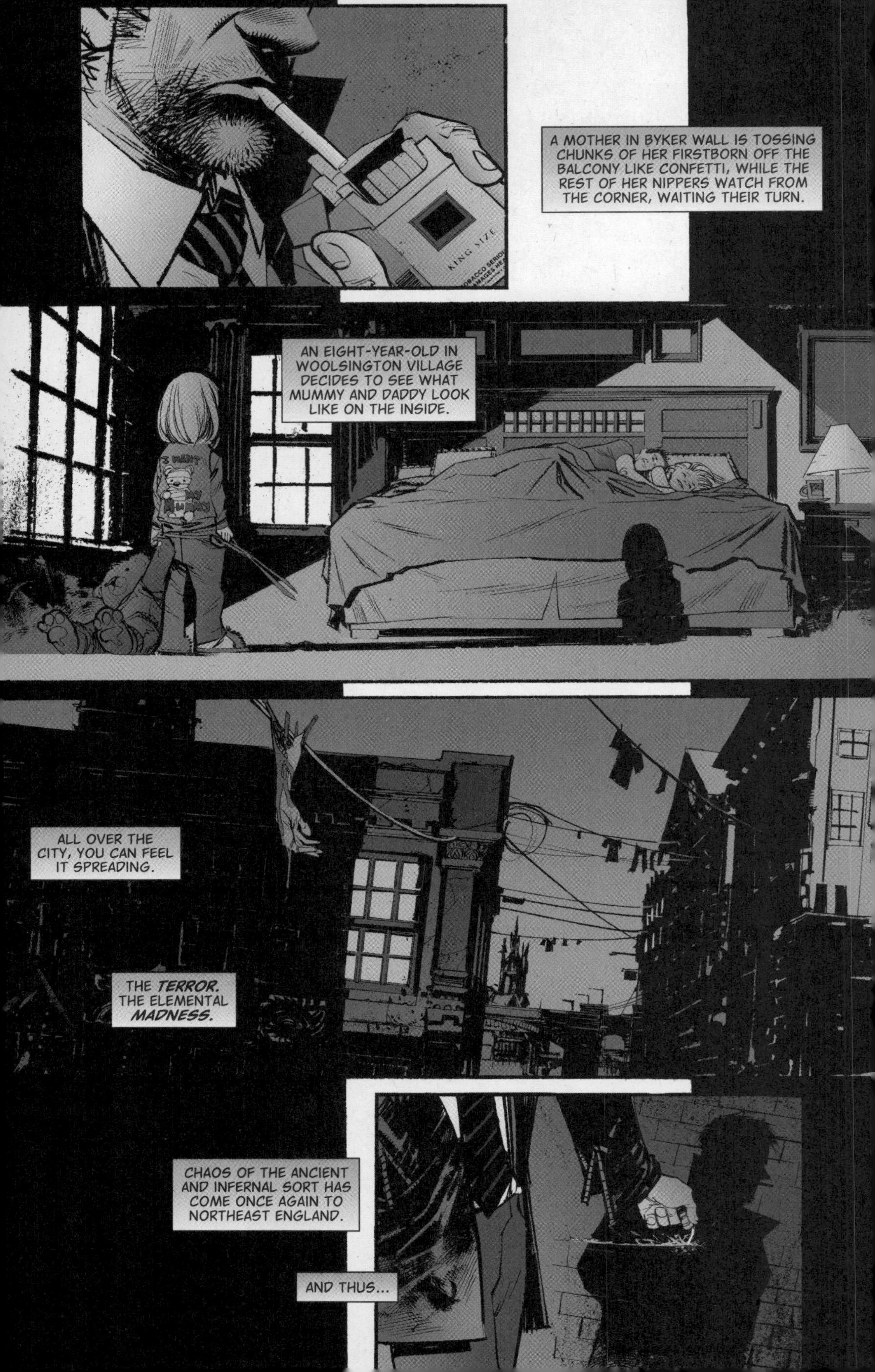

A MOTHER IN BYKER WALL IS TOSSING CHUNKS OF HER FIRSTBORN OFF THE BALCONY LIKE CONFETTI, WHILE THE REST OF HER NIPPERS WATCH FROM THE CORNER, WAITING THEIR TURN.
KING SIZE
AN EIGHT-YEAR-OLD IN WOOLSINGTON VILLAGE DECIDES TO SEE WHAT MUMMY AND DADDY LOOK LIKE ON THE INSIDE.
ALL OVER THE CITY, YOU CAN FEEL IT SPREADING.
THE *TERROR.* THE ELEMENTAL *MADNESS.*
CHAOS OF THE ANCIENT AND INFERNAL SORT HAS COME ONCE AGAIN TO NORTHEAST ENGLAND.
AND THUS...

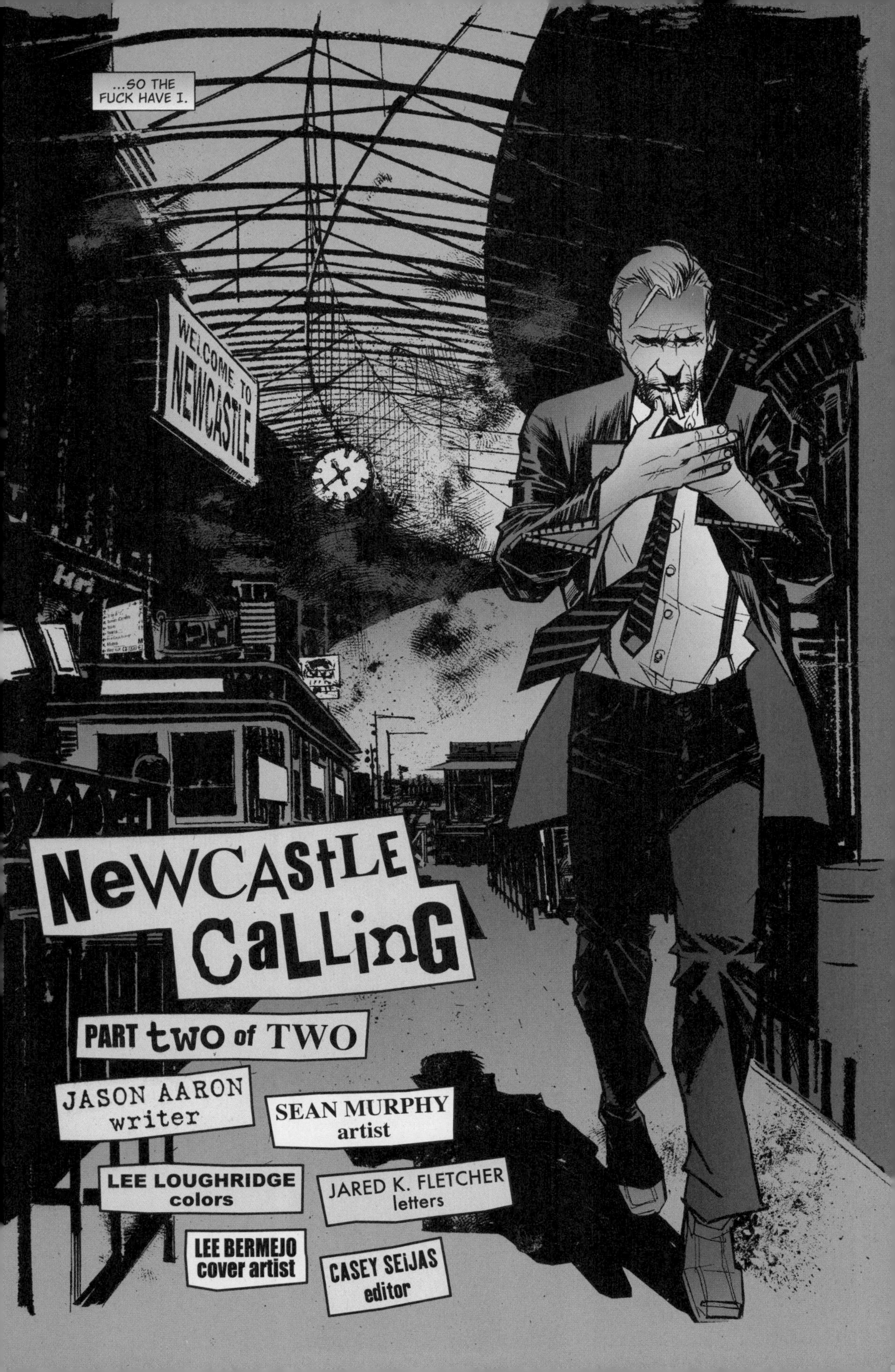
...SO THE FUCK HAVE I.
WELCOME TO NEWCASTLE
NEWCASTLE CALLING
PART two of TWO
JASON AARON writer
SEAN MURPHY artist
LEE LOUGHRIDGE colors
JARED K. FLETCHER letters
LEE BERMEJO cover artist
CASEY SEIJAS editor

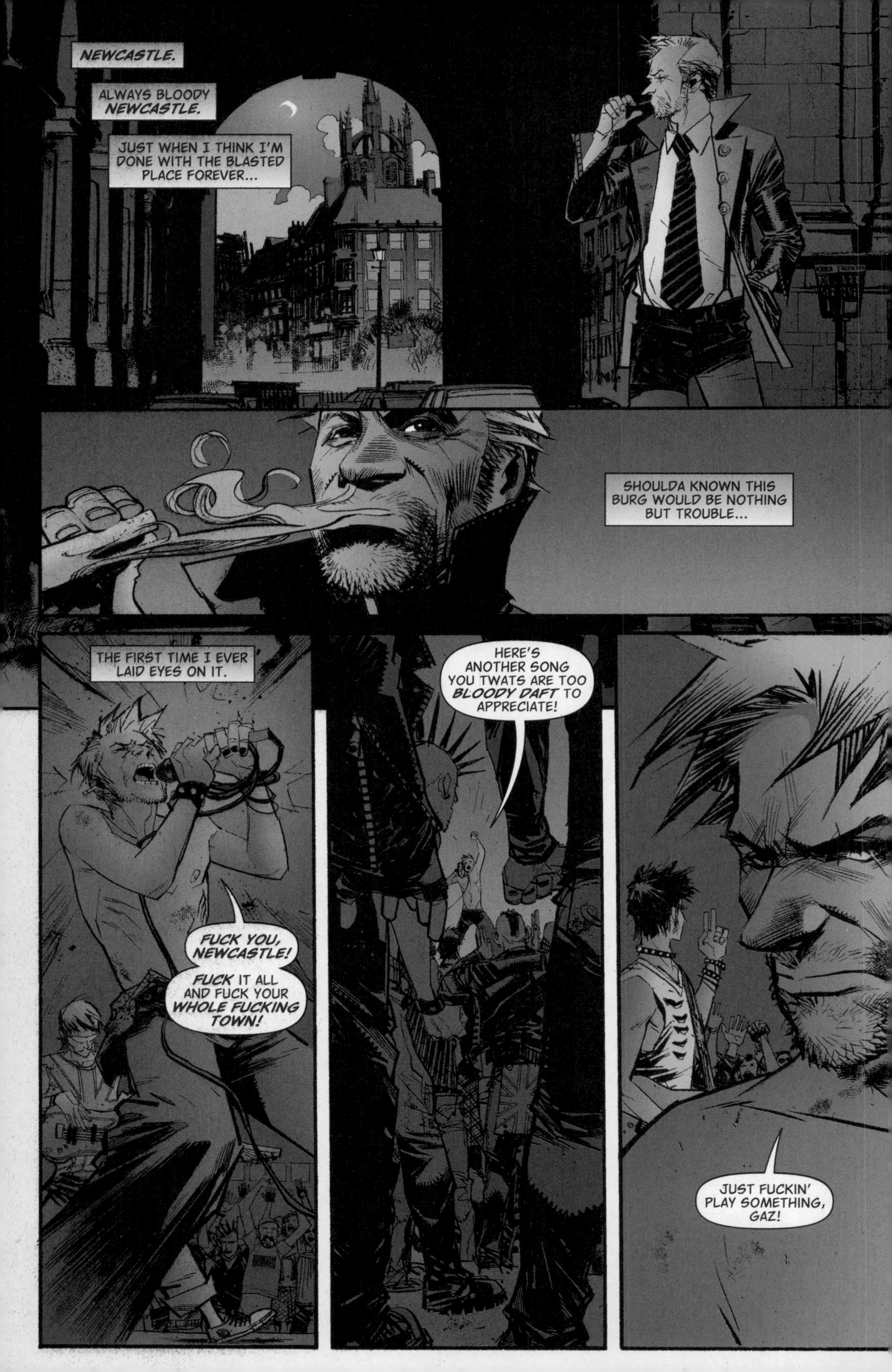
NEWCASTLE.
ALWAYS BLOODY NEWCASTLE.
JUST WHEN I THINK I'M DONE WITH THE BLASTED PLACE FOREVER...
SHOULDA KNOWN THIS BURG WOULD BE NOTHING BUT TROUBLE...
THE FIRST TIME I EVER LAID EYES ON IT.
FUCK YOU, NEWCASTLE!
FUCK IT ALL AND FUCK YOUR WHOLE FUCKING TOWN!
HERE'S ANOTHER SONG YOU TWATS ARE TOO BLOODY DAFT TO APPRECIATE!
JUST FUCKIN' PLAY SOMETHING, GAZ!

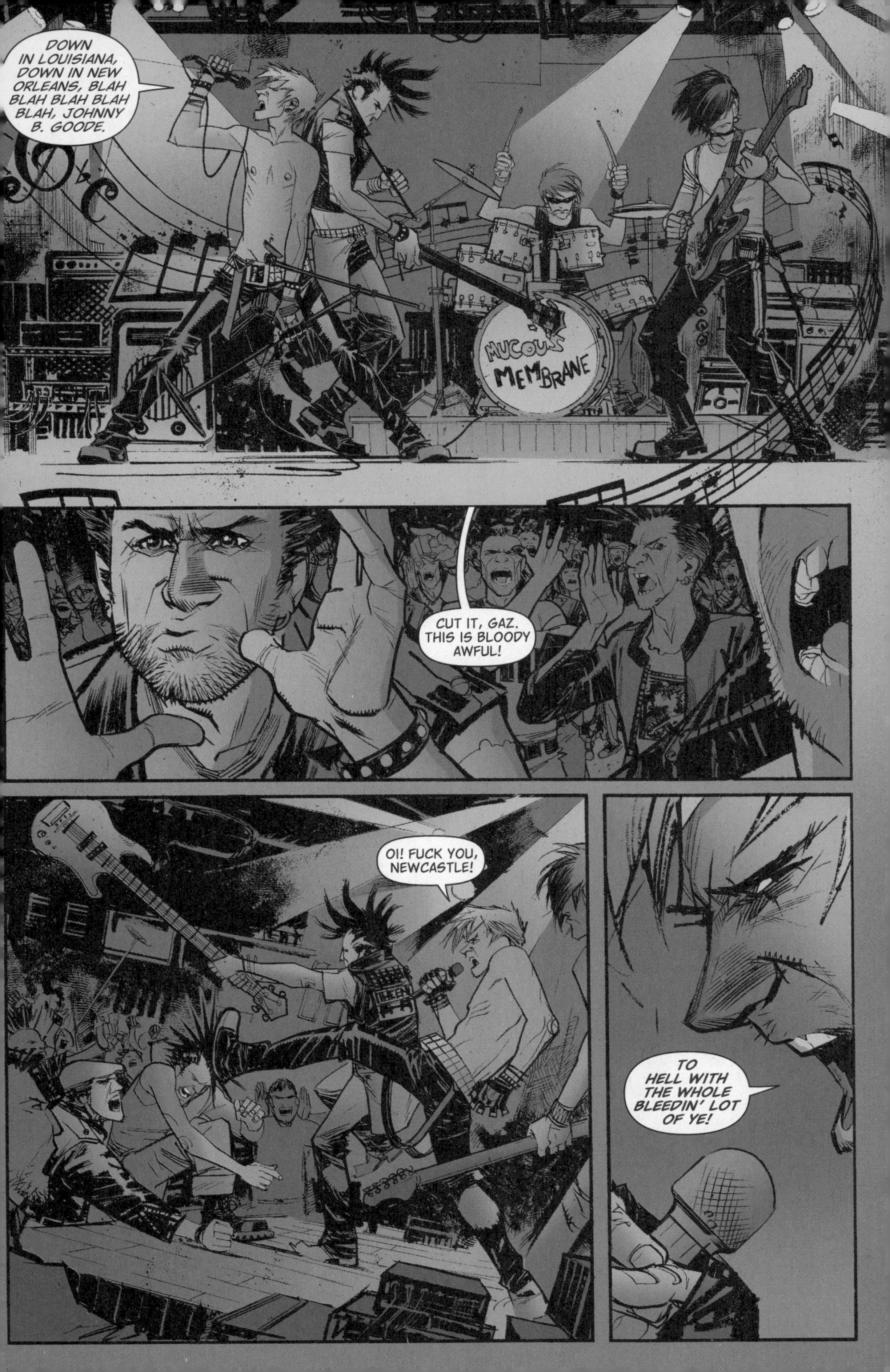
DOWN IN LOUISIANA, DOWN IN NEW ORLEANS, BLAH BLAH BLAH BLAH BLAH, JOHNNY B. GOODE.
MUCOUS MEMBRANE
CUT IT, GAZ. THIS IS BLOODY AWFUL!
OI! FUCK YOU, NEWCASTLE!
TO HELL WITH THE WHOLE BLEEDIN' LOT OF YE!

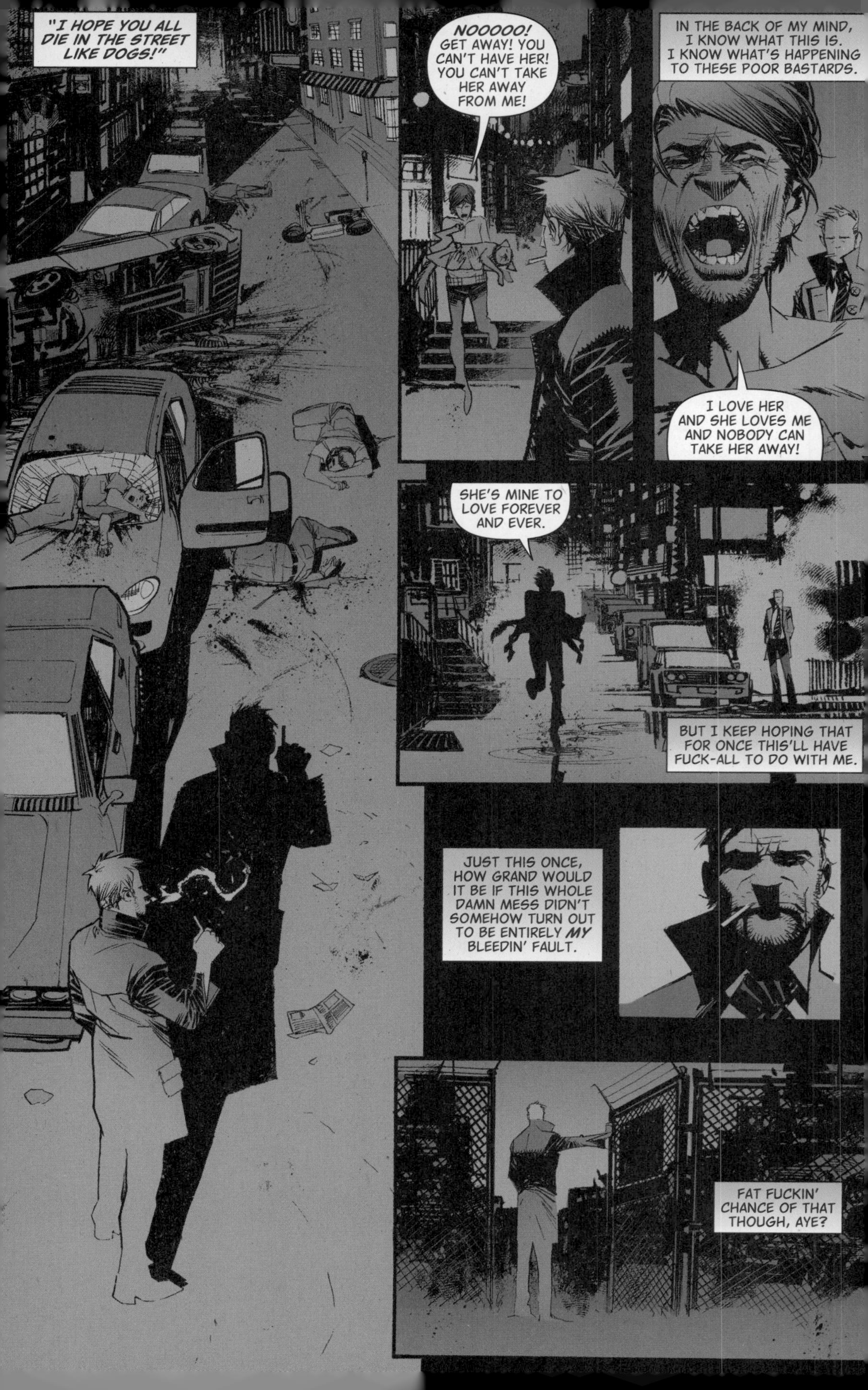
"I HOPE YOU ALL DIE IN THE STREET LIKE DOGS!"
NOOOOO! GET AWAY! YOU CAN'T HAVE HER! YOU CAN'T TAKE HER AWAY FROM ME!
IN THE BACK OF MY MIND, I KNOW WHAT THIS IS. I KNOW WHAT'S HAPPENING TO THESE POOR BASTARDS.
I LOVE HER AND SHE LOVES ME AND NOBODY CAN TAKE HER AWAY!
SHE'S MINE TO LOVE FOREVER AND EVER.
BUT I KEEP HOPING THAT FOR ONCE THIS'LL HAVE FUCK-ALL TO DO WITH ME.
JUST THIS ONCE, HOW GRAND WOULD IT BE IF THIS WHOLE DAMN MESS DIDN'T SOMEHOW TURN OUT TO BE ENTIRELY MY BLEEDIN' FAULT.
FAT FUCKIN' CHANCE OF THAT THOUGH, AYE?

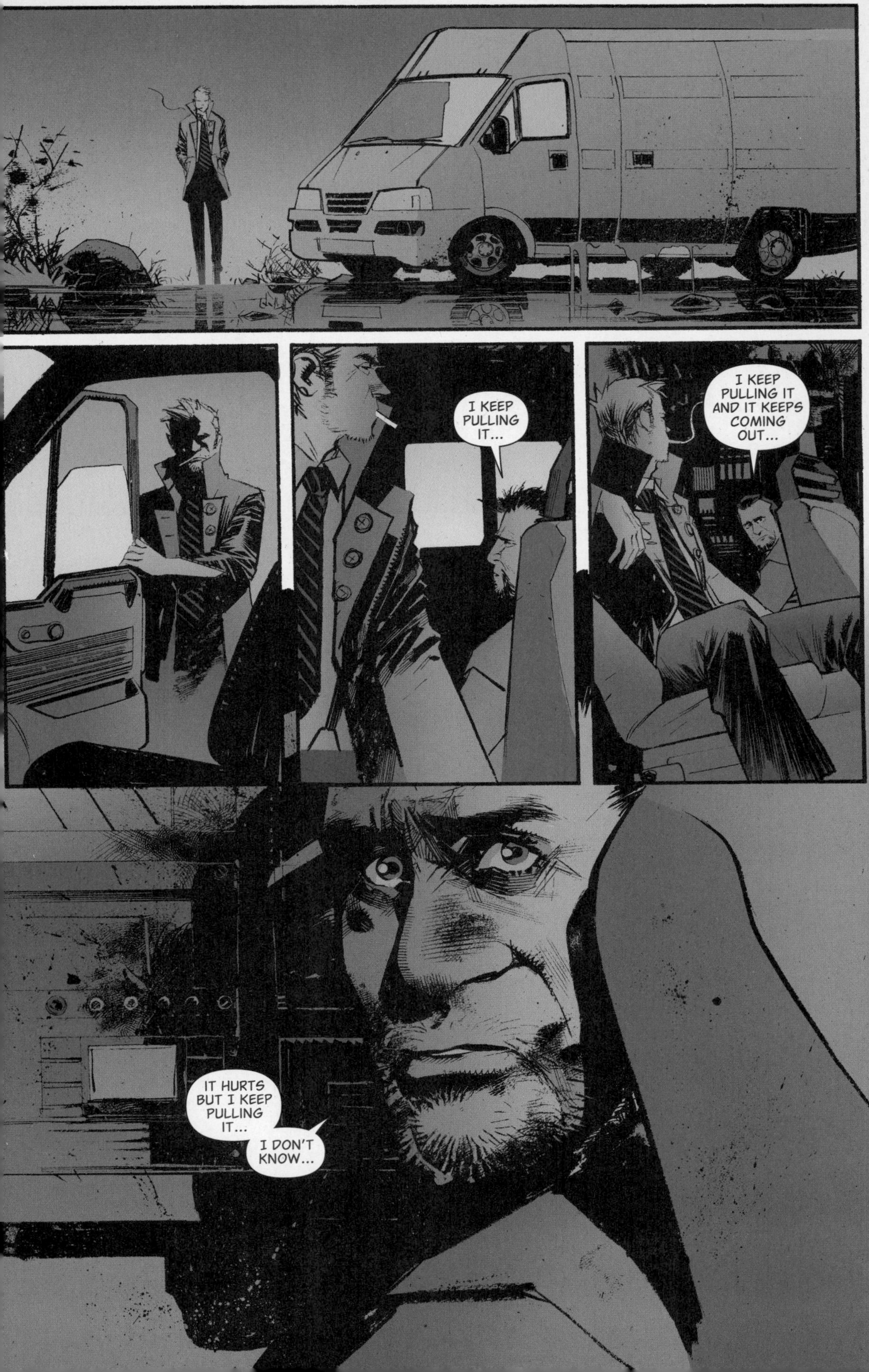
I KEEP PULLING IT...
I KEEP PULLING IT AND IT KEEPS COMING OUT...
IT HURTS BUT I KEEP PULLING IT...
I DON'T KNOW...

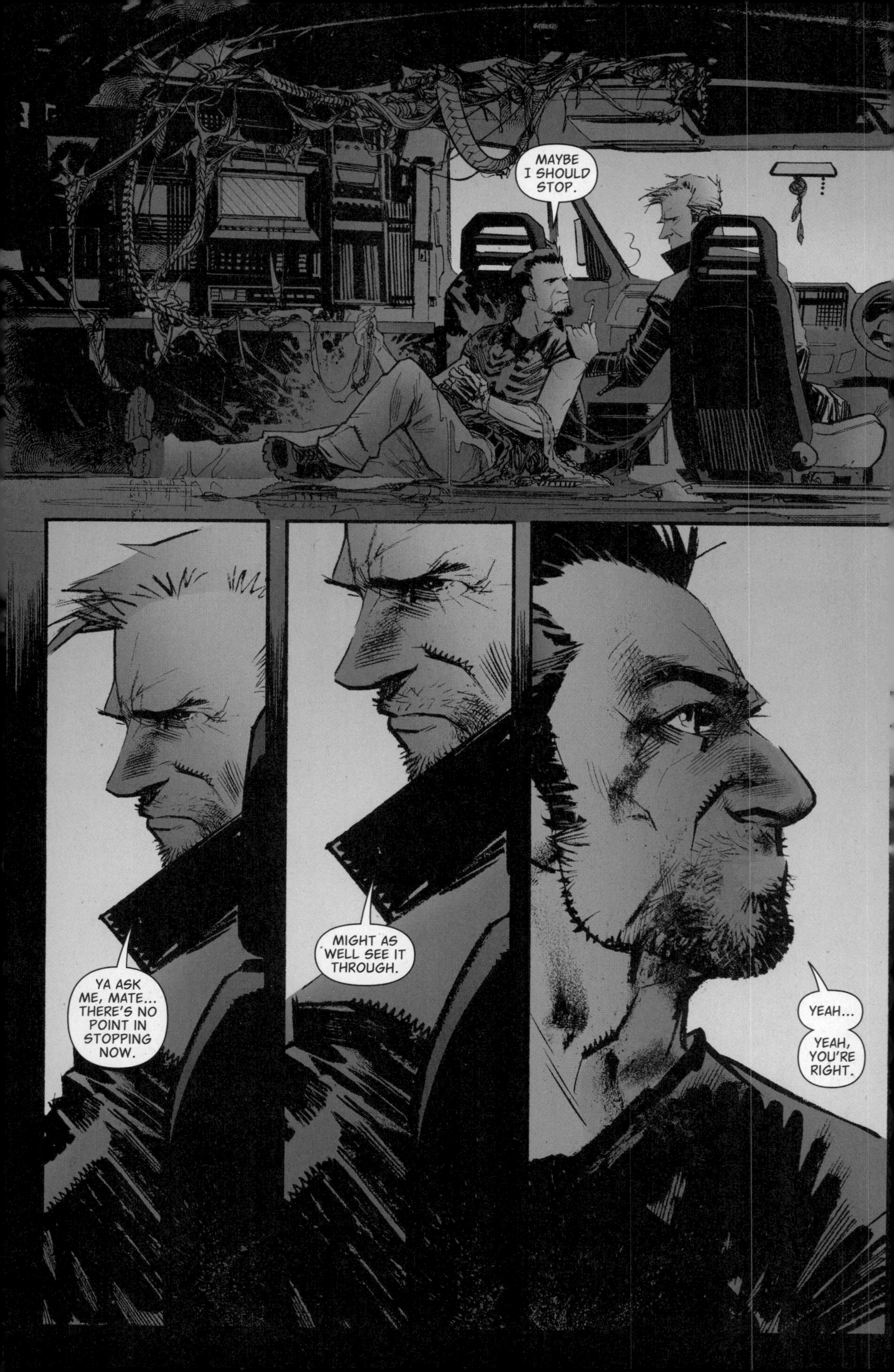
MAYBE I SHOULD STOP.
YA ASK ME, MATE... THERE'S NO POINT IN STOPPING NOW.
MIGHT AS WELL SEE IT THROUGH.
YEAH...
YEAH, YOU'RE RIGHT.

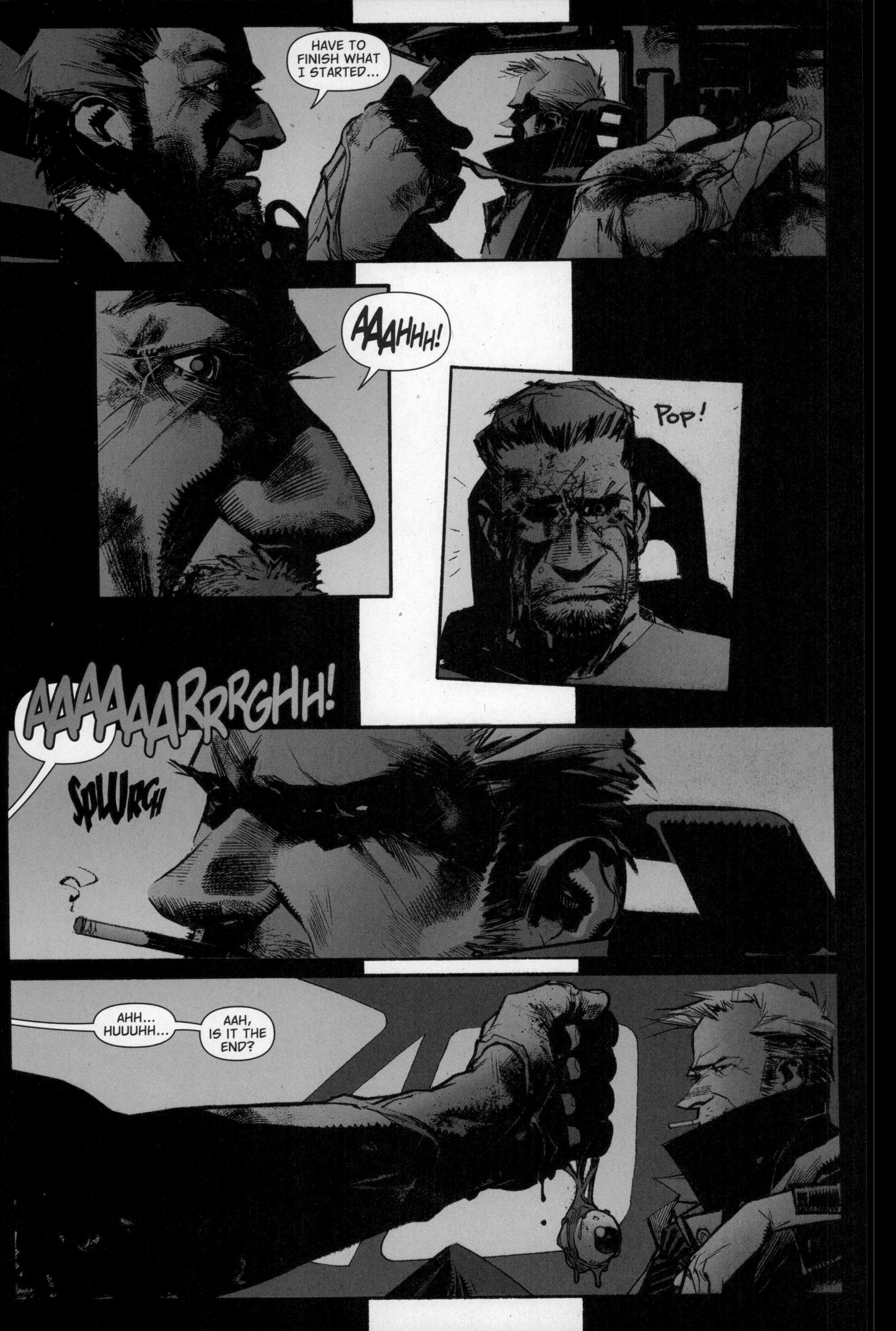
HAVE TO FINISH WHAT I STARTED...
AAAHHH!
POP!
AAAAAARRRGHH!
SPLURGH
AHH... HUUUHH...
AAH, IS IT THE END?

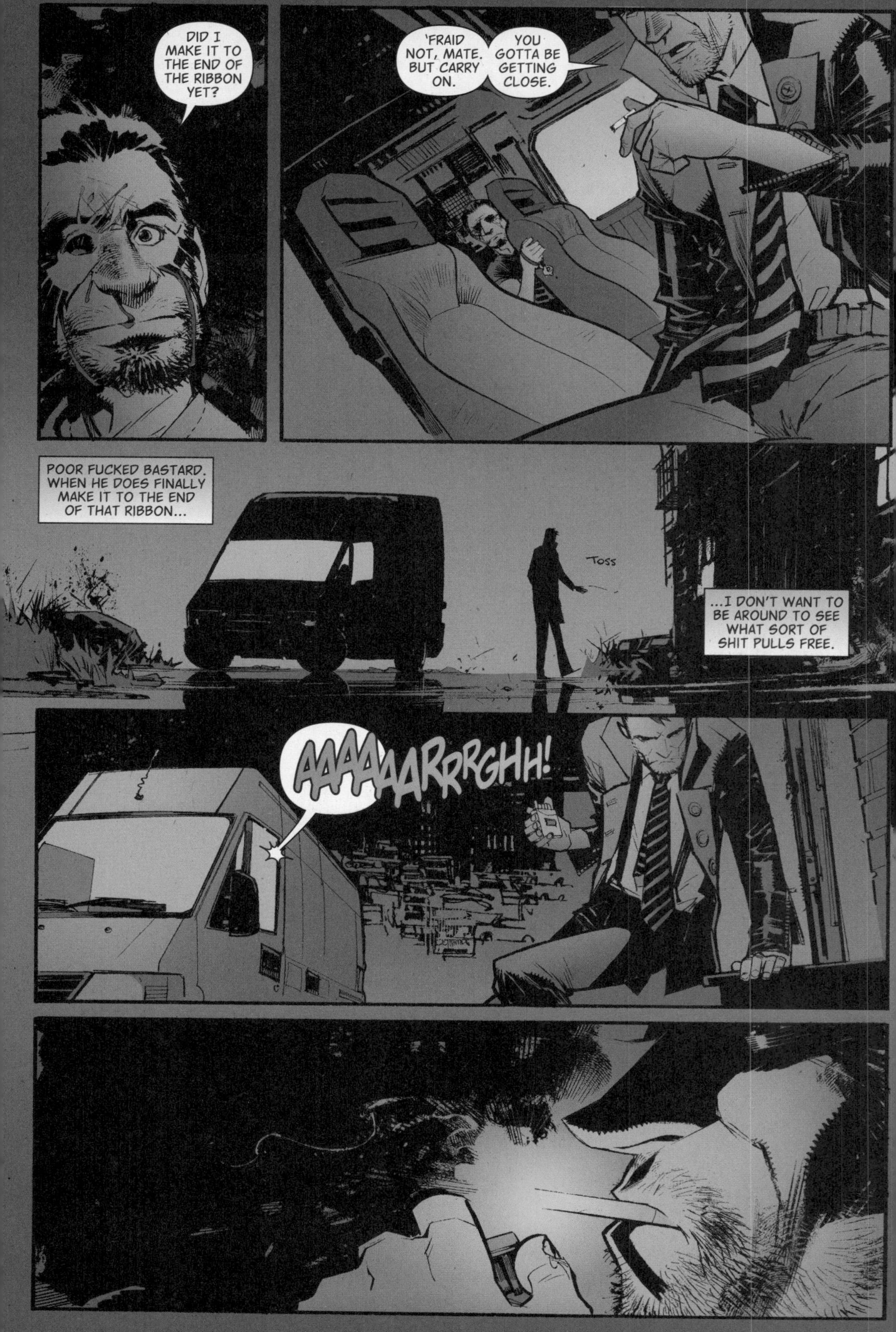
DID I MAKE IT TO THE END OF THE RIBBON YET?
'FRAID NOT, MATE. BUT CARRY ON.
YOU GOTTA BE GETTING CLOSE.
POOR FUCKED BASTARD. WHEN HE DOES FINALLY MAKE IT TO THE END OF THAT RIBBON...
TOSS
...I DON'T WANT TO BE AROUND TO SEE WHAT SORT OF SHIT PULLS FREE.
AAAAAARRRGHH!

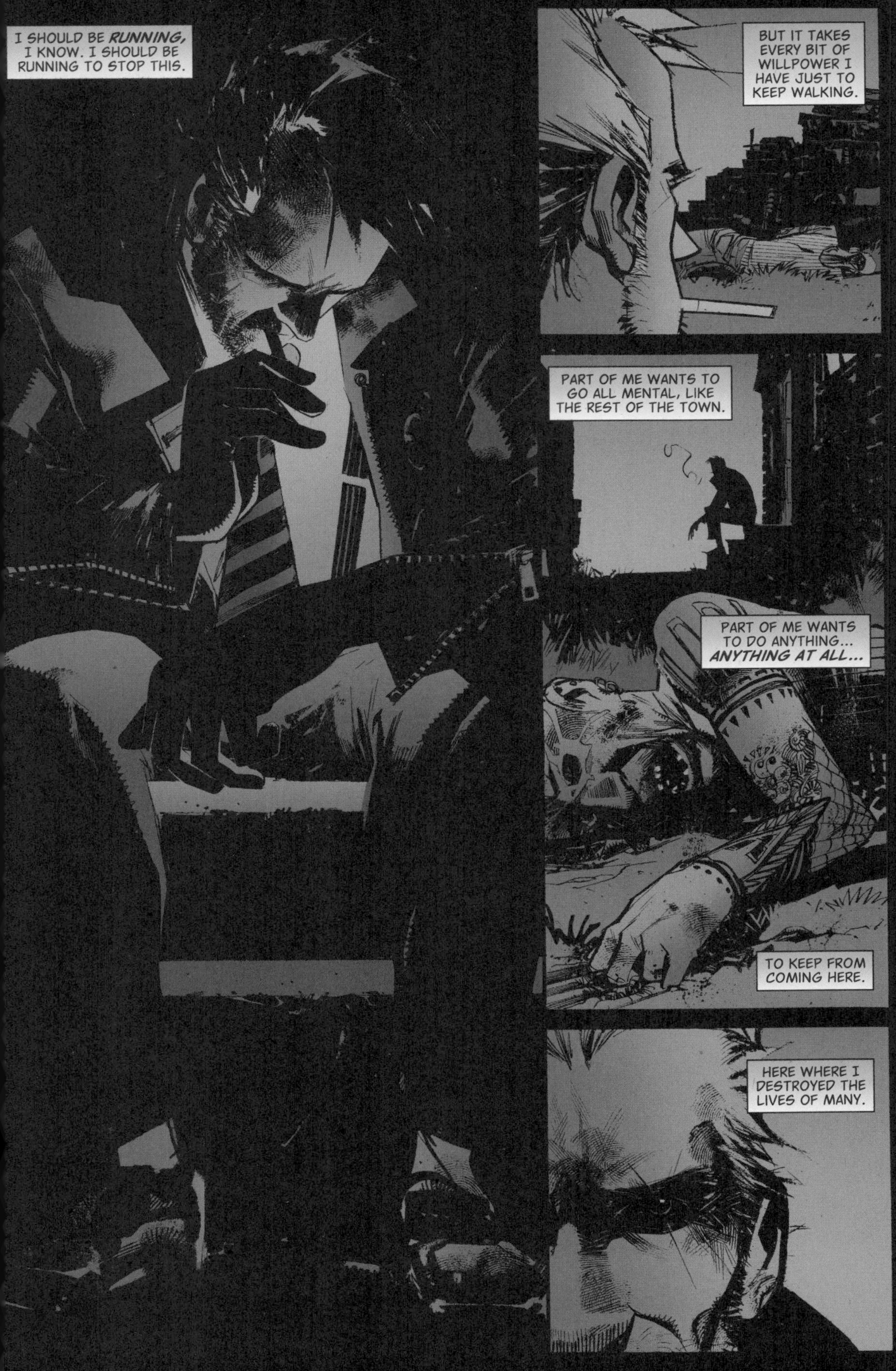

I SHOULD BE *RUNNING,* I KNOW. I SHOULD BE RUNNING TO STOP THIS.
BUT IT TAKES EVERY BIT OF WILLPOWER I HAVE JUST TO KEEP WALKING.
PART OF ME WANTS TO GO ALL MENTAL, LIKE THE REST OF THE TOWN.
PART OF ME WANTS TO DO ANYTHING... *ANYTHING AT ALL...*
TO KEEP FROM COMING HERE.
HERE WHERE I DESTROYED THE LIVES OF MANY.

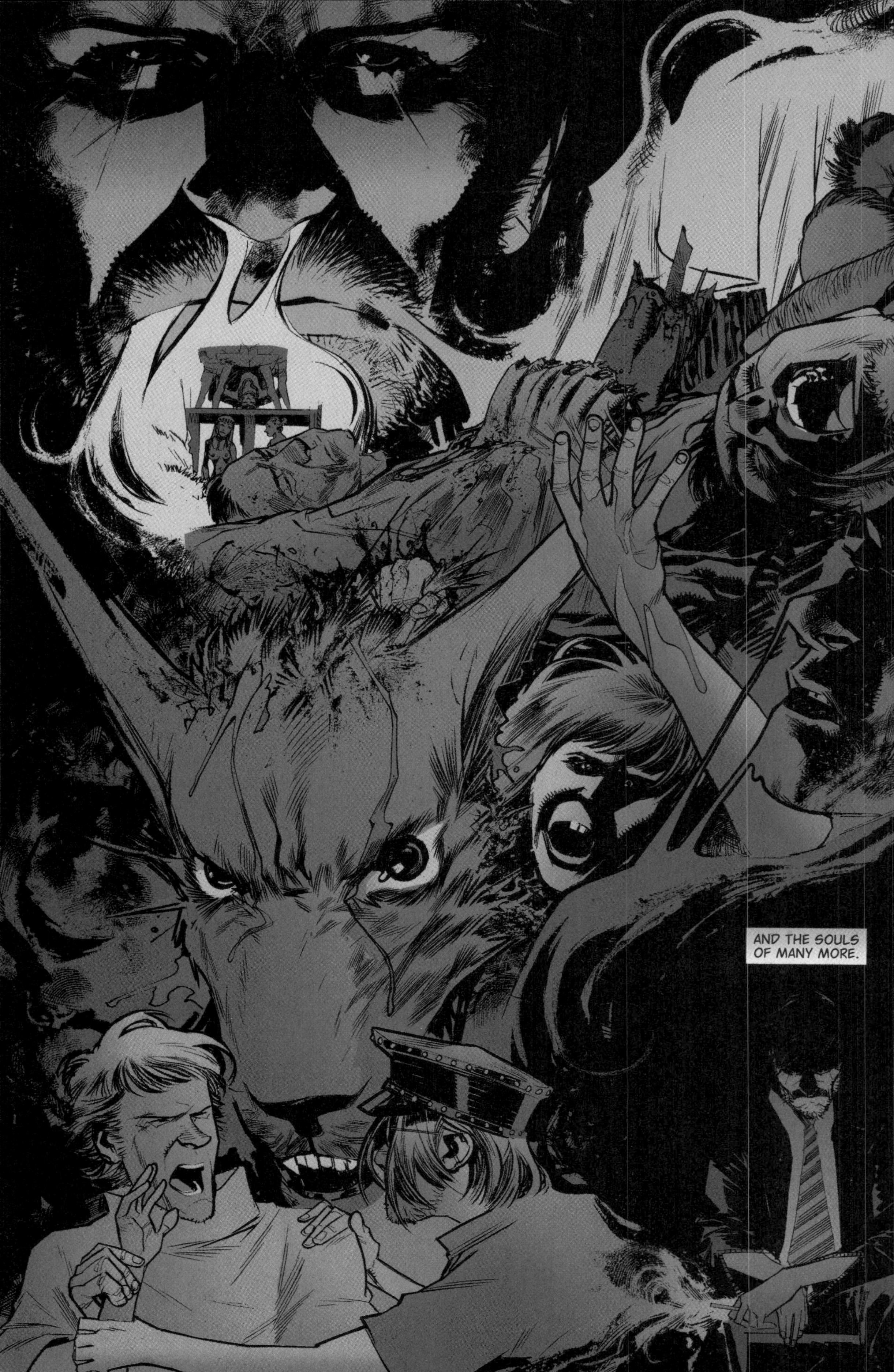
AND THE SOULS OF MANY MORE.

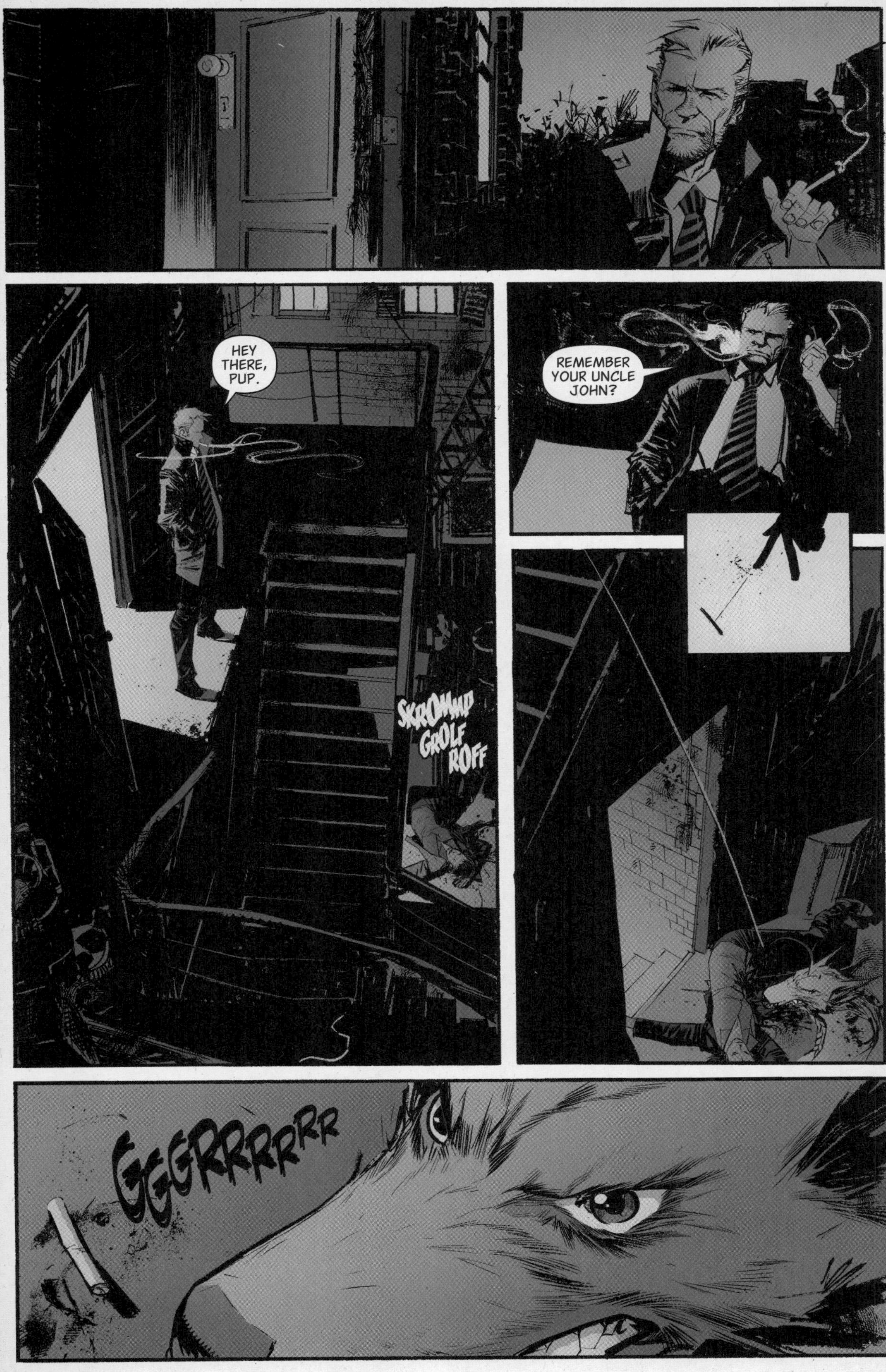
HEY THERE, PUP.
SKROMMP GROLF ROFF
REMEMBER YOUR UNCLE JOHN?
GGGRRRRRR

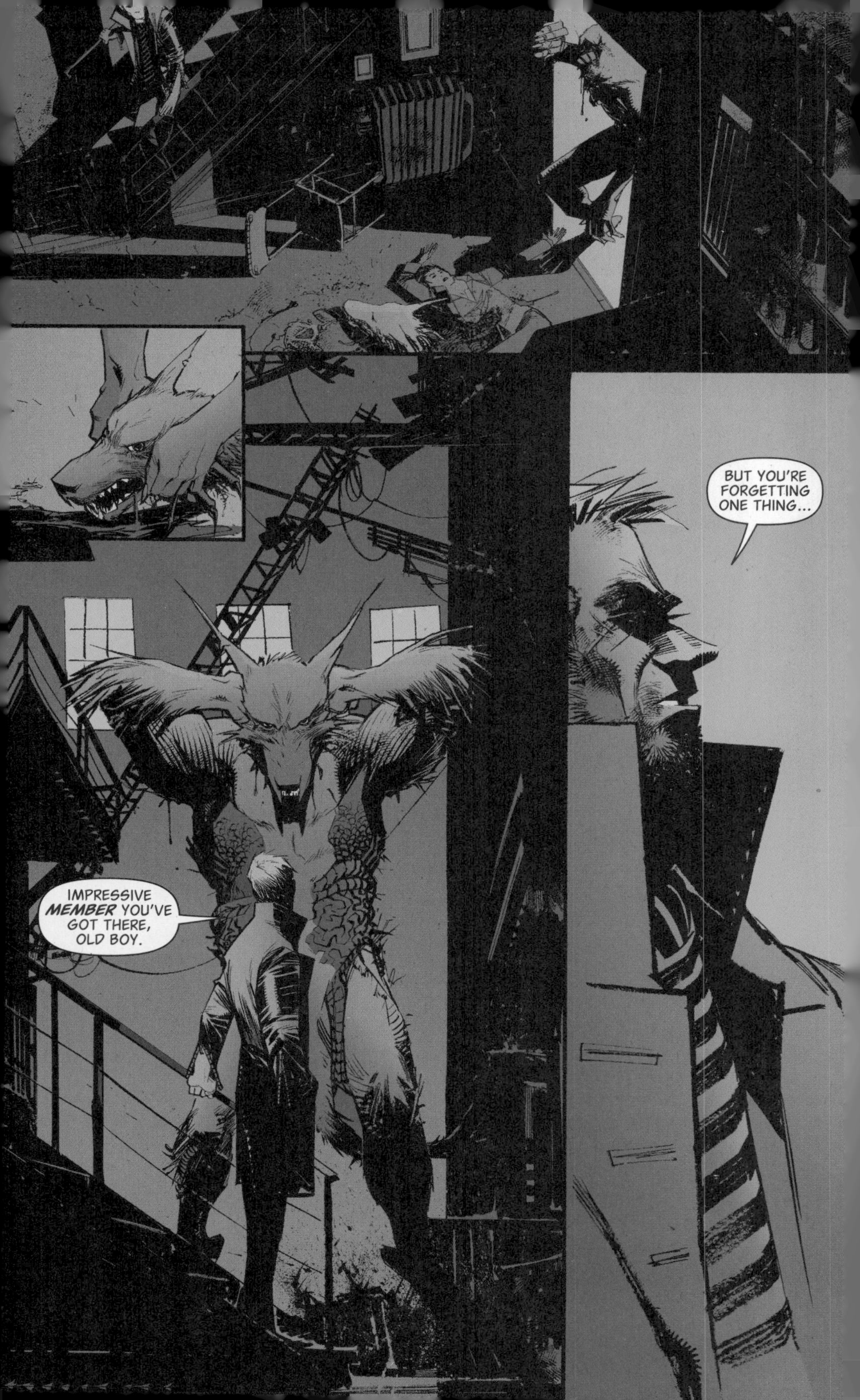
BUT YOU'RE FORGETTING ONE THING...
IMPRESSIVE *MEMBER* YOU'VE GOT THERE, OLD BOY.

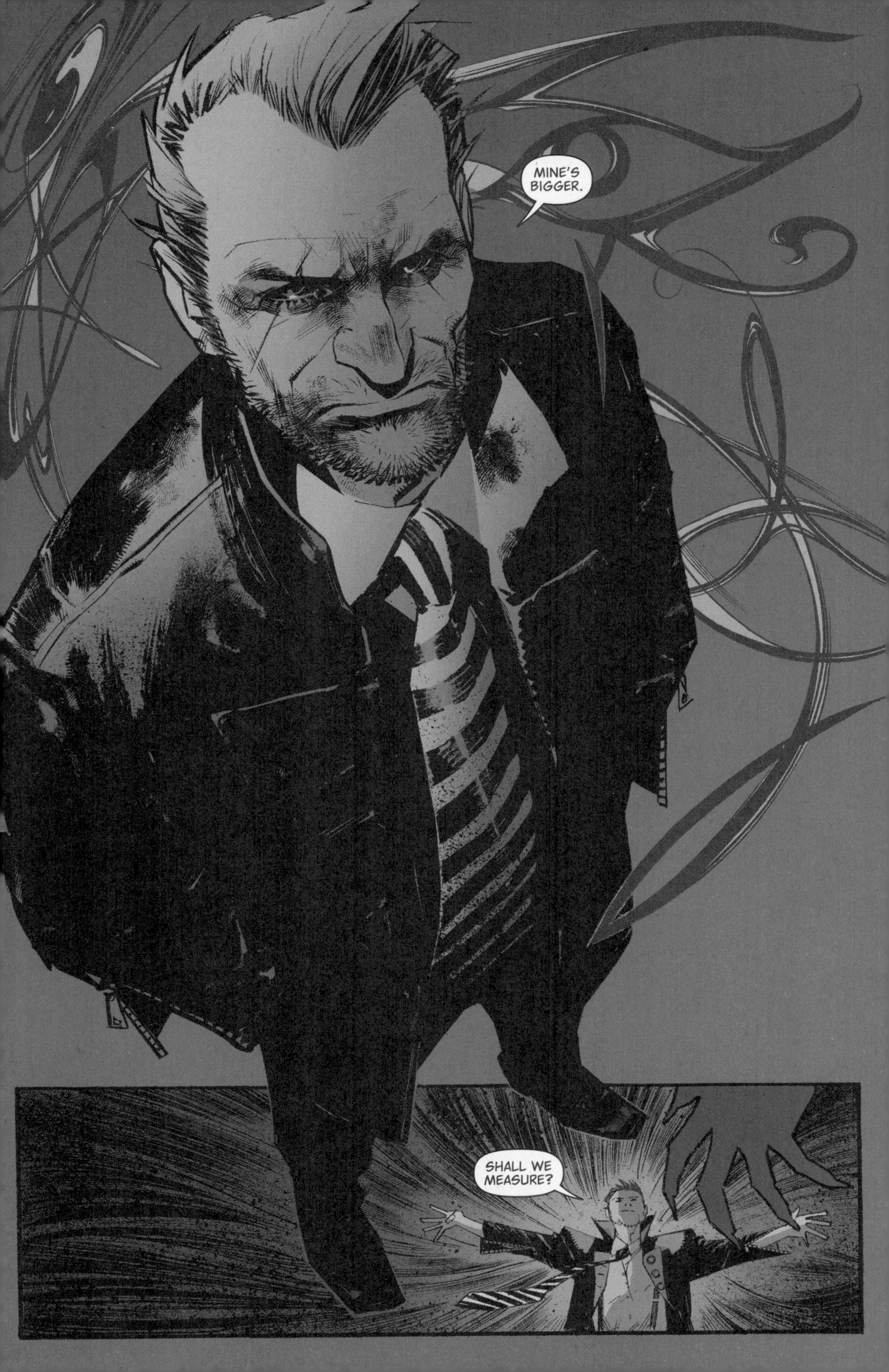
MINE'S BIGGER.
SHALL WE MEASURE?

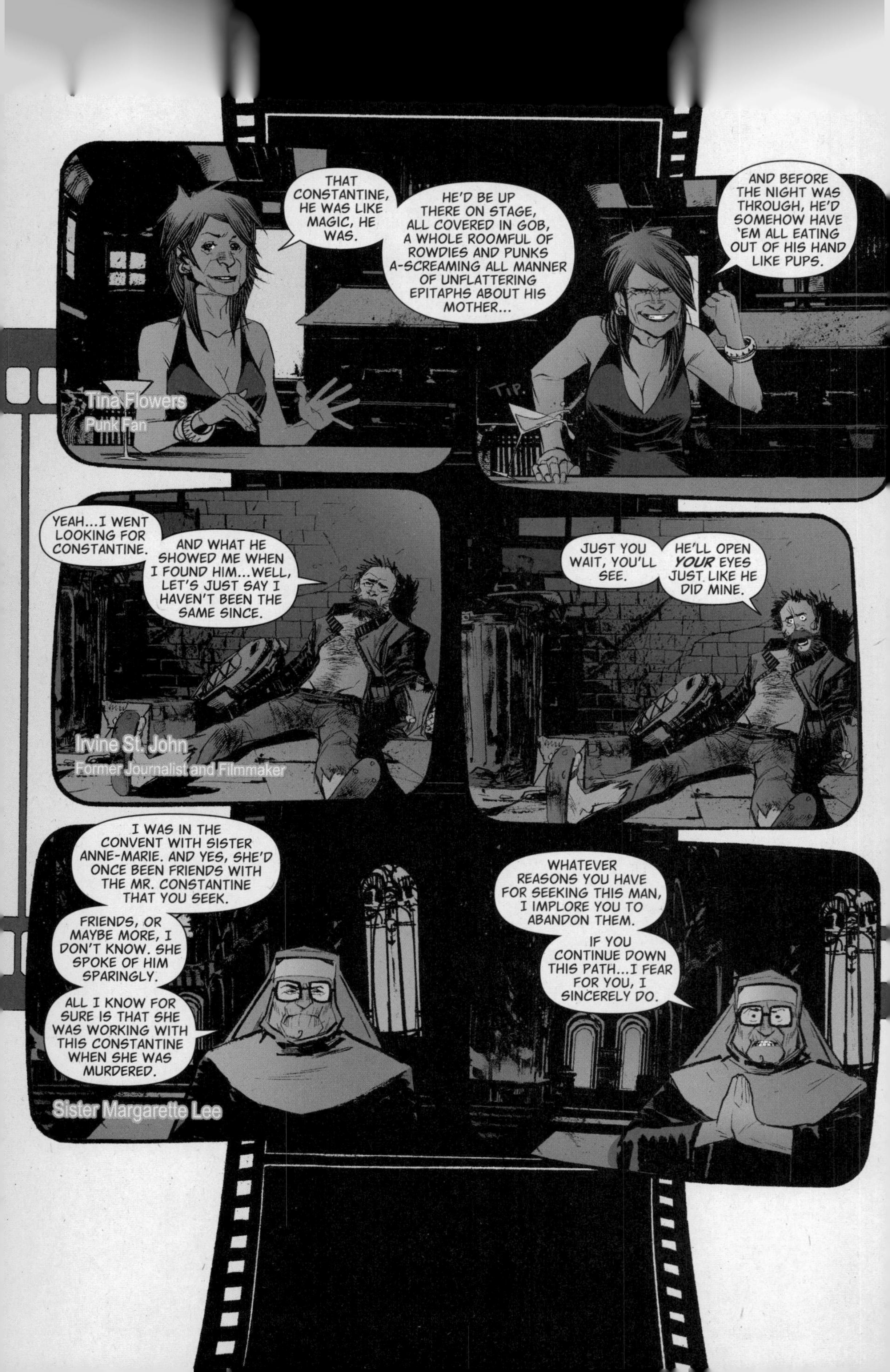
THAT CONSTANTINE, HE WAS LIKE MAGIC, HE WAS.
HE'D BE UP THERE ON STAGE, ALL COVERED IN GOB, A WHOLE ROOMFUL OF ROWDIES AND PUNKS A-SCREAMING ALL MANNER OF UNFLATTERING EPITAPHS ABOUT HIS MOTHER...
Tina Flowers
Punk Fan
AND BEFORE THE NIGHT WAS THROUGH, HE'D SOMEHOW HAVE 'EM ALL EATING OUT OF HIS HAND LIKE PUPS.
TIP.
YEAH...I WENT LOOKING FOR CONSTANTINE.
AND WHAT HE SHOWED ME WHEN I FOUND HIM...WELL, LET'S JUST SAY I HAVEN'T BEEN THE SAME SINCE.
Irvine St. John
Former Journalist and Filmmaker
JUST YOU WAIT, YOU'LL SEE.
HE'LL OPEN *YOUR* EYES JUST LIKE HE DID MINE.
I WAS IN THE CONVENT WITH SISTER ANNE-MARIE. AND YES, SHE'D ONCE BEEN FRIENDS WITH THE MR. CONSTANTINE THAT YOU SEEK.
FRIENDS, OR MAYBE MORE, I DON'T KNOW. SHE SPOKE OF HIM SPARINGLY.
ALL I KNOW FOR SURE IS THAT SHE WAS WORKING WITH THIS CONSTANTINE WHEN SHE WAS MURDERED.
Sister Margarette Lee
WHATEVER REASONS YOU HAVE FOR SEEKING THIS MAN, I IMPLORE YOU TO ABANDON THEM.
IF YOU CONTINUE DOWN THIS PATH...I FEAR FOR YOU, I SINCERELY DO.

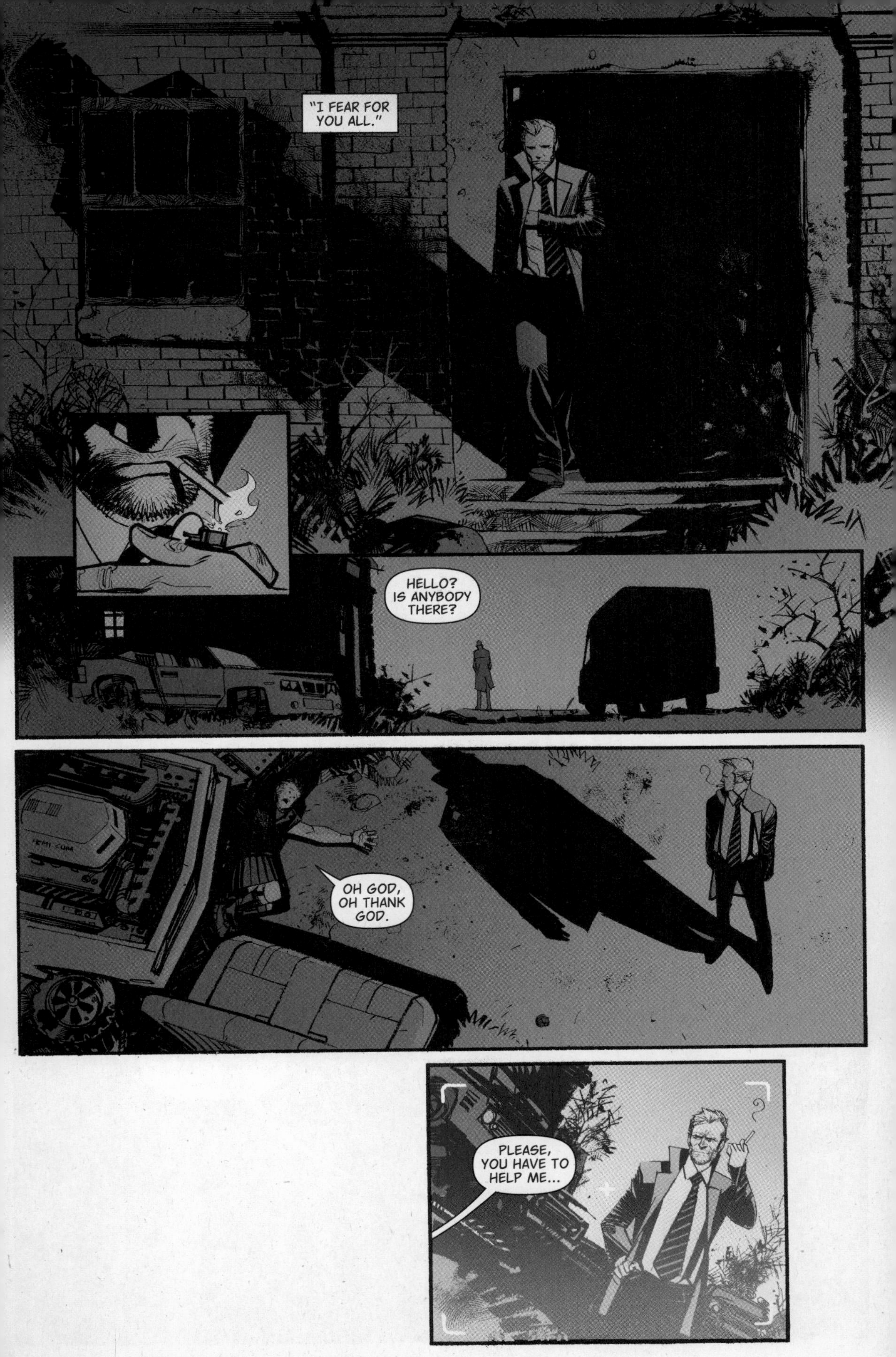
"I FEAR FOR YOU ALL."
HELLO? IS ANYBODY THERE?
OH GOD, OH THANK GOD.
PLEASE, YOU HAVE TO HELP ME...

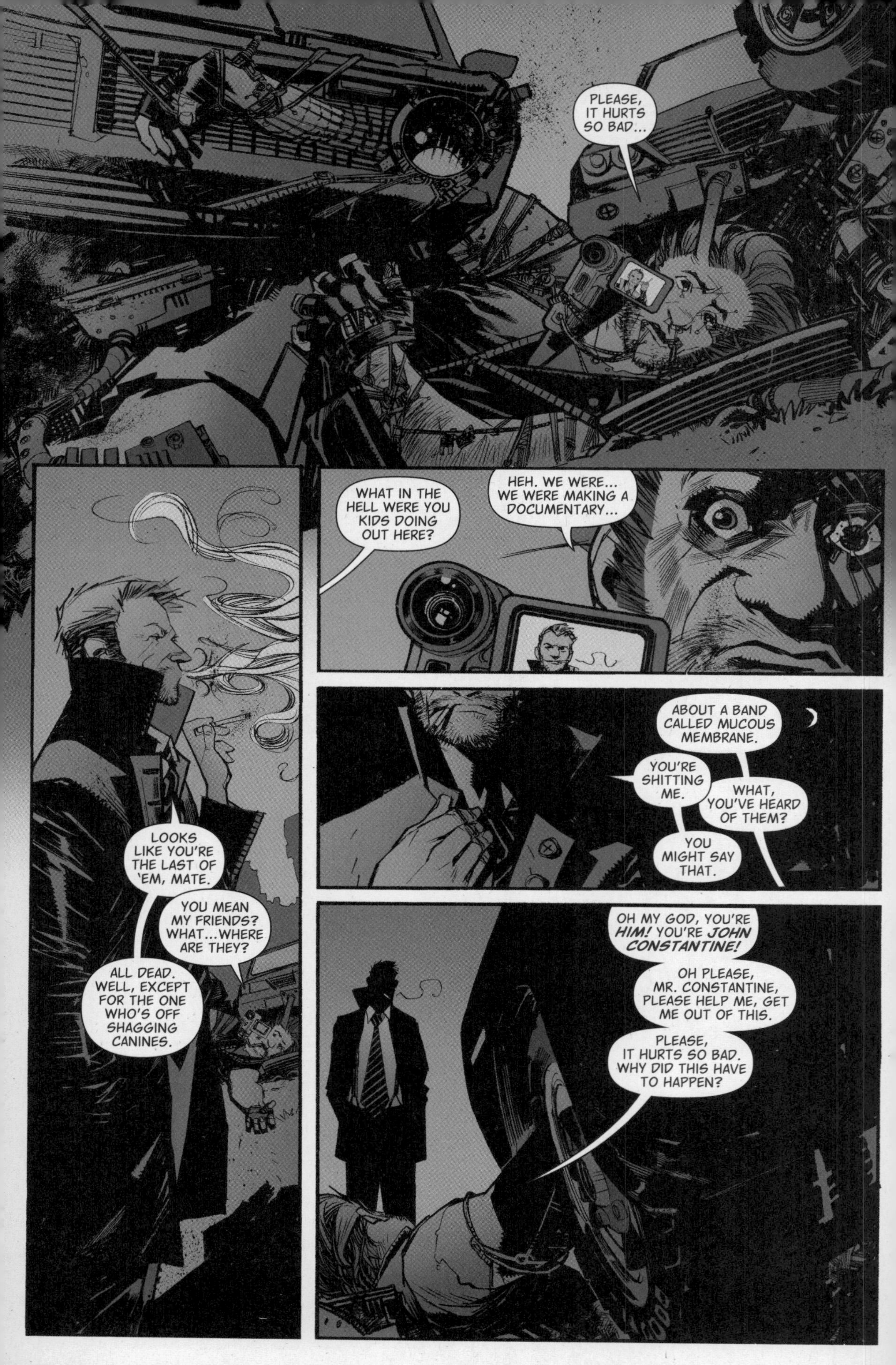

PLEASE, IT HURTS SO BAD...
WHAT IN THE HELL WERE YOU KIDS DOING OUT HERE?
HEH. WE WERE... WE WERE MAKING A DOCUMENTARY...
ABOUT A BAND CALLED MUCOUS MEMBRANE.
YOU'RE SHITTING ME.
WHAT, YOU'VE HEARD OF THEM?
YOU MIGHT SAY THAT.
LOOKS LIKE YOU'RE THE LAST OF 'EM, MATE.
YOU MEAN MY FRIENDS? WHAT...WHERE ARE THEY?
ALL DEAD. WELL, EXCEPT FOR THE ONE WHO'S OFF SHAGGING CANINES.
OH MY GOD, YOU'RE *HIM!* YOU'RE *JOHN CONSTANTINE!*
OH PLEASE, MR. CONSTANTINE, PLEASE HELP ME, GET ME OUT OF THIS.
PLEASE, IT HURTS SO BAD. WHY DID THIS HAVE TO HAPPEN?

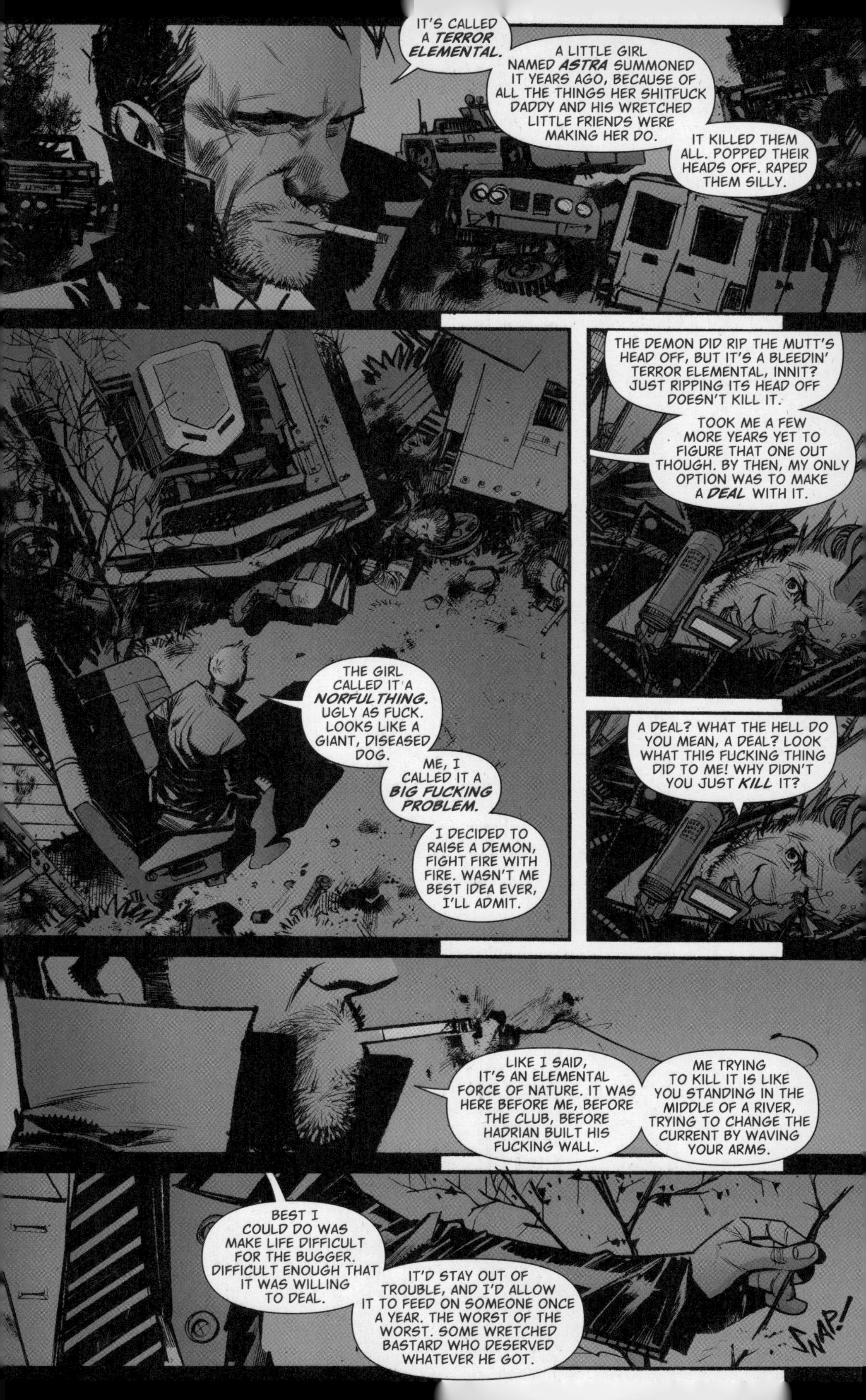
IT'S CALLED A TERROR ELEMENTAL.
A LITTLE GIRL NAMED ASTRA SUMMONED IT YEARS AGO, BECAUSE OF ALL THE THINGS HER SHITFUCK DADDY AND HIS WRETCHED LITTLE FRIENDS WERE MAKING HER DO.
IT KILLED THEM ALL. POPPED THEIR HEADS OFF. RAPED THEM SILLY.
THE GIRL CALLED IT A NORFULTHING. UGLY AS FUCK. LOOKS LIKE A GIANT, DISEASED DOG.
ME, I CALLED IT A BIG FUCKING PROBLEM.
I DECIDED TO RAISE A DEMON, FIGHT FIRE WITH FIRE. WASN'T ME BEST IDEA EVER, I'LL ADMIT.
THE DEMON DID RIP THE MUTT'S HEAD OFF, BUT IT'S A BLEEDIN' TERROR ELEMENTAL, INNIT? JUST RIPPING ITS HEAD OFF DOESN'T KILL IT.
TOOK ME A FEW MORE YEARS YET TO FIGURE THAT ONE OUT THOUGH. BY THEN, MY ONLY OPTION WAS TO MAKE A DEAL WITH IT.
A DEAL? WHAT THE HELL DO YOU MEAN, A DEAL? LOOK WHAT THIS FUCKING THING DID TO ME! WHY DIDN'T YOU JUST KILL IT?
LIKE I SAID, IT'S AN ELEMENTAL FORCE OF NATURE. IT WAS HERE BEFORE ME, BEFORE THE CLUB, BEFORE HADRIAN BUILT HIS FUCKING WALL.
ME TRYING TO KILL IT IS LIKE YOU STANDING IN THE MIDDLE OF A RIVER, TRYING TO CHANGE THE CURRENT BY WAVING YOUR ARMS.
BEST I COULD DO WAS MAKE LIFE DIFFICULT FOR THE BUGGER. DIFFICULT ENOUGH THAT IT WAS WILLING TO DEAL.
IT'D STAY OUT OF TROUBLE, AND I'D ALLOW IT TO FEED ON SOMEONE ONCE A YEAR. THE WORST OF THE WORST. SOME WRETCHED BASTARD WHO DESERVED WHATEVER HE GOT.
SNAP!

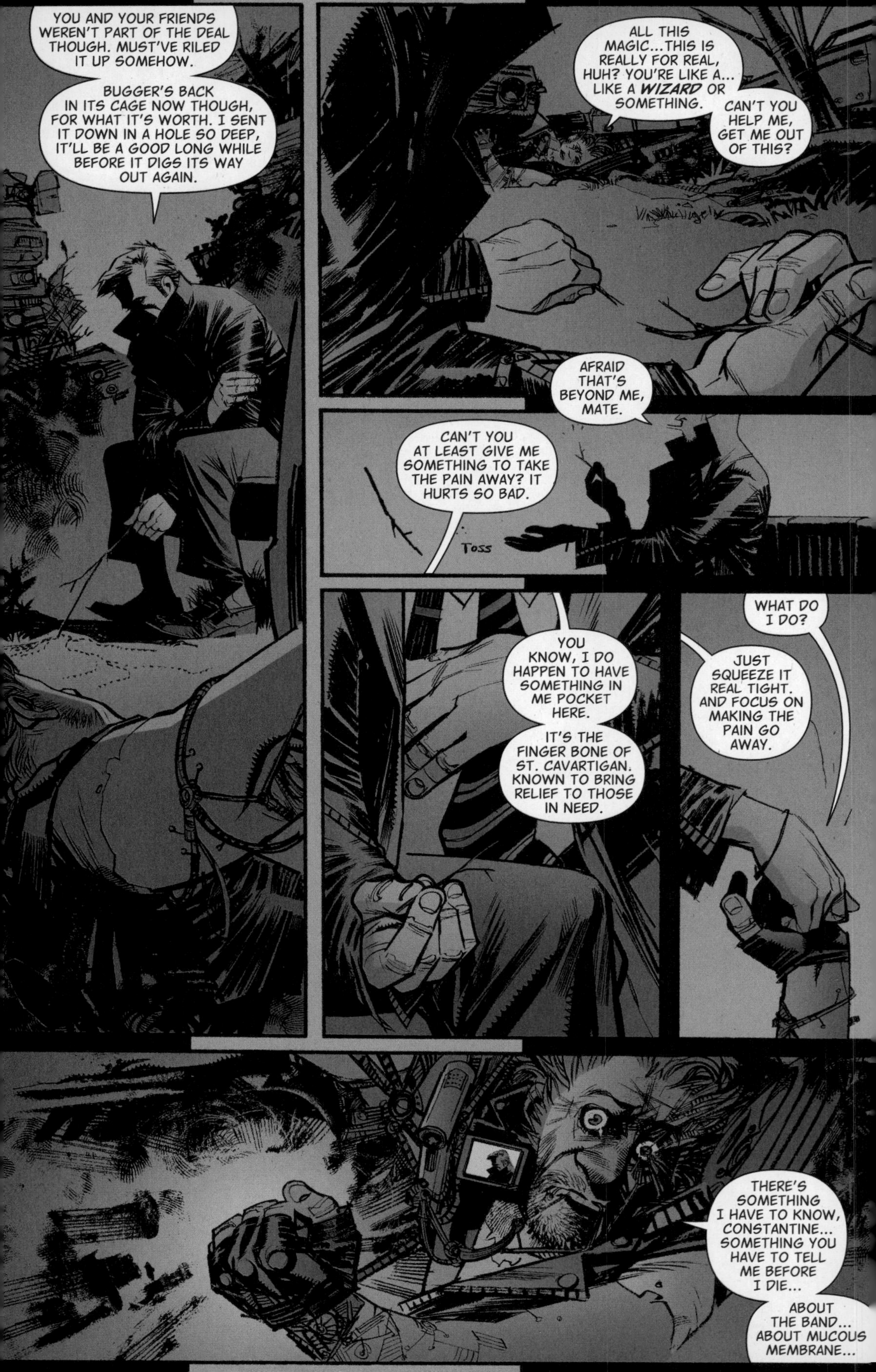
YOU AND YOUR FRIENDS WEREN'T PART OF THE DEAL THOUGH. MUST'VE RILED IT UP SOMEHOW.
BUGGER'S BACK IN ITS CAGE NOW THOUGH, FOR WHAT IT'S WORTH. I SENT IT DOWN IN A HOLE SO DEEP, IT'LL BE A GOOD LONG WHILE BEFORE IT DIGS ITS WAY OUT AGAIN.
ALL THIS MAGIC...THIS IS REALLY FOR REAL, HUH? YOU'RE LIKE A... LIKE A **WIZARD** OR SOMETHING.
CAN'T YOU HELP ME, GET ME OUT OF THIS?
AFRAID THAT'S BEYOND ME, MATE.
CAN'T YOU AT LEAST GIVE ME SOMETHING TO TAKE THE PAIN AWAY? IT HURTS SO BAD.
TOSS
YOU KNOW, I DO HAPPEN TO HAVE SOMETHING IN ME POCKET HERE.
IT'S THE FINGER BONE OF ST. CAVARTIGAN. KNOWN TO BRING RELIEF TO THOSE IN NEED.
WHAT DO I DO?
JUST SQUEEZE IT REAL TIGHT. AND FOCUS ON MAKING THE PAIN GO AWAY.
THERE'S SOMETHING I HAVE TO KNOW, CONSTANTINE... SOMETHING YOU HAVE TO TELL ME BEFORE I DIE...
ABOUT THE BAND... ABOUT MUCOUS MEMBRANE...

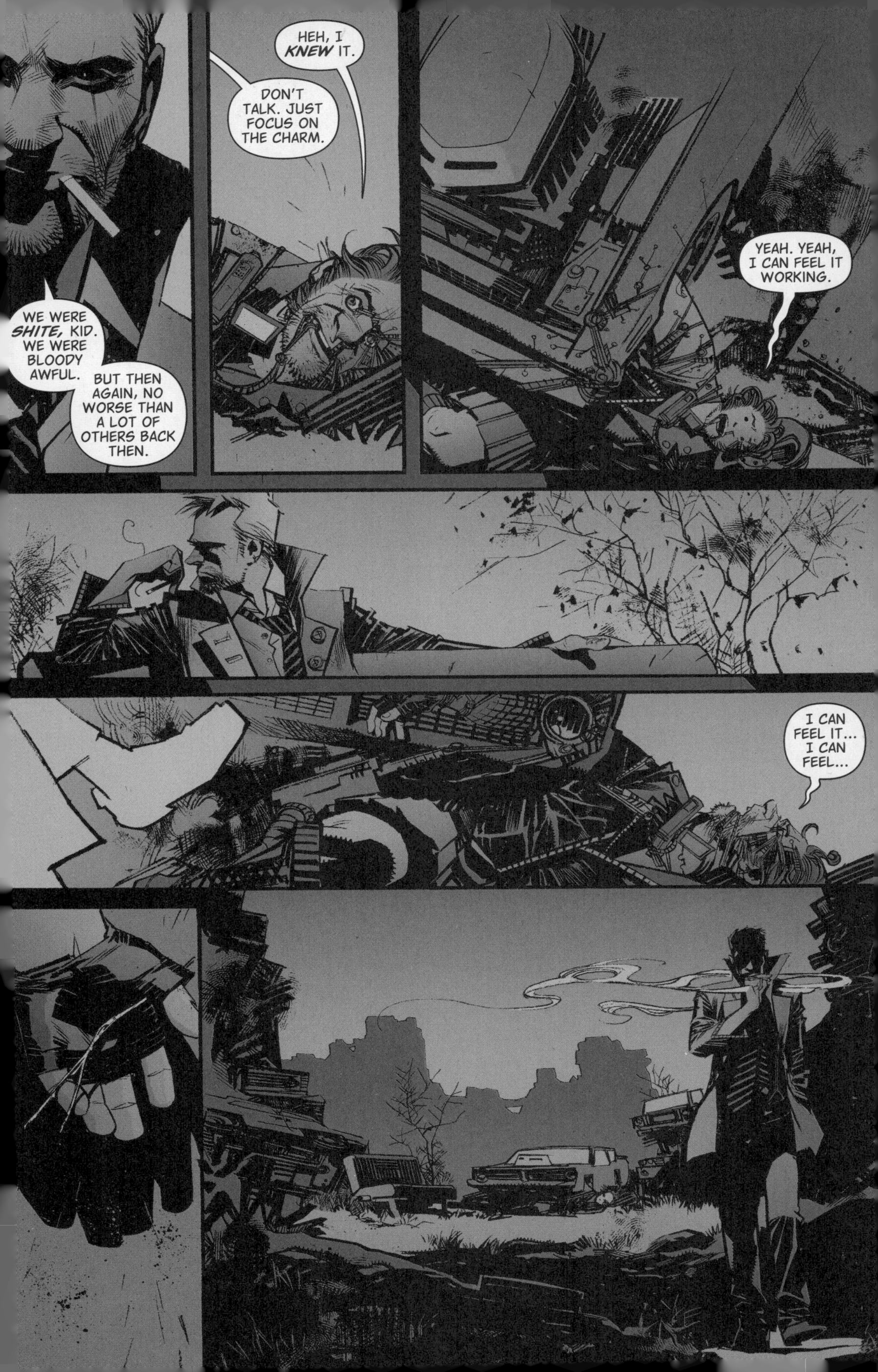
WE WERE *SHITE,* KID. WE WERE BLOODY AWFUL.
BUT THEN AGAIN, NO WORSE THAN A LOT OF OTHERS BACK THEN.
HEH, I *KNEW* IT.
DON'T TALK. JUST FOCUS ON THE CHARM.
YEAH. YEAH, I CAN FEEL IT WORKING.
I CAN FEEL IT... I CAN FEEL...

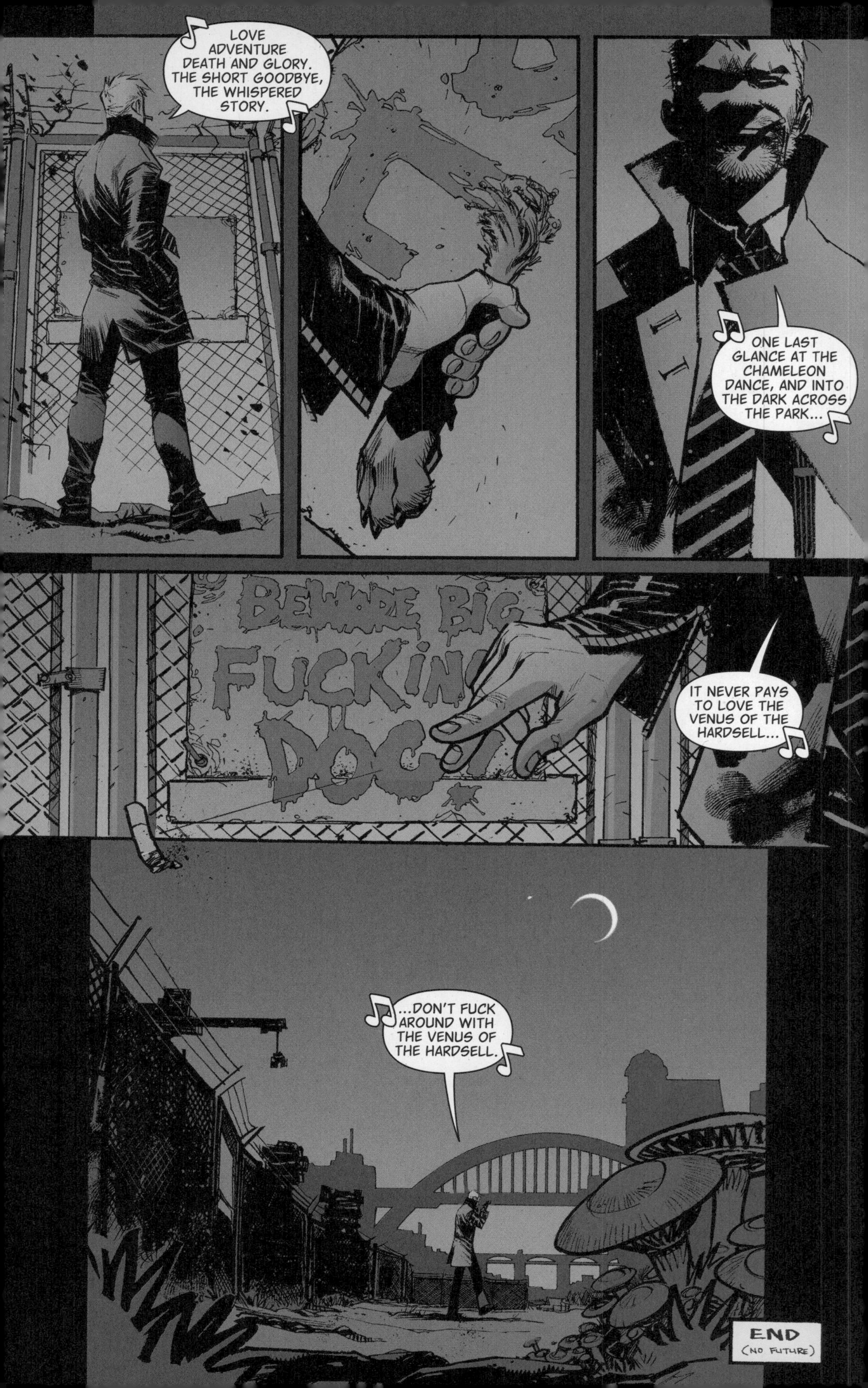
LOVE ADVENTURE DEATH AND GLORY. THE SHORT GOODBYE, THE WHISPERED STORY.
ONE LAST GLANCE AT THE CHAMELEON DANCE, AND INTO THE DARK ACROSS THE PARK...
BEWARE BIG FUCKIN DOG
IT NEVER PAYS TO LOVE THE VENUS OF THE HARDSELL...
...DON'T FUCK AROUND WITH THE VENUS OF THE HARDSELL.
END
(NO FUTURE)

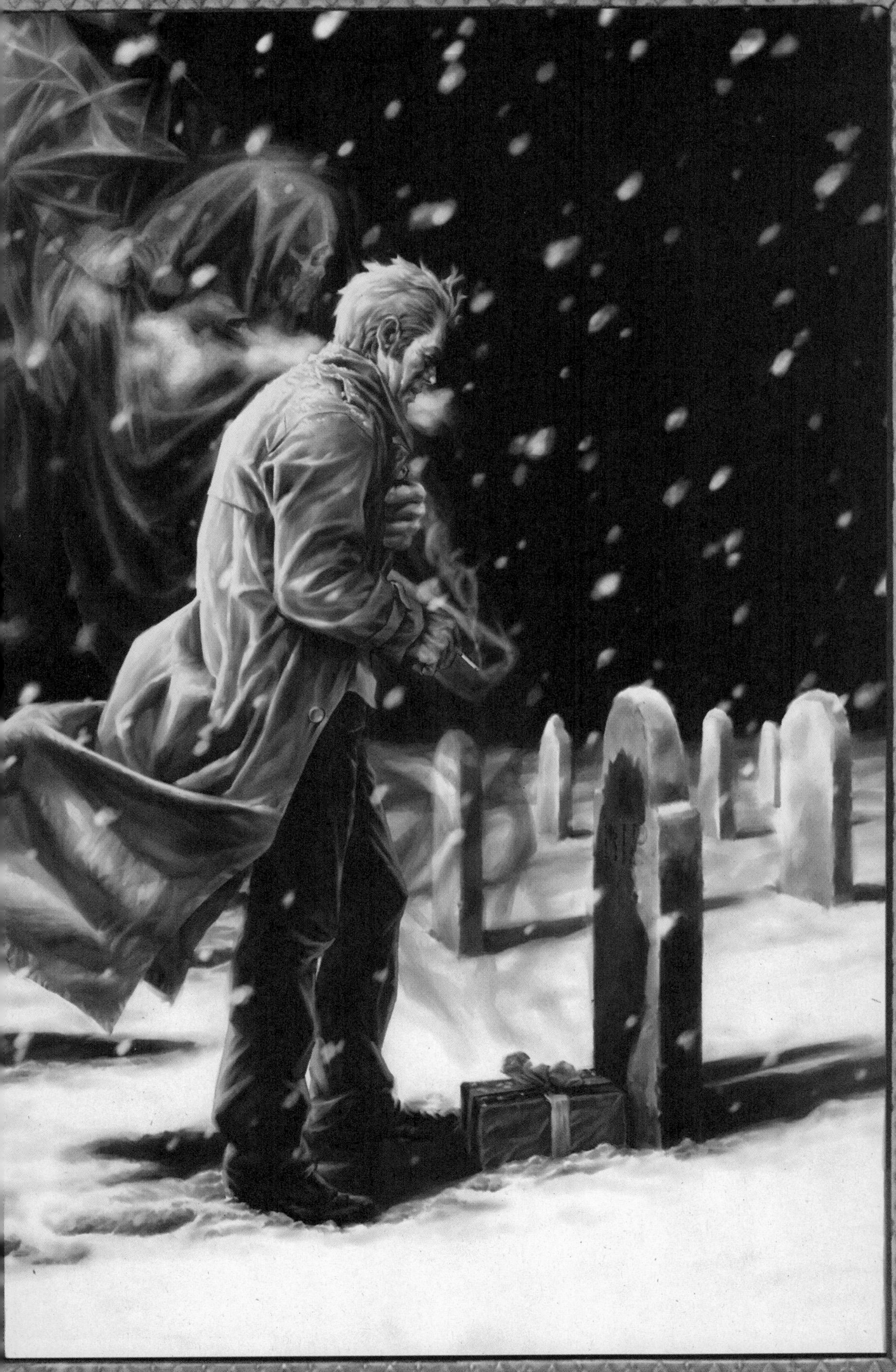

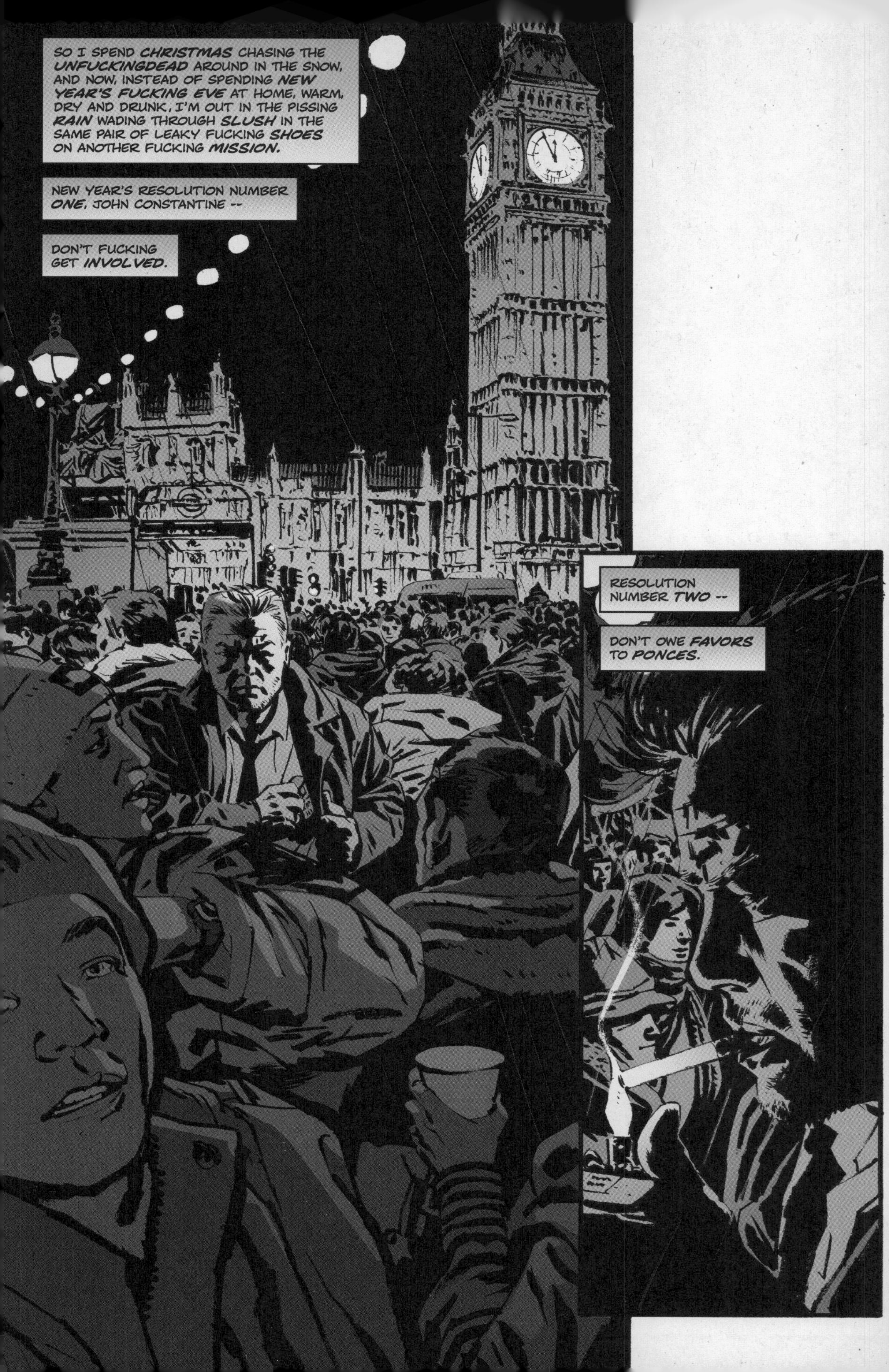
SO I SPEND CHRISTMAS CHASING THE UNFUCKINGDEAD AROUND IN THE SNOW, AND NOW, INSTEAD OF SPENDING NEW YEAR'S FUCKING EVE AT HOME, WARM, DRY AND DRUNK, I'M OUT IN THE PISSING RAIN WADING THROUGH SLUSH IN THE SAME PAIR OF LEAKY FUCKING SHOES ON ANOTHER FUCKING MISSION.
NEW YEAR'S RESOLUTION NUMBER ONE, JOHN CONSTANTINE --
DON'T FUCKING GET INVOLVED.
RESOLUTION NUMBER TWO --
DON'T OWE FAVORS TO PONCES.

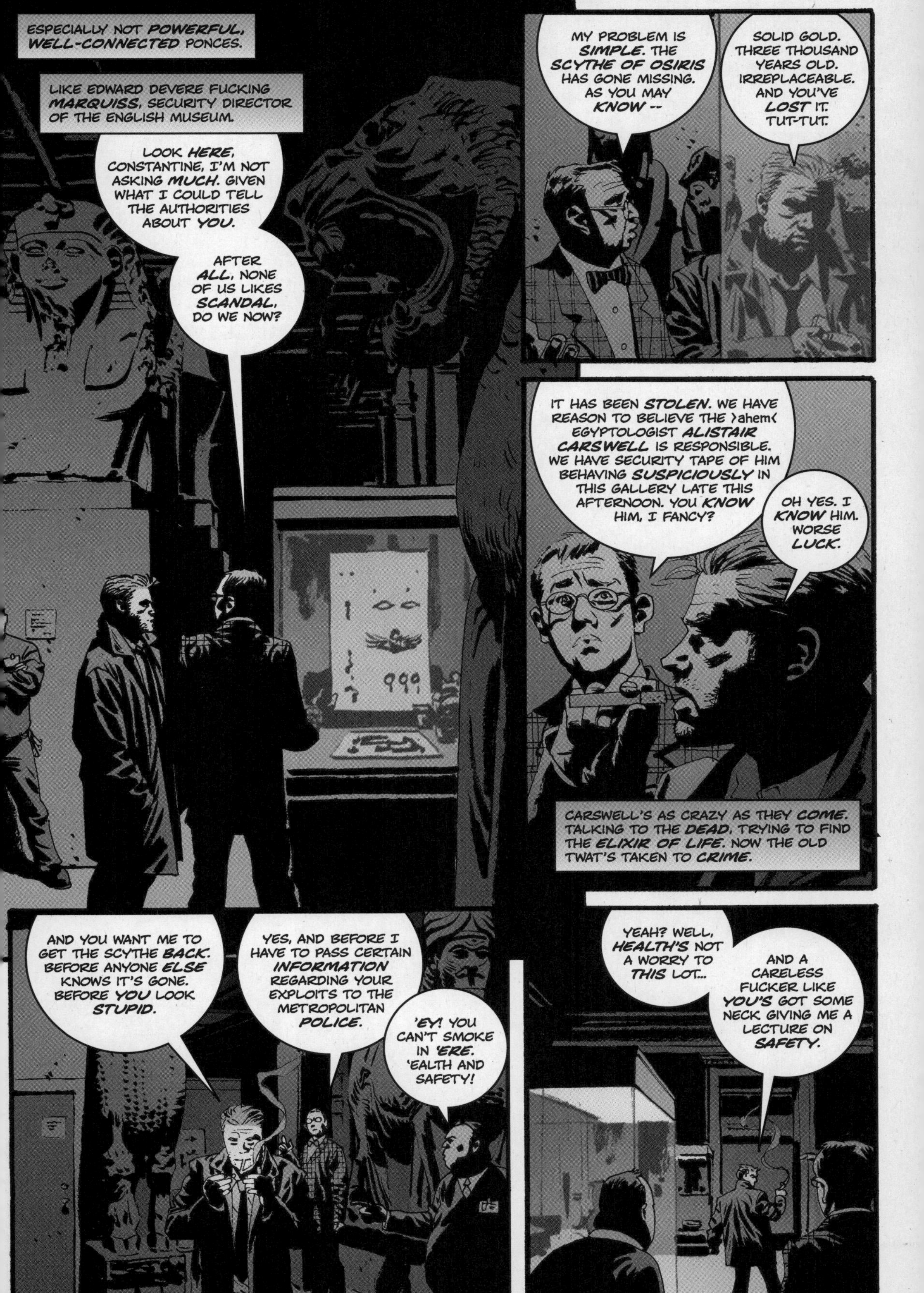
ESPECIALLY NOT POWERFUL, WELL-CONNECTED PONCES.
LIKE EDWARD DEVERE FUCKING MARQUISS, SECURITY DIRECTOR OF THE ENGLISH MUSEUM.
LOOK HERE, CONSTANTINE, I'M NOT ASKING MUCH. GIVEN WHAT I COULD TELL THE AUTHORITIES ABOUT YOU.
AFTER ALL, NONE OF US LIKES SCANDAL, DO WE NOW?
MY PROBLEM IS SIMPLE. THE SCYTHE OF OSIRIS HAS GONE MISSING. AS YOU MAY KNOW --
SOLID GOLD. THREE THOUSAND YEARS OLD. IRREPLACEABLE. AND YOU'VE LOST IT. TUT-TUT.
IT HAS BEEN STOLEN. WE HAVE REASON TO BELIEVE THE ›ahem‹ EGYPTOLOGIST ALISTAIR CARSWELL IS RESPONSIBLE. WE HAVE SECURITY TAPE OF HIM BEHAVING SUSPICIOUSLY IN THIS GALLERY LATE THIS AFTERNOON. YOU KNOW HIM, I FANCY?
OH YES. I KNOW HIM. WORSE LUCK.
CARSWELL'S AS CRAZY AS THEY COME. TALKING TO THE DEAD, TRYING TO FIND THE ELIXIR OF LIFE. NOW THE OLD TWAT'S TAKEN TO CRIME.
AND YOU WANT ME TO GET THE SCYTHE BACK. BEFORE ANYONE ELSE KNOWS IT'S GONE. BEFORE YOU LOOK STUPID.
YES, AND BEFORE I HAVE TO PASS CERTAIN INFORMATION REGARDING YOUR EXPLOITS TO THE METROPOLITAN POLICE.
'EY! YOU CAN'T SMOKE IN 'ERE. 'EALTH AND SAFETY!
YEAH? WELL, HEALTH'S NOT A WORRY TO THIS LOT...
AND A CARELESS FUCKER LIKE YOU'S GOT SOME NECK GIVING ME A LECTURE ON SAFETY.

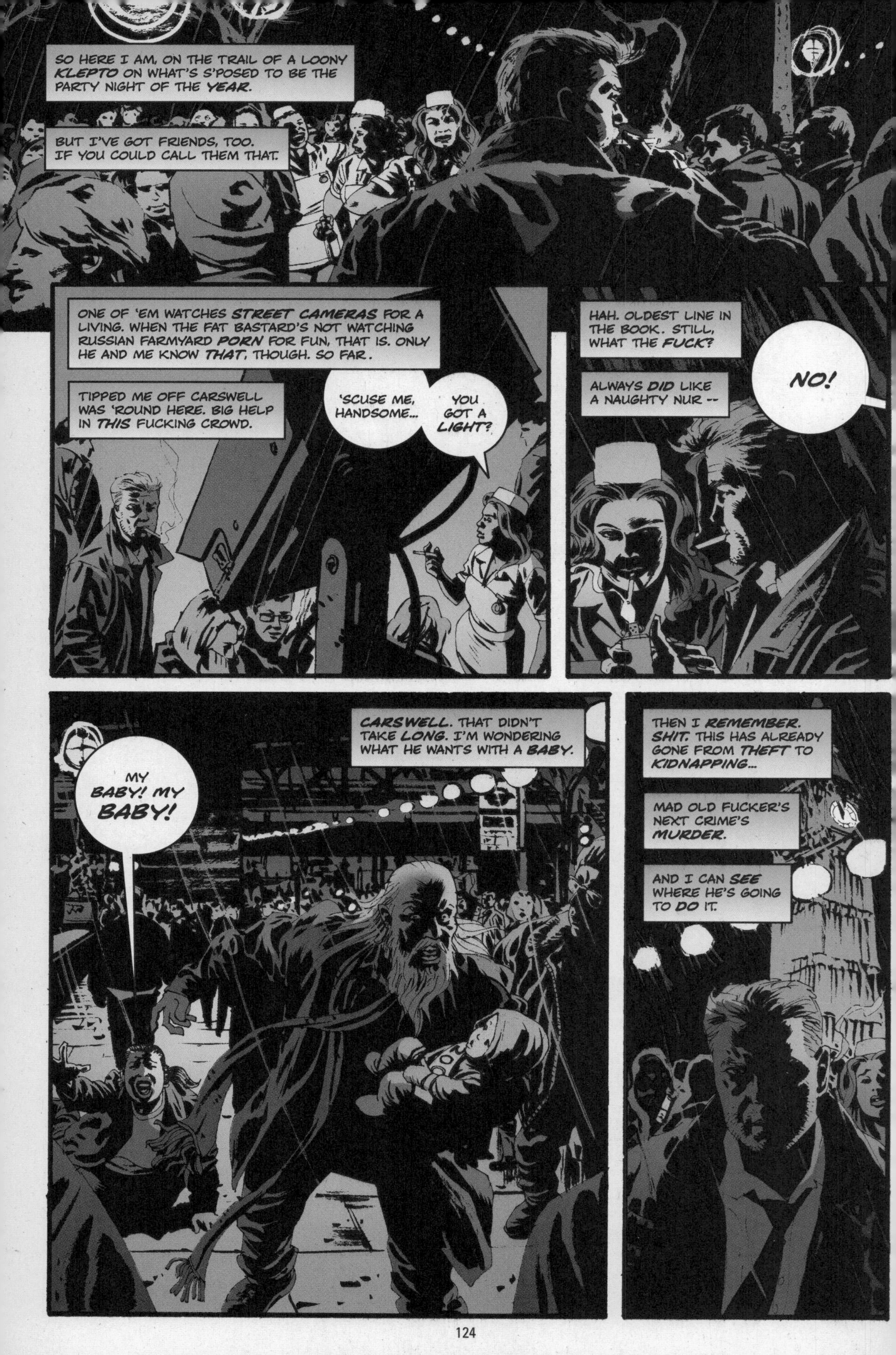

SO HERE I AM, ON THE TRAIL OF A LOONY KLEPTO ON WHAT'S S'POSED TO BE THE PARTY NIGHT OF THE YEAR.
BUT I'VE GOT FRIENDS, TOO. IF YOU COULD CALL THEM THAT.
ONE OF 'EM WATCHES STREET CAMERAS FOR A LIVING. WHEN THE FAT BASTARD'S NOT WATCHING RUSSIAN FARMYARD PORN FOR FUN, THAT IS. ONLY HE AND ME KNOW THAT, THOUGH. SO FAR.
TIPPED ME OFF CARSWELL WAS 'ROUND HERE. BIG HELP IN THIS FUCKING CROWD.
'SCUSE ME, HANDSOME...
YOU GOT A LIGHT?
HAH. OLDEST LINE IN THE BOOK. STILL, WHAT THE FUCK?
ALWAYS DID LIKE A NAUGHTY NUR --
NO!
MY BABY! MY BABY!
CARSWELL. THAT DIDN'T TAKE LONG. I'M WONDERING WHAT HE WANTS WITH A BABY.
THEN I REMEMBER. SHIT. THIS HAS ALREADY GONE FROM THEFT TO KIDNAPPING...
MAD OLD FUCKER'S NEXT CRIME'S MURDER.
AND I CAN SEE WHERE HE'S GOING TO DO IT.

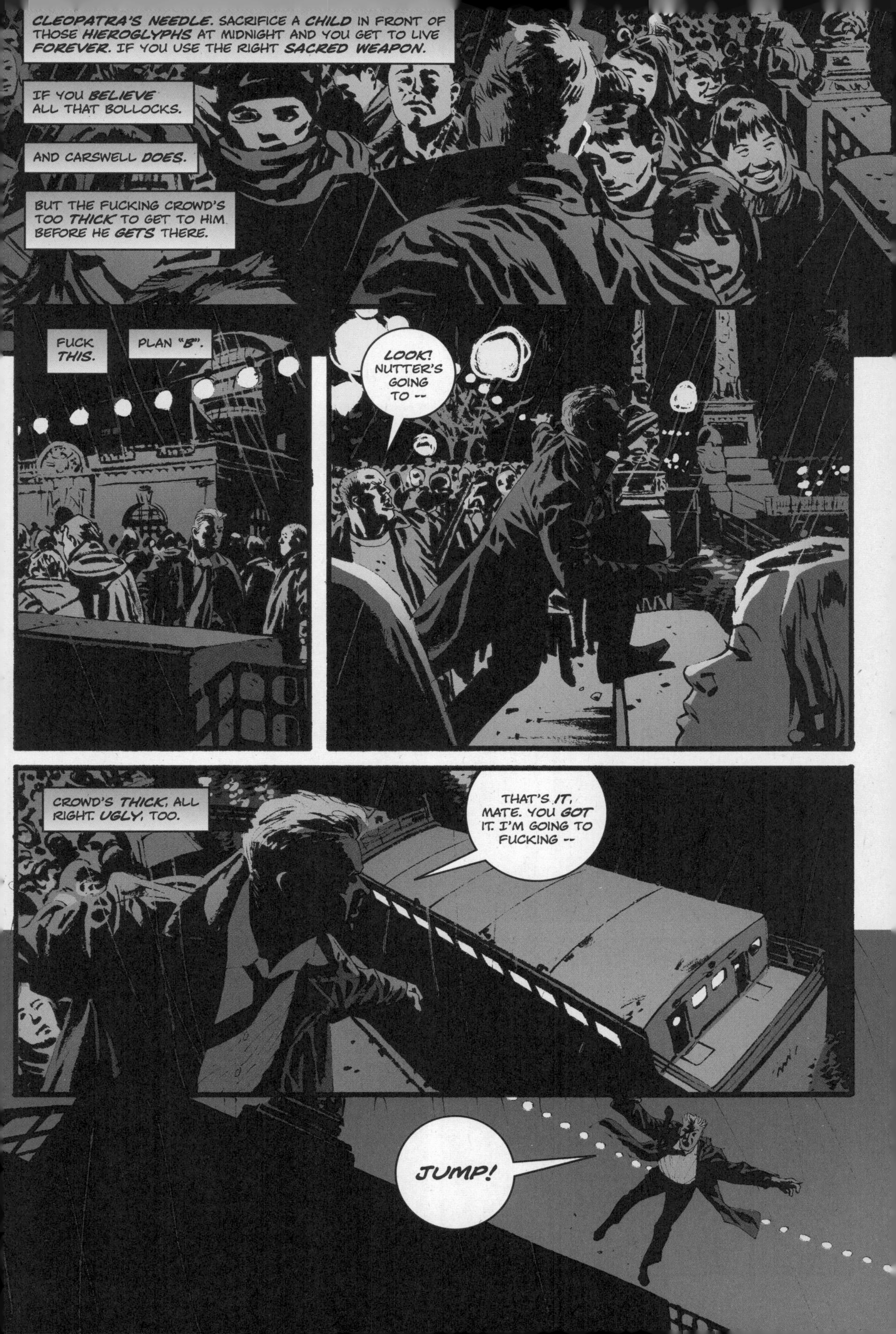
CLEOPATRA'S NEEDLE. SACRIFICE A CHILD IN FRONT OF THOSE HIEROGLYPHS AT MIDNIGHT AND YOU GET TO LIVE FOREVER. IF YOU USE THE RIGHT SACRED WEAPON.
IF YOU BELIEVE ALL THAT BOLLOCKS.
AND CARSWELL DOES.
BUT THE FUCKING CROWD'S TOO THICK TO GET TO HIM BEFORE HE GETS THERE.
FUCK THIS.
PLAN "B".
LOOK! NUTTER'S GOING TO --
CROWD'S THICK, ALL RIGHT. UGLY, TOO.
THAT'S IT, MATE. YOU GOT IT. I'M GOING TO FUCKING --
JUMP!

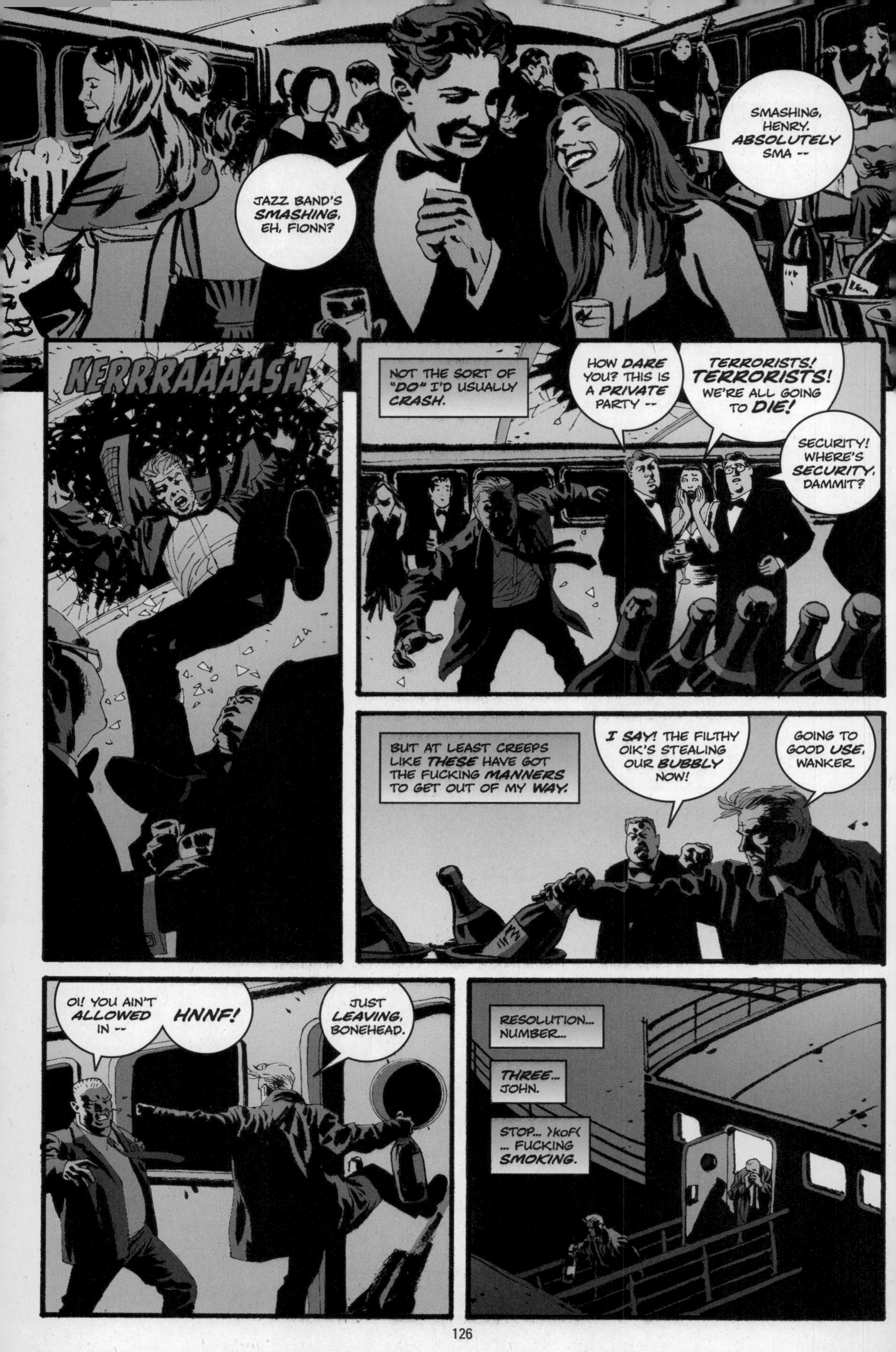

JAZZ BAND'S SMASHING, EH, FIONN?
SMASHING, HENRY. ABSOLUTELY SMA --
KERRRAAAAASH
NOT THE SORT OF "DO" I'D USUALLY CRASH.
HOW DARE YOU? THIS IS A PRIVATE PARTY --
TERRORISTS! TERRORISTS! WE'RE ALL GOING TO DIE!
SECURITY! WHERE'S SECURITY, DAMMIT?
BUT AT LEAST CREEPS LIKE THESE HAVE GOT THE FUCKING MANNERS TO GET OUT OF MY WAY.
I SAY! THE FILTHY OIK'S STEALING OUR BUBBLY NOW!
GOING TO GOOD USE, WANKER.
OI! YOU AIN'T ALLOWED IN --
HNNF!
JUST LEAVING, BONEHEAD.
RESOLUTION... NUMBER...
THREE... JOHN.
STOP... ›kof‹ ... FUCKING SMOKING.

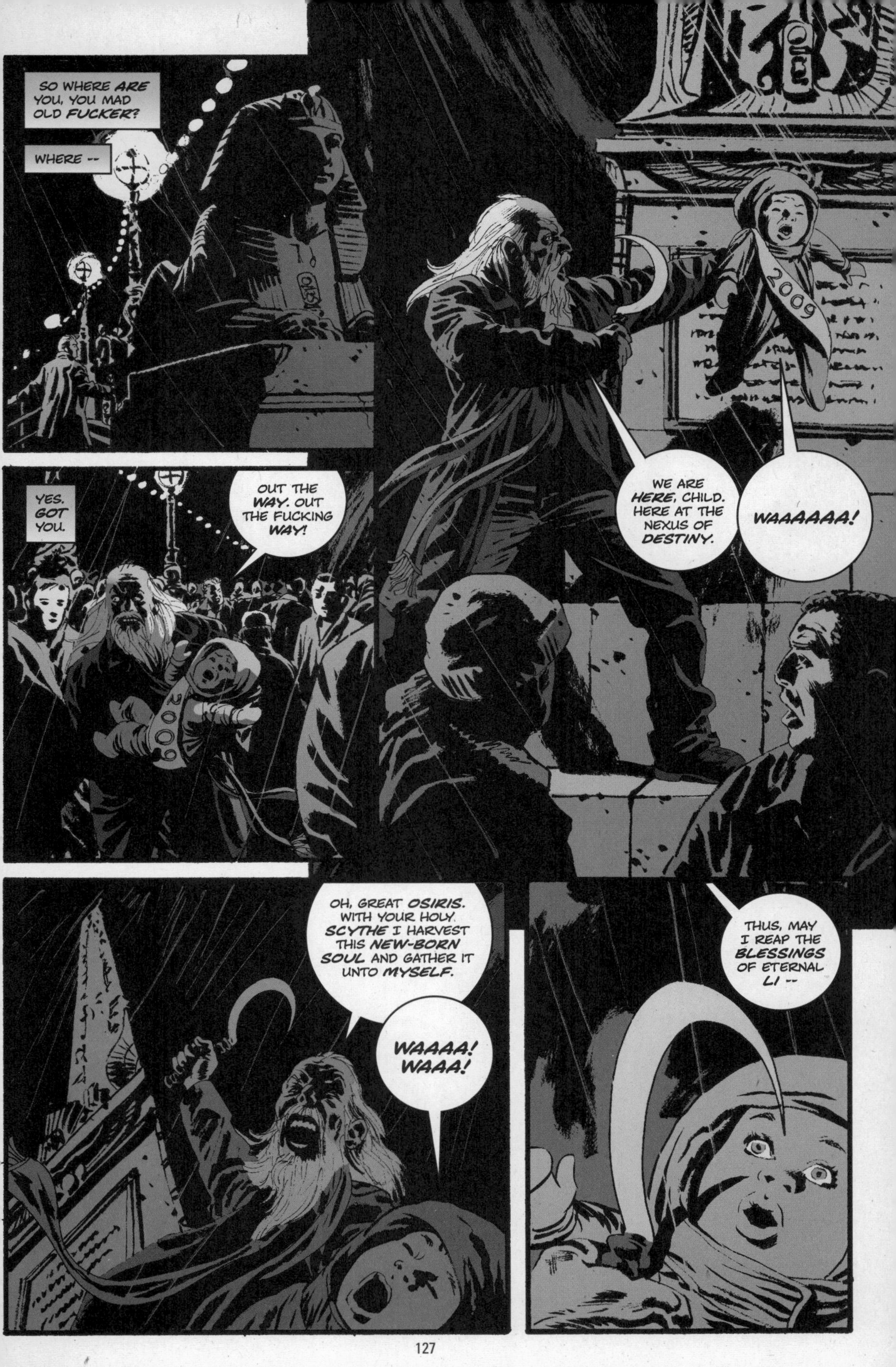
SO WHERE ARE YOU, YOU MAD OLD FUCKER?
WHERE --
YES. GOT YOU.
OUT THE WAY. OUT THE FUCKING WAY!
WE ARE HERE, CHILD. HERE AT THE NEXUS OF DESTINY.
WAAAAAA!
OH, GREAT OSIRIS. WITH YOUR HOLY SCYTHE I HARVEST THIS NEW-BORN SOUL AND GATHER IT UNTO MYSELF.
WAAAA! WAAA!
THUS, MAY I REAP THE BLESSINGS OF ETERNAL LI --

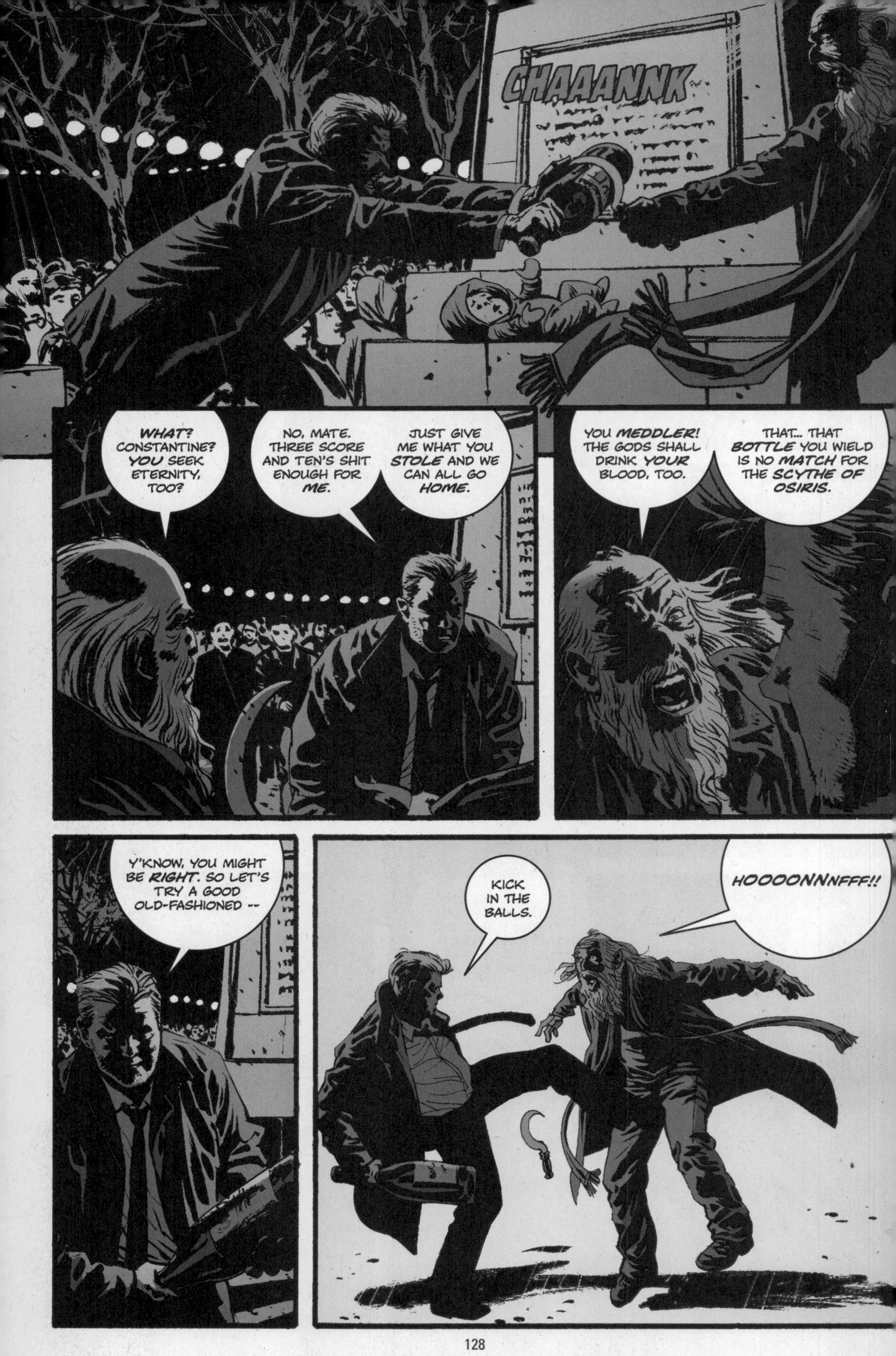
CHAAANNK
WHAT? CONSTANTINE? YOU SEEK ETERNITY, TOO?
NO, MATE. THREE SCORE AND TEN'S SHIT ENOUGH FOR ME.
JUST GIVE ME WHAT YOU STOLE AND WE CAN ALL GO HOME.
YOU MEDDLER! THE GODS SHALL DRINK YOUR BLOOD, TOO.
THAT... THAT BOTTLE YOU WIELD IS NO MATCH FOR THE SCYTHE OF OSIRIS.
Y'KNOW, YOU MIGHT BE RIGHT. SO LET'S TRY A GOOD OLD-FASHIONED --
KICK IN THE BALLS.
HOOOONNNFFF!!

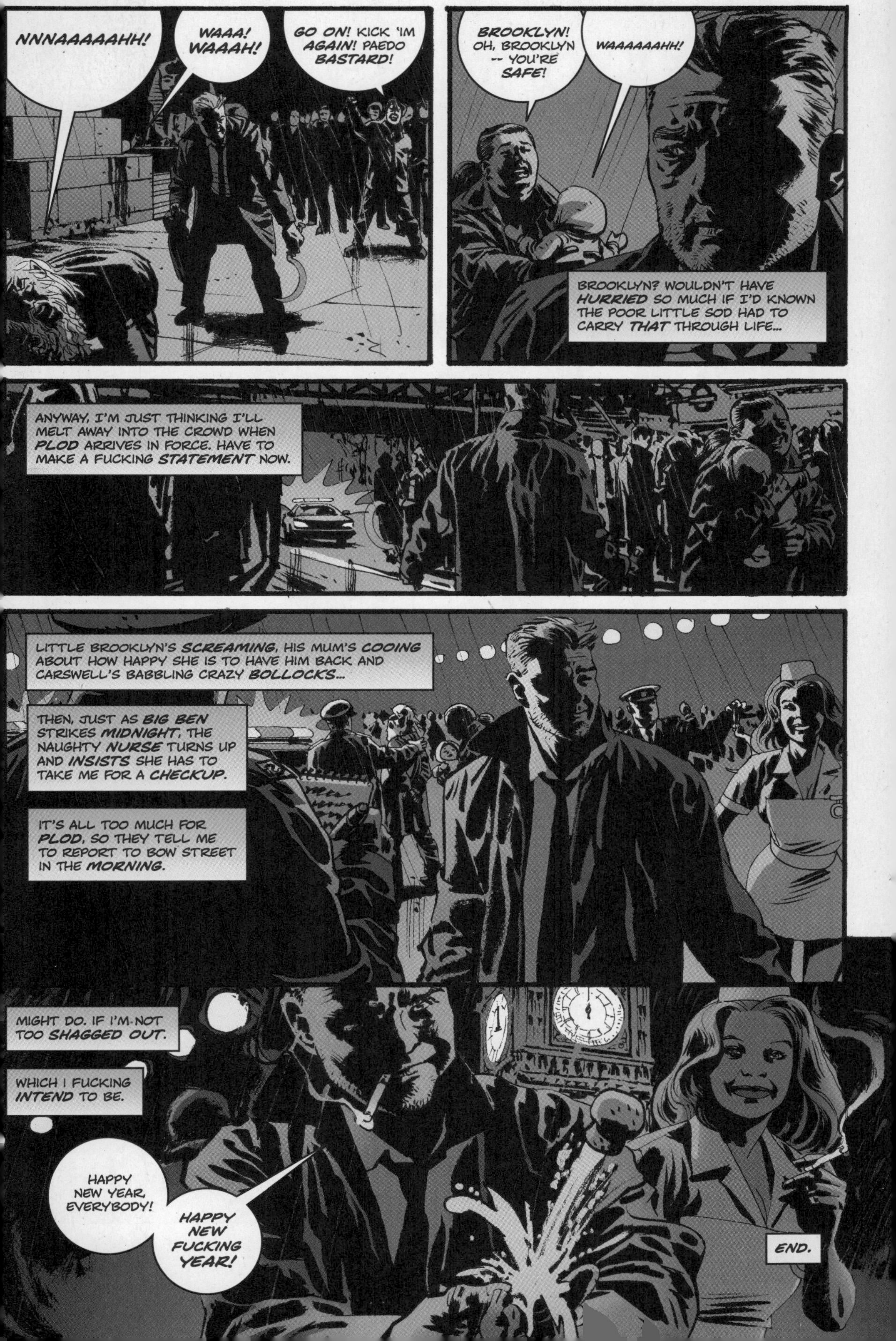
NNNAAAAAAHH!
WAAA! WAAAH!
GO ON! KICK 'IM AGAIN! PAEDO BASTARD!
BROOKLYN! OH, BROOKLYN -- YOU'RE SAFE!
WAAAAAAAHH!
BROOKLYN? WOULDN'T HAVE HURRIED SO MUCH IF I'D KNOWN THE POOR LITTLE SOD HAD TO CARRY THAT THROUGH LIFE...
ANYWAY, I'M JUST THINKING I'LL MELT AWAY INTO THE CROWD WHEN PLOD ARRIVES IN FORCE. HAVE TO MAKE A FUCKING STATEMENT NOW.
LITTLE BROOKLYN'S SCREAMING, HIS MUM'S COOING ABOUT HOW HAPPY SHE IS TO HAVE HIM BACK AND CARSWELL'S BABBLING CRAZY BOLLOCKS...
THEN, JUST AS BIG BEN STRIKES MIDNIGHT, THE NAUGHTY NURSE TURNS UP AND INSISTS SHE HAS TO TAKE ME FOR A CHECKUP.
IT'S ALL TOO MUCH FOR PLOD, SO THEY TELL ME TO REPORT TO BOW STREET IN THE MORNING.
MIGHT DO. IF I'M NOT TOO SHAGGED OUT.
WHICH I FUCKING INTEND TO BE.
HAPPY NEW YEAR, EVERYBODY!
HAPPY NEW FUCKING YEAR!
END.

CHRISTMAS CARDS

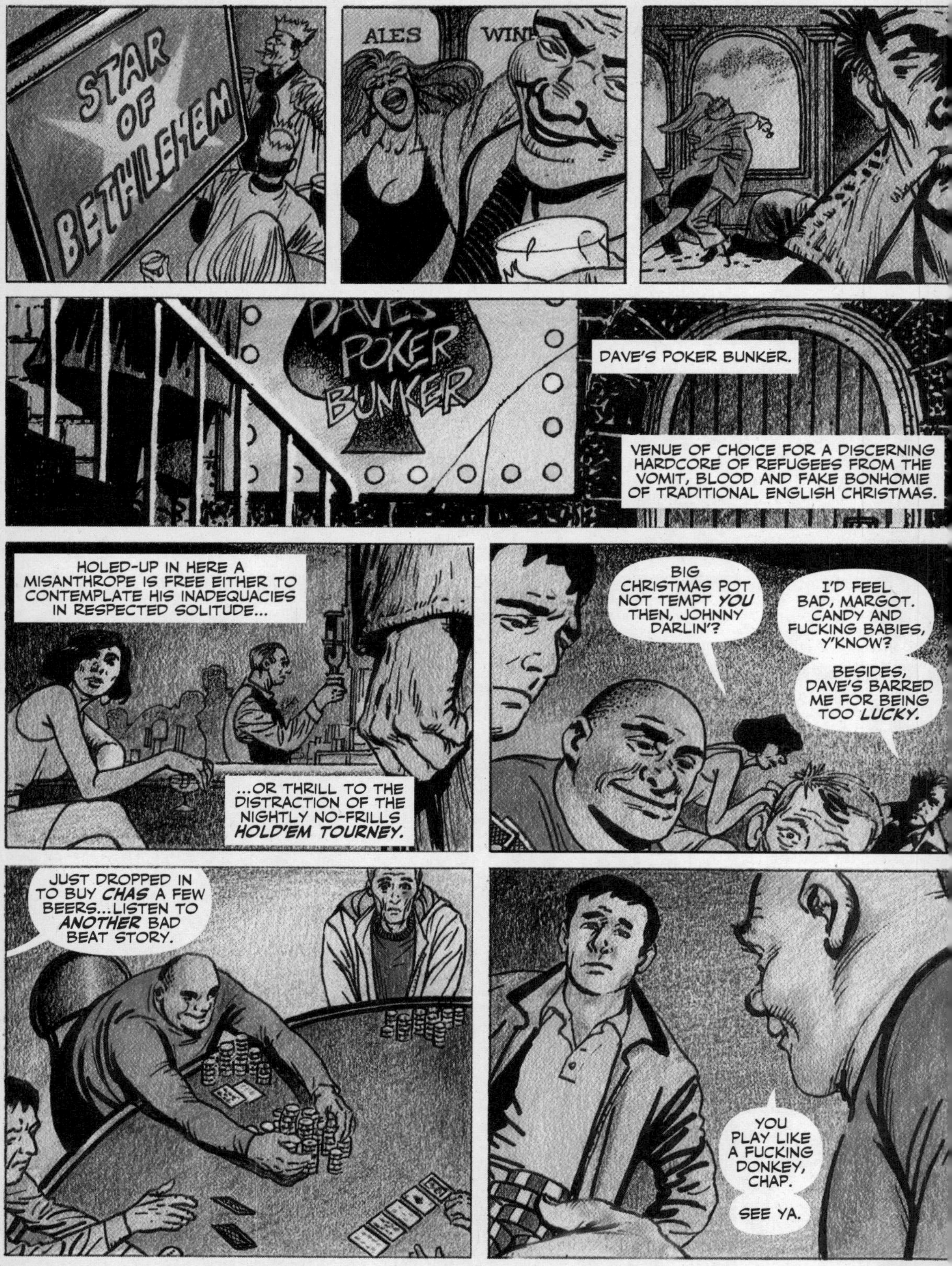
STAR OF BETHLEHEM
ALES
DAVE'S POKER BUNKER
DAVE'S POKER BUNKER.
VENUE OF CHOICE FOR A DISCERNING HARDCORE OF REFUGEES FROM THE VOMIT, BLOOD AND FAKE BONHOMIE OF TRADITIONAL ENGLISH CHRISTMAS.
HOLED-UP IN HERE A MISANTHROPE IS FREE EITHER TO CONTEMPLATE HIS INADEQUACIES IN RESPECTED SOLITUDE...
...OR THRILL TO THE DISTRACTION OF THE NIGHTLY NO-FRILLS *HOLD'EM TOURNEY.*
BIG CHRISTMAS POT NOT TEMPT *YOU* THEN, JOHNNY DARLIN'?
I'D FEEL BAD, MARGOT. CANDY AND FUCKING BABIES, Y'KNOW?
BESIDES, DAVE'S BARRED ME FOR BEING TOO *LUCKY.*
JUST DROPPED IN TO BUY *CHAS* A FEW BEERS...LISTEN TO *ANOTHER* BAD BEAT STORY.
YOU PLAY LIKE A FUCKING DONKEY, CHAP.
SEE YA.

SCRIPT BY JAMIE DELANO - ART BY DAVID LLOYD

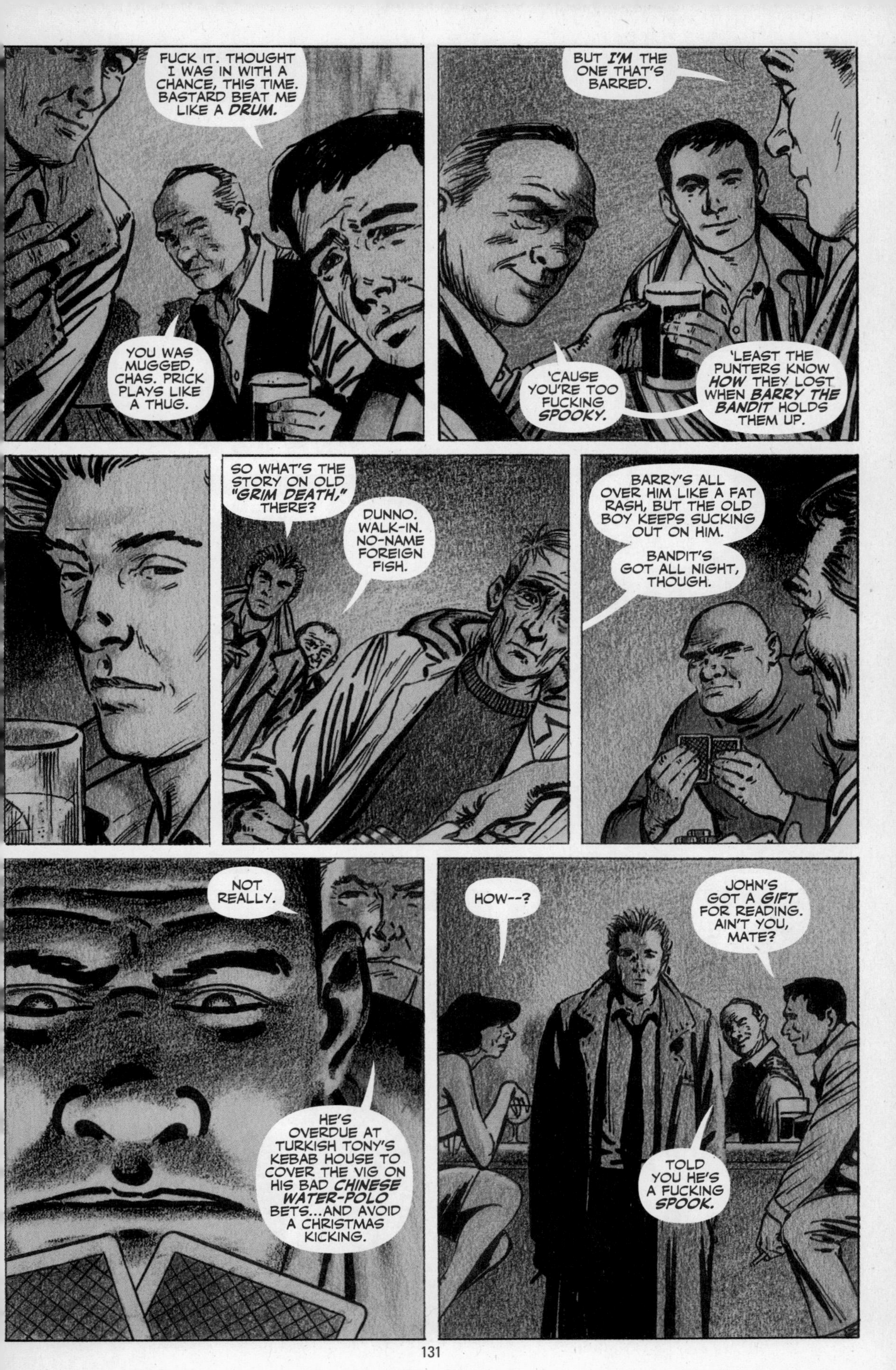
FUCK IT. THOUGHT I WAS IN WITH A CHANCE, THIS TIME. BASTARD BEAT ME LIKE A DRUM.
YOU WAS MUGGED, CHAS. PRICK PLAYS LIKE A THUG.
BUT I'M THE ONE THAT'S BARRED.
'CAUSE YOU'RE TOO FUCKING SPOOKY.
'LEAST THE PUNTERS KNOW HOW THEY LOST WHEN BARRY THE BANDIT HOLDS THEM UP.
SO WHAT'S THE STORY ON OLD "GRIM DEATH," THERE?
DUNNO. WALK-IN. NO-NAME FOREIGN FISH.
BARRY'S ALL OVER HIM LIKE A FAT RASH, BUT THE OLD BOY KEEPS SUCKING OUT ON HIM.
BANDIT'S GOT ALL NIGHT, THOUGH.
NOT REALLY.
HE'S OVERDUE AT TURKISH TONY'S KEBAB HOUSE TO COVER THE VIG ON HIS BAD CHINESE WATER-POLO BETS...AND AVOID A CHRISTMAS KICKING.
HOW--?
JOHN'S GOT A GIFT FOR READING. AIN'T YOU, MATE?
TOLD YOU HE'S A FUCKING SPOOK.

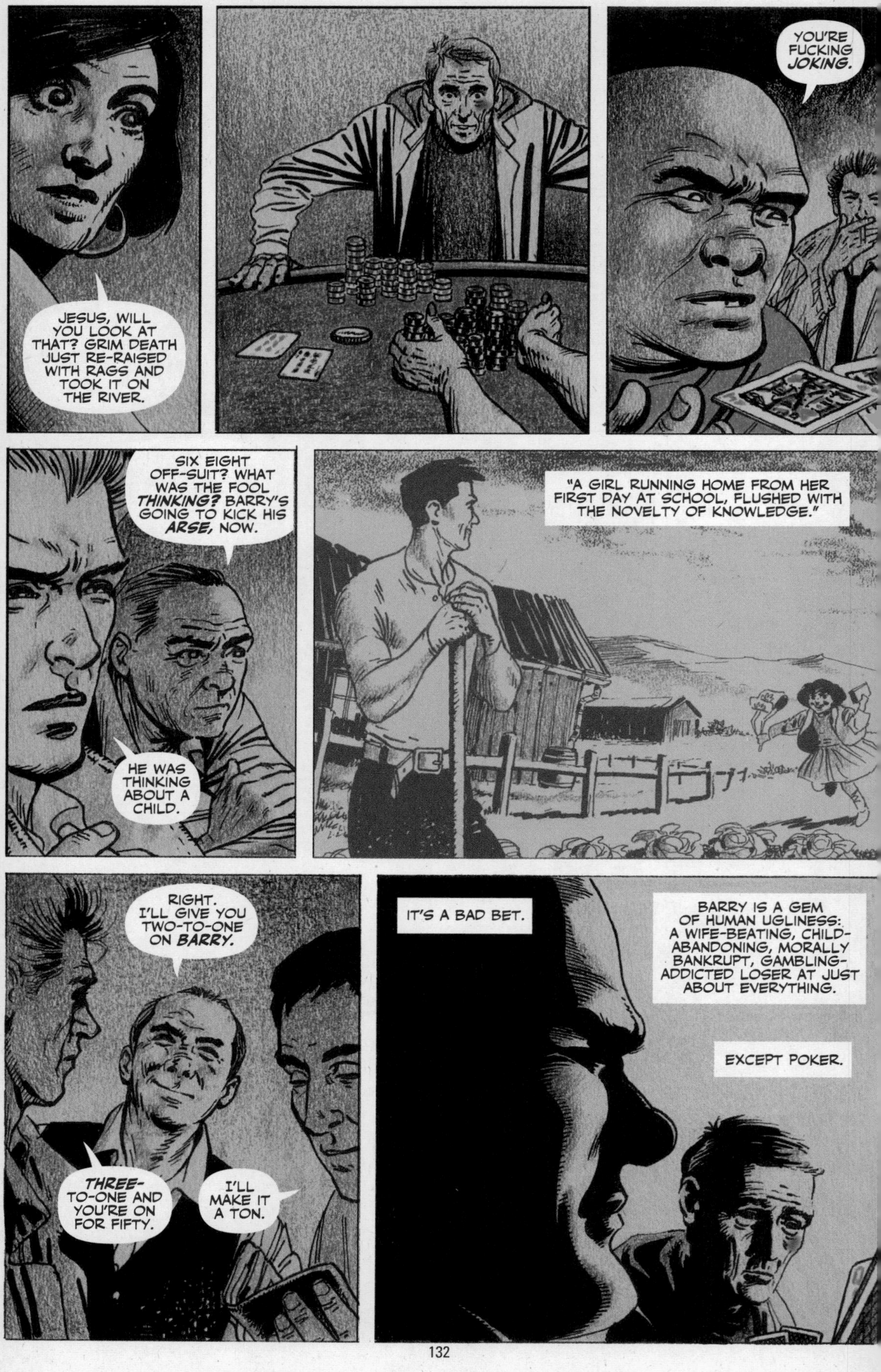
JESUS, WILL YOU LOOK AT THAT? GRIM DEATH JUST RE-RAISED WITH RAGS AND TOOK IT ON THE RIVER.
YOU'RE FUCKING *JOKING.*
SIX EIGHT OFF-SUIT? WHAT WAS THE FOOL *THINKING?* BARRY'S GOING TO KICK HIS *ARSE,* NOW.
HE WAS THINKING ABOUT A CHILD.
"A GIRL RUNNING HOME FROM HER FIRST DAY AT SCHOOL, FLUSHED WITH THE NOVELTY OF KNOWLEDGE."
RIGHT. I'LL GIVE YOU TWO-TO-ONE ON *BARRY.*
THREE- TO-ONE AND YOU'RE ON FOR FIFTY.
I'LL MAKE IT A TON.
IT'S A BAD BET.
BARRY IS A GEM OF HUMAN UGLINESS: A WIFE-BEATING, CHILD-ABANDONING, MORALLY BANKRUPT, GAMBLING-ADDICTED LOSER AT JUST ABOUT EVERYTHING.
EXCEPT POKER.

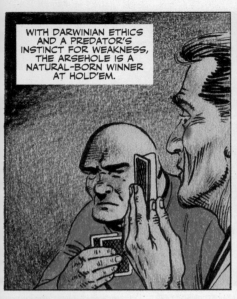

WITH DARWINIAN ETHICS AND A PREDATOR'S INSTINCT FOR WEAKNESS, THE ARSEHOLE IS A NATURAL-BORN WINNER AT HOLD'EM.

LUCKY FOR HIM, BECAUSE STEALING THE HARD-EARNED FROM BAFFLED NO-HOPERS, LIKE CHAS, IS ALL THAT MAINTAINS THE BANDIT'S SELF-RESPECT AND KEEPS THE WOLF FROM HIS DOOR, THESE DAYS.

WANT THIS PRETTY *BAD*, EH? BIG CHANCE TO CHANGE YOUR LIFE?

DREAM ON, FISH. *DUMB LUCK* DON'T LAST FOREVER.

THE FAT MAN'S LIPS FLAP, BUT THE SOUND HAS NO MEANING. THE OLD MAN CLOSES HIS EYES.

AND WATCHES HIS ACHINGLY HOPEFUL ALMOST-WOMAN-CHILD LEAVE HOME, PROUD TO SUPPORT HER FAMILY WITH HONEST WORK ABROAD.

OLD GRIM DEATH CLINGS ON, PLAYING ON A WING AND A PRAYER, HIS MOVES NO MORE THAN RANDOM ACTS OF *FAITH*.

CHRIST. THAT WAS MY LAST FIFTY, JOHN.

LET'S HOPE THE POKER GODS ARE FEELING *SENTIMENTAL*.

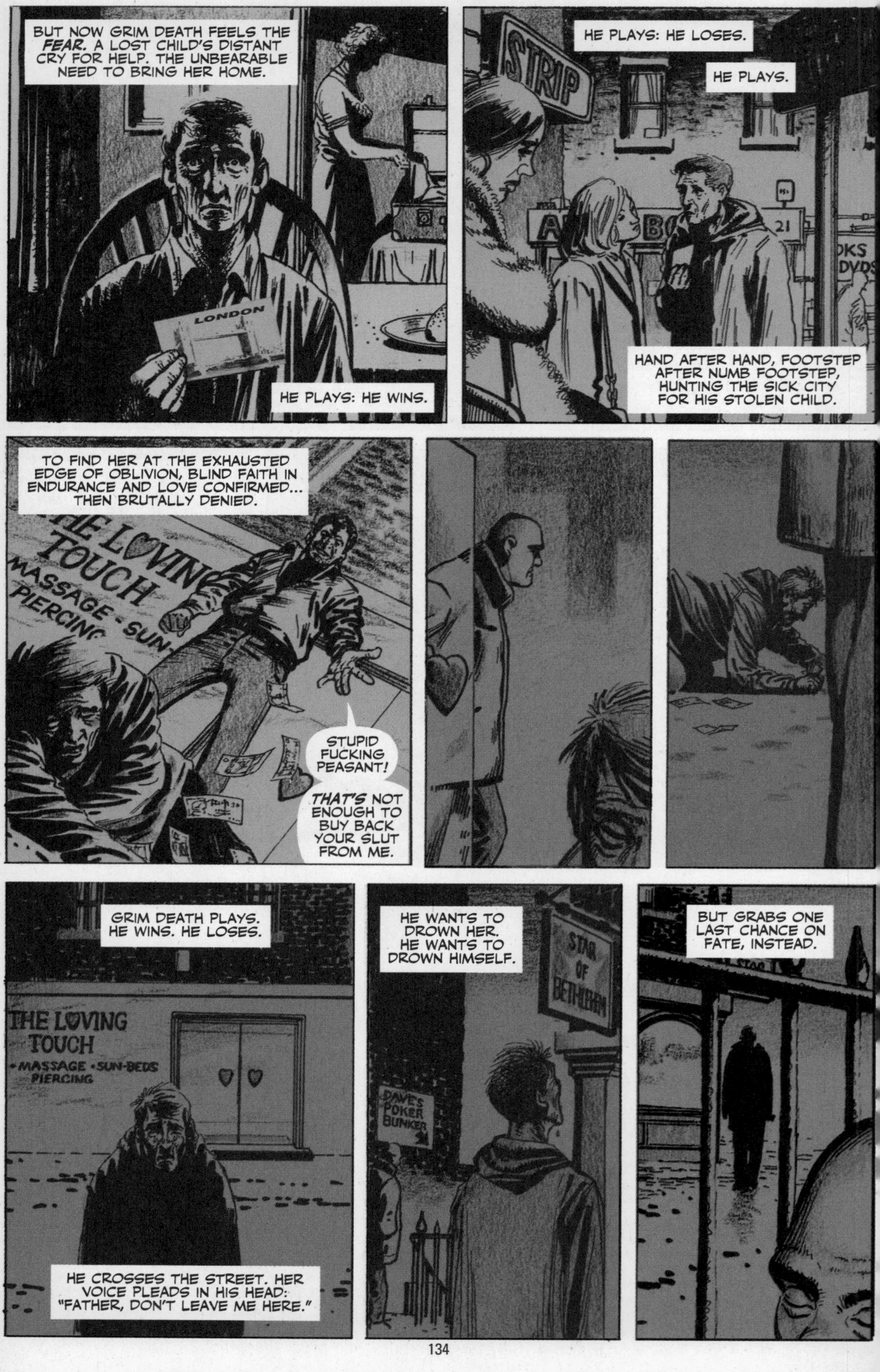
BUT NOW GRIM DEATH FEELS THE *FEAR.* A LOST CHILD'S DISTANT CRY FOR HELP. THE UNBEARABLE NEED TO BRING HER HOME.
LONDON
HE PLAYS: HE WINS.
STRIP
HE PLAYS: HE LOSES.
HE PLAYS.
HAND AFTER HAND, FOOTSTEP AFTER NUMB FOOTSTEP, HUNTING THE SICK CITY FOR HIS STOLEN CHILD.
TO FIND HER AT THE EXHAUSTED EDGE OF OBLIVION, BLIND FAITH IN ENDURANCE AND LOVE CONFIRMED... THEN BRUTALLY DENIED.
STUPID FUCKING PEASANT!
THAT'S NOT ENOUGH TO BUY BACK YOUR SLUT FROM ME.
GRIM DEATH PLAYS. HE WINS. HE LOSES.
THE LOVING TOUCH
•MASSAGE •SUN-BEDS
PIERCING
HE CROSSES THE STREET. HER VOICE PLEADS IN HIS HEAD: "FATHER, DON'T LEAVE ME HERE."
HE WANTS TO DROWN HER. HE WANTS TO DROWN HIMSELF.
STAR OF BETHLEHEM
DAVE'S POKER BUNKER
BUT GRABS ONE LAST CHANCE ON FATE, INSTEAD.

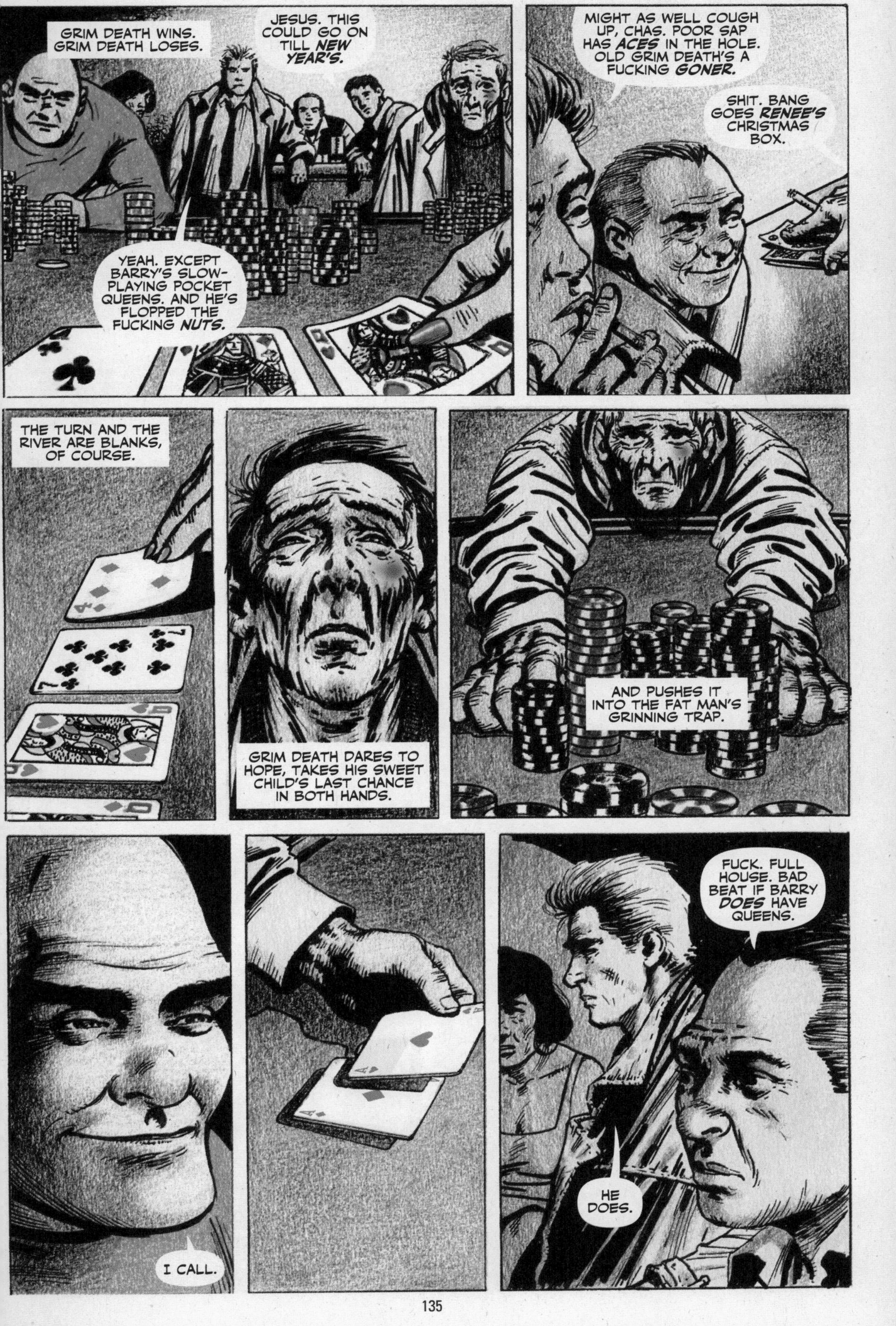
GRIM DEATH WINS. GRIM DEATH LOSES.
JESUS. THIS COULD GO ON TILL NEW YEAR'S.
YEAH. EXCEPT BARRY'S SLOW-PLAYING POCKET QUEENS. AND HE'S FLOPPED THE FUCKING NUTS.
MIGHT AS WELL COUGH UP, CHAS. POOR SAP HAS ACES IN THE HOLE. OLD GRIM DEATH'S A FUCKING GONER.
SHIT. BANG GOES RENEE'S CHRISTMAS BOX.
THE TURN AND THE RIVER ARE BLANKS, OF COURSE.
GRIM DEATH DARES TO HOPE, TAKES HIS SWEET CHILD'S LAST CHANCE IN BOTH HANDS.
AND PUSHES IT INTO THE FAT MAN'S GRINNING TRAP.
I CALL.
FUCK. FULL HOUSE. BAD BEAT IF BARRY DOES HAVE QUEENS.
HE DOES.

THE BANDIT SLIPS A FAT FINGER UNDER THE SKIRTS OF HIS PRETTY LADIES... RELISHES THEIR REVELATION.

BUT DESIRE SHRIVELS, DISSOLVES IN A SUDDEN CHURNING VOID OF SELF-DISGUST.

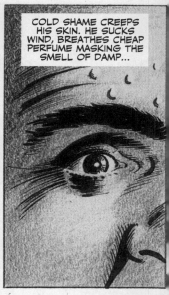

COLD SHAME CREEPS HIS SKIN. HE SUCKS WIND, BREATHES CHEAP PERFUME MASKING THE SMELL OF DAMP...

...AND A GRUBBY MASSAGE-PARLOR PRE-GAME SHAG...LIMP, LIFELESS, DISAPPOINTING.

SHIT. HIS *DAUGHTER* IS PROBABLY OLDER NOW, THAN THIS SULLEN GIRL YEARNING TO SHOWER OFF HIS SWEAT.

FUCKING SCREW-FACED FOREIGN TART. HE *GAVE* HER AN EXTRA TWENTY. WHY SHOULD HE FEEL *GUILTY?*

TIME TO FLIP 'EM OVER, PUT THIS FUCK OUT OF HIS MISERY AND CLAIM A PAIN-FREE CHRISTMAS.

SO *WHY* HAS HE JUST TOSSED SWEET VICTORY INTO THE *MUCK?*

OKAY. YOU GOT ME.

AND PUT HIMSELF IN FUCKING *TRACTION?*

136

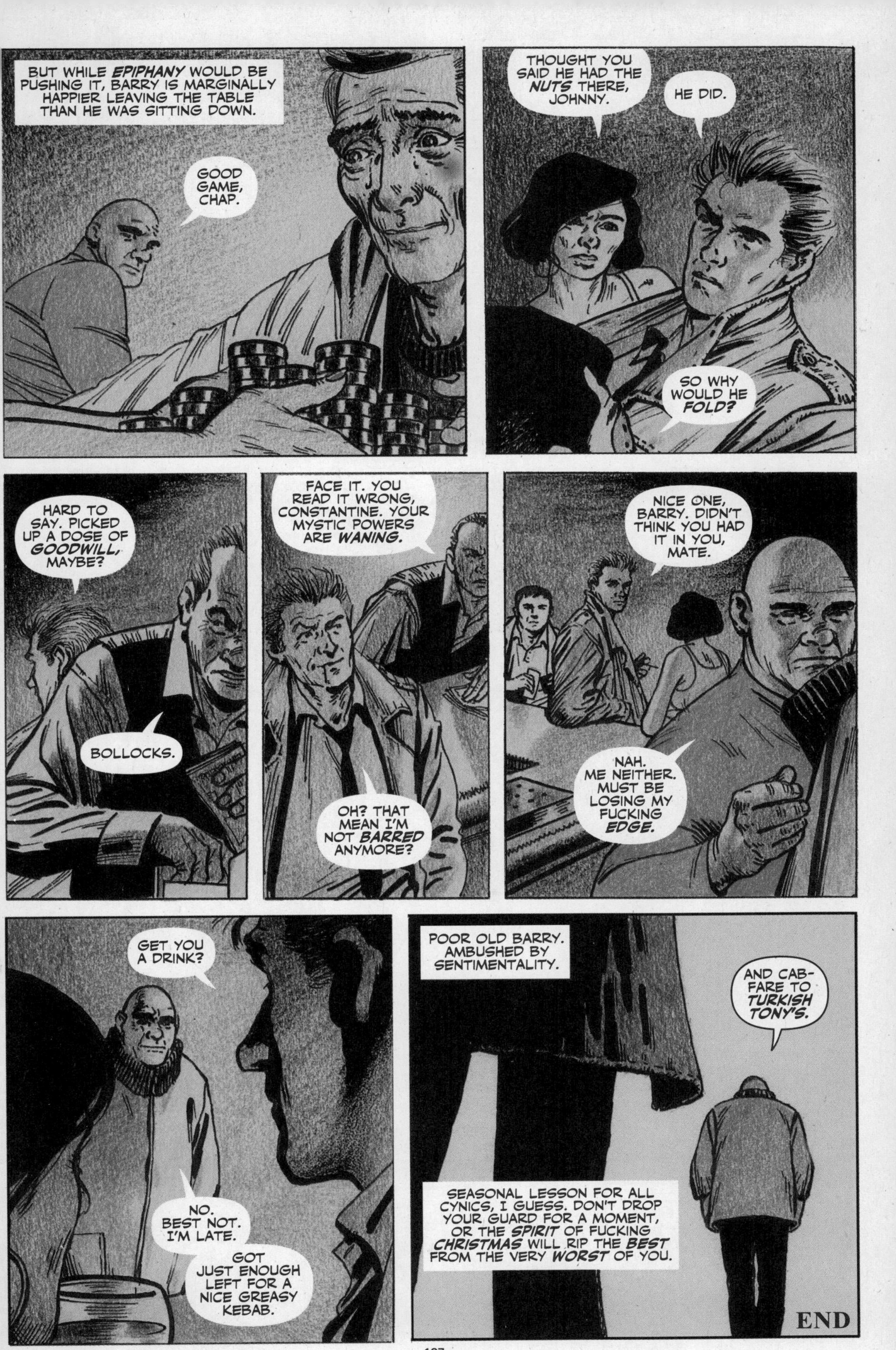
BUT WHILE EPIPHANY WOULD BE PUSHING IT, BARRY IS MARGINALLY HAPPIER LEAVING THE TABLE THAN HE WAS SITTING DOWN.
GOOD GAME, CHAP.
THOUGHT YOU SAID HE HAD THE NUTS THERE, JOHNNY.
HE DID.
SO WHY WOULD HE FOLD?
HARD TO SAY. PICKED UP A DOSE OF GOODWILL, MAYBE?
BOLLOCKS.
FACE IT. YOU READ IT WRONG, CONSTANTINE. YOUR MYSTIC POWERS ARE WANING.
OH? THAT MEAN I'M NOT BARRED ANYMORE?
NICE ONE, BARRY. DIDN'T THINK YOU HAD IT IN YOU, MATE.
NAH. ME NEITHER. MUST BE LOSING MY FUCKING EDGE.
GET YOU A DRINK?
NO. BEST NOT. I'M LATE.
GOT JUST ENOUGH LEFT FOR A NICE GREASY KEBAB.
POOR OLD BARRY. AMBUSHED BY SENTIMENTALITY.
AND CAB-FARE TO TURKISH TONY'S.
SEASONAL LESSON FOR ALL CYNICS, I GUESS. DON'T DROP YOUR GUARD FOR A MOMENT, OR THE SPIRIT OF FUCKING CHRISTMAS WILL RIP THE BEST FROM THE VERY WORST OF YOU.
END

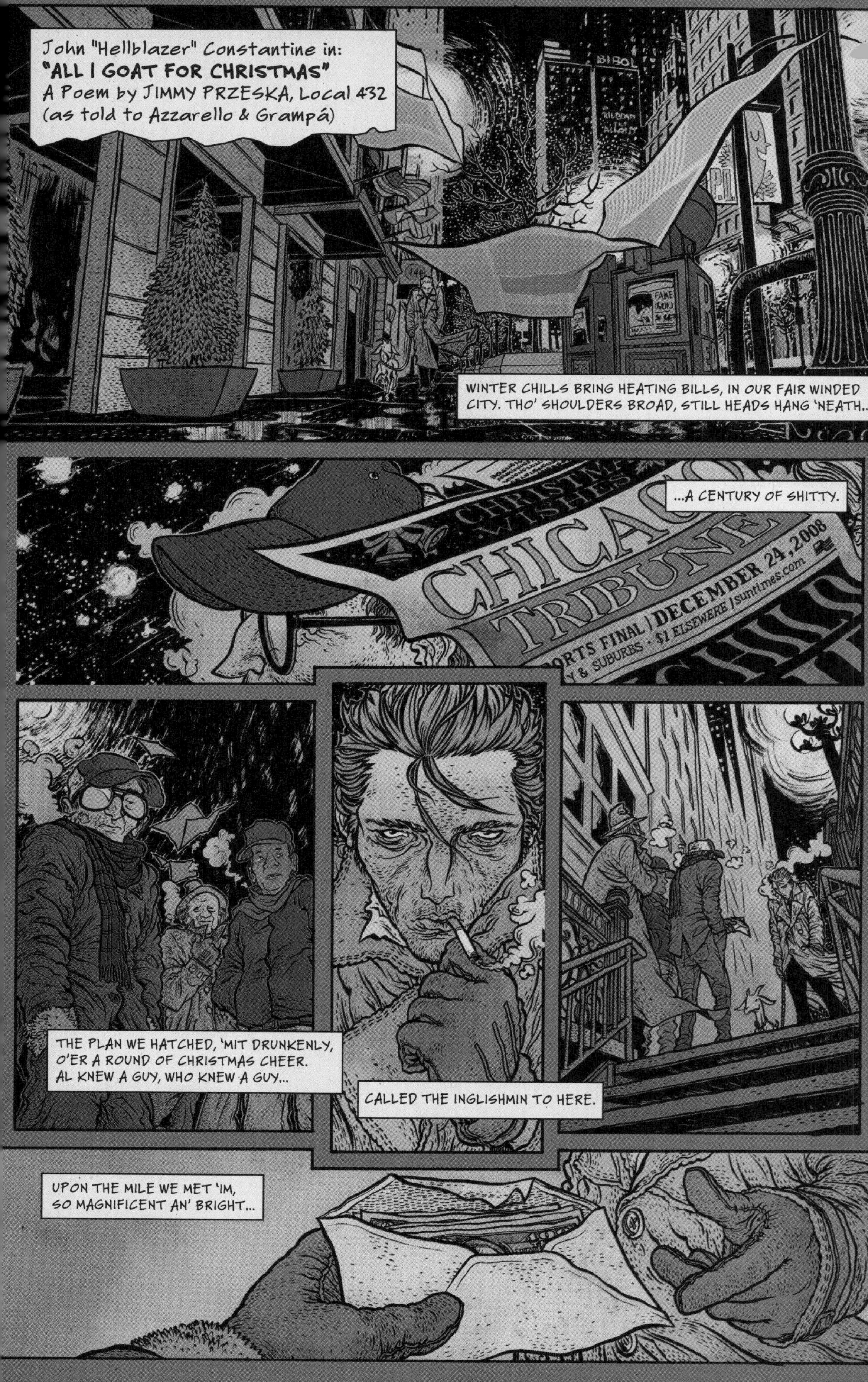

John "Hellblazer" Constantine in:
"ALL I GOAT FOR CHRISTMAS"
A Poem by JIMMY PRZESKA, Local 432
(as told to Azzarello & Grampá)
WINTER CHILLS BRING HEATING BILLS, IN OUR FAIR WINDED CITY. THO' SHOULDERS BROAD, STILL HEADS HANG 'NEATH...
...A CENTURY OF SHITTY.
CHICAGO TRIBUNE
SPORTS FINAL | DECEMBER 24, 2008
CITY & SUBURBS · $1 ELSEWERE | suntimes.com
THE PLAN WE HATCHED, 'MIT DRUNKENLY, O'ER A ROUND OF CHRISTMAS CHEER. AL KNEW A GUY, WHO KNEW A GUY...
CALLED THE INGLISHMIN TO HERE.
UPON THE MILE WE MET 'IM, SO MAGNIFICENT AN' BRIGHT...

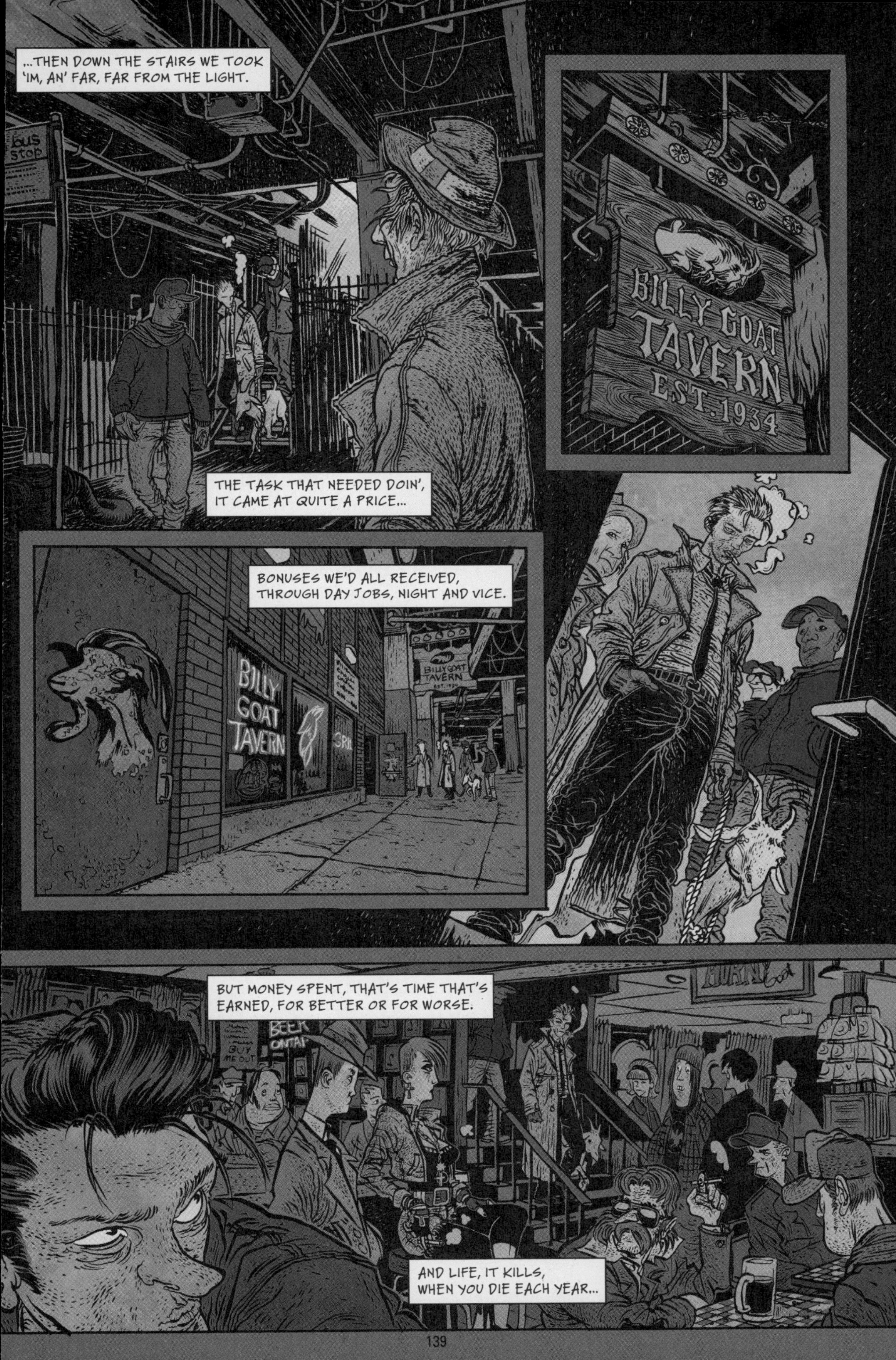
...THEN DOWN THE STAIRS WE TOOK 'IM, AN' FAR, FAR FROM THE LIGHT.
BUS STOP
BILLY GOAT TAVERN EST. 1934
THE TASK THAT NEEDED DOIN', IT CAME AT QUITE A PRICE...
BONUSES WE'D ALL RECEIVED, THROUGH DAY JOBS, NIGHT AND VICE.
BILLY GOAT TAVERN
BILLY GOAT TAVERN
BUT MONEY SPENT, THAT'S TIME THAT'S EARNED, FOR BETTER OR FOR WORSE.
BEER
BUY ME OUT
AND LIFE, IT KILLS, WHEN YOU DIE EACH YEAR...

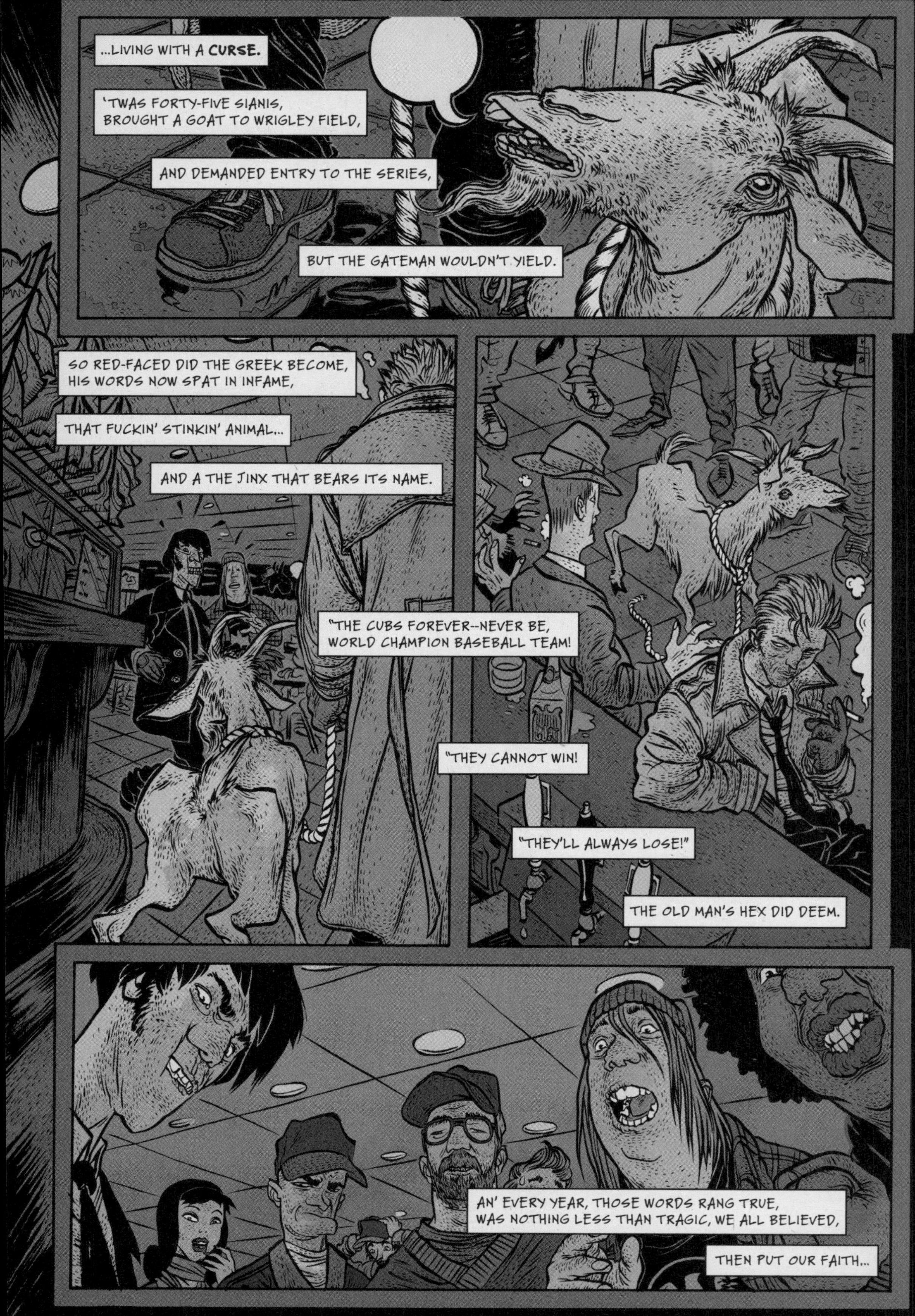

...LIVING WITH A CURSE.
'TWAS FORTY-FIVE SIANIS, BROUGHT A GOAT TO WRIGLEY FIELD,
AND DEMANDED ENTRY TO THE SERIES,
BUT THE GATEMAN WOULDN'T YIELD.
SO RED-FACED DID THE GREEK BECOME, HIS WORDS NOW SPAT IN INFAME,
THAT FUCKIN' STINKIN' ANIMAL...
AND A THE JINX THAT BEARS ITS NAME.
"THE CUBS FOREVER--NEVER BE, WORLD CHAMPION BASEBALL TEAM!
"THEY CANNOT WIN!
"THEY'LL ALWAYS LOSE!"
THE OLD MAN'S HEX DID DEEM.
AN' EVERY YEAR, THOSE WORDS RANG TRUE, WAS NOTHING LESS THAN TRAGIC, WE ALL BELIEVED,
THEN PUT OUR FAITH...

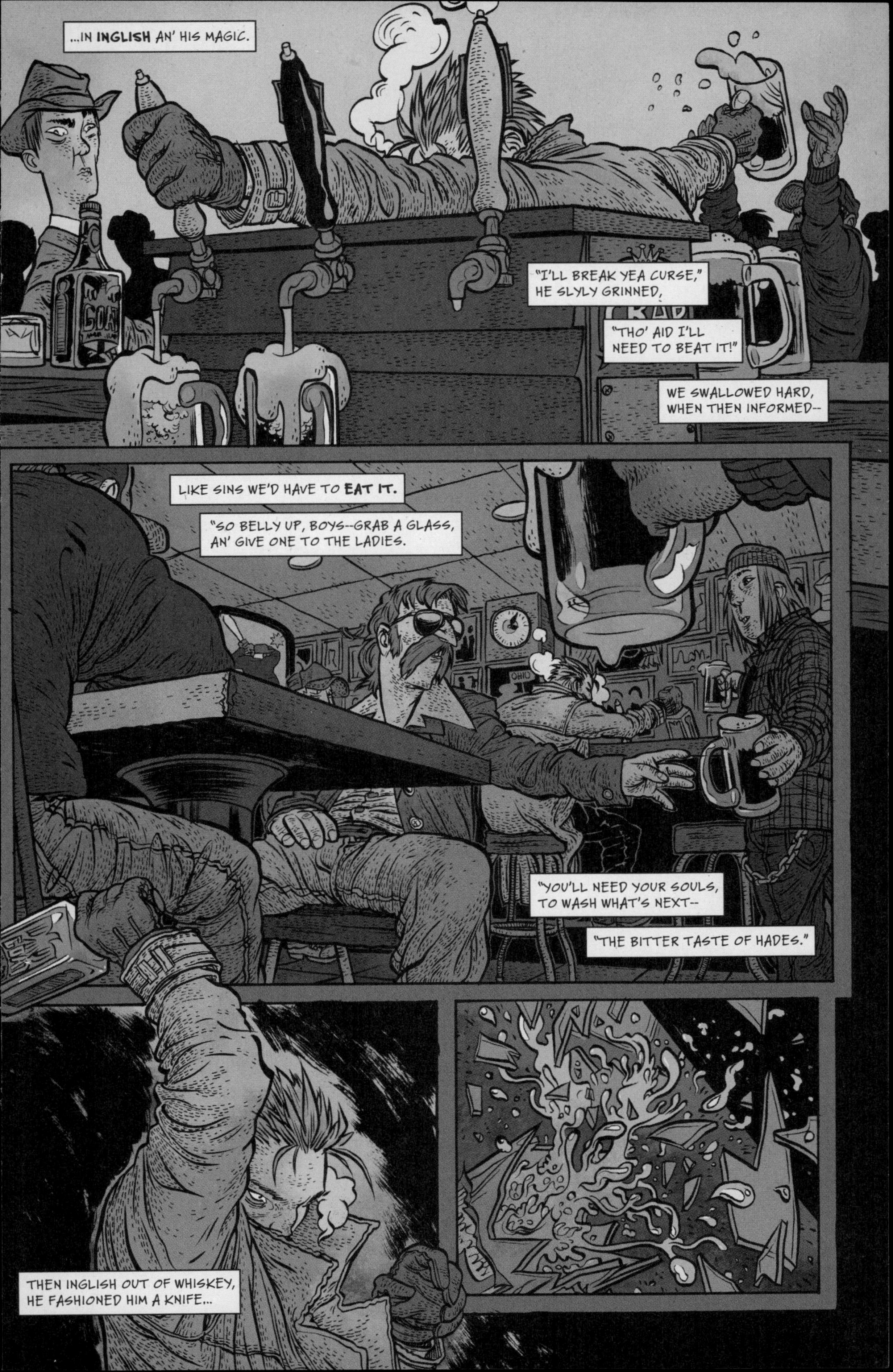
...IN INGLISH AN' HIS MAGIC.
"I'LL BREAK YEA CURSE," HE SLYLY GRINNED,
"THO' AID I'LL NEED TO BEAT IT!"
WE SWALLOWED HARD, WHEN THEN INFORMED--
LIKE SINS WE'D HAVE TO EAT IT.
"SO BELLY UP, BOYS--GRAB A GLASS, AN' GIVE ONE TO THE LADIES.
"YOU'LL NEED YOUR SOULS, TO WASH WHAT'S NEXT--
"THE BITTER TASTE OF HADES."
THEN INGLISH OUT OF WHISKEY, HE FASHIONED HIM A KNIFE...

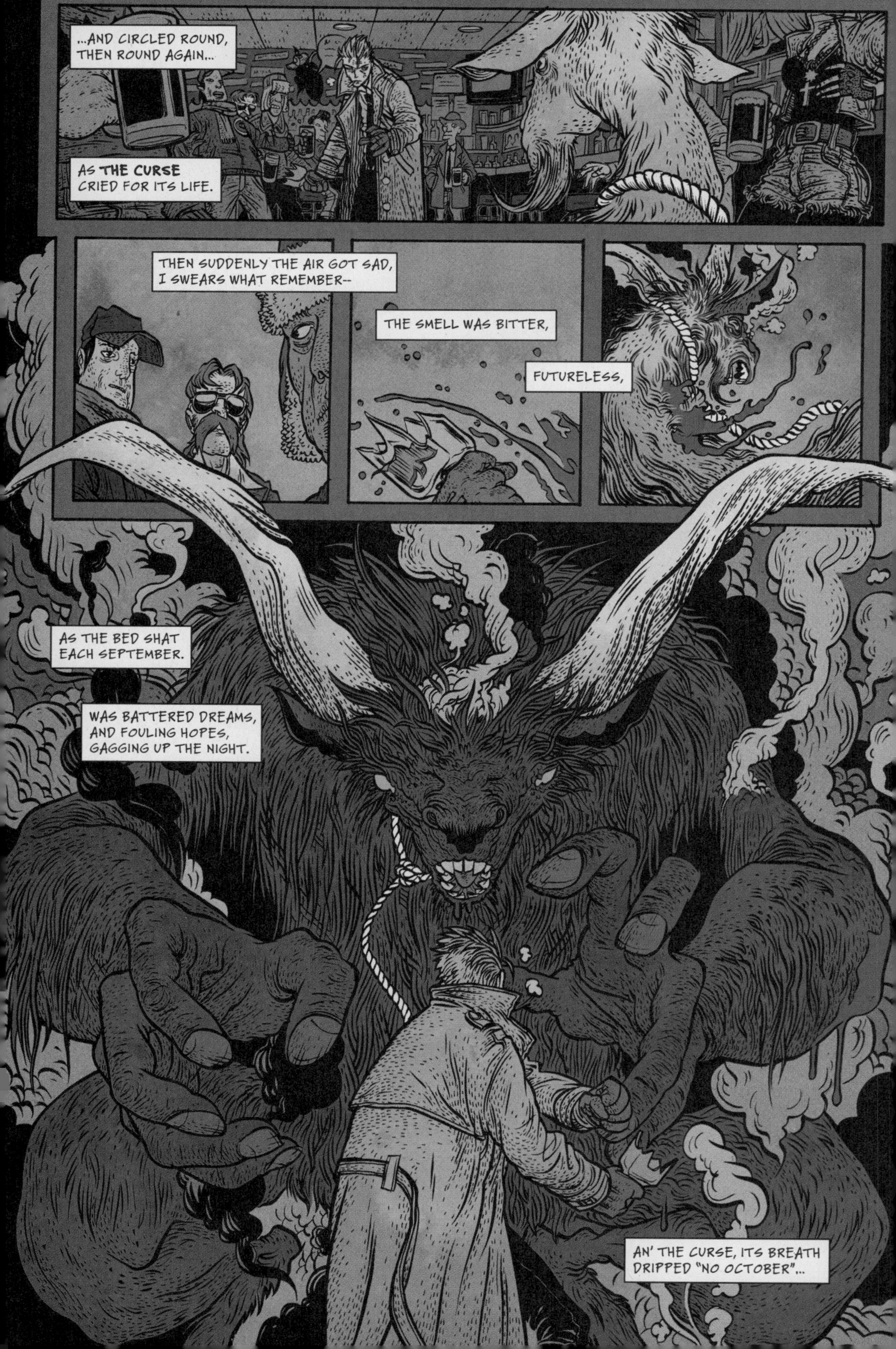
...AND CIRCLED ROUND, THEN ROUND AGAIN...
AS THE CURSE CRIED FOR ITS LIFE.
THEN SUDDENLY THE AIR GOT SAD, I SWEARS WHAT REMEMBER--
THE SMELL WAS BITTER,
FUTURELESS,
AS THE BED SHAT EACH SEPTEMBER.
WAS BATTERED DREAMS, AND FOULING HOPES, GAGGING UP THE NIGHT.
AN' THE CURSE, ITS BREATH DRIPPED "NO OCTOBER"...

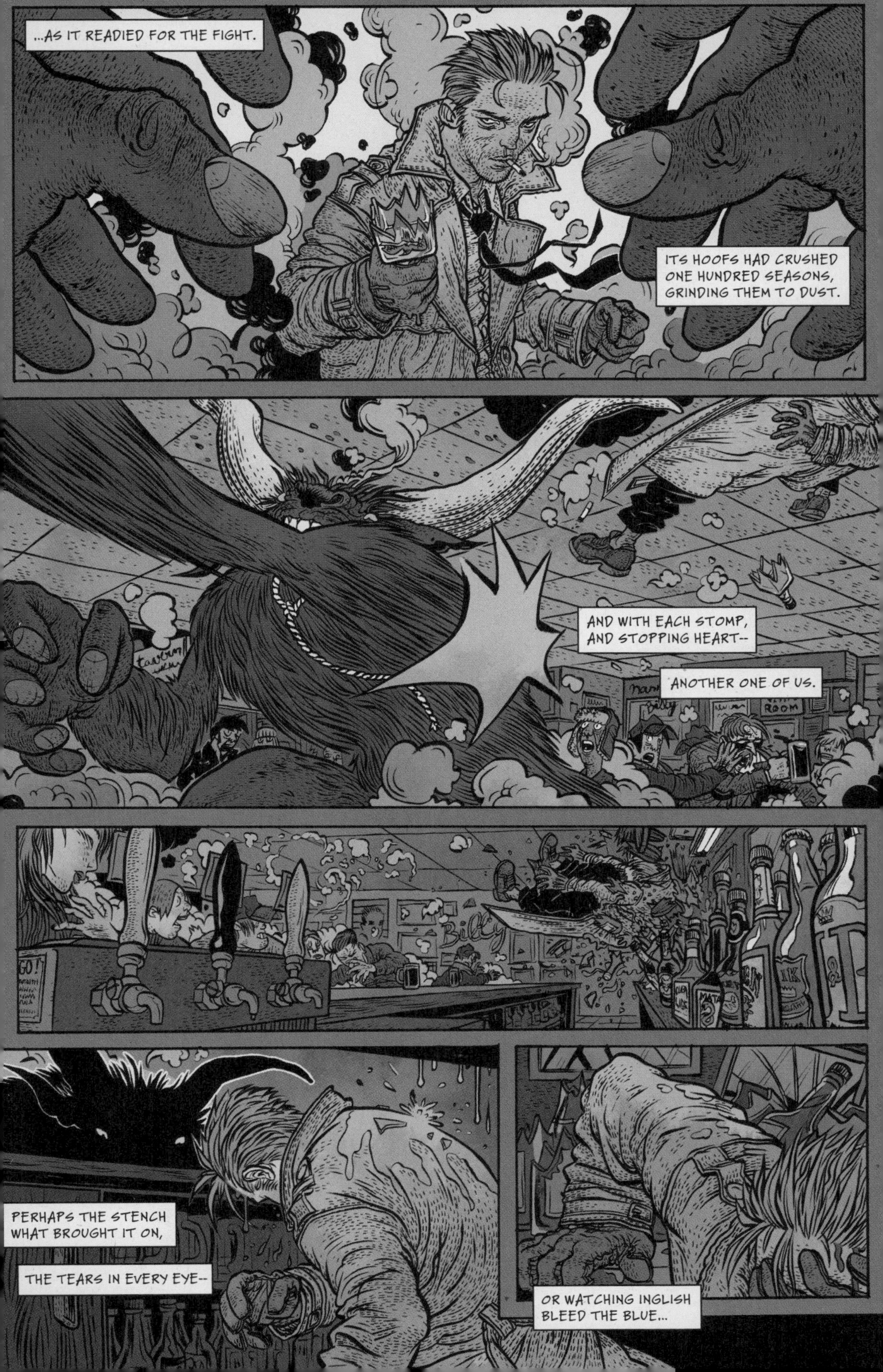
...AS IT READIED FOR THE FIGHT.
ITS HOOFS HAD CRUSHED ONE HUNDRED SEASONS, GRINDING THEM TO DUST.
AND WITH EACH STOMP, AND STOPPING HEART--
ANOTHER ONE OF US.
PERHAPS THE STENCH WHAT BROUGHT IT ON,
THE TEARS IN EVERY EYE--
OR WATCHING INGLISH BLEED THE BLUE...

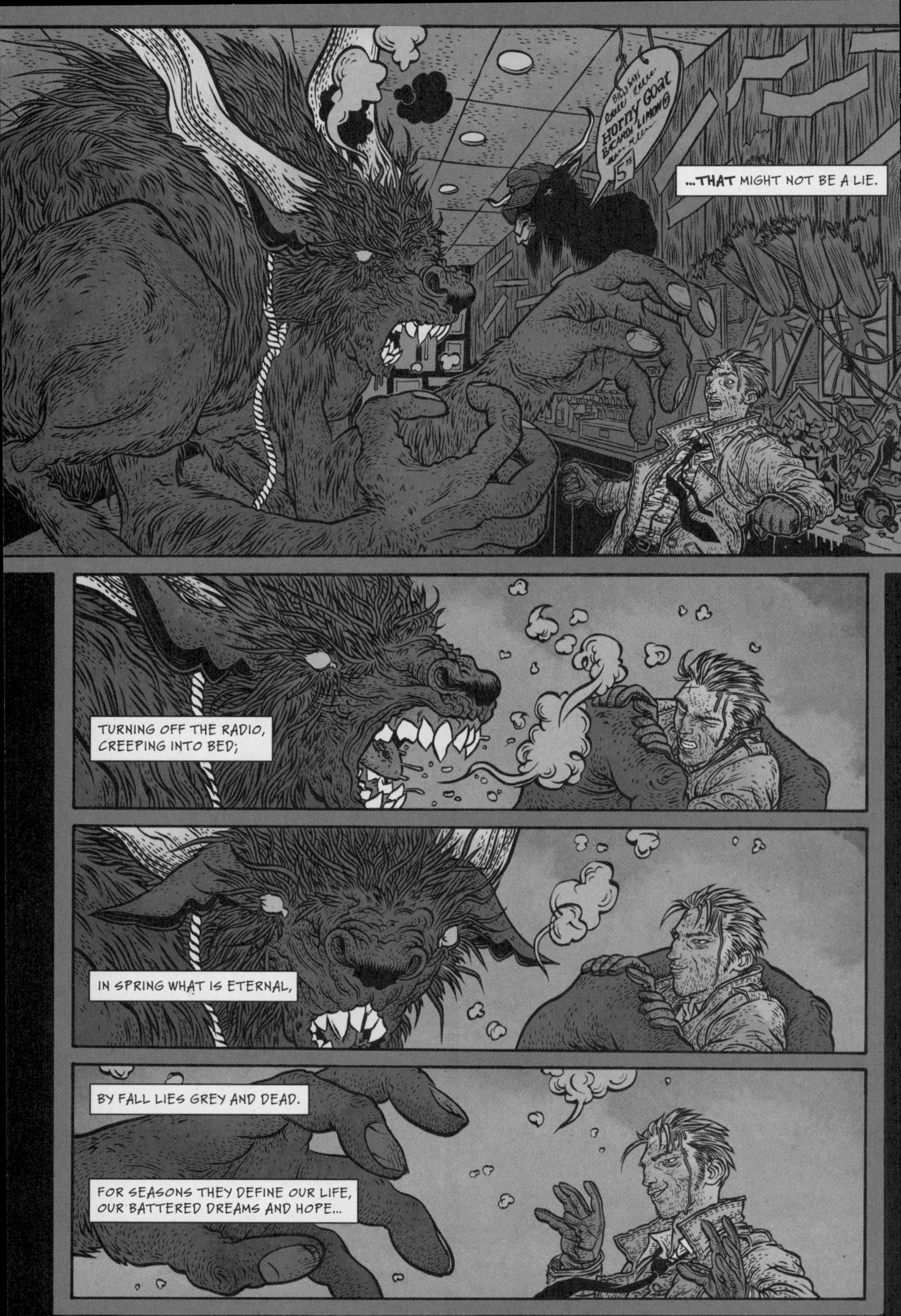

Horny Goat
BACARDI LIMON
...THAT MIGHT NOT BE A LIE.
TURNING OFF THE RADIO,
CREEPING INTO BED;
IN SPRING WHAT IS ETERNAL,
BY FALL LIES GREY AND DEAD.
FOR SEASONS THEY DEFINE OUR LIFE,
OUR BATTERED DREAMS AND HOPE...

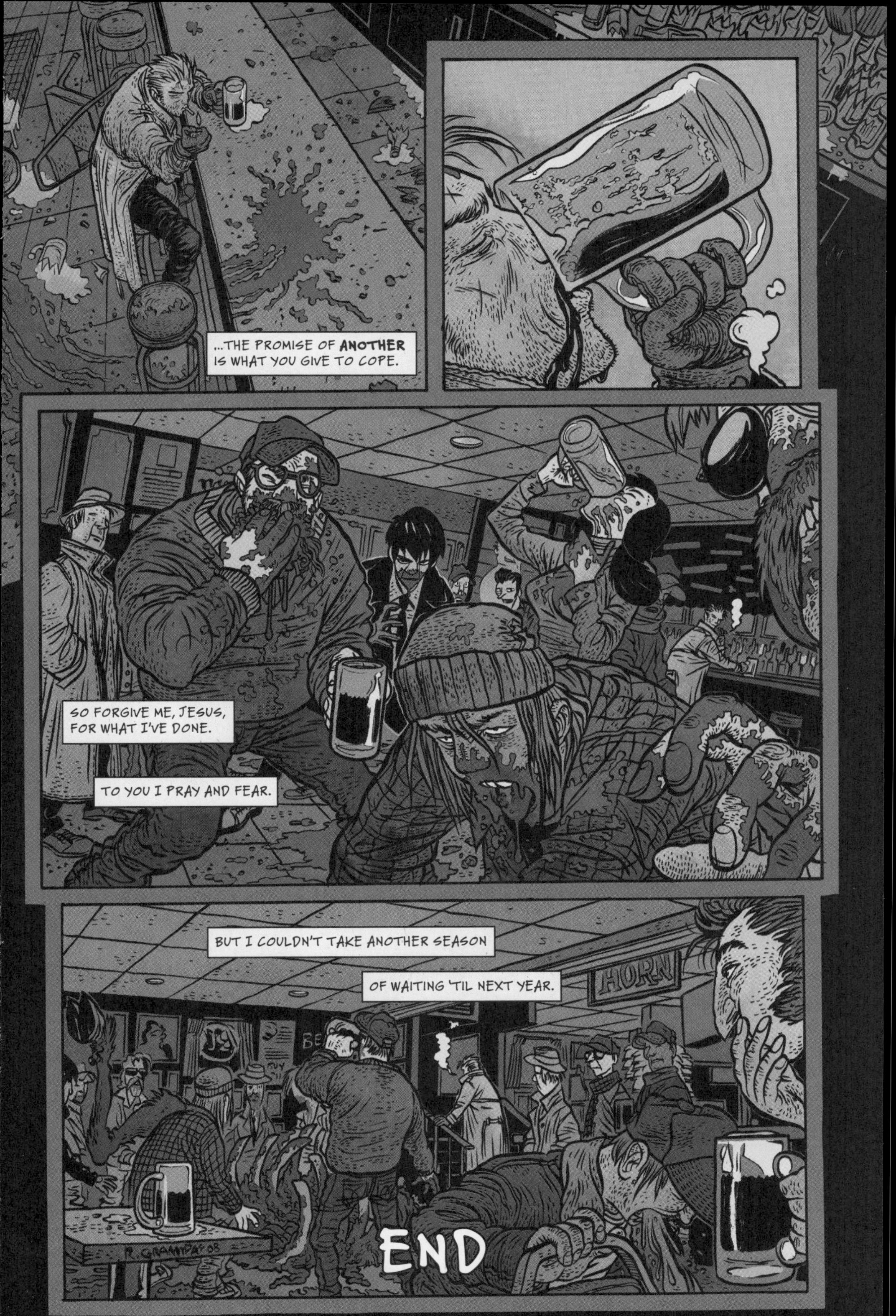
...THE PROMISE OF **ANOTHER** IS WHAT YOU GIVE TO COPE.
SO FORGIVE ME, JESUS, FOR WHAT I'VE DONE.
TO YOU I PRAY AND FEAR.
BUT I COULDN'T TAKE ANOTHER SEASON
OF WAITING 'TIL NEXT YEAR.
HORN
END

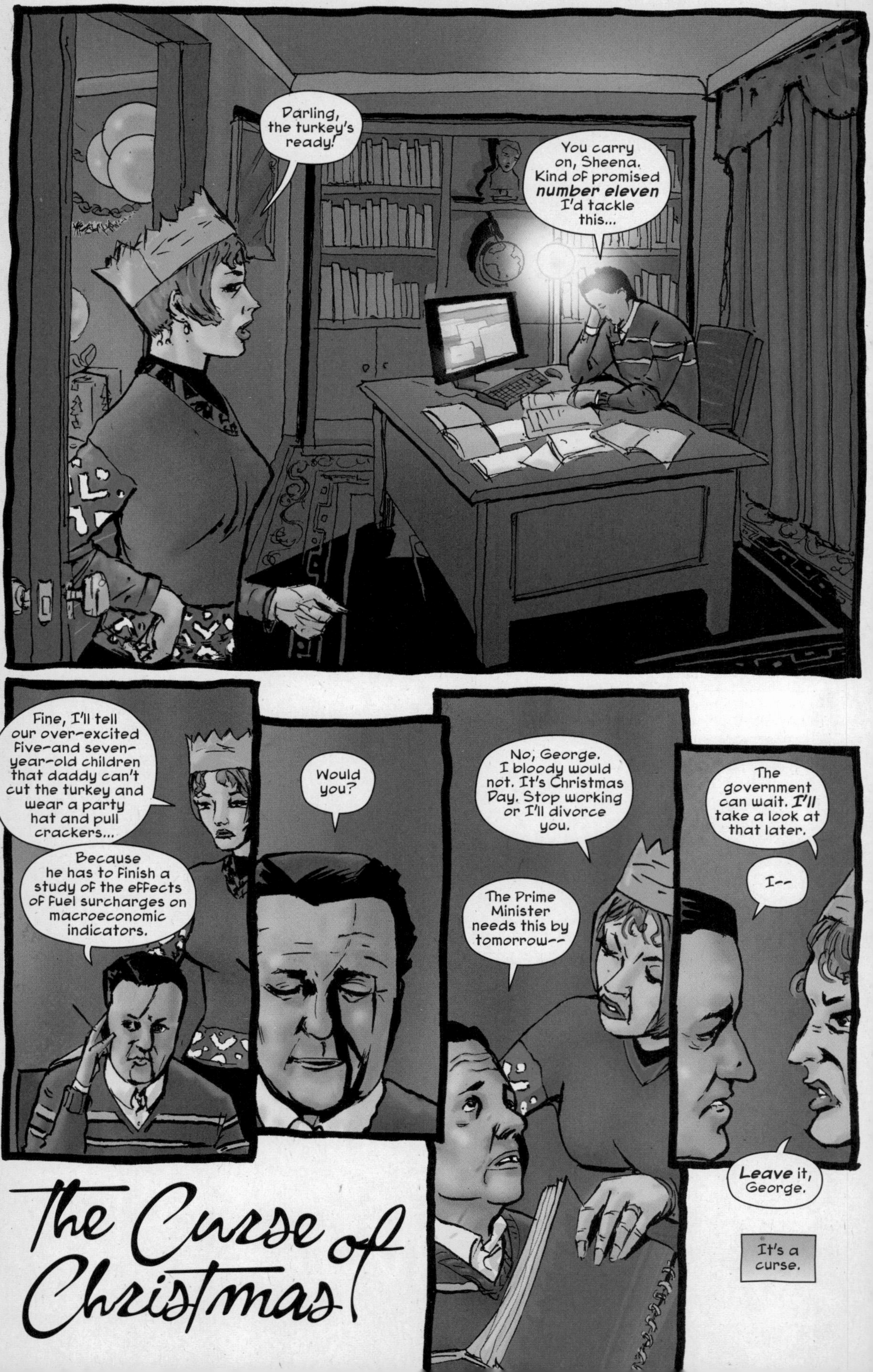
Darling, the turkey's ready!
You carry on, Sheena. Kind of promised **number eleven** I'd tackle this...
Fine, I'll tell our over-excited five-and seven-year-old children that daddy can't cut the turkey and wear a party hat and pull crackers...
Because he has to finish a study of the effects of fuel surcharges on macroeconomic indicators.
Would you?
No, George. I bloody would not. It's Christmas Day. Stop working or I'll divorce you.
The Prime Minister needs this by tomorrow--
The government can wait. *I'll* take a look at that later.
I--
Leave it, George.
The Curse of Christmas
It's a curse.

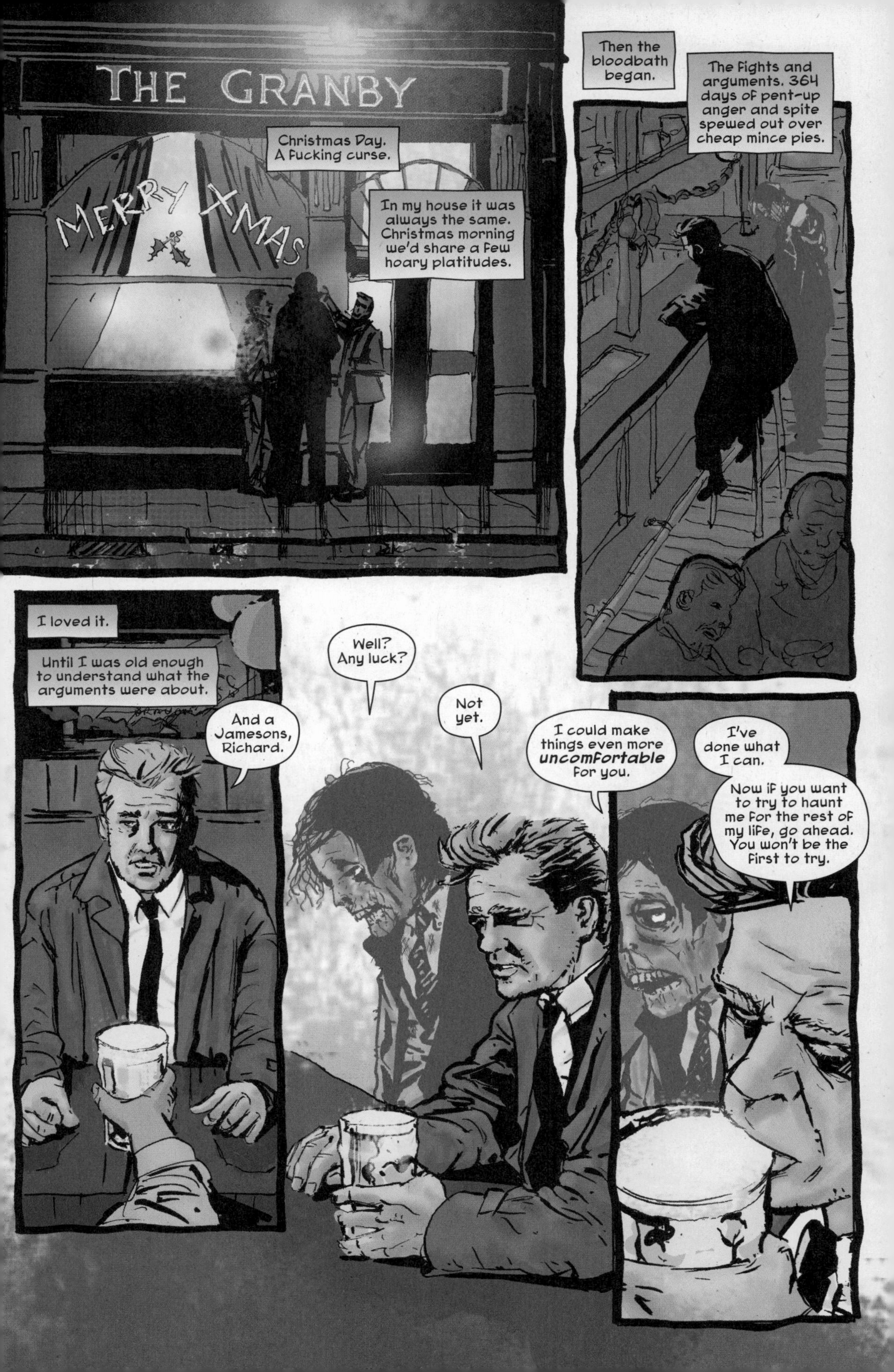
THE GRANBY
Christmas Day. A fucking curse.
MERRY XMAS
In my house it was always the same. Christmas morning we'd share a few hoary platitudes.
Then the bloodbath began.
The fights and arguments. 364 days of pent-up anger and spite spewed out over cheap mince pies.
I loved it.
Until I was old enough to understand what the arguments were about.
And a Jamesons, Richard.
Well? Any luck?
Not yet.
I could make things even more *uncomfortable* for you.
I've done what I can.
Now if you want to try to haunt me for the rest of my life, go ahead. You won't be the first to try.

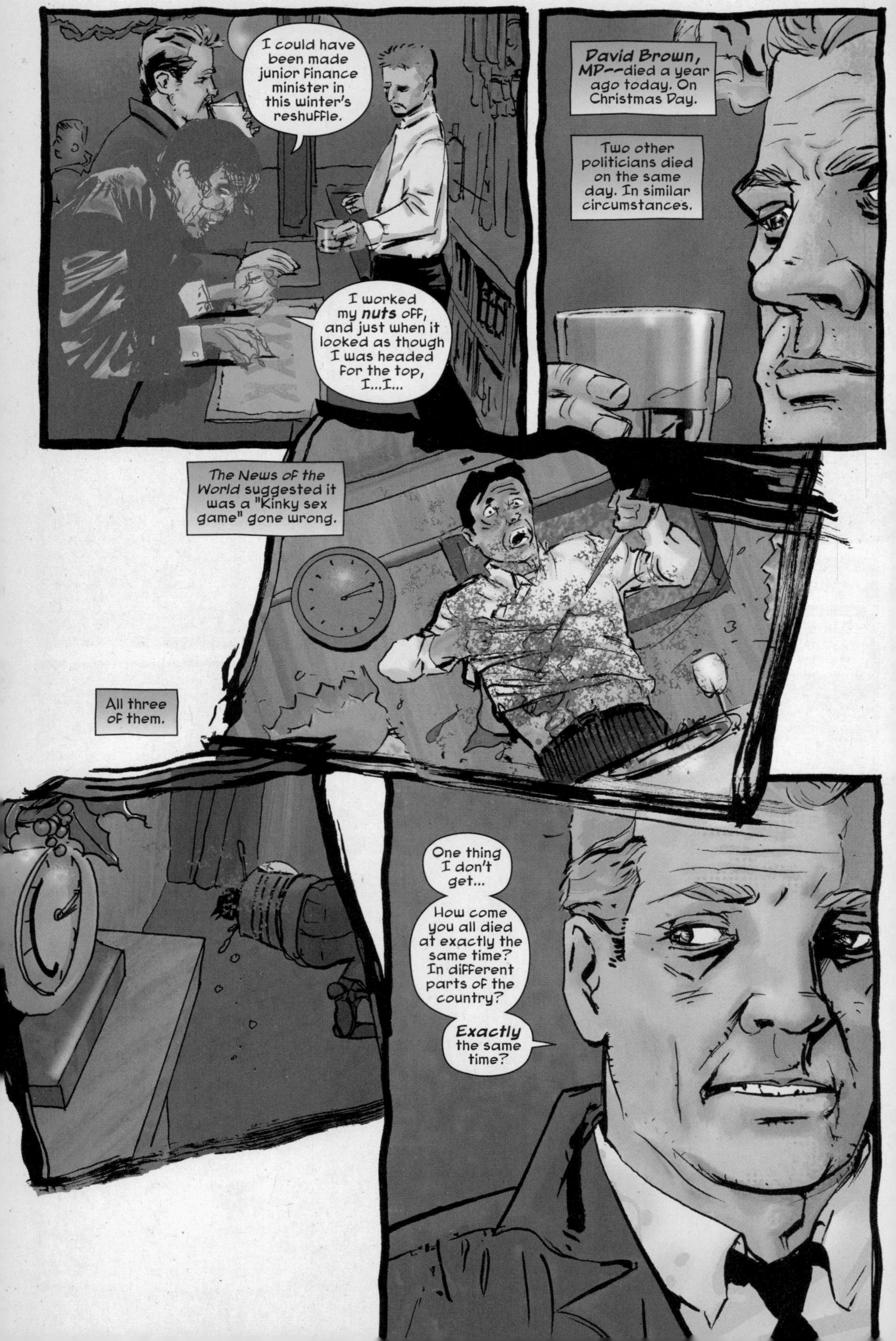
I could have been made junior finance minister in this winter's reshuffle.
I worked my *nuts* off, and just when it looked as though I was headed for the top, I...I...
David Brown, *MP*--died a year ago today. On Christmas Day.
Two other politicians died on the same day. In similar circumstances.
The News of the World suggested it was a "Kinky sex game" gone wrong.
All three of them.
One thing I don't get...
How come you all died at exactly the same time? In different parts of the country?
Exactly the same time?

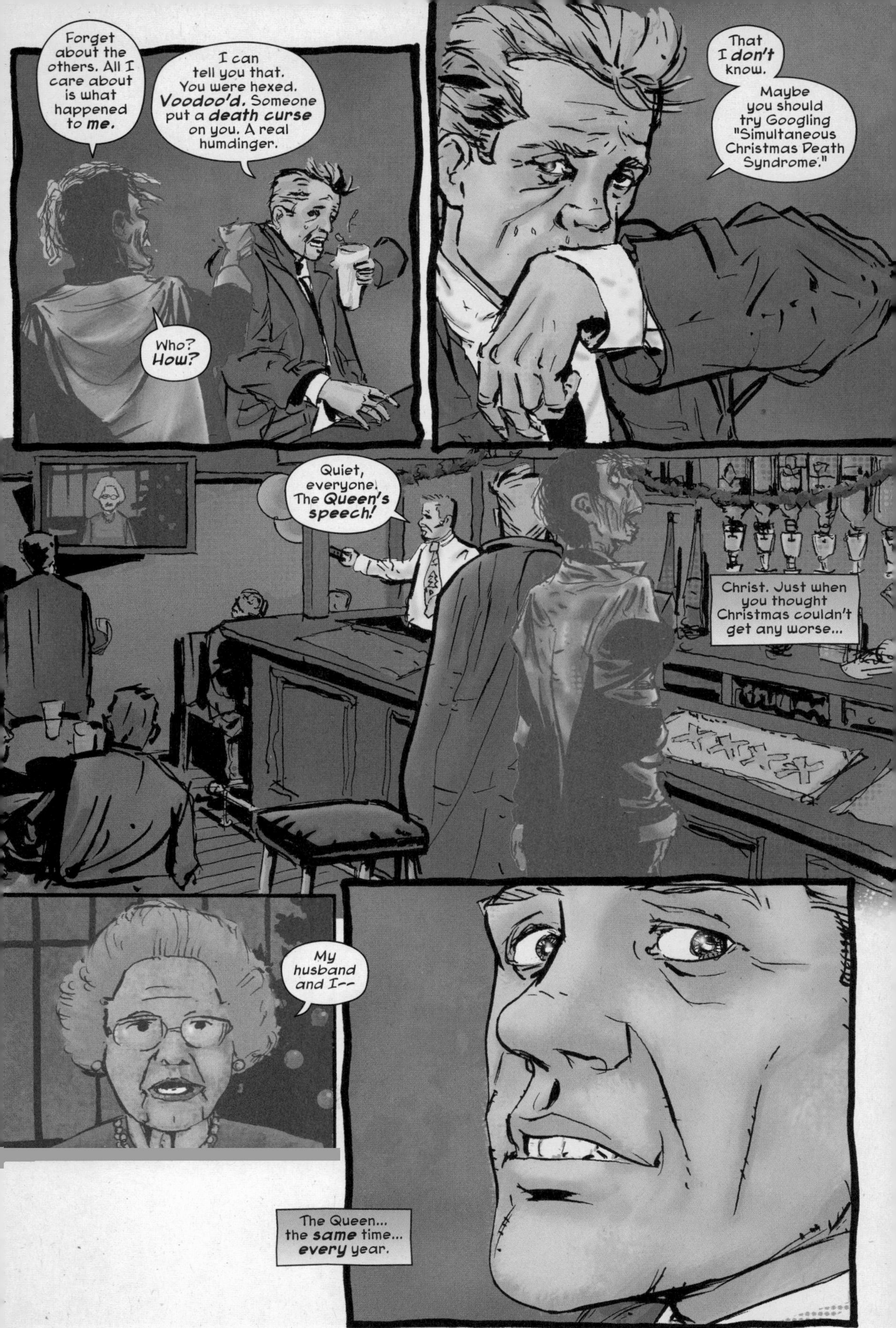

Forget about the others. All I care about is what happened to *me*.
I can tell you that. You were hexed. *Voodoo'd.* Someone put a *death curse* on you. A real humdinger.
Who? *How?*
That I *don't* know.
Maybe you should try Googling "Simultaneous Christmas Death Syndrome."
Quiet, everyone! The *Queen's speech!*
Christ. Just when you thought Christmas couldn't get any worse...
My husband and I--
The Queen... the *same* time... *every* year.

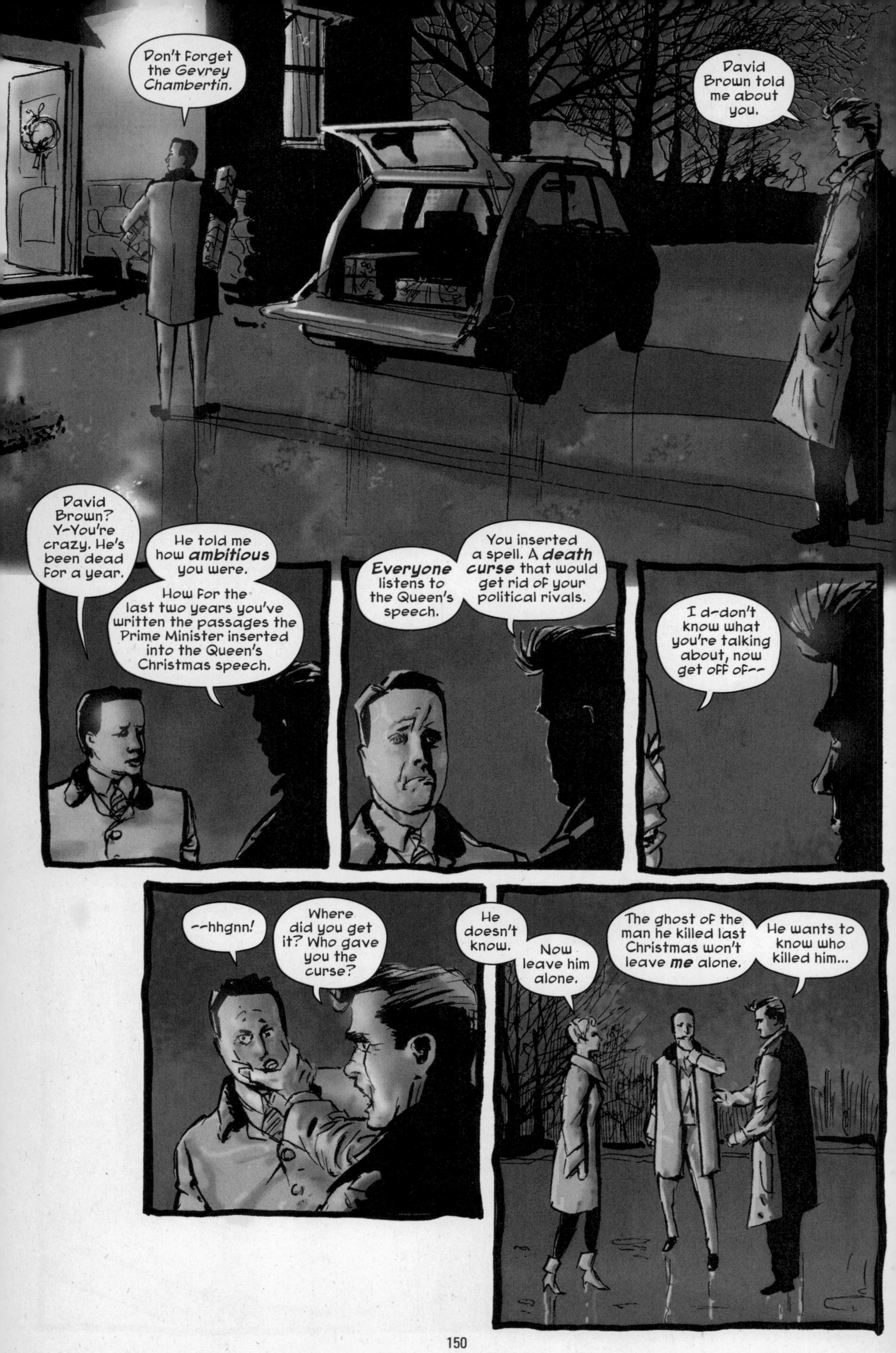

Don't forget the Gevrey Chambertin.
David Brown told me about you.
David Brown? Y-You're crazy. He's been dead for a year.
He told me how **ambitious** you were.
How for the last two years you've written the passages the Prime Minister inserted into the Queen's Christmas speech.
Everyone listens to the Queen's speech.
You inserted a spell. A **death curse** that would get rid of your political rivals.
I d-don't know what you're talking about, now get off of--
--hhgnn!
Where did you get it? Who gave you the curse?
He doesn't know.
Now leave him alone.
The ghost of the man he killed last Christmas won't leave **me** alone.
He wants to know who killed him...

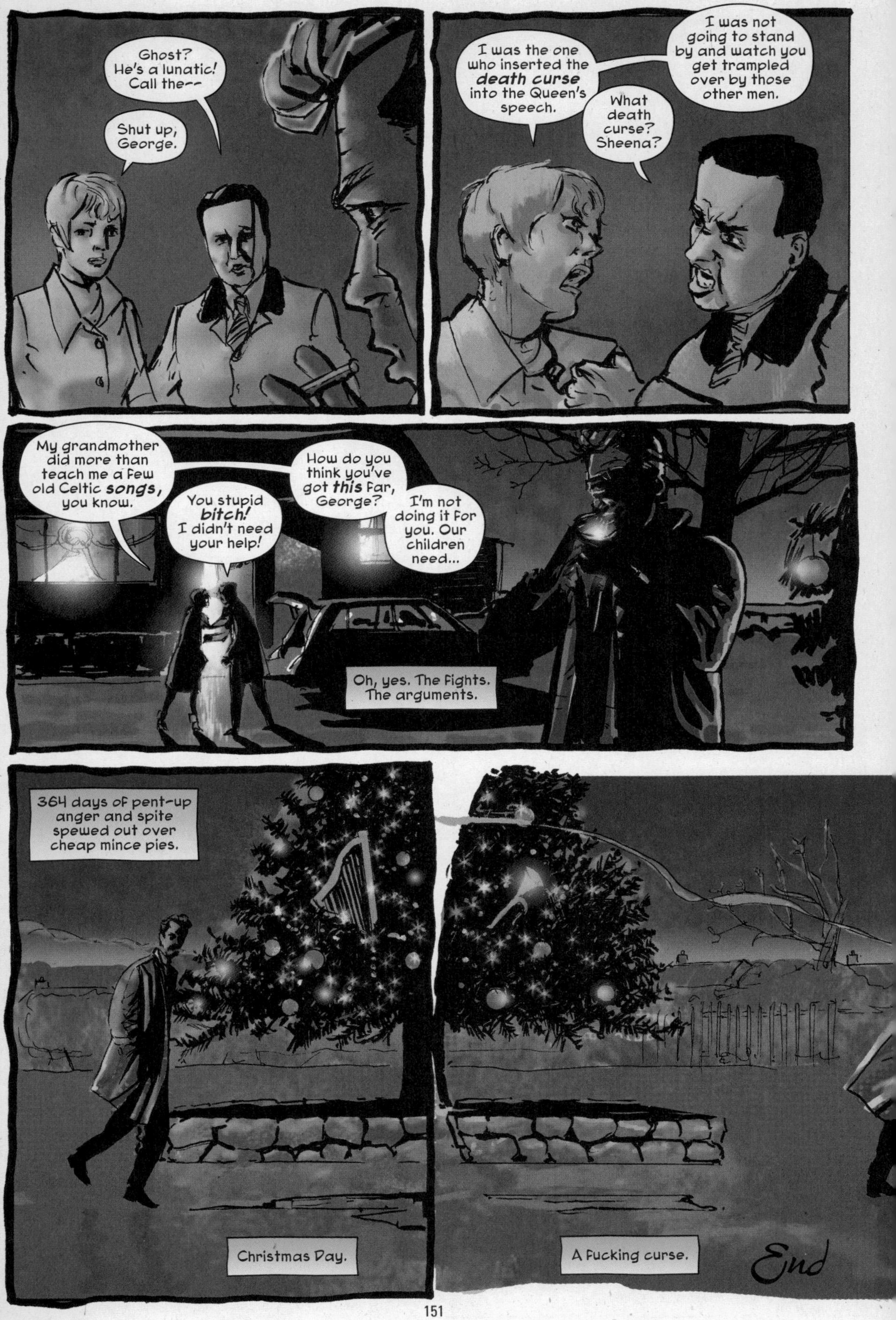
Ghost? He's a lunatic! Call the--
Shut up, George.
I was the one who inserted the death curse into the Queen's speech.
I was not going to stand by and watch you get trampled over by those other men.
What death curse? Sheena?
My grandmother did more than teach me a few old Celtic songs, you know.
You stupid bitch! I didn't need your help!
How do you think you've got this far, George?
I'm not doing it for you. Our children need...
Oh, yes. The fights. The arguments.
364 days of pent-up anger and spite spewed out over cheap mince pies.
Christmas Day.
A fucking curse.
End

SNOW had FALLEN

"IN THE BLEAK MIDWINTER, FROSTY WIND MADE MOAN..."

"EARTH STOOD HARD AS IRON, WATER LIKE A STONE..."

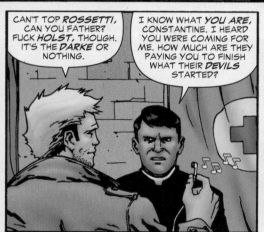

CAN'T TOP *ROSSETTI*, CAN YOU *FATHER*? FUCK *HOLST*, THOUGH. IT'S THE *DARKE* OR NOTHING.

I KNOW WHAT *YOU ARE*, CONSTANTINE. I HEARD YOU WERE COMING FOR ME. HOW MUCH ARE THEY PAYING YOU TO FINISH WHAT THEIR *DEVILS* STARTED?

WHOA, *PADRE*...

I'M JUST HERE SNOOPING FOR A MATE. IT'S NOT MY REGULAR THING BUT HE THINKS THERE'S SOMETHING *UNUSUAL* ABOUT YOUR LOCAL BHOPAL. AND I WAS TOLD YOU MIGHT HAVE SOME INFO...

WHY WOULD THE LIKES OF *YOUR* FRIENDS GIVE A DAMN FOR *US*?

HAVE YOU EVEN *HEARD* WHAT HAPPENED?

"SNOW HAD FALLEN, SNOW ON SNOW..."

OH, I HEARD. EVERYBODY HEARD.

MULTINATIONAL WHATEVERTHEFUCK PLANT GOES BOOM. *DAYS* TILL THEY ADMIT THE SHIT IT SPREAD WAS ANYTHING TO *WORRY* ABOUT.

WE TRIED TO GET THE KIDS INSIDE, BUT...

WE JUST HAD SOME OLD *CHRISTMAS* BOOKS DONATED TO THE CHURCH. THEY COPIED THE PICTURES THEY'D SEEN, OF CHILDREN *PLAYING*. THEY THOUGHT THE ASH WAS *SNOW*. THEY THOUGHT IT WAS A *MIRACLE*.

"SNOW ON SNOW..."

"IN THE BLEAK MIDWINTER, LONG AGO."

AND NOW AFTER THAT... *POISON* MADE THEM SICK...

NOW *DEVILS* ARE COMING FOR THEM.

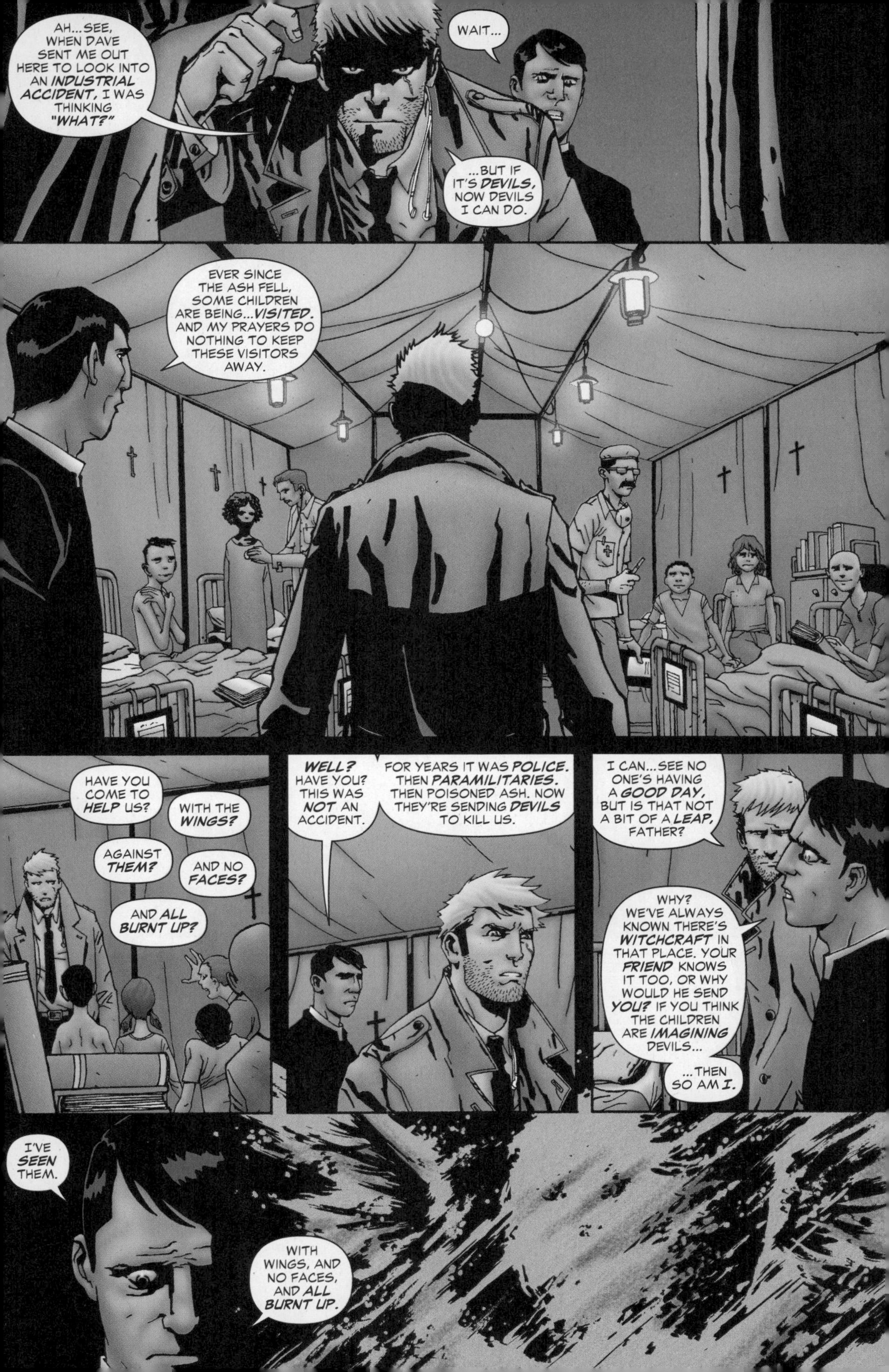
AH...SEE, WHEN DAVE SENT ME OUT HERE TO LOOK INTO AN INDUSTRIAL ACCIDENT, I WAS THINKING "WHAT?"
WAIT...
...BUT IF IT'S DEVILS, NOW DEVILS I CAN DO.
EVER SINCE THE ASH FELL, SOME CHILDREN ARE BEING...VISITED. AND MY PRAYERS DO NOTHING TO KEEP THESE VISITORS AWAY.
HAVE YOU COME TO HELP US?
WITH THE WINGS?
AGAINST THEM?
AND NO FACES?
AND ALL BURNT UP?
WELL? HAVE YOU? THIS WAS NOT AN ACCIDENT.
FOR YEARS IT WAS POLICE. THEN PARAMILITARIES. THEN POISONED ASH. NOW THEY'RE SENDING DEVILS TO KILL US.
I CAN...SEE NO ONE'S HAVING A GOOD DAY, BUT IS THAT NOT A BIT OF A LEAP, FATHER?
WHY? WE'VE ALWAYS KNOWN THERE'S WITCHCRAFT IN THAT PLACE. YOUR FRIEND KNOWS IT TOO, OR WHY WOULD HE SEND YOU? IF YOU THINK THE CHILDREN ARE IMAGINING DEVILS...
...THEN SO AM I.
I'VE SEEN THEM.
WITH WINGS, AND NO FACES, AND ALL BURNT UP.

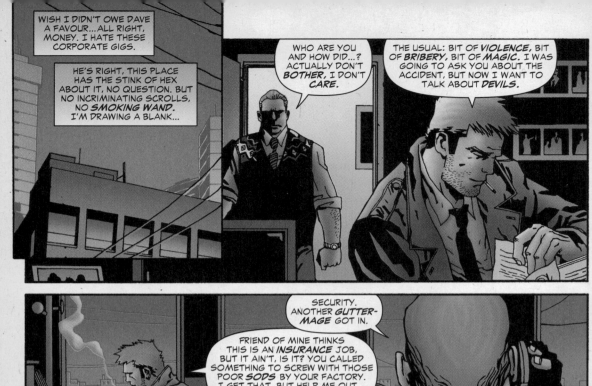

WISH I DIDN'T OWE DAVE A FAVOUR... ALL RIGHT, MONEY. I HATE THESE CORPORATE GIGS.

HE'S RIGHT, THIS PLACE HAS THE STINK OF HEX ABOUT IT, NO QUESTION. BUT NO INCRIMINATING SCROLLS, NO SMOKING WAND. I'M DRAWING A BLANK...

WHO ARE YOU AND HOW DID...? ACTUALLY DON'T BOTHER, I DON'T CARE.

THE USUAL: BIT OF VIOLENCE, BIT OF BRIBERY, BIT OF MAGIC. I WAS GOING TO ASK YOU ABOUT THE ACCIDENT, BUT NOW I WANT TO TALK ABOUT DEVILS.

SECURITY. ANOTHER GUTTER-MAGE GOT IN.

FRIEND OF MINE THINKS THIS IS AN INSURANCE JOB, BUT IT AIN'T, IS IT? YOU CALLED SOMETHING TO SCREW WITH THOSE POOR SODS BY YOUR FACTORY. I GET THAT. BUT HELP ME OUT... I'VE BEEN AT THE HELL GAME A WHILE...

AND WHATEVER YOU'VE INVOKED IS RINGING NO BELLS AT ALL.

YOU'VE BEEN TALKING TO THE PRIEST. AS I SAID TO HIM, MR. ABOUT-TO-BE-SAVAGELY-BEATEN, WHY WOULD I BLOW UP MY OWN FACTORY? DO YOU HAVE THE SLIGHTEST IDEA HOW MUCH THIS COCK-UP IS COSTING ME?

COME ON. CLEARING UP A TOXIC SPILL: GAJILLIONS OF BUCKS. COWED LOCAL POPULACE? PRICELESS.

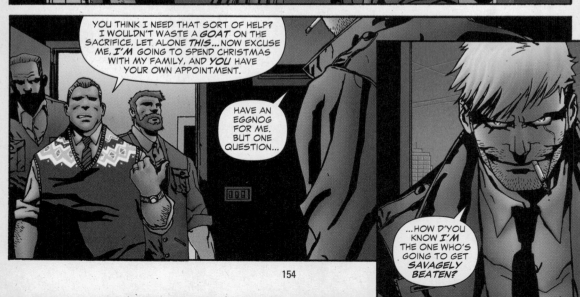

YOU THINK I NEED THAT SORT OF HELP? I WOULDN'T WASTE A GOAT ON THE SACRIFICE, LET ALONE THIS... NOW EXCUSE ME, I'M GOING TO SPEND CHRISTMAS WITH MY FAMILY, AND YOU HAVE YOUR OWN APPOINTMENT.

HAVE AN EGGNOG FOR ME. BUT ONE QUESTION...

...HOW D'YOU KNOW I'M THE ONE WHO'S GOING TO GET SAVAGELY BEATEN?

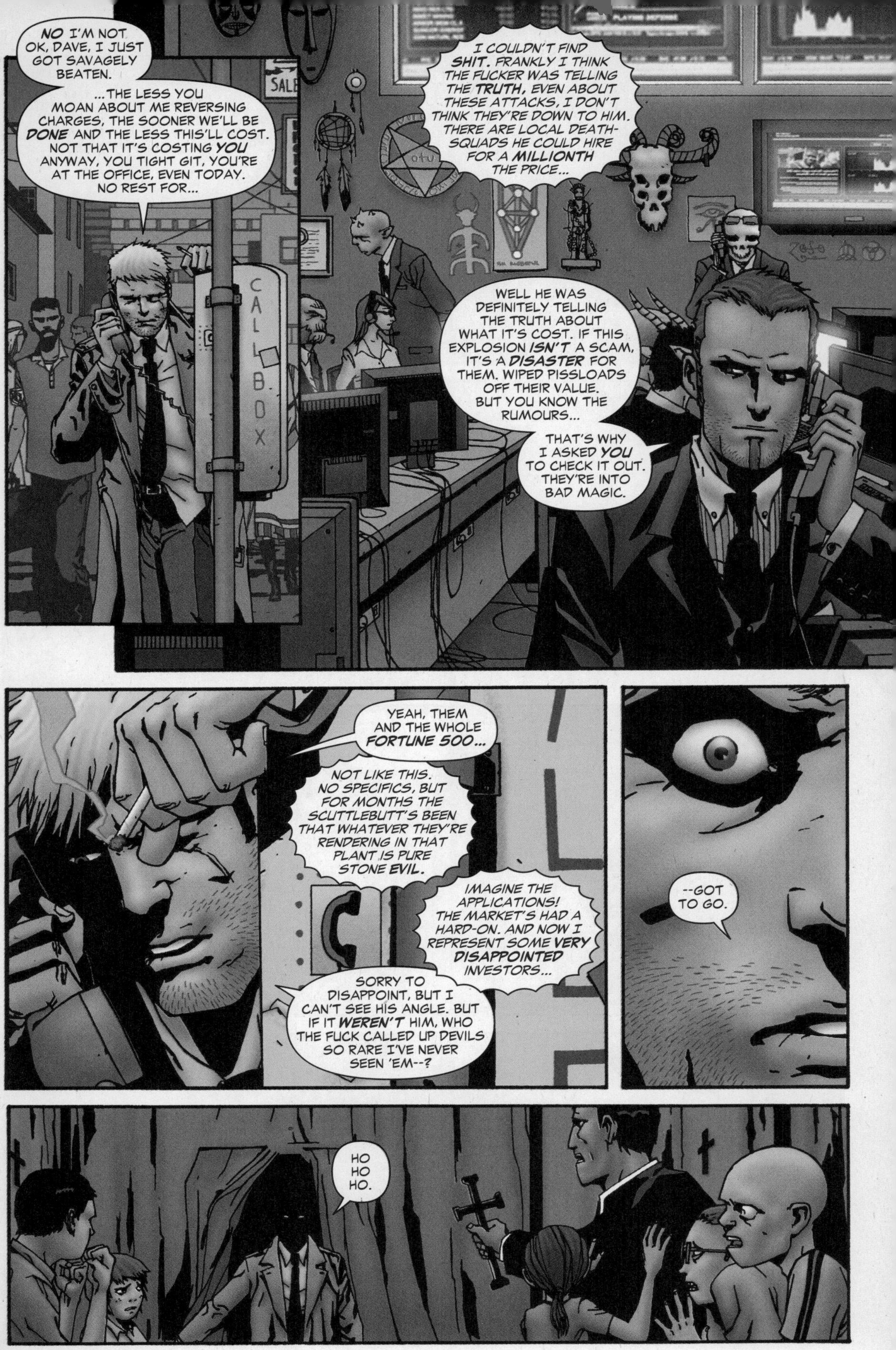
NO I'M NOT OK, DAVE, I JUST GOT SAVAGELY BEATEN.
...THE LESS YOU MOAN ABOUT ME REVERSING CHARGES, THE SOONER WE'LL BE DONE AND THE LESS THIS'LL COST. NOT THAT IT'S COSTING YOU ANYWAY, YOU TIGHT GIT, YOU'RE AT THE OFFICE, EVEN TODAY. NO REST FOR...
I COULDN'T FIND SHIT. FRANKLY I THINK THE FUCKER WAS TELLING THE TRUTH, EVEN ABOUT THESE ATTACKS, I DON'T THINK THEY'RE DOWN TO HIM. THERE ARE LOCAL DEATH-SQUADS HE COULD HIRE FOR A MILLIONTH THE PRICE...
WELL HE WAS DEFINITELY TELLING THE TRUTH ABOUT WHAT IT'S COST. IF THIS EXPLOSION ISN'T A SCAM, IT'S A DISASTER FOR THEM. WIPED PISSLOADS OFF THEIR VALUE. BUT YOU KNOW THE RUMOURS...
THAT'S WHY I ASKED YOU TO CHECK IT OUT. THEY'RE INTO BAD MAGIC.
YEAH, THEM AND THE WHOLE FORTUNE 500...
NOT LIKE THIS. NO SPECIFICS, BUT FOR MONTHS THE SCUTTLEBUTT'S BEEN THAT WHATEVER THEY'RE RENDERING IN THAT PLANT IS PURE STONE EVIL.
IMAGINE THE APPLICATIONS! THE MARKET'S HAD A HARD-ON. AND NOW I REPRESENT SOME VERY DISAPPOINTED INVESTORS...
SORRY TO DISAPPOINT, BUT I CAN'T SEE HIS ANGLE. BUT IF IT WEREN'T HIM, WHO THE FUCK CALLED UP DEVILS SO RARE I'VE NEVER SEEN 'EM--?
--GOT TO GO.
HO HO HO.

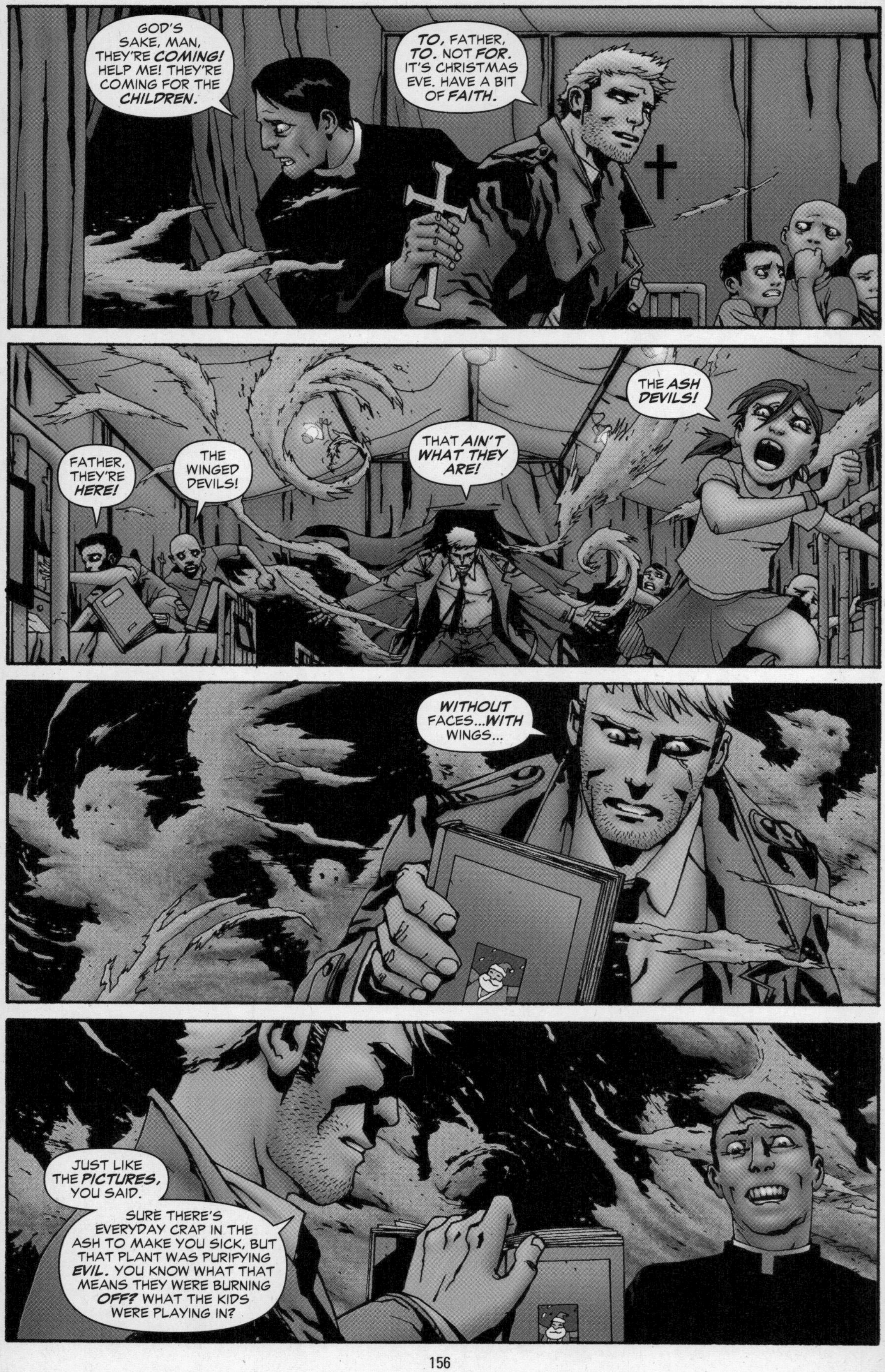
GOD'S SAKE, MAN, THEY'RE COMING! HELP ME! THEY'RE COMING FOR THE CHILDREN.
TO, FATHER, TO. NOT FOR. IT'S CHRISTMAS EVE. HAVE A BIT OF FAITH.
FATHER, THEY'RE HERE!
THE WINGED DEVILS!
THAT AIN'T WHAT THEY ARE!
THE ASH DEVILS!
WITHOUT FACES...WITH WINGS...
JUST LIKE THE PICTURES, YOU SAID.
SURE THERE'S EVERYDAY CRAP IN THE ASH TO MAKE YOU SICK, BUT THAT PLANT WAS PURIFYING EVIL. YOU KNOW WHAT THAT MEANS THEY WERE BURNING OFF? WHAT THE KIDS WERE PLAYING IN?

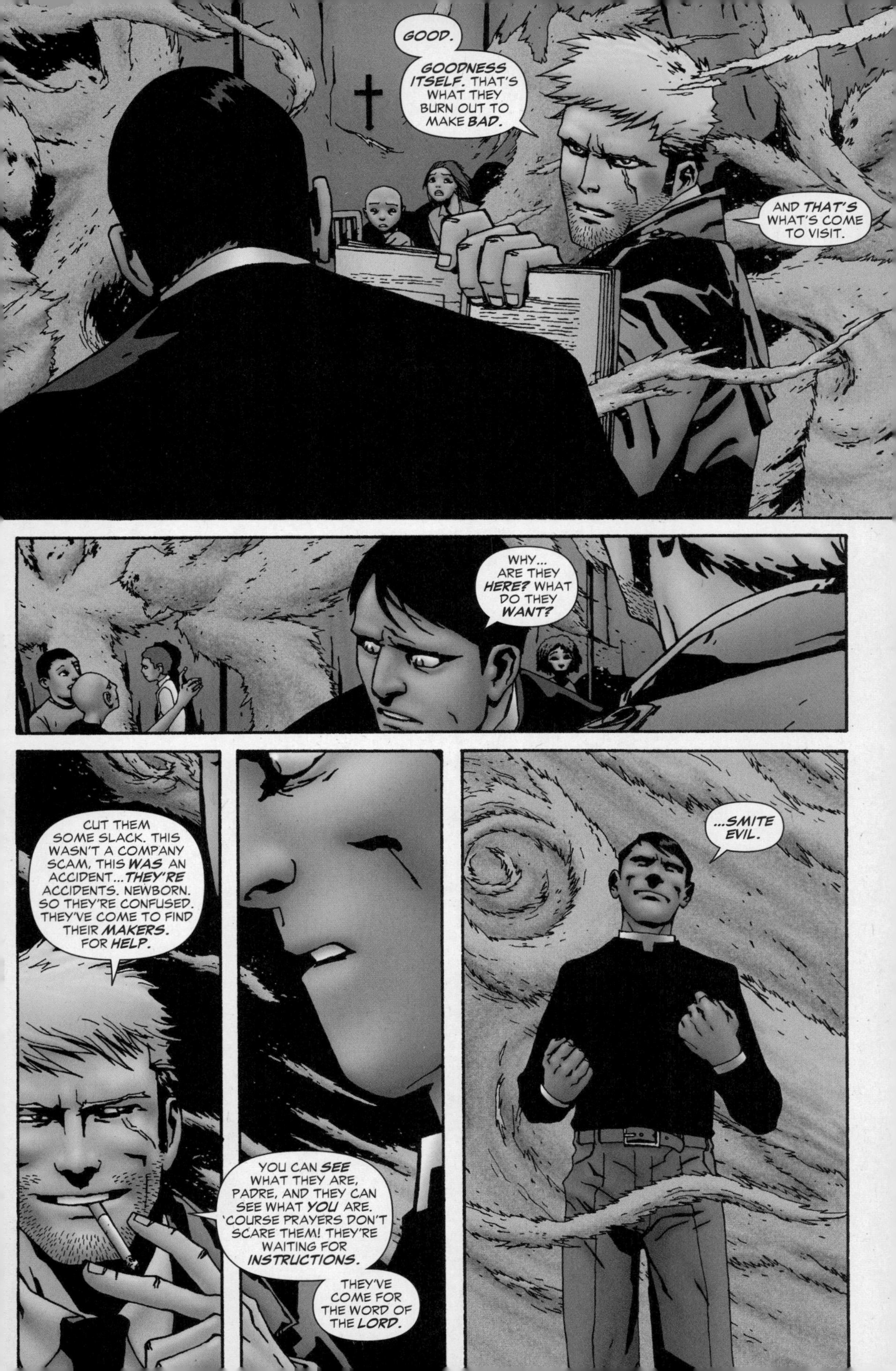
GOOD.
GOODNESS ITSELF. THAT'S WHAT THEY BURN OUT TO MAKE BAD.
AND THAT'S WHAT'S COME TO VISIT.
WHY... ARE THEY HERE? WHAT DO THEY WANT?
CUT THEM SOME SLACK. THIS WASN'T A COMPANY SCAM, THIS WAS AN ACCIDENT...THEY'RE ACCIDENTS. NEWBORN. SO THEY'RE CONFUSED. THEY'VE COME TO FIND THEIR MAKERS. FOR HELP.
YOU CAN SEE WHAT THEY ARE, PADRE, AND THEY CAN SEE WHAT YOU ARE. 'COURSE PRAYERS DON'T SCARE THEM! THEY'RE WAITING FOR INSTRUCTIONS.
THEY'VE COME FOR THE WORD OF THE LORD.
...SMITE EVIL.

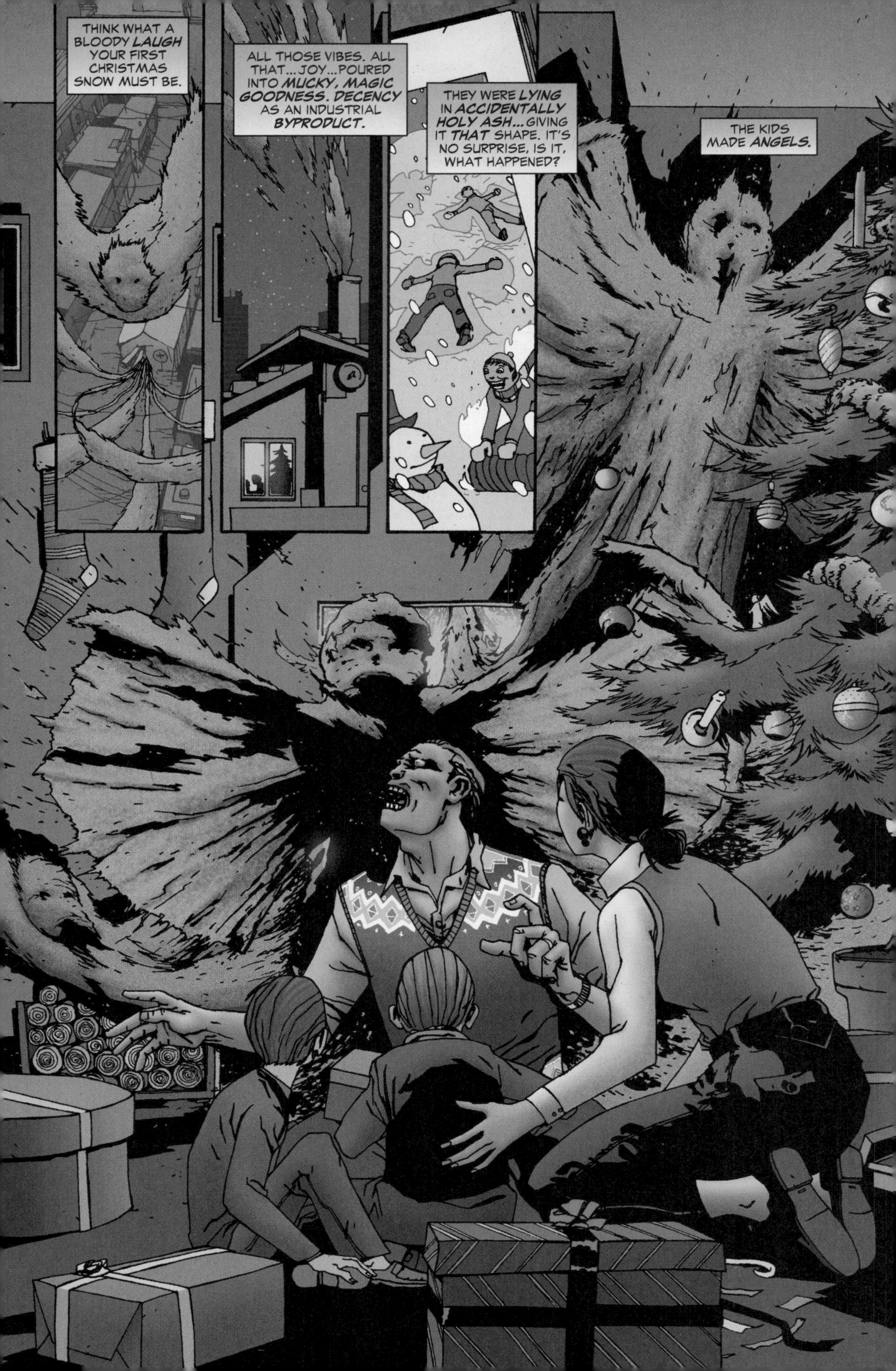
THINK WHAT A BLOODY *LAUGH* YOUR FIRST CHRISTMAS SNOW MUST BE.
ALL THOSE VIBES. ALL THAT...JOY...POURED INTO *MUCKY, MAGIC GOODNESS. DECENCY* AS AN INDUSTRIAL *BYPRODUCT.*
THEY WERE *LYING* IN *ACCIDENTALLY HOLY ASH...* GIVING IT *THAT* SHAPE. IT'S NO SURPRISE, IS IT, WHAT HAPPENED?
THE KIDS MADE *ANGELS.*

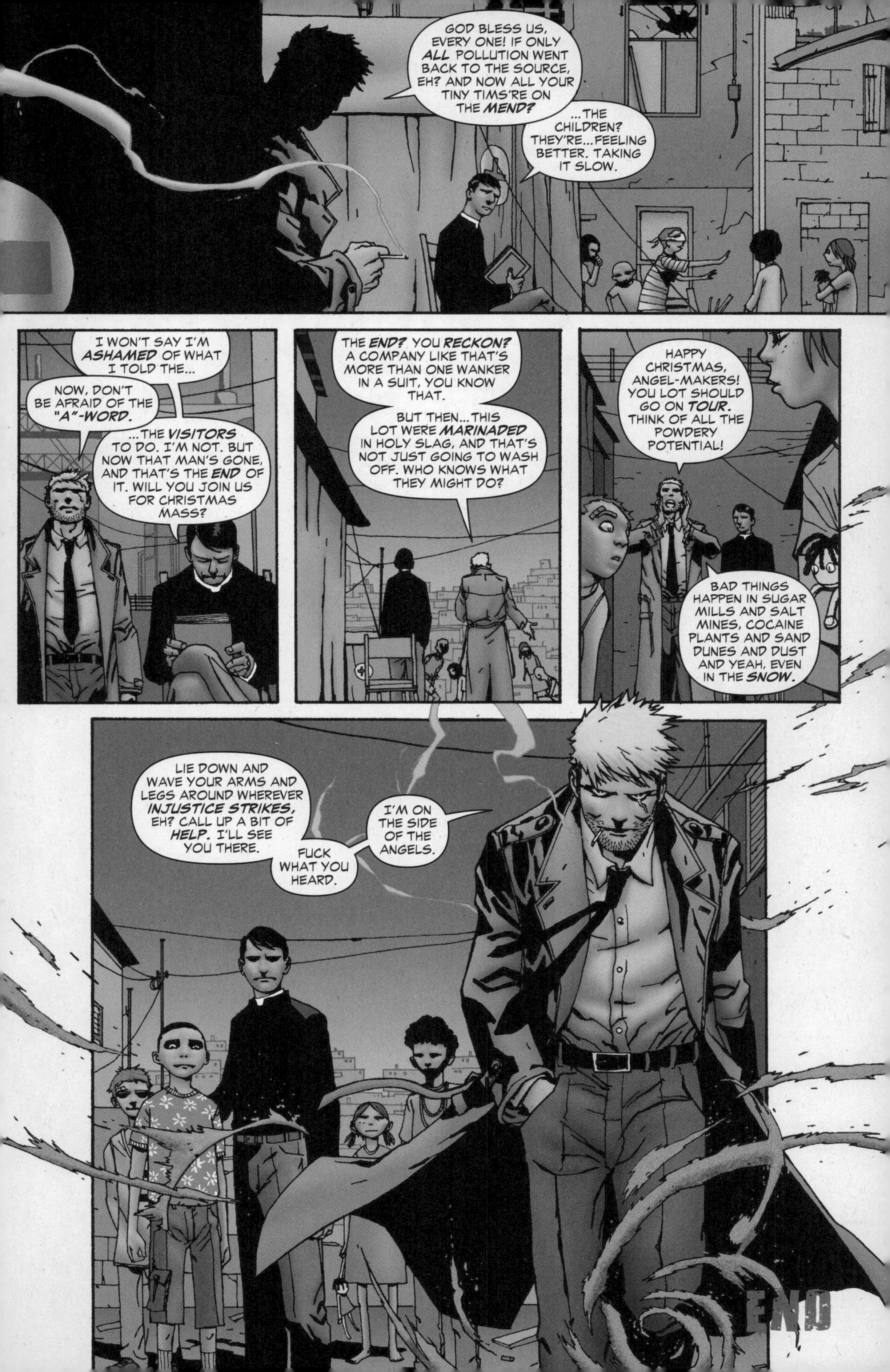
GOD BLESS US, EVERY ONE! IF ONLY ALL POLLUTION WENT BACK TO THE SOURCE, EH? AND NOW ALL YOUR TINY TIMS'RE ON THE MEND?
...THE CHILDREN? THEY'RE...FEELING BETTER. TAKING IT SLOW.
I WON'T SAY I'M ASHAMED OF WHAT I TOLD THE...
NOW, DON'T BE AFRAID OF THE "A"-WORD.
...THE VISITORS TO DO. I'M NOT. BUT NOW THAT MAN'S GONE, AND THAT'S THE END OF IT. WILL YOU JOIN US FOR CHRISTMAS MASS?
THE END? YOU RECKON? A COMPANY LIKE THAT'S MORE THAN ONE WANKER IN A SUIT, YOU KNOW THAT.
BUT THEN...THIS LOT WERE MARINADED IN HOLY SLAG, AND THAT'S NOT JUST GOING TO WASH OFF. WHO KNOWS WHAT THEY MIGHT DO?
HAPPY CHRISTMAS, ANGEL-MAKERS! YOU LOT SHOULD GO ON TOUR. THINK OF ALL THE POWDERY POTENTIAL!
BAD THINGS HAPPEN IN SUGAR MILLS AND SALT MINES, COCAINE PLANTS AND SAND DUNES AND DUST AND YEAH, EVEN IN THE SNOW.
LIE DOWN AND WAVE YOUR ARMS AND LEGS AROUND WHEREVER INJUSTICE STRIKES, EH? CALL UP A BIT OF HELP. I'LL SEE YOU THERE.
I'M ON THE SIDE OF THE ANGELS.
FUCK WHAT YOU HEARD.
END